The Anxiety Code:

Deciphering the Purposes of Neurotic Anxiety

Dr. Roger Di Pietro, Psy.D.

with special contribution from

Dr. Harold H. Mosak, Ph.D., ABPP

Dedication

Dr. Harold H. Mosak, Ph.D., ABPP

Multinational professor, prolific author, friend, polymath, Adlerian cognoscenti
and clinician, as well as philanthropic mentor who generously provided
unparalleled instruction and encouragement.

Acknowledgments

Thank you to my family for their support, as well as
David "Two weeks" Baker, M.A., Dr. Anthony DiGiovanni, M.D.,
and Dr. Joseph Fullone, M.D. for their feedback and technical knowledge.

Introduction

People often consider anxiety as the result of some cause, say genetic, biological, social, occupational, or financial. Accordingly, pharmacological and talk therapy approaches employ prescriptions and procedures to alleviate symptoms by searching for and treating the perceived precipitants. Yet, what if this cause and effect mindset has inherent limitations and risks?

Then it would be wise, indeed necessary and beneficial, to discuss a viewpoint that could detect and resolve those concerns, as well as point the way to more comprehensive assessment and treatment. To that end, perhaps it's best that I briefly describe my academic and clinical perspectives as well as this publication's predominant theoretical underpinnings.

Psychology is the principal discipline of my triple major bachelor's degree. I subsequently earned two master's degrees in psychology. The first is a Master of Arts in the Social Sciences (Behavior Modification); a course of study and practice that primarily focused on the individual and less on the medical and social factors of psychological symptoms. Although I continue to value and apply the advantages of that theoretical orientation in my practice, I sought more comprehensive training in Europe. I earned a Master of Science in Social Psychology from the London School of Economics and Political Science (LSE), University of London. While there, my interactions with people from diverse countries multiplied my understanding and appreciation of the social influences on individual functioning as well as the need to adopt many lenses to comprehend humanity. Upon completion of my studies in London, I moved to Chicago and earned a Doctorate in Clinical Psychology from the Adler School of Professional Psychology (known as Adler University after January 2015). My postdoctoral training at the University of Rochester Medical Center at Strong Memorial Hospital provided additional instruction in individual, couples, marital, and family therapy. Presently, I'm a clinical psychologist in private practice in Upstate New York.

Although this text is a synthesis of my scholarship, clinical experiences, and supportive material from various disciplines, it's foremost Adlerian in its construction. As you may be unfamiliar with that theoretical perspective and practice, some clarification can helpfully illuminate this book's direction and scope.

Dr. Alfred Adler was one of the three founding fathers of psychotherapy (the others being Sigmund Freud and Carl Jung). He created a distinct approach and treatment style: Individual Psychology. Dr. Adler contended that people are active, goal oriented, social, and creative. In addition to his practice, he disseminated knowledge about the etiology and characteristics of neuroses to assist in prevention and assessment.[1] To be equally accessible for laypersons as well as professionals, he communicated his theories and practices openly and clearly.

The *Diagnostic and Statistical Manual of Mental Disorders* (DSM) contains the common diagnostic language of psychiatry and psychology. Although founded some time ago, Adlerian theory and practice is compatible with current DSM understanding and implementation.[2] Also, its unique perspective is consistent with a biopsychosocial approach wherein genetic, physical, familial, environmental, as well as an individual's cognitive and psychological factors can explain, and be used in treating, psychopathology.[3] This book investigates Generalized anxiety disorder as it's classified in the DSM as well as in the International Classification of Diseases (ICD), but it's also known as Neurotic anxiety.

Under Dr. Adler's firsthand instruction was Dr. Rudolf Dreikurs, a psychiatrist who, among other achievements, was renown for applying Individual Psychology to the comprehension and treatment of children as well as parent training. In 1952, Dr. Dreikurs and others founded what became the Adler School of Professional Psychology in Chicago. One of these founders was his student and eventual colleague and co-therapist, Dr. Harold H. Mosak.

Dr. Mosak's encyclopedic contribution to Adlerian theory and practice includes teaching and lecturing at more than 70 colleges and universities around the world, publishing a combination of more than 130 articles and books, and practicing for approximately six decades. He and I previously co-authored a textbook on the history and use of childhood memories as a personality assessment: *Early Recollections: Interpretative Method and Application*. Additionally, Dr. Mosak identified the personality constituents that I've nicknamed the *Anxiety Code*. To honor his request to build on his achievements, interdisciplinary and intradisciplinary contributions fortify and advance this book's Adlerian ancestry.

Given neurotic anxiety's kindred characteristics with neurotic depression (Dysthymic disorder) it may be most appropriate to view this text as the second born, fraternal twin to *The Depression Code: Deciphering the Purposes of Neurotic Depression*. Although the presented information has been used successfully in therapy, for reasons that will become apparent, this book isn't a self-help text nor is it to be used for diagnosis. Rather, this work provides a perspective that may shatter myths, inspire dialogue, enhance comprehension and care, as well as stimulate research.

Consistent with Dr. Adler's recipe for accessibility, this book's instructive, yet conversational style palatably blends its ingredients of art and sciences. The format is similar to a classroom or therapy session: personalized and with direct questions to prompt contemplation and involvement. Clinical, archaic, uncommon, or unmanageable terminology has been translated into clearer, easier, and perhaps more memorable, terms. Also, to avoid mind-numbing repetition, multiple identifiers are used interchangeably (e.g., neurotic individuals, neurotically anxious persons, those with generalized anxiety).

Individual Psychology with its perspective that people are active, goal oriented, social, consistent, and creative, poses an intriguing question about generalized anxiety disorder — one that this book sets forth to answer.

Dr. Roger Di Pietro, Psy.D.

Table of Contents

Chapter 1: A Different Perspective

What is Anxiety?

People commonly consider anxiety as the aftershock of a traumatizing experience (e.g., being barbarically brutalized), worry about a possible outcome (e.g., job application) or general nervousness about life (e.g., vague apprehension, long-term financial concerns, existential angst). Anxiety can be related to a small stressor, such as a disorganized room or running late to work, or something massive, like unexpectedly receiving a stage four cancer diagnosis, or being in the midst of a terrifying wartime battle. It can occur when things are out of control, as when in a car careening down an ice-slicked road. Conversely, anxious thoughts and images can inexplicably appear when all is calm. Moreover, anxiety can incongruously erupt when matters are favorable and well managed, merely by thinking; for instance, about possible failure or rejection. In addition, anxiety can contagiously and vicariously arise, say as when interacting with a panicking individual or by empathizing with a predated victim in a horror movie.

Anxiety varies in scope, intensity, frequency, and duration. It's a common experience and an inherent part of existence. It's important to note that anxiety becomes a diagnosable problem when it significantly degrades people's quality of life. Anxiety can be pervasive, start in early childhood, extend throughout the life span, and exist in every area of life. Individuals can fear things outside of themselves as well as their inner functioning (e.g., anomalies in bodily actions, thoughts, or emotions).[4]

Among a crowd of anxiety diagnoses, this book spotlights one: Generalized anxiety disorder, also referred to as Neurotic anxiety. This long term (six months or more) constellation of symptoms can include excessive worry that's difficult to control, apprehension, a sense of restlessness or feeling keyed up or on edge, being easily fatigued, experiencing difficulty concentrating or mind going blank, irritability, muscle tension, sleep disturbance, muscular tension (e.g., fidgeting, tension headaches, trembling, inability to relax), lightheadedness, sweating, rapid heart rate and/or breathing, epigastric discomfort, dizziness, and dry mouth.[5] In addition, generalized anxiety may coexist with panic disorder, social phobia, and depression.[6]

Neurotically anxious individuals may painstakingly deliberate about what's right or wrong and good or bad. They often think several steps ahead and contemplate the outcome of countless courses of action, attempt to anticipate others' thoughts, responses, and behaviors, be perpetually apprehensive, vigilant, and perhaps produce a perception that people are caustically and callously judgmental. They might worry to the point of indecision and immobility. Also, some have a pervasive feeling of inadequacy, being overwhelmed, and that failure and rejection are endlessly imminent. They may be driven perfectionists who resist rest, as well as self-monitor and measure themselves. Unfortunately, those with generalized anxiety may experience symptoms for years before seeking treatment — and often only after they experience significant impairment in their functioning.[7]

Anxiety can be emotionally, cognitively, and physically exhausting, limit or prohibit employment, socializing, and intimacy, and disallow anything other than fleeting glimpses of peace. Alarming thoughts can unpredictably trigger an avalanche of anxiety. Symptom duration may be curiously and frustratingly disproportionate to the perceived cause. Anxiety can ruin everyday experiences and outlaw otherwise pedestrian tasks, say air travel, driving on the thruway, routine medical tests, or talking with others. It can feel like being inextricably tethered to a temperamental ticking time bomb, with carelessness hastening a volatile conclusion.

So why does this clinical level of anxiety occur?

Cause and Effect

Anxiety existed well before the birth of psychology as an official field of practice and psychologists as healthcare practitioners. However, this doesn't mean that people were left untreated. Medical doctors transplanted their understanding of physical illness and disease to the assessment and treatment of psychological symptoms.[8] This shouldn't be a surprise given their place in society as effective and revered healers. Consequently, during psychology's first steps as a dedicated field much of the terminology, conceptual models, and approaches that clothed it were hand-me-downs from its older sibling medical science, for example, the use of diagnosis, viewing individuals as sick or ill, searching for symptom causes, and the use of medications.[9]

So how might this medical mindset guide the conceptions of mental functioning and anxiety as well as the direction of psychology as a discipline?

Medical science primarily works with a cause and effect mentality of "this causes that to happen." Accordingly, successful medical intervention often has a boomerang-like trail that starts and ends with symptom assessment. Practitioners may identify symptoms, search for their precipitants, then implement treatment to resolve symptoms. For instance, in the case of a broken thumb, symptoms (pain, limited range of movement) prompt an examination for a cause (fractured proximal phalanx), which dictates treatment (realign bone, set with cast), with symptom alleviation the sign of restored health and a job well done.

Medical science has advanced anxiety assessment and intervention; for example, examinations for neurophysiological issues within the brain, genetic factors, or inappropriate neurotransmitter amounts that produce anxiety. Also, there's the commendable formulation of medicines and practices that effectively soothe and silence symptoms.

When psychologists and other mental health practitioners employ the cause and effect paradigm they often investigate patients' thoughts that generate symptoms as well as search for historical and external triggers such as traumatic events, childhood abuse or neglect, living in a volatile home and witnessing chaotic events or violence, being in a friction-filled or unfulfilling relationship, loneliness, work stress, financial stressors, or deceitful friends.

Pitfalls and Doubts

Indisputably, humanity would be much worse off if people never questioned the flat-world conception or the belief that the earth is the center of the universe. Likewise, unexamined acceptance of any psychological theory (or the measurement and therapy born from it) can counterproductively conceal contradictory evidence that would discredit it or lessen its applicability. While the causal perspective can have tremendous clinical usefulness, how might it obscure revealing clues essential for comprehensive treatment?

Recording and Recall

Some neurotically anxious individuals readily recollect one or more childhood events they're certain fathered their anxiety. Others may persistently proclaim there must be an incident or circumstance responsible for their symptoms, but are frustratingly unable to unearth it. And with the devout belief that anxiety is caused, some therapists undertake digging through patients' memories in an attempt to excavate an assumedly buried event that once disinterred would demystify the genesis of anxiety and illuminate a treatment path. All of this seems reasonable given that neurotically anxious patients' recollections from their childhood contain more themes of fear and trauma than other assessed groups' memories.[10] Although this data appears to provide incontestable and conclusive proof of how early events plant the seed of anxiety that subsequently sprouts symptoms, what are the problematic factors?

First, how might you view the memories' validity if you found out that when the remembered event occurred those individuals were exhausted, had the flu, or on medications that influenced attention, cognition, or mood? These and other variables can decrease the fidelity of the memories' recording, which makes accurate recall impossible.

Second, by definition childhood memories are encoded from children's physical, cognitive, and psychological point of view. Therefore, how might variables such as an underdeveloped ability to understand complex speech, tone of voice, and body language (among other behavior), and their shorter physical perspective cap or corrupt situational awareness and bias the memory?

Third, consider how you might conceive of air travel if your first flight were a turbulent nightmare. It's likely that this one-time, emotionally-laden event would etch in your memory that a particular airline or, possibly, all flights are deadly, which may lead you to consider the train the next time you travel.[11] In addition, contemplate children who regularly witness verbal and physical family conflict. Could accruing years of those memories, directly or indirectly, infuse the belief that life is unpredictable or people are unnervingly conflictual (regardless of how people act with that perspective, say perpetually guarded due to expecting conflict or relentlessly driven to keep the peace)?

Whether the memory is of a unique dramatic event or an accumulation of mild, but consistent experiences, people can forge a perspective of themselves, others, and the world. So how might this influence recollection?

Well, consider how those with low self-esteem might be inclined to recognize the times they failed rather than when they succeeded. Likewise, if people believe that bad things happen to them, might they perceive and remember when unfortunate events occur and not observe the positive ones? Or, contemplate how driven, anxious individuals may predominantly encode those profitable outcomes that occurred because they worried (e.g., anxiety prompted intense study that enabled passing when others flunked). *Neurotically anxious persons have an attentional bias that can prime them to perceive situations that are in accord with their mindset.*[12] Also, they may recollect authentic anxiety-soaked memories and hold onto them throughout their lives.[13]

Fourth, consider how two people can have dramatically different memories of the same event.[14] (This is often exhibited in marital therapy, as you might imagine.) Although each believes what's respectively remembered is reality and therefore resistant to change, at least one is wrong. *As people believe their recollections are genuine, they may be tenacious to them — even when they're incorrect.*

Fifth, as fantastical as it may seem, others can make suggestions — or merely ask questions — that distort or implant memories.[15] So if others' perceptions or statements are biased, corrupted, or inaccurate in some other way, then anxious persons' memories may be slanted or utterly false. Nevertheless, they may mistakenly believe them to be true and act in accord with those misperceptions.

Sixth, memories aren't exact replays from an exhaustive library. Rather, people's current perspective can be so powerful as to influence recollection selection and presentation.[16] Anxious individuals can recast neutral or pleasant times as anxiety filled or traumatic and horrific.[17] People's current mindset may influence recall to the point where they may deem a memory true when it's adulterated or fabricated.[18] And false recollections don't solely occur with people who have average to poor recall ability; it happens just as often for those with highly superior autobiographical memory.[19]

What people recollect, and how it's remembered, is from their present point of view.[20] Might this explain why neurotically anxious persons have more frequent themes of fear and trauma in their childhood memories? Consequently, perhaps the best use of early recollections is to assess current mindset and implement that understanding in treatment.[21]

Largely, human memory is imperfect and unreliable.[22] Memories can be fluid and flexible — more like rivers than rocks. *Nevertheless, a cause and effect mindset may urge people to dwell on the past and risk inadvertently employing biased, corrupted, or counterfeit memories that may misguide attention, misinform, and degrade assessment and treatment.* Sometimes, memories aren't a window to the past that afford a clear understanding, but rather are a distorted, stained-glass window, colored by personality and present functioning. Fair enough, but wouldn't searching for authentic peaceful and agreeable memories reduce anxiety?

Not necessarily. Some anxious individuals have difficulty finding such remembrances due to their current mindset. Paradoxically, pleasant recollections may aggravate anxiety when people compare those events with their current selves and interpret those memories as heartbreakingly distant and hopelessly irretrievable. They may quickly dismiss or discount serene and cheerful memories others offer, as they're not in accord with an anxious mindset.

Insight

Some people are convinced they cognitively possess a hidden trove of information that once discovered will flood them with a revelation of self-awareness that scuttles their anxiety. Consequently, they enthusiastically embark upon an exploratory treasure hunt for insight. Yet, what does the following suggest about awareness, emotions, and behavior change?

• In dozens of countries there are warnings on cigarette packages (e.g., "Cigarettes cause fatal lung disease," "Cigarettes cause cancer," "Cigarettes cause strokes and heart disease"[23]). Moreover, some cigarette packages have pictures of cancer, dead fetuses, hemorrhaging brains, blinded eyeballs, or gangrenous feet.[24] Yet, people continue to smoke.

• Those who perceive themselves as entitled to buy whatever they want, can swiftly and indifferently dismiss collection agencies' abundant feedback to stop overspending and start paying their bills.

• There are people who choose to continue to eat after their bodies send the message that additional food is unnecessary. Relatedly, consider how an unbiased, yet incriminating bathroom scale often leads people to avoid it rather than adjust their eating habits.

As people regularly engage in behavior they're fully aware is potentially hazardous, what implication does this have for those who believe that mere self-awareness resolves anxiety?

Insight doesn't guarantee behavior change or symptom resolution.

Searching for a Cause

Being able to quickly identify and learn associations increases the likelihood of safety as people can pair particular behaviors with healthy outcomes and other actions with painful, unhealthy consequences that should be avoided. (Odds are, you only had to touch a hot stove once to learn your lesson.)

As the causal mindset asserts there *has to be* a cause of anxiety, it's perfectly logical, indeed compulsory, to seek that which is believed to spawn symptoms as a means to stop them — like looking for the source of a house's water leak to halt further damage. Accordingly, people, and often their therapists, investigate various factors that might simultaneously explain symptoms and suggest a course of treatment. However, what problems lurk?

First, given that people have kaleidoscopic experiences from joy to fear, love to indifference, exhilaration to boredom, acceptance to anger, contentment to dissatisfaction, and all colors in-between, there's a bountiful spectrum of memories from which they can always pick a cause — regardless of accuracy. Honestly, who *couldn't* recall an anxious or worrisome experience?

Second, have you ever thought about a person who then called you shortly thereafter? While you might have thought there was a connection (perhaps even a supernatural one) between the two factors, did you thoroughly examine it?

Consider the following:

• How many people did you think about that day?

• How many of those people did not call?

• How many people called you that you didn't recently think about?

• How often does this event occur throughout a year and is it greater than chance?

People's ability to recognize associations and patterns is so strong as to be susceptible to finding relationships *where none exist*. Perceiving non-existent relationships is called illusory correlation.[25] Apophenia and patternicity are terms that highlight how people have a tendency to find patterns in meaningful as well as meaningless data.[26] Some can be amusing, such as finding images in random, indistinct things (e.g., clouds), or downright unhealthy as when people develop superstitions.[27] For instance, people may believe in a causal relationship between a full moon and bizarre, unhealthy, or illegal behavior (a.k.a. lunar effects), however, there isn't any reliable or notable correlation.[28] Some people believe that sugar makes children hyperactive. In actuality, sugar lowers activity and it's other factors such as social and physical settings (e.g., a party) that can increase energy — nevertheless expectations of a specific cause (a false correlation) can maintain the myth.[29] With that in mind, how might people's perception patterns negatively impact the search for a symptom cause?

Third, when the cause and effect perspective whets people's appetite for an initiating event they may hungrily sift through various factors to determine what stirs their anxiety. But what might happen when they're unable to identify any personal, social, financial, health, occupational, or legal stressor?

They can become frustrated and conclude their symptoms must be biological, chemical, or genetic in origin — whether or not that's true.

Fourth, please take a moment and count how often the letter "e" appears in the previous sentence. Take your time and be precise. You can reread the sentence as many times as you wish. *After* you're done counting and are confident in your number, continue reading. Go!

Without looking back at that sentence, how many times does the letter "i" appear?

Although you read that sentence at least twice, it's because you weren't looking for the "i"s that you didn't attend to them. Therefore, you were unable to accurately acknowledge their presence. This is an example of inattentional blindness.[30] Similarly, when the cause and effect perspective of symptoms is people's sole conception, they chance becoming unaware of other points of view that may augment their comprehension.

Fifth, people may seek authentic anxiety-producing memories, events, and conditions to explain symptoms and direct treatment. However, might frequent focusing on anxiety-riddled material precipitate, maintain, or escalate symptoms?

Searching for symptom causes may lead people to misidentify them or reduce the likelihood of searching for and finding things that are incompatible with a causal mindset. This reduces the breadth of assessment and treatment as well as risks sustaining anxiety.

Genetics

Anxiety can prohibit and poison necessary and rewarding experiences, such as relationships, friendships, employment, and a sense of peace. Consequently, people often perceive it as pointless, irrepressible, and counterproductive. Some individuals state that they've "always been anxious" and report having symptoms since adolescence or for as long as they can remember. You can see how these factors tip the scales towards a genetic conception of generalized anxiety. With that in mind, think about how individuals often look for easily-identifiable genetic parallels among family members (e.g., hair color, eye color, height, facial features, allergies). Similarly, some symptomatic persons identify anxious family members and use that as evidence that their anxiety has a genetic origin. In fact, in many instances generalized anxiety has an identifiable genetic association or predisposition.[31] Yet, if that applied to every case…

• Might medical science have more certainty in identifying those prone to developing it and be better able to explain, predict, and control it?

• How could symptom resolution occur solely through the process of talk therapy?

• Why would symptoms arise in individuals with no family history of anxiety?

• Genes can be turned on and off due to a colorful palette of epigenetic (i.e., external, non-genetic) influences.[32] Yet, does that account for the gallery of symptom portraits that vary in type, duration, and severity among people or various symptomatic hues within a single person?

• How might you explain selective symptom generation associated with non-genetic factors such as when specific others are nearby, in the face of certain tasks, and only in particular environments?

• If generalized anxiety were entirely due to an off-key genetic composition that lessens or prohibits social interaction, relationships, and intimacy, might the process of natural selection have notably reduced symptom potency or prevalence?

Now, select one of your non-genetic characteristics, say a passion for gardening or sports, pet ownership, type of books or movies you enjoy, or desire to play video games. Does someone in your extended family have matching interests or behaviors? If the number of persons or characteristics is large enough, correlations can always be made. Certainly, a genetic basis of anxiety could explain its seemingly dissociated existence from people's goals, yet think about the following. Although genetic causes of, or predispositions to, generalized anxiety are present and have a significant association, they may play a modest role, are somewhat ambiguous and may be related to several diagnoses, open to interpretation, and influenced by environmental factors.[33] Moreover, even if specific genes are present, that may not determine whether they're expressed.

In other words, the same diagnosis or characteristics among family members can sometimes give a false impression that symptoms are inherited when symptomatic similarities are due to the setting, interactions, as well as individual choice and perspective. Also, note that when people hear the same statements repeatedly, they tend to rate them as truer than new statements.[34] Just consider this in regard to those situations where relatives or others frequently tell a neurotic individual "Your anxiety is genetic," "Your brain is wired differently," or "You have a chemical imbalance."

Medical Correlation and Symptom Suppression

Generalized anxiety is associated with a number of medical and physical conditions, for example tension headaches, chronic fatigue, heart disease, chest pain, heart palpitations, upset stomach, nausea, heartburn, flatulence, dry mouth, perspiring, frequent urination, shortness of breath, belching, dizziness, tremor, hypertension diabetes, Sjögren's syndrome, vaginismus, premature ejaculation, neck and back pain, as well as irritable bowel syndrome.[35] In addition, there are numerous medical concerns and organic issues (e.g., endocrine system disorders, brain tumors) that mimic generalized anxiety symptoms.[36] Additionally, people may misidentify their anxiety-related physical symptoms as medical complaints. (Indeed, medical doctors regularly refer patients to me for psychological assessment and treatment when tests are negative for a heart attack or other physical malady.)

Determining causes can be daunting. Just ponder the array of disparate factors that might produce symptoms, such as childhood experiences, neurotransmission activity, neurotransmitter levels, financial difficulties, social rejection, physiological functioning, infidelity, social status, job instability, health concerns, as well as innumerable other variables including how things such as caffeine can intensify anxiety. Note that it's unfeasible to identify and comprehend all possible precipitants simultaneously as well as their potential interactions. Consequently, researchers routinely dissect states, things, and events, systematically eliminating as many extraneous variables as possible to get to the root cause or a fundamental understanding. They may distill a complex and confounding condition down to microscopic causes (e.g., genetic, physiological, biological, chemical) to explain, control, or predict anxiety, and formulate pharmaceutical or biological therapies. When medications subdue symptoms, it can fortify the belief that biochemical or physiological issues cause anxiety.

As people commonly have natural and innate variation in functioning and composition (e.g., vision, allergies, intelligence, hearing, disease susceptibility), it's understandable why anxious individuals may believe their brains, bodies, and neurotransmitter levels, for instance, are different from non-symptomatic persons.

While respectfully not trespassing too far into psychiatry's front yard, it's important to examine data that supports that claim.

Although the research on the neurobiology of generalized anxiety is somewhat limited, particular brain regions and neurotransmitters are of note.[37] There are many regions and systems of the brain (e.g., frontal cortex, limbic and paralimbic regions, neuroendocrine) associated with generalized anxiety.[38] Research has found differences in the amygdala (nuclei in the brain associated with emotion and memory) for those diagnosed with generalized anxiety disorder compared to those without that diagnosis.[39] Neurotically anxious individuals have differences in serotonin metabolism and regulation of serotonin transporters than non-anxious individuals, and serotonin medicines (e.g., SSRIs) reduce symptoms.[40] Benzodiazepines can immediately reduce generalized anxiety symptoms by influencing gamma-aminobutyric acid (GABA) neurotransmitter activity.[41] In addition, neurotic anxiety has been associated with elevated levels of catecholamines as well as changes in cortisol levels.[42]

Perhaps an analogy may best illustrate how psychotropic medicines can help. It's likely your car has electronic stability control and traction control, which assist or control braking and steering when your vehicle loses grip on a slippery road. These systems disengage when your car is out of jeopardy and you're able to resume safe operation. Comparably, when people experience symptom acceleration prior to and during a stressor, they may use anxiolytics (anxiety-reducing medicine) to curb symptoms until matters are less stressful or they're better able to manage their thoughts, emotions, and actions, then medication use can be stopped.

The concurrence of anxiety and specific microscopic variables (e.g., neurotransmitter amounts, brain region activation, hormone levels), along with how anxiolytics can blot out symptoms, appears to provide ample evidence that imperfect and renegade innate constituents cause anxiety. Yet, does a correlation between microscopic gremlins and anxiety prove that the former always causes the latter?

Well, imagine someone told you that fire trucks cause house fires and then provided the following evidence:

1. Whenever a house is on fire at least one fire truck is nearby.

2. Fire trucks are almost never present in front of houses that are not on fire.

However, you *know* that fire trucks don't set homes ablaze. So you quickly conclude that just because something is present or absent concurrently with an event, doesn't mean that you can accurately infer cause. *A correlation between two conditions doesn't prove causation.*[43]

Now take this a step further. What can happen when people visualize appetizing foods such as lasagna, bacon-wrapped filet mignon, cookies, pizza, or warm cinnamon rolls?

They may salivate, the neurons in the hunger centers of their brains start firing, and possibly their stomachs growl.[44] Likewise, consider how imagining sexually stimulating images, sounds, or memories may initiate specific physiological responses such as activating the sexual response areas of the brain, secretion of lubricating fluid, and tumescence.[45] Certainly there's a correlation, and indeed a cause, *but it's people's thoughts that generate specific microscopic, physiological, and behavioral events.* This provides a revealing clue about neurotic anxiety, medical correlation, and anxiolytic-suppressed symptoms.

Consider how even though the amygdala is often noted for its association with generalized anxiety, its role is uncertain.[46] In addition, while the hormones norepinephrine and cortisol are related to anxiety, the role of norepinephrine is currently ill-defined, and the research findings on what part cortisol plays are inconsistent.[47]

Although the neurotransmitter GABA is associated with anxiety, and anxious persons may have diminished benzodiazepine receptor sensitivity, the therapeutic benefit of benzodiazepines that act on GABA approaches that of placebo after 4 to 6 weeks of use, about 25 to 30% of patients do not experience a therapeutic effect, and some risk tolerance and dependence.[48] And while a decrease in benzodiazepine function is correlated with generalized anxiety disorder, it's unclear whether it's a state or trait characteristic.[49]

Intriguingly, established antidepressants such as selective serotonin reuptake inhibitors (SSRIs), tricyclic antidepressants (TCAs), and monoamine oxidase inhibitors (MAOIs) may effectively treat anxiety symptoms.[50] However, less troublesome SSRIs have mostly displaced TCAs and MAOIs as first-line treatment.[51] And, while serotonin is a neurotransmitter implicated in generalized anxiety, be mindful that the amount of serotonin people have does not explain the onset of anxiety, exactly how serotonin is involved remains a mystery, and research findings of serotonin in generalized anxiety are varied and inconclusive.[52] Yet if that's the case why are SSRIs effective for generalized anxiety? Their effectiveness may be accounted for by the diverse role of serotonin.[53] Given the complexity of biological functioning and limited research, more investigation of other variables (e.g. second messenger systems) may improve comprehension and treatment.

Unavoidable natural variation in functioning, composition, neurotransmitter presence, hormone level, and telltale neuronal activity, among numerous other things, may explain different medication responses. Thankfully, when one medication fails to provide relief, another may be successful. But at this time, there's uncertainty about the role of various factors in symptom development and maintenance. Indeed, no specific neurotransmitter system makes itself prominent in generalized anxiety.[54] Simply, more research is needed to better understand what is, and is not, involved.[55] Research suggests that pharmaceutical advertisements may provide too little information and exaggerate the merits of medication while encouraging its use to address symptoms.[56] There's some debate whether such ads are beneficial or harmful, and if the regulations are too flexible and insufficiently enforced.[57] Perhaps tellingly, most countries do not permit direct to consumer pharmaceutical advertisements.[58] Some individuals believe that advertising directly to symptomatic consumers may prompt them to leapfrog or disregard their medical doctors' advice and prompt the prescription of specific medications and dosages.

Although anxiety may be correlated to specific microscopic variables and medication that addresses those factors lowers or eliminates symptoms, doesn't guarantee that those coexisting innate elements universally breed anxiety. In fact, it's uncertain whether neurotransmitter anomalies precede neurotic anxiety, arrive in concert with it, or are caused by it.[59] So, for instance, might focusing on anxiety-producing material generate symptoms as well as the corresponding characteristic neuronal activity, hormone levels, and neurotransmitter presence? Possibly, just consider how neurotic anxiety can change the autonomic nervous system (which controls various areas of functioning such as heart rate, respiration, breathing, swallowing, and sexual arousal).[60]

Now think about if you were to have surgery, you would logically and rightfully expect anesthesia before the first incision. In addition, consider how medication can be a treasured means by which to make life more tolerable or enjoyable, say by diminishing chronic pain, or brief, but intense discomfort, say headaches or muscle sprains. Pain reduction can be a good and useful thing. Anesthesia is incredibly advantageous and mandatory for things such as surgery and insufferable medical conditions, enabling what may be unlikely or impossible. However, while some types can reduce inflammation that permanently stops pain;

in general, it doesn't cure anything (e.g., it's the surgery, not the anesthesia, that solves the problem).

Take a moment to reflect on those with a congenital insensitivity to pain. They may be free — or nearly so — from pesky problems like an achy back, joint pain, toothaches, and sunburns. However, pain-free living isn't as liberating and merry as you might imagine. They're unable to determine what people who can experience pain would immediately know. Consequently, they're prone to biting their tongue or cheek, consuming scalding hot meals or beverages, breaking bones, lacerations, and freezing.[61] So rather than be carefree, they must remain protectively vigilant for threats as well as take extra precautions to avoid injury from even the most commonplace risks.[62] With this in mind, when can medically suppressing pain be counterproductive?

It's when people engage in behavior they should avoid. For example, trying to walk on an insufficiently-mended broken leg because their attention is off of their symptoms or they misperceive themselves as healed and healthy. In addition, there are some who use analgesics to suppress the pain that would otherwise prompt them to visit their doctor. Perhaps they wish to avoid incurring a bill, scolding for unhealthy practices, the notion they aren't as young or strong as they believe, or grave news. However, physical pain can arise from a number of internal problems that impact people's quality of life or threaten it outright. Consider how dentition fractures or infections, lacerations, heart attacks, dehydration, skeletal breaks, starvation, and drowning, blare a loud and rapid pain feedback mechanism that alerts people to a problem. Accordingly, imagine the ill effects of avoiding proper care and merely suppressing symptoms for a variety of medical issues that may turn serious or deadly (e.g., an infected tooth, chest pain, high fever, persistent cough). Pain can be the sharp-tongued educator who reprimands misbehavior and whose discipline guides future action (e.g., shin splints are the body's extended reminder to stretch the next time you go for a run). Whereas pain is most uncomfortable, and at times debilitating, it's the body's useful and necessary feedback channel that aids survival.[63] Therefore, if people were to voluntarily anesthetize their pain to the point of stifling a safety mechanism, their lives rapidly become dangerous. *Although there can be advantages, merely anesthetizing symptoms doesn't cure anything, and for some it ultimately may be a counterproductive and life-threatening tactic.*

Analogously, anti-anxiety medications can relatively quickly, and with little effort, ameliorate or eliminate uncomfortable or painful symptoms. As people often use medications to alleviate various medical symptoms it's no surprise they use anxiolytics to quell anxiety. After all, people needn't suffer. Medication allows people to function in ways that might otherwise be difficult, improbable, or impossible such as working, socializing, or dating. Like an oven mitt, anxiolytics can prevent painful symptoms and allow task completion. In fact, they're often used in conjunction with talk therapy so individuals can face their fears with less stress than if they were unassisted by medication. However, similar to analgesics, anxiolytics aren't curative. Knowing that, how might suppressing anxiety with psychotropic medications be counter therapeutic?

First, imagine a stormy marriage wherein one spouse uses anxiolytics to quiet anxiety. Such treatment isn't uncommon when people believe their symptoms are inborn...or that the spouse won't change. Unfortunately, as the tidal wave of tension is unlikely to ebb, the symptomatic person may continue medication consumption merely to dam the rising sea of marital concerns and deprioritize their resolution with anxiolytic-authorized apathy. Yet once you recognize that anxiety can signal a problem, might medically submerging symptoms perpetuate anxiety, as well as sustain or swell psychotropic use given that the undercurrent of issues remain? In such cases harbored symptoms may swiftly resurface once medication is cast away.

Silencing symptoms with psychotropics may be like muzzling a barking watchdog. In addition, it risks sidestepping responsibility for changing unhealthy behavior or mindset, like children who stick their fingers in their ears and shout "I'm not listening! I'm not listening!" when addressed for their mischief. *Medicating symptoms does not necessarily improve finances, relationships, family dynamics, work conditions, faulty logic, or other contributors to anxiety. This can perpetuate symptoms as long as the main issue remains unaddressed.* This is why psychiatrists often encourage their patients to seek psychotherapy while medication reduces symptoms.

Second, while medication may muffle shrill anxiety, what's a troubling associated risk?

Some who are currently on, or previously used, anxiety-reducing medication complain about a reduction in sexual desire, or experience boredom and depressive symptoms.[64] (Patients describe it to me as being "zombified" — numbly and indifferently detached, incapable of happiness or excitement.) Ruling out overmedication, why might those symptoms arise?

It's because *the physiological response for anxiety is the same for exhilaration, and it's the cognitive interpretation of that physiological arousal that gives meaning*.[65] Medicating anxiety's underlying mechanics doesn't yield joy any more than an absence of debt means that one's wealthy, and it may bankrupt the ability to experience interest and exhilaration.

Third, how might those with low self-esteem perceive themselves when various non-medical attempts to resolve their symptoms are ineffective with medication the only means of relief?

Some view it as undeniable proof they're innately flawed (e.g., genetically, biochemically, physiologically), their condition is incurably chronic, and they're eternally and inextricably shackled to their pill bottle — especially if they're unable to discern any external symptom cause. It's an anxiety-producing perception that can erode self-esteem.

Fourth, think about how people often drink coffee or alcohol to attain a desired outcome. However, with continued consumption they brew a tolerance for the active ingredients and may progressively imbibe greater quantities to reach previous results. Over time, physiological and psychological cravings may escalate and there may be withdrawal symptoms when people are unable to, or choose not to, consume. And, if you think it may be near impossible for people to forgo their morning coffee, how difficult might it be for some to abandon their anxiolytics?

Unfortunately, not only do particular anti-anxiety medications risk habituation, dependency, and abuse, certain individuals may experience symptoms when they discontinue treatment.[66]

Fifth, consider how people automatically and mechanically engage in various behavioral obligations, like brush their teeth or run on a treadmill, while their thoughts pleasantly vacation elsewhere. In addition, some of these behaviors may become intertwined with their identity (e.g., "I'm a runner"). Likewise, individuals may reliably and robotically take their medicine at a scheduled time of day, perhaps at breakfast or before going to bed, anticipating and experiencing the medicinal effects like clockwork. However, what might be an accompanying danger?

Well, imagine that you cut your hand and used an adhesive bandage to protect the wound and accelerate healing. Likely, you'd check the progression of healing when you replace the bandage, testing whether it's needed and discontinue use when the cut is healed.

Now reflect on how individuals may state they feel fine while on anti-anxiety medication and don't feel any drive to terminate its use, sometimes fearing their symptoms will return. However, do they risk taking pharmaceuticals ritualistically without assessing the symptomatic need for continued use?

Sixth, in all likelihood you or someone you know had a childhood illness such as a sore throat or ear infection that an antibiotic cured by slaying the invading army of bacteria. Such experiences create a roughhewn template of medication as curative. Regrettably, anxious individuals who maintain only that conception may believe anxiolytics cured their symptoms as they had anxiety, took pharmaceuticals for a while, and became symptom free. But how can this be if anxiolytics, like analgesics, merely suppress symptoms?

Often there are unexamined confounding variables. Perhaps they settled bills, found fulfilling employment, lost stubborn body fat, removed a suspicious mole, changed their worldview, or started an intoxicating new relationship. Such factors may be difficult to see, indeed even to know what to look for, when people perceive and expect anti-anxiety medication to be curative.

Many medications treat generalized anxiety disorder and there's support for their usefulness; however, with the knowledge that more research is needed, psychosocial interventions may be more effective, and the combination of psychopharmacology and psychotherapy doesn't necessarily improve outcome.[67] Treating generalized anxiety with only pharmacotherapy has varied clinical outcomes, higher rates of attrition from treatment, and difficultly in sustaining benefits.[68] Nevertheless, anti-anxiety psychotropic medication can be beneficial in many circumstances. Like those who take medications to ease their medical symptoms, people may use anxiolytics as an efficient and effective means of to lessen or quell their psychological symptoms. This can improve functioning and enable people to go on about their day with less stress. Indeed, anti-anxiety medications can chemically convince symptoms to quiet down or cease until the therapeutic effect of the medication wears off.

While anxiolytics virtuously and quickly allow functioning that might be otherwise improbable or impossible, medicating without healing may perpetuate underlying issues (and associated symptoms) and, for some, risk being a prescription for long-term pharmaceutical consumption.

Perceiving People as Passive Victims

What may occur when anxiety is seen solely as the repercussion of some external event, say a relationship failure, a disintegrated friendship, or job loss, or as the natural and uncontrollable result of internal causes such as genetic anomalies or chemical imbalances?

Anxious persons may be perceived as passive victims. As innocuous and accurate as this sounds, what are the related dangers?

• Disallowing or minimizing the knowledge that people can influence their symptoms as revealed in declarations such as, "I'm certain it's genetic and there's nothing I can do to change it. So why try?"

• Limiting the number and types of assessment and treatment.

• Surrounding others may imprison symptomatic persons with the arresting indictment of innate deficiency: a seemingly inescapable life sentence.

• Believing uncontrollable symptoms will unpredictably and relentlessly assail them can increase anxiety.

• Obscuring anxious persons' role in symptom development; for example, what they said or did that resulted in the termination of a relationship, friendship, or employment.

What might you do if you see a friend or family member worrying about retirement savings, ruthlessly self-critical about a minor mistake, or crying about a lost love?

You might pause what you're doing, listen attentively, reassure, and fill a much-needed role, for instance, play cupid. *An individual's anxiety can influence others and lead to specific results.* Remember this, for it has tremendous importance and relevance to neurotic anxiety.

Science moves forward when it improves its logic and practice, perhaps by discarding false assumptions and counterproductive and harmful methodologies. Augmenting comprehension and treatment, either in breadth or with finer precision, also can advance science. With that in mind, please note that none of the preceding sections is an attack against insight development, medical or genetic understanding and intervention, or the field of psychiatry and its principled practitioners who provide indispensable medication. Each discipline can be beneficial and will improve over time; however, all have inherent weaknesses or incomplete conceptions. Simply, the preceding illustrates the need for more research and comprehensive understanding, as well as highlights the complexity of human functioning. Like an electric bill, generalized anxiety may have many contributors that vary over time. This underscores the necessity of a biopsychosocial approach, which recognizes multiple factors in symptom development as well as the necessity of diverse assessment and treatment paths.

Broadening the Symptom Paradigm

Whereas some theories wilt in the light of contradictory evidence and new ones flourish in their place, some merely have to accommodate novel information and practice. Yet, why might it be significantly difficult for people to change their perspectives and take in new knowledge?

First, they may gravitate toward simplistic shortcuts and neat explanations, which are economical but may be inaccurate or counterproductive as they make decisions with insufficient information.[69] Accordingly, some patients make unsubstantiated statements they unquestionably accept and evangelize (e.g., assumption of genetic links, unverified chemical imbalances).

Second, individuals may confirm what they believe (even if it's unsupported, incorrect, or bizarre) rather than look for alternative hypotheses and change their perspectives and understanding. *It's easier for people to accept something that's in accord with their perspective than for them to challenge their understanding.*[70] (This is known as confirmation bias.[71]) Accordingly, they may be reluctant to adapt or surrender their theories in the face of incompatible information or when they experience intermittent success.

Third, problems arise when people act reflexively without thoroughly investigating what's said. Unfortunately, unexamined statements may be taken as universal truths and applied to an entire population equally. While simple, easy, and common, uncritically using shortcuts and applying blanket terms neglects to take into account variations and exceptions to the rule. Such stereotyping blurs the conception of generalized anxiety as well as those suffering with it, which may imperil treatment. In other words, some people may apply a fact or half-truth in all circumstances without investigating the limits of what's said or implied, and seek treatment in accord with a misunderstanding. For instance, some believe that all forms of anxiety are caused by an event or are genetic or biochemical in origin because they saw an advertisement or a trusted relative made an uninformed statement.

Now think about how magic tricks and three-dimensional optical illusions teasingly mislead you into believing the impossible. Although you're certain they're just clever deceptions, it can be difficult to grasp how they work given your point of view and expectations. However, once you take a different psychological or physical perspective, what was magic and inexplicable becomes science and intelligible. So, how might this apply to psychological theories of anxiety?

First, people are prone to maintain their mindset and may be unaware they need to look for alternative perspectives to gain greater understanding. Second, it can be exponentially more difficult to know which theories to question, as some are accurate while others are not. Third, it's challenging to change or add to the causal mindset while standing in the same theoretical spot, especially when it's accepted, prevailing, and productive. Peering through the cause and effect lens makes it difficult to perceive its failings and unanswered questions.

Consider how from within the causal mindset it's perfectly logical that people would put forth strong, consistent effort to quickly alleviate their painful, unnerving, and unpredictable anxiety by searching for a cause and then cure (or medicate) the symptoms. Yet, knowing this, why might they do the following?

- Avoid therapy.

- Refuse anxiolytics.

- Sit in silence during therapy sessions.

- Frequently disagree with the therapist.

- Fruitlessly search for symptom causes.

- Forget to take their medication regularly.

- Neglect to do their therapeutic homework.

- Terminate therapy when issues and symptoms remain.

- Not find even a hint of relief in any brand or dose of anxiolytic.

- Visit a number of therapists, but never make any significant progress.

- Label themselves with a different, and perhaps more severe, diagnosis.

- Prematurely stop medication usage (even when it was reducing symptoms).

- Set regular, but infrequent appointments (e.g., once a month, semiannually).

- Routinely make late cancellations or repeatedly fail to attend appointments.

- Go to a few therapy sessions, cease treatment, and then restart months or years later.

• Fail to make changes in thought or behavior that could lessen or eliminate symptoms.

• Attend treatment regularly, but repeatedly change the conversation to irrelevant topics.

• Terminate medication use fearing possible side effects (even if they haven't endured one).

• Receive treatment for many years (sometimes decades) with little or no anxiety reduction.

• Emphatically state their symptoms are genetic or biochemical in origin when they haven't been tested and lack supportive data.

• Contend that their medication is ineffective or has become inadequate, but refrain from seeking a change in pharmaceutical dosage or type.

• Detest the pressure of taking anxiolytics at specific times or with food, but suffer with intolerable symptoms for periods much longer than it would take to consume medication.

• Declare they don't want to become "hooked on drugs" before the possibility of prescription, when they take the lowest dose available, medicate as needed, or habitually use drugs such as caffeine, nicotine, alcohol, or marijuana.

There are various possible reasons for the above. For example, there can be a variation in medication response, insufficient insurance to fund treatment, inadequate practitioners, frequent out-of-town travel, belief that mental health treatment is stigmatizing, religious prohibitions, relying on alternative and non-scientific treatments (e.g., talking with a priest or faith healer, acupuncture, homeopathy, magnetic therapy, Reiki), reluctance to retell painful, yet pertinent historical events and information when repeatedly transferring to new therapists (as may happen at a university or hospital training site), or unreliable transportation. Yet, could that list of behaviors provide clues that unravel a preconception and simultaneously point to a solution?

While the cause and effect approach works well for medical issues, consider how it's applied to psychological symptoms. Broadly, psychiatry focuses on how the brain works chemically, electrically, biologically, and physiologically, as well as the functions of neurons and parts of the brain and how they're related to symptoms. In their graduate training, psychiatrists may study these areas virtually exclusively and from the cause and effect theoretical orientation. They examine symptoms, focus on thought patterns and epigenetic causes as well as assess possible innate initiators, make a diagnosis (which is placed under the umbrella term "mental illness"), and prescribe medication.

Psychologists and other mental health providers evaluate symptoms, predominantly attend to ways of thinking and various psychosocial stressors, diagnose, offer support and employ cognitive and behavioral interventions. While overlaps exist, a simple analogy may better illustrate the differences.

Consider how computers and phones have various physical parts referred to as hardware, such as memory, central processing unit (CPU), graphics chip, long-term storage, antennas, and screen. However, they also have intangible computer code known as software (the operating system and applications), which provide the rules for action and presentation.

Knowing that, you can see how psychiatry may view hardware issues (e.g., neurotransmission, neurotransmitters, ganglion, hormones) as causing anxiety, with treatment focused on addressing symptoms physically (e.g., medication, surgery). And just as it's impossible that all computer or phone problems are hardware based, all anxiety symptoms cannot be psychiatric. Now think of psychology as focused on software functioning, and identifying anxiety as often related to software issues: thinking, perceptions, and rules for living (among other intangible factors such as self-esteem and acceptance) that can influence the body's hardware (e.g., upset stomach, trembling, behavior). Operating within the cause and effect paradigm, psychologists and psychiatrists look for symptom causes and implement their respective forms of intervention. But is that the only way to comprehend and treat symptoms?

What is Neurotic Anxiety?

How might you address the aforementioned trapdoors, doubts, curiosities, and shortcomings associated with maintaining only a cause and effect perspective of generalized anxiety or the conception that there's just a biological or genetic or physiological origin of symptoms?

Well, no doubt you've solved a taxing puzzle or problem after employing a different point of view or novel technique. Fortunately, the field of psychology has many and diverse theoretical orientations.[72] Consequently, there are numerous ways to approach, assess, and treat psychological conditions.

This book is primarily based on Adlerian theory and practice, wherein people are comprehended as active, resourceful, goal-oriented persons functioning within a social field. Adlerian theory and treatment is influential, incorporating individual, genetic, familial, and environmental factors in understanding and treating psychopathology and is therefore consistent with the current biopsychosocial approach in psychology.[73] In addition, it's been one of the main influences on the formation of cognitive behavior therapy.[74] Although more research is needed, it's been effective in treating generalized anxiety and increasing people's quality of life.[75]

Practitioners working from the Adlerian growth model avoid the "mental illness" label and dwelling on the detrimental aspects of functioning. Rather, they view psychological symptoms as a function of development, and concentrate on and increase people's strengths, encourage more beneficial thoughts and actions as well as define healthier goals.[76] This is similar to how a personal trainer teaches people how to exercise safely and effectively or how a nutritionist urges healthier eating. Moreover, it endorses and encourages therapy for personal development as well as for preventive measures.[77]

Although you have a snapshot of anxiety, what does "neurotic" mean?

The term isn't pejorative. It's used to differentiate from biological, chemical, physiological, physical, or genetic factors that may cause anxiety. The Adlerian perspective views neuroses as akin to non-psychotic, personality disorders.[78] Personality can be quickly conceptualized as one's perception of, and rules for, life, self, others, the world, ethical convictions, and goal attainment. It's each person's distinct and defining operating system, so to speak. Neurotic anxiety is seen as personality based with personality characteristics influencing symptom presentation. The Adlerian viewpoint asserts that people are creative, active individuals who through the unique lens of their respective personalities select and move toward countless objectives. With this in mind, you arrive at a compelling and irresistible mystery:

What if anxiety symptoms aren't merely the effect of some cause, but also personality-based and purposeful means to achieve goals?

Chapter 2: Goal Orientation

Given that those with generalized anxiety genuinely suffer, the postulation that their symptoms can be purposeful is predictably controversial as it risks appearing unsympathetic and accusatory. Nevertheless, it's a premise that requires addressing an inescapable and crucial question: How inherent, significant, and pervasive is goal achievement for human functioning and survival?

Importance and Variety

Goals can be conceptualized as the attainment of a different state than the current one (e.g., get married) *as well as the preservation of a particular condition or way of functioning and the avoidance of a loss* (e.g., maintain a marriage and dodge divorce). But that's just the beginning of a vast array of ways to comprehend goals. Fortunately, a collage of snapshot examples can efficiently expose goals' prevalence and power.

People may have tiny intentions such as scratching an itch or life-defining ones like being a movie star, becoming a multi-millionaire, or having a family. *Goal variety varies vastly.*

Contemplate how dedicated individuals may repeatedly take an essential exam before working at their career of choice or how couples earnestly try for a prolonged period before conceiving a child. *Goal achievement might not happen when expected and people may tenaciously maintain their objectives and persevere through failure to achieve what they desire.*

Think about children who dream of driving an expensive, exotic supercar, yet later are content owning a respected, but more affordable sports car. *Approximate goal achievement may be satisfactory.* This may also appear when one desire is willingly altered so that other objectives are achieved. For example, buying a less expensive car will leave money to remodel the kitchen.

When restaurant patrons are informed that what they ordered is no longer available they can select another entrée to sate their hunger. *People may revise the means to reach their goal.*

Now consider how individuals may have particular aspirations, like attend a coveted university or play professional football, which go unfulfilled. However, life continues and they adapt to particular requirements or prohibitions and let earlier desires lie fallow and cultivate new (and perhaps immensely different) ones. *People can select alternative goals when they're unable to achieve their original objectives or become disinterested in pursuing them.*

What's common among asking for a raise, being promiscuous, serving in the military, choosing to be childfree, and minimizing hygiene? As these goals influence health, financial stability, longevity, obligations, appearance, self-esteem, as well as the ability to thrive and reproduce, you arrive at another conclusion: *An individual's goals can have a social impact.*

When people describe themselves, they often start by identify what they do for a living. If retired they state what they used to do or have difficulty characterizing themselves.[79] Also, they may label themselves by their possessions or pastimes (e.g., BMW owner, skier). *People can define themselves by their goals.*

Given that desires such as becoming wealthy, popular, or physically fit can be a means to something else say, a mansion, getting a date, or longevity, you realize that *one goal can enable the attainment of another.* Also, those that complete a crossword puzzle or learn how to play the piano, show that *people can set and attain goals beyond their basic needs.*

What do sex, symphonies, and sports reveal about desires?

Certain goals can only be achieved in cooperation with others who have the same aim.

As people select different careers to support themselves, and raise children in contrasting ways (even within the same family), you can conclude that *individuals with identical goals do not necessarily achieve them in the same manner.*

What might wanting to "do nothing" while on vacation, during a lazy Sunday, or after a strenuous day reveal? *Inaction can enable individuals to achieve their intentions.* When people escape a lifeless party or burning building without deciding on a specific destination they illustrate how *individuals can reach goals by retreating from places, people, and activities.* (That also implies that they're moving toward something, even if it's vague.)

Note that in the United States for about every two marriages there's one divorce.[80] (Note, the takeaway from this often misunderstood statistic is that many people get divorced.) Moreover, factor in those intact marriages that are miserable, emotionally and physically distant, or conflictual. Nevertheless, individuals wed without any assurance of a successful marriage. *People can accept unknowns willfully and gleefully — even for major decisions with relatively poor probability of achieving the desired outcome — as they move toward their goal.*

Consider how individuals may delegate decisions when they're uninterested in the presented choices, don't value the outcome or topic, want to avoid conflict, have no genuine preference, or fear failing. Also, as people cannot be competent in all areas of life, some tasks are left to experts. *People can choose what goals to pursue and which to pass onto others.*

When people vacillate in indecision, say when choosing a restaurant or what relatives to visit on an important holiday, what happens when hunger mounts and inevitable deadlines arrive?

Friends and family members may make the decision. *Some goals can be met by indecision or default* (e.g., students sitting in the back row of a cavernous classroom are unlikely to be called upon for an answer or contribution).

As the preceding slideshow of points suggests, goals are important, varied, and prevalent. So why do some exist and others do not?

Self-determination, Genetics, and Social Factors

Although some individuals believe innate factors cause their symptoms and alibi their actions, how vital is individual choice in human functioning?

Well, perhaps you've had the experience of feeding an infant food that was quickly deemed unpalatable and unceremoniously relocated, seen a toddler single-mindedly kick off uncomfortable and restrictive footwear, or a youngster perseveringly angling for a sought-after toy. Evidently, even the youngest of children can choose and express their preferences and the means to achieve them even if they're counter to what others want. "Sure individual choice occurs," you may say, "but how influential is it compared to genetic factors?"

There are innumerable — and somewhat totalitarian — genetic goals. For instance, after conception and during gestation embryonic cells must divide with extraordinary precision of timing and place to create neuronal pathways and organ development, construct systems for respiration, elimination, circulation, and so on, and operate those systems unerringly. Evidently, DNA-based objectives are necessary for life to exist, and given DNA's influential reign, this underlines goals' importance and prevalence. Moreover, there are countless DNA-based behavioral goals such as reflexes and biological responses. However, even though people often attribute their thoughts, actions, and emotions to their genetic foundation, do genetically-alike family members have identical hobbies, indistinguishable careers, and the same favorite movies?

Not usually. Now examine how although notable similarities exist between identical twins and are significantly greater than those for less genetically-similar fraternal twins, there's debate as to whether some of that correspondence may be due to various non-genetic factors (e.g., others treating them similarly, twins can spend more time together, they may strive to act more alike, they experience similar parenting styles).[81] In addition, identical twins aren't as mirrored as the name implies, and can be rather dissimilar.[82] Obversely, have you ever met people who are unrelated to you, yet have the same distinctive mannerisms as your family members?

The difference between and among siblings may be referred to as the Teeter-totter effect (regardless of twinship), as siblings can choose different objectives and become competent in life differently based on how each sibling chooses to attain significance.[83] The teeter-totter analogy references how one child is superior in one area (e.g., athletics) whereas another sibling may rank lower in that arena but is elevated in another (e.g., academics). This underscores the importance of individual choice and simultaneously relaxes the grip of genetic determinism.

Genetic similarity, and even being reared in the same house, doesn't guarantee that siblings will choose the same career, hobbies, social groups, among other things, no matter how the social environment may shape perception and influence individual choice or how genetic parallels provide particular benefits and limitations (e.g., intelligence, appearance). *Regardless of the genetic and upbringing similarities, each child demonstrates autonomy and individual choice by accepting or rejecting what's available, and by creating new options.*

Recognize that if the genes to prompt eating and sex weren't evolutionarily fortified to the point of fostering two enticing, enjoyable, and universal behavioral goals, humanity would have gone extinct a long time ago. Yet, what can you conclude from the fact that individuals can deliberately decide to starve themselves of food and sex?

People can voluntarily influence at least a few of their genetically-based objectives.

Odds are you know someone who engages in unsafe or unhealthy behavior such as eating or drinking excessively, using illicit drugs, or is in a relationship with an abusive, neglectful, or exploitive person. However, if you offered sound advice, did it go unheeded?

People can choose goals and actions that override vital innate objectives such as health, even to the point where they become perilously obstinate and impervious to argument.

Now consider the social factors in an individual's choice of goals as well as the means to them. For example, examine how parents may prompt things such as feeding and nap times, or later on, how schools, employers, and government agencies provide rules and goals for functioning (e.g., how to solve math problems, traffic conventions and laws). *Individuals impose goals and means to attain them onto others.*

Although parents, teachers, neighbors, characters in books, movies, and television shows, Internet content, fads and fashion and the like may role model behavior and sway goal selection, those things can also be individually dismissed or rebelled against. *From early in life, goal orientation is prevalent and subject to individual choice as well as social influence.*

What might you determine when people follow instructions because they had a sibling who routinely broke the rules and got in trouble or injured? Or, what about those children who learned that ambition allows financial security and status from parents who role modeled successful drive and determination? *People can select goals and ways to attain them from witnessing others' experiences.*

Each culture (or subculture) can influence the value of particular physical characteristics (say through media exposure and promotion).[84] People may change their physical appearance to conform to what's socially encouraged, for instance, by getting into better physical shape or having cosmetic surgery. This desire to adhere to social expectations can extend to tangible goods and services (e.g., clothes, landscaping). Also, keep in mind that individuals may accept or reject culturally-promoted goals, even to the point of doing the opposite of what society promotes. Moreover, just as one person can accept or reject someone else's or a culture's values or objectives, what one culture or subculture appreciates may be something another ridicules or rebuffs.

Although family members can guide crucial matters such as career, study habits, customs, and diet, what does an impassioned couple demonstrate when they excitedly elope despite their families' prohibitions?

When people pursue action in the face of disapproval and possible penalty from family members and friends, they provide incontestable evidence for the power of goal orientation and individual choice. *People may tenaciously stick to their goals even if loved ones sanction them.*

What might you conclude when individuals choose to violate the law or rebel against widely held convictions, such as those who steal, rape, or murder?

Although there are unambiguous laws, promoted moral guidelines, and societal expectations and rules, people can select and rationalize illegal, unhealthy, and socially-sanctioned goals.

When people are ineffective in reaching their objectives or experience a loss of self-determination they may feel helpless and become physically ill.[85] *People need to be able to make their own decisions and choose their own behaviors, often to become competent within their environment.*[86] Although goal orientation is indisputably essential to human functioning, are people always aware of their decisions as well as their related goal-attaining actions?

Conscious and Unconscious

Conscious and unconscious functioning has particular relevance to neurotic anxiety. Although people commonly speak of the "unconscious mind" or the "conscious part of the brain" as if they were two distinct and often conflictual physical territories, that's incorrect.

So what does conscious and unconscious mean?

Simply, that of which you're conscious is that of which you're presently aware. For instance, at this moment you're conscious of the fact that you're reading these words, *aren't you?*

That of which you're unconscious is something of which you're unaware, but could become cognizant. For example, a moment ago you were probably not conscious of your breathing or blinking, but upon attending to those behaviors you become mindful of them. Because the terms conscious and unconscious tend to get confused, an analogy can facilitate understanding.

Note that when you're sitting at a desk, everything on the desktop is in view and readily accessible. The same can be said for that of which you are conscious. However, what's an inherent problem with a desktop? It's limited in how much it can accommodate. Similarly, you can be conscious of only a finite number of things at any particular moment. At first this may seem like a tremendous disadvantage, but must you always be aware of everything you know?

Of course not. If you were constantly aware of all the information in your mind, everything would be a priority, every detail impulsively and distressingly clamoring for your attention, interrupting functioning, and making life unnerving and perplexing, obscuring what you're trying to focus on like rude moviegoers who shout or block your view of the screen. Moreover, just imagine if people were continually conscious of all the times they failed or were rejected. Unbearable memories would persistently and devastatingly savage them and create a relentlessly painful existence that would erode self-esteem and inevitably jeopardize goal achievement including safety and survival. (Besides, the massive firestorm of chemical and electrical activity in the brain required for such omniscience makes it impossible.) Yet, people often need precise information such as addresses, people's names, work figures, and birthdays as well as awareness of the current environment with its perils and benefits. So how might individuals hold a library of knowledge, yet select specific data from their cognitive archives?

Well, what's the solution to the problem of restricted desktop space?

Drawers. What you cannot fit on the desktop, don't want counterproductively cluttering that space, or don't need immediately, is stored in welcoming drawers underneath. You pragmatically migrate items from drawers to the desktop and repatriate them when they're no longer needed.

Yet, note that as you cannot see what's in the drawers when looking at the desktop, you may be unaware that those articles are within reach. You may suspect something is in a drawer, but are uncertain. However, with a cursory glance or a bit of rummaging around you can find the desired item. With this in mind, you can equate those physical objects in desk drawers to that information which is psychologically unconscious. People avoid dangerous and draining information overload by being unaware of data and call it up when necessary, either readily or with some dedicated exploration. *In accord with goal orientation, people may become conscious or unconscious of information based on usefulness.* But that isn't always the case.

Think about when someone asks you a trivia question and the solution is ticklingly hazy and intangible. You may plead, "Give me a clue!" Sometimes, that's enough to resurrect that otherwise apparitional answer. If that doesn't help, you may frustratingly plea for the solution outright; however, once it's given you may say, "I can't believe I forgot that, but I know it's right." Hearing it revived your memory and you became aware of the connection between the question and the answer. The answer was never gone; it was buried deep in some metaphorical drawer in your mind. Sometimes external events or cues bring thoughts or emotions to the forefront of your mind; for example, when looking at old photos and having long forgotten toys immediately spring up in your mind like a Jack-in-the-box. *Internally or externally instigated cues and searches can prompt recollection.* This doesn't imply that everything is unconscious only to be retrieved later with the proper technique. Memories can fade into oblivion.[87]

Consider how individuals may be completely unaware that they back away or pull their belongings near when a stranger approaches. *Some automatic thoughts and behaviors can be instigated consciously or unconsciously.*[88] However, such behavior has an aim (e.g., safety).

Undoubtedly, the first time you drove a car you had to be keenly attentive to how the steering wheel reacted, how much pressure to put on the accelerator and the brake and how fast to do so. However, down the road you can drive with less attention paid to those aspects of driving and shift your focus to other things, such as a song, a conversation, or some future task. *Well-learned actions can become automatic, done without being conscious of doing them, which allows people to attend to other things.*[89] (Have you ever driven somewhere on "autopilot" and not remembered much, if any, of the trip?)

Sometimes people say or do social things without being fully conscious of it until they make a mistake. For example, have you ever dined at a restaurant and when the server said, "Enjoy your dinner," you reflexively said, "Thanks, you too"? Clearly, that person isn't having dinner and you recognized your error a moment after you uttered the phrase. *Much social behavior occurs without people being conscious of its occurrence, but can be predominantly suitable.*[90] When it's inappropriate individuals may realize how much their social actions kick in like an unconscious reflex.

When people consciously work toward their goals they view their behavior as willful; yet, how might they perceive the actions they execute unconsciously?

Often people view their unconscious behavior as being unintentional.[91] This should make perfect sense. When individuals operate in an unconscious way they may not take ownership for their actions, and deem them foreign and accidental. Yet, why is that untrue?

Well, start by thinking about how your dreams take an unpredictable trajectory, a serpentine path that may leave you curious, surprised, alarmed, delighted, peaceful, passionate, distraught, or some other emotion. So why can't you foresee the uncanny turns taken in those nocturnal narratives given that it's *your* brain that's simultaneously generating and viewing the imagery?

The unconscious operates stealthily, and people are often unable to predict what their minds will generate. In fact, there are many ways in which this occurs. For instance, anxious persons frequently have distressing or horrific thoughts appear unexpectedly.

How come people often don't notice the the error that's right in front of them?

If you didn't catch the inaccuracy in the previous sentence you have an example of how *perceptual habits can make unconscious that which doesn't fit your established patterns of perception.*[92] It's a process that secretly organizes material by editing out information that doesn't fit into your rules or experience. Consider how a typo doesn't match your understanding of how a word is correctly spelled and your brain automatically makes unconscious that which isn't in accord with your established patterns. *You may see your intentions,* and be unaware of that which isn't in agreement with your goal for the sentence or word.

Some people mindlessly drive around and "randomly" end up at an old lover's house, pastry shop, or another off-limits, yet alluring, destination that's otherwise impossible to justify to themselves or others. Their goal was protectively and purposefully veiled until they achieved it. *People may engage in goal-achieving movement or immobility unknowing of the purpose.*

Why might people think it shouldn't take them more than 15 minutes to rake the autumn leaves off their lawn when it actually takes them two hours to complete the task?

Clarity about their inaccurate prediction comes from examining their goals. First, they intensely want a tidy yard. Second, they want to avoid doing a tedious chore for hours. So what's their psychological solution to this standoff? They unconsciously distort their perception of the barrier by altering their time estimation.[93] They can start raking by erasing the hurdle that would exist if they correctly estimated the time required. *This unconscious influence reveals their preference.* But why might those individuals keep raking for hours? They may not want an embarrassingly incomplete job, for instance. (And even if they did walk away from the task, in what's known as the Zeigarnik Effect people may recall and have intrusive thoughts about unfinished tasks, which can prompt completion.[94])

Why when people desperately want to meet someone at a bar one lustful night, yet find the patrons unappetizing, there's a notable revision in their appraisal as closing time approaches, seeing those recently disqualified as increasingly attractive?

To attain their desires people must give themselves license to take action and overcome obstacles. This can occur by unconsciously modifying perception. In so doing, people can convince themselves that their randy ruse is authentic attraction, thereby legitimize their intentions and actions. Similarly, those with matrimony on their minds or desire to have a child may reappraise and return to lovers who they've dated and dismissed, perhaps only dimly aware of their own (perceived) time-sensitive flaws like advancing age or thinning hair. Relatedly, some married couples shortly after their children are born or reach school age have increasingly icy or conflictual interactions that precede their divorce. So why did they get married and then divorced and experience such variation in emotion in so few years? Some people want children during the socially-acceptable precursor of marriage and have childrearing assistance during the challenging initial years, but ultimately not give up control, accept long-term vulnerability, associate with the spouse longer than necessary, etc. *Goals can shape perception, thoughts, emotions, and actions in ways that people are unconscious.*

Have you ever been at a party where others' discussions drone on indistinctly as part of the background noise, but you become immediately aware of when someone states your name?

People are able to identify their name when it's mentioned in conversations within earshot when they aren't consciously paying attention.[95] This is an example of selective auditory attention.[96] *The brain can unconsciously filter information and instantly and automatically make you aware of it.*

Have you've ever purchased a car and then saw that type of vehicle with much greater frequency or learned a new word then heard it repeatedly thereafter? It's not because those cars or words suddenly appeared. Rather, you went from being unconscious of their presence to being conscious of them (a.k.a. Baader-Meinhof Phenomenon, Frequency Illusion[97]).

Did you ever watch a movie and suspect that something was odd, but were unable to identify it until you viewed that curious scene again?

Unconscious processing allows information to cross from the unconscious wings to the center stage of consciousness.

Have you ever fell asleep on a couch?

Probably. But, did you ever roll off and tumble onto the floor?

Probably not. But *why* not?

People regularly move during sleep.[98] However, moving on a narrow couch while asleep imperils the unspoken goal of remaining on it to avoid crashing onto the floor. So although you were unconscious of your goal selection, as well as your movement and position on the couch relative to its edge, rather remarkably you never fell off. Evidently, you set and achieved your objective unconsciously.

Now, think about how sleeping during a summer night's light rain may not wake you up...unless you left your windows open. Similarly, exhausted parents may sleep through the most horrific din of their children's play, but wake like a shot upon the first cry. *People can unconsciously monitor and adjust their thoughts and physical actions in accord with their goals.* (Reportedly, Friedrich August Kekulé's dream of a snake eating its own tail helped resolve the mystery of benzene's chemical structure — a circle.[99]) Fascinatingly, people can unconsciously process some forms of information and make decisions while asleep.[100]

The unconscious is only those parts of consciousness that people are unable to completely understand.[101] They can become cognizant of particular aspects of what's unconscious, but as with all things human, insight has natural variation, but that doesn't mean that there's an unconscious mind.[102] Especially one that mischievously or maliciously works against their goals. *Conscious and unconscious functioning work harmoniously, complementarily, and without defining and separating territorial boundary lines.*[103] In addition, *people can act, make decisions, and select goals consciously and unconsciously.* Please note that not every act, slip of the tongue, or memory lapse reveals a secret objective. The error is in overanalyzing what's essentially a mistake or accident.

Significance

When children compare their intelligence, physical abilities, and judgment to others they may feel a disagreeable sense of inadequacy to them as well as to a presenting challenge. It's at this point that children often demonstrate an extraordinary capacity. As children are limited in their ability to achieve their aims, they're motivated to compensate for this deficiency.[104] So, for instance, when children feel incompetent in comparison to others who know how to ride a bike, this sense of inferiority may motivate learning. This is an illustration of direct compensation.[105] On the other hand, if they're poor at math they may excel at, and take pride in, achieving in another arena such as sports, being helpful around the house, or being funny. This is an example of indirect compensation.[106]

Like everyone else, neurotic persons strive toward goals they believe grant significance.[107] It's an overarching goal defined and achieved in different and countless ways, for example:

• Satiation, e.g., "I'm no longer hungry.", "I've played enough Tic-Tac-Toe for a lifetime."

• Competence or Proficiency, e.g., "I know I can speak, read, and write French fluently."

• Safety, e.g., "I can provide clothing, food, shelter, and healthcare for my family."

• Being or having things that are "good enough," e.g., "I'm in a respectable financial position (without needing to be a billionaire)," "I'm reasonably fit (although not an Olympic athlete)."

• Superiority compared to others, e.g., Chess master, have more friends, more industrious, healthier, stronger, smarter, richer, have higher achieving children.

With that in mind, consider the following:

First, *location and movement along the significance yardstick can be defined objectively*. Say, something measurable and universal, like able to lift more weight, or income level. Second, *significance can be a subjective personal preference that may not mirror others' conception of it* (e.g., knowledge of sports or books, kindness, alcohol tolerance). Third, *individuals can measure their significance in comparison to others in infinite areas, subjectively and objectively* (e.g., being single, monogamous, or promiscuous, spotlighted employee or working in the shadows). Like musicians who have the same desire to play in an orchestra, but each choses a different instrument; *people have uniquely-defined subjective goals of significance*. So, how might these areas be categorized and compared?

The Life Tasks

Consider how various animal species enter the world with a notably high percentage of their brains complete with instincts and preprogrammed behavior.[108] Fascinatingly, DNA can orchestrate goal-achieving actions such as building nests, constructing dams, courting rituals and actions, migration, spinning webs, swimming, and walking. These hardwired phenomena increase the likelihood of survival and reproduction, especially for newborn animals that have to fend for and feed themselves. While people have DNA-directed innate behaviors, for example, reflexes (e.g., gag, grasp, blink, pupillary response to changes in light[109]) and sexual arousal responses (secretion of lubricating fluid and tumescence[110]), the amount of preprogrammed behavior is small and simple compared to most wildlife. Although this appears to be a catastrophic disadvantage, what's the upside?

Humans can live in a multitude of environments: jungles, deserts, cosmopolitan cities, cold and desolate tundra, in the countryside, and high in the mountains. Moreover, they have the unique ability to learn different languages, foster distinct cultures, and make use of local materials and adapt to unique environmental advantages and constraints (e.g., what resources are available to build shelter). In other words, a reduced number of hardwired, preprogrammed behaviors allows for extraordinary variation within one species and beneficial adaptation to various surroundings. This allows humanity greater growth and dispersion that exponentially increases the likelihood of survival and reproduction. In addition, when different individuals, indeed disparate cultures, have multiple perspectives they can pool their knowledge and provide abundant ways in which to enjoy life (e.g., different food, art, architecture) and solve problems. However, what's a prominent downside?

People are faced with the obligation of addressing those areas without innate solutions. For instance, people must attain food, clothing, housing, and safety to survive. During infancy and childhood, others provide these necessities. However, as children age they're obligated to assume these responsibilities. This challenge can be defined as the Work Task.[111] While people often select a career goal (e.g., airline pilot) and manner to attain it (e.g., flight school), the Work Task doesn't mandate employment. Sometimes, people rely on others, perhaps parents, relatives, friends, or government agencies, to fulfill those obligations and make life more manageable and pleasurable. The Work Task also encompasses what people do when they aren't working, for example, vacationing, reading a novel, or playing sports.

The Social Task is how individuals associate and interact with others, if at all.[112] Part of this task is how they address the need to belong (e.g., groups, family, friendships).

There's also the Sexual Task.[113] Four subtasks compose the Sexual task.

• Sexual role definition. This is how individuals define being a man or a woman, biologically and socially.

• Sex role identification. This is how people perceive themselves in comparison to their conception of an ideal man or woman. Individual, social, and cultural factors shape this definition.

• Sexual development. This is the achievement and perception of sexual development milestones.

• Sexual behavior. Sexual feelings, sexual activity, dating, marriage, family, physical closeness, acceptance, and love comprise this category. People can approach others or choose to be alone.

The Self Task is how people define and evaluate themselves from a third-person perspective, and it has four subtasks.[114]

• Survival. Individuals' physical and mental health, self-esteem, and sense of belonging constitute this subtask.

• Body image. This is how people perceive and evaluate their bodies.

• Opinion. This is what individuals think of themselves, in whole or in part.

• Self-evaluation (the self-conception of how others receive them, for example, with warmth and understanding, discouragement, or indifference).

The Spiritual Task is how people give meaning to their lives, such as how they define their place in the universe, what they do about such things as religion, and conceptions about life and death.[115] Note that this task does not assume the existence of invisible supernatural beings, magical thinking, or the mystical. The Parenting and Family Task is how individuals regard their families and interact (or not) with them.[116]

The life tasks are inescapable challenges which people lack inborn answers, therefore must select goals and what paths to take to achieve them. *How they choose to address the life tasks is revealing.*

"Real" Man and "Real" Woman

The concepts of natural selection and evolution essentially state that those genes that have a neutral or positive influence on the ability to survive or flourish remain while those that reduce the likelihood of survival or thriving reduce in number or do not remain in the gene pool.[117] Now think about this in regard to how, starting in infancy, people learn what goals to select and how to achieve them. They retain strategies that work and discard those that are inefficient or ineffective. The process of an individual's development is the acquisition of strategies and tactics to achieve objectives in the life tasks. This perspective of life as a progression from an inferior position (physically, cognitively, emotionally, behaviorally, linguistically, and a limited ability to achieve goals) to a competent one by adapting to the environment is Darwinian in character.[118] Indeed, using evolution as the foundation for understanding you can see that people strive toward their goals physically and psychologically.[119] *Thoughts and actions that enable goal achievement become stronger and more likely while those that are unproductive or grossly inefficient become weaker, less common, and may go extinct.* (For instance, you can readily suspect the long-term developmental differences between a child who regularly gets a desired toy after having a nuclear meltdown of emotions in the store versus the child who consistently works diligently on chores and schoolwork to earn the same toys.)

When goals require action to move from one state to another (e.g., get a job promotion), the initial state can be perceived as a minus situation and the final state as a plus situation. Given social influence, individual choice, and problem solving skills, people have the goal to overcome real and perceived minus conditions in creative ways.[120] Keep in mind that what goals people have and how they plan their movement from inferiority to significance is their choice. Perhaps you can imagine how someone might say, "If I work hard, be kind, keep on top of things, go to the right university, and make strategic connections, I'll become a successful businessperson, fall in love and find the right person to marry, have children, develop friendships, be respected, buy a vacation home, and grow old gracefully." When you put these individual choices and plot points together you have a story with a beginning, middle, and end, an overarching goal, character development, twists and turns, unique themes, and all the related elements. People's ideals and means of how to attain their goals are known as "Fictional finalism," something that helps them makes sense of the world and get through life.[121] Yet, why is it a *fiction*?

Well, consider how the person in the preceding example acts as if going to the right university and networking will lead to professional, personal, and financial success, and acts in accord with that conception. However, there may be overwhelming student loan debt (or some other condition) that prohibits the ability to socialize with popular and influential others, get married, have a family, or buy a vacation home. In addition, as people have different goals and means to attain them, there isn't one right way of living. With that in mind, you can see how each person's ideals, paths to significance and goal attainment are a creation, a *fiction* that's acted upon as if those beliefs were true or realistic. Consequently, their accuracy, effectiveness, or long-term impact on themselves or others may go unexamined. In fact, people may attribute failure to their insufficient devotion to, or straying from, their "formula for success," then renew their vows to it — even when it's faulty.

Individuals create their conceptions of a "Real" man and a "Real" woman, which basically represent each person's distinct description of ideal attributes that enable goal attainment.[122] Note that they can include unhealthy as well as socially and environmentally detrimental characteristics and goals; for instance, those who believe they must have things their way can eventually alienate their friends and family. Although these characterizations are individually chosen, imperfect, vary among people, influenced by life experiences, and subject to social pressure, people may defiantly defend their conceptions. It's also important to register how individuals may measure and accept or reject themselves and others against their unique ideal conceptions of a "Real" man and a "Real" woman. Knowing this, how and why might anxiety be generated when people compare themselves to their conception of a "Real" man or "Real" woman and find themselves falling short?

Goals are indispensable, inherent, inescapable, omnipresent, defining, influential, and play a prominent role in safety and survival. People consciously and unconsciously select and achieve objectives to attain significance in the life tasks. And, when you combine goal prevalence with the commonness of anxiety, you arrive at an interesting possibility. Rather than be an inscrutable, pointless, and painful anomaly of human functioning, could neurotic anxiety be a means of goal achievement?

Chapter 3: Emotions

Those with generalized anxiety experience lacerating emotions such as dread, hurt, worry, sadness, depression, frustration, angst, fear, anger, jealousy, shame, and embarrassment. Disquieting sensations gradually saturate and spoil various areas of functioning, say by sabotaging sleep and the ability to concentrate. Unnerving emotional eruptions may flare up without warning, with seemingly inexplicable timing, or without apparent provocation. Moreover, mood swings appear uncontrollable as well as unpredictable in duration and severity. Anxiety can spark frenzied action as well as bully sufferers into retreat or paralyze them. In addition, insecurity, sensitivity, irritability, agitation, restlessness, and confusion can act as an accelerant on emotions and leave anxious persons — as well as nearby others — feeling virtually shredded and perpetually exhausted, with little to no peace. So why might neurotic individuals experience emotions in this way?

Causal, Primal, Embarrassing, and Counterproductive?

What do the following have in common?

- Winning the lottery.

- Seeing a loved one die.

- Listening to a hilarious story.

- Finding out an unscrupulous salesperson swindled you.

Each illustrates that external stimuli can reflexively precipitate emotions, say exhilaration, grief, amusement, and anger.

Emotions such as inconsolable and broken-hearted despair, vein-popping rage, fervid and unrestrained lust show how emotions can appear to have a lightning-fast onset, be primal in their presentation, and dethrone logic. People often believe that intellect elevates humanity and emotions debase it to more primitive level.[123] For instance, the accusation "You're acting like an animal!" may follow someone's intense and unseemly emotion. As intelligent decisions, patience, and logic are valued characteristics, some people may reject or devalue emotions. Correspondingly, suppressing emotions is often encouraged and praised for consideration, composure, usefulness, and superior cognition (e.g., "Be cool,"

"Remain civil," "Keep calm and carry on"). Knowing this, why might people say the following?

"My emotions overwhelmed me."

"I was doing fine, until *you* made me angry!"

"I was completely out of control and irrational."

When people apologize for their emotional displays or characterize them as alien, random, externally caused, or irrepressible they may distance what could imperil self-esteem and acceptance. Now consider how people may fret about their loved ones' fidelity to the point of driving them away or be so anxious that they have to excuse themselves from a sought after job interview, anticipated party, or important meeting. At this point, you might insist that emotions are caused, primal, cringeworthy, foreign, illogical, and antithetical to any purpose, yet how would life be if people didn't have emotions?

Individuals could go about their lives in a practical and consistent way, achieving goals efficiently and effectively. Whole industries would be transformed. People would resolve their differences and propel civilization forward with unprecedented speed and fluidity. There wouldn't be any more crimes of passion or emotional outbursts. Individuals would be liberated from painful emotions, and wouldn't face the choice of chemically restraining them. While this may seem ideal, what's the problem with this hypothetical existence?

Emotions Fuel Behavior

Imagine an elementary school teacher instructing students who — after enduring a biting winter — longingly look out upon the sun-soaked grass under a cloudless blue sky. The educator quickly surmises the lesson is without an audience. Knowing this, why might the following be said animatedly?

"Who's interested in watching a new *3D movie* about dinosaurs? Some dinosaurs were *bigger than a five-story building* and others could run up to *40 miles per hour!*"

Start by looking at the teacher's goal: It's to get the students to attend to the lecture. But is there a bland appeal to the students' sense of practicality and logic with statements such as, "This is important material that you need to learn so you can appreciate life on multiple levels"?

No…but do you know why?

Well, think about how even though people may be fully aware of the numerous benefits associated with regular exercise, some sidestep it with utter indifference. *Logic and facts don't necessarily initiate or sustain action.* So what might?

Consider how by enthusiastically generating emotion, the teacher attempts to energize the students to engage in the lesson. *Emotions can stimulate action toward a goal.*[124] Arousal (mild anxiety) can facilitate performance, depending on the complexity of the task, up to a point where it becomes overwhelming.[125] Without emotion people would be little more than drones doing only what's necessary to survive. After all, how could art, music, sports, and dating move such apathetic creatures?

Although it may be tempting to consider that just children are influenced by such simple emotional ploys, swaying emotions to motivate behavior is used on people of all ages. For instance, why do news shows — forums for delivering facts — have music soundtracks? Facts don't need musical accompaniment. Nevertheless, there's a reason why news programs incorporate music. It's to generate a particular mood or shape a mindset.[126] Now reflect on how inspirational music played at sporting events, political rallies, and religious services may precipitate particular emotions to spur specific conduct (e.g., cheer for a team, vote for a candidate, donate money). The same can be said for a charismatic leader who inspires action. *External factors can initiate positive sentiment that prompts behavior.*

Relatedly, why might people caustically describe those on an opposing side of a conflict or challenge whether it's a sporting event, debate, or war as idiotic, detestable, suspicious, exploitive, or dangerous?

By doing so they can provoke fear, hatred, worry, uncertainty, desperation, peril, or fury, which may incite an otherwise inert audience to take action against others. *People can foster negative, painful emotions in others that can be as motivational as positive and pleasant ones, perhaps more so.*

How might you energize yourself to do a boring or burdensome obligation that you'd rather not do, say filing your taxes, visiting the dentist, or doing the laundry?

You may ponder the positive aspects of the task like getting a tax return, having healthier teeth and gums, or wearing clean clothes. Conversely, you may think about being audited, tooth loss or an excruciating root canal, or going to work in wrinkled, reeking clothes that draw derision. Either way you may be sufficiently motivated to file your taxes, go to the dentist, or do your laundry. *People may focus on conditions or factors that generate positive or negative emotions that spur action.* That to which people attend guides their emotions. (Indeed, perhaps you've seen a child's mood and behavior pivot abruptly when an artful parent smoothly distracts or re-focuses the kid's attention.)

When people dwell on danger, crime, disease, rejection, and failure, they generate fear, worry, apprehension as well as other pungent emotions that can lessen the likelihood of engaging in action such as drinking and driving, walking down a dark alley, having risky sex, applying for a job, or asking someone out on a date. *Emotions can lead to inaction.*[127]

Even though emotions may appear to be caused, primal, embarrassing, counterproductive, and illogical, the preceding offers counter testimony. In fact, when you correctly connect all of the puzzle pieces you get a coherent and revealing picture that's central to neurotic anxiety.

Start with goal orientation. To reach their objectives, people need to either take action or refrain from it. They determine (consciously or unconsciously) which to do, but that's just the beginning. Now factor in the inextricably-intertwined relationship between emotions and action. The former can influence the latter. Accordingly, people must not only select a goal and the means to achieve it (action or inaction), but also must kindle the relevant emotions that initiate the desired behavior. So how might they do that?

People can focus on whatever is necessary to generate specific emotions that energize movement in any direction, or immobilize them from taking action, to reach a goal. (Please remember this, as it's vital to human functioning.) Although emotions may appear to conflict with logic, they aren't rogue agents. People can create and arrange their emotions to be in agreement with their goals.[128] *Logic and emotion can work harmoniously to achieve objectives.*[129] Yet if this is so, why might emotions appear counterproductive, foreign, or irrational?

Well, if the emotion (e.g., anger) fuels behavior which allows a goal (e.g., coworkers' compliance), but it threatens something valuable (e.g., employment), then to achieve the desired outcome plus protect their job, individuals may attempt to distance themselves from their emotion by labeling it as alien and/or becoming unconscious of the relationship between their emotion and their behavior. In addition, people may misperceive their emotions as irrational and counterproductive when they're unfamiliar with the psychodynamics involved and are told their emotions are due to a chemical imbalance, "bad wiring," genetics, outside influences, etc. *Emotions can reveal underlying goals and perspectives, and appear to clash with intellect only when people want to hide their convictions and beliefs.*[130]

Evidently, emotions are natural, necessary, and can be purposeful means to various objectives. So, although emotions are often viewed as animalistic, it's apathy and indifference that make people inhumane.[131] Although this may explain emotional universality you soon face a follow-up question: How do you explain the variation in emotional displays either among people or within an individual?

Controlling and Filtering Emotions

Although the human body can be perplexing, countless clues about its function and structure help resolve riddles. For instance, why might people have different emotional responses to things that would appear to spark a universal, innate emotional reaction (e.g., riding a roller coaster)?

Various individuals experience different emotions about the same thing. First, there are diverse temperaments among children — even siblings — well before learning occurs, and perhaps genetic differences account for various emotional responses to a specific condition or event.[132] Second, and more relevant to psychology, is that people may acclimate to those things that initially generate a particular emotion like an apprehensive youngster who warms to a barking, frenetic puppy or those who conquer their inborn fear of heights and falling to become skydivers. This suggests that people can learn emotional responses, and may overcome genetic loading for specific emotional reactions. Emotions aren't merely a thoughtless reflex. In fact, *feelings and thoughts comprise emotions.*[133] Stately differently, people's physical sensations combined with their cognition foster particular emotions. How people interpret their inner states defines their emotions. Fascinatingly, *the same biological system (sympathetic) is used for anxiety and excitement, it's how the signals are perceived and interpreted cognitively that determines their meaning.*[134] This demystifies those times when people experience different emotions during the same activity, say as when one pilots a speedboat rapidly over choppy water with exhilaration, while the terrified passenger pleads for the boat to stop.

So, how might you explain the following apparent disconnect between emotion and action?

• An employee merely seethes with anger at an insufferable boss rather than assert himself.

• While at a party, a hurt and infuriated wife refrains from responding to her husband's insult.

Clarity requires factoring in the primacy of goal orientation. By swallowing his bitter anger, the employee avoids a long and gloomy wait in the unemployment line among other unenviable outcomes. Similarly, if the wife's desire is to avoid divorce (and the related risks of returning to dating as well as not seeing the children everyday), financial difficulties, poisoning a party, conflict, or further ridicule, she abstains from asserting herself. *People can suppress their emotions, and related action, to reach a goal (including maintaining the status quo).*

In what's known as Impact bias, people can overestimate the positive or negative impact of future events on their emotions.[135] While this poor predictive ability appears to be a human failing, how might it make sense? First, after an event people may be disproportionately focused on it and pay less attention to other matters. So, for example, during a divorce people may disproportionately anticipate the future negative impact on their mood far greater than what actually occurs. Second, examine how this may trigger particular behavior, such as stopping — or slowing down — the divorce proceedings.

Now consider how a foreboding movie soundtrack, experience of someone's inappropriate humor, a change in a person's face or body language, or mindfulness of who's around you, may guide your emotional response, perhaps by amplifying your awareness, setting the mood, or in some other way prepare you for what's about to happen. Knowing this, what might you guess from the following?

• Individuals who refrain from laughing at a racist or sexist joke, not because they don't find it funny, but rather the subject of such invective is within earshot.

• People who curse reflexively and forcefully when something doesn't go as expected, but never swear in front of children when in similarly stressful conditions.

First, as long as individuals wish to avoid conflict, ridicule, or making someone else uncomfortable they'll refrain from laughing at an offensive joke they find humorous. Second, people can restrain their otherwise unregulated emotional expression of expletives when they deem them inappropriate and detrimental.

Changes in the social environment and people's different perspectives can influence emotional responses.[136] Although some emotions can be spontaneous, at least some cognition and judgment may occur before what's often seen as an irrepressible and natural emotional response. *At times, emotions may be cognitively overruled if it assists with goal achievement.* All it takes is a moment's reflect on what's known as displaced aggression (e.g., a supervisor harshly and publicly criticizes an employee, who later goes home and yells at the dog), to recognize that emotions can be channeled and redirected.

But what about those who determinedly (yet without evidence) profess that a chemical imbalance or "bad wiring" generates their emotions and actions? Unquestionably, conditions such as brain injury, dementia, or changes in neurotransmitters and hormones can alter people's functioning, emotional abilities and displays.[137] However, consider the following.

What might a drunk and disorderly college student do when receiving an unplanned call from temperance-advocating parents or the campus police?

If the student's goal is to avoid disappointing others or getting into trouble if found intoxicated, there may be a dedicated attempt to act sober by controlling and filtering behavior that could reveal the level of intoxication; for example, moderating emotional display, speaking clearly, being polite, minimizing speech, as well as remaining upright and stationary (perhaps with the assistance of a nearby wall). As unpolished as the presentation is, might this example demonstrate the possibility that *goals, social assessment, knowledge of proper behavior, and individual choice may partly nullify a "chemical imbalance" (as when there's a strong concentration of alcohol) in the brain?*

Though this seems a bit specific, one-sided, and irrelevant to generalized anxiety, look a bit deeper. For example, the obverse of the above exists. Those who consume non-alcoholic beverages assuming they contain alcohol tend to act inebriated.[138] People can unconsciously modify their behavior based on their perceptions and rules and give the false impression of a chemical imbalance. Also, do all intoxicated people act the same way? For instance, some become loud, others get quiet. (Relatedly, I've seen graduate students drink a pot of coffee, yet *still* not have the energy to work on their intimidating dissertations. Perhaps their desire to avoid the grueling task outran the obligation to get working — despite their caffeine-altered brain chemistry.)

While countless chemically-swayed conditions exist, consider how some people blame their hormones for their behavior and emotions as if they had absolutely no agency over their decisions and actions. Yet, would a spouse accept that assertion when the better half is caught flirting with a coworker? Just consider how often people are encouraged to cognitively overcome their hormonally-influenced behavior (say, indelicately instructed to not think with parts of their anatomy). While certain neurochemicals and brain functioning can play a central and legitimate role in symptom development, these indirect illustrations illuminate a question that may initially appear inappropriate and incriminating: Might some neurotically anxious individuals attribute emotions, thoughts, and actions to internal factors to simultaneously permit them while avoiding accountability for them?

Decongesting Logic Gridlock

Think about how long it would take you to contemplate every element and possible outcome for decisions with innumerable and undisclosed components. For instance, choosing which house to buy contains inherently unknowable factors that would otherwise influence your selection (e.g., the house was built above what would eventually become a sinkhole, hidden poor workmanship compromised its structural integrity, inconsiderate neighbors would allow their dog to bark ceaselessly and use your lawn as a maintenance-free litter box). As most decisions have inestimable factors, there could always be some element that went wrong or wasn't considered. With an increase in the number of variables, there's an exponential magnification of time and effort required to arrive at a sound judgment. This may paralyze people from making a choice. *Contemplating all the possible factors and consequences of each decision would be too taxing and counterproductive.*[139] Yet, why are such cognitive traffic jams so rare?

Well, examine what people do when reasoning is too time consuming or overwhelmingly immense, when there are several equivalent options, or how they resolve common decisions like where to eat, what movie to watch, what painting to buy, or what music to play. They have to make a choice, but don't have the time or resources to take everything into account. They may engage in particular behavior because "it feels right," or they're "in the mood" for a particular option, or they have a "gut feeling." *When logic is insufficient or cumbersome, emotions can tip the scales in the decision-making process and decongest logic gridlock.* Contrary to the belief that emotions contradict logic, *emotions can have practical effects on decision-making.*[140] In fact, anxiety can prompt healthy decisions, such as do an excellent job at work, bring food to an ill neighbor, or protectively monitor children's safety. However, does this mean that anxious people always arrive at the healthiest or most advantageous solution?

Absolutely not. People can multiply their emotional intensity and work themselves up into a frenzy and take action "without thinking." Neurotic persons' emotions can fuel frantic action that's decidedly irresponsible or risky (e.g., breaking their diet, buying something that's unaffordable, having an affair) or paralyze them from healthy actions (e.g., not get a physical, refrain from asking out a desired other). So does this mean that emotions are unrelated to their goals?

No. While it can appear that way, clarity comes from examining people's objectives. When individuals have a yearning that's unjustifiable, their anxiety may allow them to swiftly and forcefully overrule prudence and authorize irresponsible or dangerous endeavors. This prohibits them from taking the time to examine their actions — for if they did, they wouldn't be able to permit themselves to do it. (In other words, it's easier to wolf down a doughnut or two than to pause and think about the long-term and undesired consequences of that consumption, as that would forbid eating the doughnuts. You can imagine how people can do this in a number of arenas, such as frenetically buying things online with a quick and easy click of a button.)

Emotions enable people to subjectively appraise options, and prioritize them.[141] *This allows them to whittle a forest of factors to a more workable amount, lessen or evade logic and spur impulsive action, and stimulate faster and more committed decisions that lead to goal-attaining action or inaction.*

Feedback and Future Decisions

Why might people experience a sense of peace or accomplishment after mowing their lawn or going to the gym? On the other hand, what are the advantages for those who have distressing guilt feelings for littering or leaving work early?

Emotions can provide feedback and be part of a behavior appraisal system that increases or decreases the likelihood of engaging in an action again, as well as provide a predictive function for what emotions to anticipate after a behavior.[142] *Emotions can reward or punish behavior, thereby guide and facilitate future decisions and actions.*

So what might this knowledge allow?

As people assess their emotions they can develop insight about how they perceive themselves, others, or life. Relatedly, registering how you feel when you interact with another person may provide a peek behind the curtain into that individual's internal state. For instance, if you feel irritated or unsettled, that may merely be a fraction of how annoyed and flustered that person feels. You can imagine how new parents might be unnerved and frustrated when they don't know what their infant wants. This may get a glimpse of what feelings the child is experiencing.

Emotions (along with bodily functions and reason) constitute one vital part of the trinity that enables full human functioning in the pursuit and maintenance of survival.[143] So even though emotions may be initially deemed caused, foreign, irrational, and counterproductive, they can be adaptive and provide future and enduring benefits.[144]

Knowing that people may unconsciously control and filter their emotions to achieve specific goals, you face another challenge: How do you decipher neurotic symptoms whose purpose may be invisible to even those who have them?

Chapter 4: Solidarity

Some neurotically anxious individuals view their bodies as comprised of ungovernable, infighting factions of biology, chemistry, neurotransmitters, and so on, which trigger insufferable symptoms. Accordingly, they may feel ceaselessly on the verge of an unprovoked attack. Yet, how might this belief of balkanized and mutinous bodily groups be a misperception?

Unable to Identify Causes

Consider neurotically anxious individuals who insist they *must always be* active and productive, and this rule for living is related to anxiety development. In their pursuit of understanding why they're anxious, there's a notable catch. If this personal directive was acquired early in life and is central to their philosophy, they may view it as natural and normal. As a result, the link between the way they think and their anxiety can remain hidden in the shadows, unexamined and unchallenged. If they're unable to discern a personal, relationship, financial, social, occupational, legal, or health stressor as responsible for their symptoms, they may misidentify unseen and uncooperative internal physical factors as the source.

A cause and effect conception of symptoms, combined with the inability to identify a stressor, along with an obstructed connection between mindset and anxiety, may make people prone to perceiving their symptoms as inborn, and their bodies as composed of rebellious, infighting, and antagonistic entities.

Learning to be Anxious?

Quiz time. Please answer the following questions as quickly and completely as possible:

1. What are your parents' names?

2. What are your siblings' names?

3. What are the names of your first grade classmates?

It's a safe bet that you instinctively answered the first two questions, but perhaps were only able to hesitatingly name a few fellow students, if any. This is rather revealing considering that there was an appreciable period in your life when you knew all their names. Thankfully, an answer is within reach. Note that learning is the action of constructing communication pathways among nerve cells in the brain.[145] Nerve communication is a physical, electrical, and chemical process.[146] Simply, nerve cells grow and associate with other neurons in a jungly thicket of intertwining trunks, branches, and roots that converse in a remarkable way. Electrical impulses rocket along the nerve and then the communication between or among nerves is accomplished by the presence or absence of neurotransmitters that excite or inhibit electrical activity in the subsequent neurons.[147] With sufficient practice or in some other way, such as a single, but emotionally-laden event, learning occurs.[148]

Being able to rapidly recall your family members' names means that your brain not only has neurons in place, but also that the proper electrical, chemical, and physical action occurs. Repeated performance and exposure to those names fostered the appropriate neurons as well as strengthened and multiplied their pathways and cultivated robust responses that enabled you to answer quickly and correctly. But if that's the case, then how do you explain your inability to remember all of your first grade classmates' names? After all, you had the neuronal associations and communication to recall them years ago, but are unable to do so presently. Odds are that you're able to remember some of those first grade classmates' names because you saw or interacted with them for years afterward or periodically encounter. Or, perhaps you were able to recall those who had a strong positive or negative emotional association such as the class clown, a bully, or your best friend, as emotional connections foster long-term learning.[149] Basically, you're able to recall family members' and specific classmates' names because you have stronger electrical, chemical, and physical actions as well as hardy neuronal connections in your brain. However, does this imply that you have a chemical imbalance or "bad wiring" for either those names remembered or forgotten?

No. Given that learning requires a change in neuronal organization and/or chemical activity, then by definition your brain is physically, or acts in a way that is, different from the way it was prior to learning. So how might this account for your failure to remember classmates' names?

Consider that when people stop exercising they lose muscle mass and strength.[150] Likewise, people's memories can weaken to the point of being irretrievable.[151]

So, what might be your verdict from the following evidence?

• Exhibit A: Given that you can speak with little or no forethought and with few errors it can be said that you can express yourself spontaneously, virtually automatically.

• Exhibit B: Likely, you've been using your native language for as long as you can remember.

• Exhibit C: You're probably unable to recall a time before speaking your mother tongue.

• Exhibit D: Your brain has language-related neuronal structures and connections.

• Exhibit E: Your brain has strong and reflexive neurotransmitter activity associated with language use.

• Exhibit F: Odds are, you speak the same language as your parents, siblings, and grandparents and share unique pronunciations, memes, and catchphrases.

Although the preceding makes a logical case that your language use is innate, it only takes a momentary reflection to see that the assertion is deceptive and flawed. Just recall how you spent years of your life at home, in the classroom, and on homework, developing your language skills. *Early learned behavior and ways of thinking can give the false impression of being inborn.* With that in mind, consider the following:

1. If people are able to activate particular areas of their brains and influence related neuronal activity and neurotransmitter presence (among other things) by merely focusing their attention, wouldn't attending to or dwelling on stressful conditions or events, whether in the past, present, or future, real or imagined, generate anxiety-related neurotransmission and the associated chemical presence in the brain?

2. If individuals attend to anxiety-producing concerns for a prolonged period, might they produce the associated neuronal development, connections, neurotransmitter levels, as well as other microscopic features and functioning?

3. Over time, would these elements enable swift and intense symptom generation that gives the impression of being virtually involuntary?

4. Accordingly, might these changes in neuronal connections and activity provide evidence that the brain can learn to generate robust and increasingly automatic anxiety as the brain is physically, or acts in a way that is, different from the way it was prior to symptom onset?

5. Is it then possible that these brain alterations could lead to identifiable differences in neuronal structures, neurotransmitter amounts, as well as other microscopic factors, from non-anxious persons?

If dwelling on stressful concerns commences a characteristic constellation of brain activity that in due course cultivates and strengthens particular neuronal structures, neurotransmission, etc. as well as enables rapid anxiety onset, might neurotic anxiety appear innately caused when in reality, it was focused thought that fostered those defining symptomatic factors?

The Unity of the Personality

Although symptomatic persons may perceive their bodies as a collection of utterly illegible, uncooperative, battling entities, is there an intelligible method to not only read the body, but also do it in a way that reveals a starkly different conclusion?

Start by acknowledging that body language has many communication channels: facial expressions, gestures, tone of voice, rate of speech, loudness, posture, and touch.[152] For instance, imagine a man arrives home from a football game, slams the door, rips off his favorite team's jersey and throws it onto the floor, then dramatically crumples his ticket and hurls it into the garbage. At which point his wife calmly asks, "They lost?"

The saying "The eyes are the mirror of the soul," suggests that peoples' eyes reveal their thoughts.[153] Is this just a relic of more superstitious and mythical times or might there be some truth to the notion? After all, lies are nothing more than people expressing false statements or withholding truthful information (a.k.a. *suggestio falsi* and *suppressio veri*[154]). They are purely immaterial thoughts, a belief of what's true or false. Yet, a change in the dilation of the iris may reveal when people are lying.[155] Also, consider how polygraph tests show autonomic nervous system activation and emotional arousal in physical means.[156] The gathered information is used to attempt to discern lies by assessing physiological and physical activity: pulse rate, skin conductivity, breathing, and blood pressure.[157] Now think about how in card games the word "tell" represents a facial expression, gesture, sound, or movement that conveys what a player is thinking or feeling, say when holding an enviable or horrible hand.[158] Micro expressions (facial expressions less than a second in duration) can reveal lies and various emotional states.[159] And, regardless of people's language or culture, emotions are identifiably associated with a mappable array of physical bodily changes and experiences with different emotions having overlapping but distinct areas.[160]

Contemplate how there are distinct types of tears (basal, reflex, and emotional) that differ by how they're activated, with emotional tears being psychologically based and related to communication.[161] Taking this a bit further, maybe you've seen worried individuals with informative sweat marks, argyle lines of anxiety on their foreheads, or they expressed having "butterflies" in their stomach (a.k.a. nervous indigestion). Or, perhaps you're familiar with the "white coat syndrome" that occurs when people's blood pressure elevates solely because of being in a clinical setting.[162] In addition, examine how psychological factors (e.g., anxiety, guilt feelings, and fear related to sexual abuse, trauma, or religious orthodoxy) may influence vaginismus, erectile dysfunction, and premature ejaculation.[163] *Measurable, bodily effects can communicate persuasive intangible thoughts.*

Knowing this, what do you think can happen when people dangle a string with a small weight on one end and visualize it moving circularly while intentionally attempting to hold the string motionless?

Tellingly, the weight swings in a circle even though they're consciously trying to immobilize their hands. If they visualize the weight moving to and fro, it will transform its movement from circular to back and forth. They sincerely believe they aren't moving their hands, yet the weight provides convincing contradictory data. This is called the ideomotor effect.[164] Perhaps you've seen people unconsciously make a fist when speaking with loathed individuals. Or, if you've ever been curious (or mistaken) about how Ouija boards and dowsing work, now you know.[165] *Thoughts or suggestions can influence unconscious or involuntary behavior.*

Have you ever wondered why people may swear in response to pain? Interestingly, swearing can increase pain tolerance.[166] This benefit isn't due to just any vocalization, as there's a difference in pain tolerance between profanity and neutral words said with the same intensity. Relatedly, those who swear more frequently do not experience the same level of pain tolerance as those that swear less often.[167] It's as if they cognitively acclimatize to profanity, thereby make it pedestrian and less impactful. The connection among thoughts, feelings, and actions is supported in many and colorful ways.

People are able to alter the activity of various biological and physical events — even those based in the hindbrain (the lower portion of the brainstem: the pons, cerebellum, and medulla oblongata) such as heart rate, blood pressure, respiration, and sexual functioning.[168] And in what may seem to some as a deflating inequity, there are women who can achieve orgasm merely by visualizing and thinking about arousing, sensual, and sexually explicit imagery and sensations.[169] In addition, consider how sword swallowers (among others) cognitively suppress their biologically-based gag and retch reflexes to achieve their feats.[170] Also, card players are aware their physical presentation may tell their thoughts and emotions and wish to refrain from communicating what might jeopardize their goal of winning. Having a "poker face" demonstrates how people can make a conscious attempt to silence revealing actions that would otherwise be expressed physically.[171] And, if you thought that lie detectors are piercingly omniscient, there are psychological countermeasures to defeat polygraph tests.[172] *People can consciously attempt to control unconscious and involuntary behavior.*

Those adopting a high-power physical pose (e.g., broadening themselves, stretching out, physically opening up) for just two minutes can demonstrate increased risk tolerance compared to those who adopt a low-power physical pose (e.g., being physically closed up, making themselves physically smaller, say by hunching over). Also, those who adopt a high-power pose have increased testosterone (a hormone related to dominance) and decreased cortisol (a hormone associated with stress) and become more assertive, confident, and comfortable.[173] *Consciously changing physical presentation can influence body chemistry, attitude, and action.*

In what's know as the clean slate effect or the MacBeth effect, washing one's hands may alleviate guilt feelings associated with unethical behavior or the impact of previous decisions or behavior (with or without moral implications).[174] *Physical actions can change mood, self-perception, and future behavior.*

Amazingly, there are instances when treatment with no clinical efficacy (e.g., a sugar pill) is dispensed to patients who nonetheless experience a significant result based on their expectation; this is called the placebo effect.[175] Additionally, the placebo effect can enhance cognitive performance.[176] *Merely the belief that something may be beneficial can have healthy effects.*

Conversely, in what's called the Nocebo effect, people experience a worsening of symptoms when given a substance that has no clinical effectiveness or even positive effects merely because they expect the substance to be harmful.[177] Now take into account how stress can compromise immune system functioning, erode the ability to heal, and resurrect latent viruses such as herpes and Epstein-Barr.[178] Moreover, there are scores of psychogenic ailments — those that originate psychologically rather than physiologically — such as bruxism (tooth grinding), psychogenic dwarfism, conversion disorders, and anxiety-related back pain, which attest to the connection among thoughts, emotions, behavior, and physiology.[179] *People can think in a way that has unhealthy physical outcomes.*

Examine how those who believe that something bad will befall them can experience certain associated emotions, and take action to prevent or minimize undesirable outcomes. For example, people may unrealistically believe that their jobs, or friends' acceptance, is in jeopardy, then worry about their presentation and go to great lengths to protect their employment and friendships. *Emotions can reveal personality, goals, and perceptions.*[180]

Neurotic anxiety can have influence beyond its emotional jurisdiction; for example, anxious individuals may experience muscle tension, chest pain, headaches, or night sweats. *Emotional tension that's prevalent in neurosis can create physical symptoms.*[181] Anxiety-based physical symptoms can be especially alarming due to their unpredictability, unfamiliarity, and intangible origins, as well as different treatment, compared to medical maladies. In addition, note that some anxiety symptoms can be identical to those associated with serious physical complaints, e.g., night sweats can be a cancer symptom, chest pain can be a symptom of a heart attack, memory loss is telltale sign of dementia. Unsurprisingly, those who curiously search the Internet for reassuring and enlightening information about their (anxiety-based) physical symptoms may stumble upon lethal or crippling diagnoses that inadvertently intensify their anxiety.

Some neurotic individuals misperceive their anxiety-based physical symptoms as genetically, physiologically, or biochemically based. Accordingly, they may set up regular appointments with their medical doctors, acupuncturists, or chiropractors, to periodically soothe their recurrent psychologically-originated physical aches and pains. Alas, overlooking the true basis of their symptoms can make them chronic concerns.

Children use metaphor in play.[182] And it appears reasonable to say that before infants and children develop their ability to speak and read fluently, metaphor may serve as their first language. After all, given their meager vocabulary they may not be able to comprehend the words, but they're able to understand and think in pictures — equating, for instance, a red droplet on a faucet with hot water and a blue one for cold. So what do metaphorical associations mean for understanding neurotic anxiety?

Well, just think about how some people say they were "scared $#!+less," then acknowledge the scientifically-valid connection between intense stress as well as generalized anxiety and irritable bowel syndrome.[183] Moreover, stressed persons may pull their hair out, bite their nails, or perhaps experience a pain in the neck when interacting with annoying others. There's even a "Broken heart syndrome" (Stress cardiomyopathy) that occurs after a stressor such as the loss of a spouse.[184] *Psychological distress may be expressed metaphorically through physical symptoms.*[185] While this may appear quirky, coincidental, and irrelevant, it may nevertheless provide clues that guide assessment and treatment.

Consider how some gamblers gratifyingly remember the times they won and not recall (or recollect as often) how many times they lost, and how this may influence their perceptions and actions. If people want to do something they'll perceive it as good, right, enjoyable, beneficial, earned, necessary, etc., which permits or prods that behavior as well as erases or discounts that which isn't in accord with their goal. (Interestingly, patients may, for instance, tell their spouse that their therapist said something in accord with the patient's goal [e.g., that the spouse should do something], when in reality the patient misperceived what the therapist said to be in agreement with what the patient wanted to hear.) Similarly, cognitions, emotions, and actions collaborate in ways people are unconscious; yet allow them to attain objectives. So, for example, people may forget to go to a boring meeting, or one where they feel exposed, completely unaware of it until after it ended. Patients may forget their appointments or to do their therapeutic homework, for instance, if either appears threatening or too difficult. *People's goals shape comprehension and memory.*[186]

Given the preceding data, the mind-body dichotomy may merely be a misperception and a misnomer. In what's known as the *unity of the personality,* each person operates as a consistent entity with the mind and body working cooperatively and indivisibly.[187] Solidarity among bodily system siblings can explain the fraternal correlation and cooperation among symptoms, neurotransmitter amounts, and brain regions activity, etc. as well as how medication can suppress symptoms. Now take that a bit further. What does such consistency among various arenas allow?

The knowledge of one can be used to predict another, as well as the ability to forecast and explain particular brain activity and neurotransmitter levels, for instance. So, seeing the physical manifestations of anxiety (e.g., pressured speech, being fidgety, perspiration) can suggest the correlated brain activity, neurotransmitter levels, among other microscopic factors and physiological actions. Also, this awareness can assist in demystifying how different body areas represent anxiety. Neuroses with physical correlates may only be comprehended when conceiving of an individual as a unified whole.[188]

Some perceive generalized anxiety as the painfully inscrutable and counterproductive result of infighting among various bodily components that sabotage functioning and aspirations. However, the unity of the personality provides clarity and corporeal comprehension. Thoughts, behaviors, and emotions can symbiotically join forces to attain goals within a social environment, each system influencing the others in any direction, consciously or unconsciously. When facing inconsistent factors or uncertainty about generalized anxiety, it's necessary to search for the missing puzzle piece that once placed makes a complete picture.[189] To understand neurotic symptoms it's important to look for the goal of the behavior, as that's part of the unity of the personality.[190]

Chapter 5: Societal Individuals

There's a common perception that anxiety pertains only to the person, has distinct innate origins, and is comprised of unique, quarantined, and therefore unrelatable, concerns. From that perspective, it's imperative to investigate an individual isolated from others…but is that possible?

Lifelong Socialization

At what point in the life span does a person become fully independent?

Indisputably, independence cannot be at conception or during gestation when the mother provides the literal lifeblood, with her health, diet, smoking, drug and alcohol use, influencing fetal development, welfare, as well as her child's DNA.[191] Likewise, newborns need compassionate others nearby to provide food, clothing, shelter, and attention.

Infants and toddlers must acquire various skills, like learning to walk and communicate. While they may theorize and experiment with their newfound physical world, decide which toys to use, etc., observing others and being taught, comprise much of their learning. In addition, others thrust goals (e.g., eating, sleeping, learning) upon them.

Children may be frustrated and stymied when trying to reach their objectives, or too impatient to experiment and learn, and soon recognize that surrounding others are more capable of attaining (often superior) goals. They may ask others for help, parrot their words, or mimic their decisions or actions. Note that anyone can serve as an educator, say family members, teachers, neighbors, and even those passing strangers who make statements or role model particular behavior. By extension, the human-created content on the radio, Internet, and in books, television shows, and movies can instill values and ways of acting. Socialization and instruction allow children to comprehend rules and modes of communication and interaction, consequences, values, concepts, functionality, and roles people play, which enable greater goal selection and achievement in multiple environments. Undoubtedly, you can recollect people who influenced you, be it an encouraging teacher, a grumpy neighbor, or even some influential, and warmly remembered, TV show or movie characters.

Children's natural curiosity and spongelike ability to soak up information offsets their insufficient knowledge and limited behavioral range. They eagerly fortify their understanding of the world and build competency by achieving increasingly challenging goals. Their successes are pleasurably reinforcing and increase the likelihood of future attempts. Indeed, you've probably seen children beam with radiant pride when they demonstrate some newfound skill. Yet, how might this marriage of intrinsic motivation and abundant energy be hazardous?

Their inquisitiveness is precariously interwoven with naiveté. Consequently, they may have insufficient caution for common dangers such as choking, drowning, falls, poisons, and burns. Fortunately, others provide safe environments as well as a watchful eye and protective hand.

Teenagers and young adults may experience reassuring camaraderie with like-minded others. It's a time when ostracism is feared and acceptance craved. Awareness of what's acceptable can be the cover charge to gain entry into a club of valued people. This knowledge can maintain status and minimize rejection. Also, from young adulthood onward, intimate relationships can grant unparalleled joy, peace, as well as exhilaration, and is essential for species survival. Relatedly, new parents regularly share responsibilities to fulfill family demands, and may rely on others to assist financially or with childrearing. So if you held the belief that adulthood is when a person is finally liberated from others — therefore the best time to assess individual functioning — you need to take a broader view. Adults have to fulfill certain life obligations, at least procure shelter, sustenance, and clothing. Pursuing a career or honing one or more disciplines allows them to contribute to society and afford life's necessities and then some (though those with children in college may dispute the latter). Yet, how does each person access countless services necessary for survival, when skill specialization prohibits self-sufficiency?

Cooperation and complementary roles allow individuals to exchange their abilities so that everyone benefits. Each person refines a skill that contributes a valuable role to the group, with others' abilities supplementing that person's weaknesses or inexperience. You may not be able to do your own surgery or electrical work, for example, but others can and it's through reciprocal effort that people achieve safer and more enjoyable living. In this way, societies develop a broader scope, become more resilient, can advance their collective knowledge, and increase the number and scale of achievements, say space exploration, healthcare, or engineering feats. (As a thought-provoking side note, under certain conditions the collective wisdom of a group may be more precise than that from the smartest individual within it.[192]) *Social interaction, cooperation, and interdependence enable a pooling of resources to attain a multitude of individual and group objectives.*[193]

Now reflect on how senior citizens may be able to bestow their accumulated wealth of experience and have the financial security to charitably enrich other's lives (or watch the grandchildren whose parents are utterly exhausted or desire uninterrupted intimacy, for instance), but may be reliant on those who can compensate for any erosion of physical and/or mental capacity that may occur with advanced age. Collaboration compensates for people's inherent physical limitations.[194] This equally applies to humanity's relative lack of hardwired instincts and strengths other species have. Obversely, people acting in self-interested ways can poison their community and ultimately jeopardize their own well-being.[195] Even when there's competition for limited resources that sparks interpersonal conflict, a global goal that encompasses all involved fosters cooperation.[196] Social problems may only be solved by those who are willing to work together.[197] Perhaps that's why all civilizations have begun communally.[198] *Throughout each life stage an individual needs to cooperate and be interdependent to address life's challenges.* (Therefore, the answer to the question posed at the top of this section is, "Probably never.")

The Game of Life

What are the common characteristics of football, cricket, baseball, hockey, and volleyball?

- There's competition between or among participants.
- Contestants have a clear objective: to win the game.
- To achieve that goal they must achieve subgoals (e.g., score points).
- Each game has common rules created by communication and consensus.
- There's cooperation among teammates for the mutual goal of winning.
- All contestants collaborate for the common desire to play the game.
- Tactics that violate the rules may be penalized.

So how might you generalize these characteristics to life?

Well, think about how life has ultimate goals: people want to survive and thrive. And similar to games, people achieve these goals by attaining subgoals, such as eating, earning a university degree or gaining skills training, securing a career, and having a family. *Achieving subgoals can be required to attain the vital objectives of surviving and thriving.*

Now examine how team players often have specific, yet complementary roles that contribute to the group's success toward winning the game. Similarly, people have various harmonizing careers and abilities that enable an individual, as well as a society, to survive and thrive. *Social cooperation with complementary skill sets benefits individuals and the larger community.*

Just like teams compete, individual team players may go head-to-head with those on the same team (e.g., MVP status). Similarly, individuals (including siblings) vie for jobs, homes, affection, or virtually anything else. *People can compete against others — even those closest to them — for the same goal.*

While games require participants, there's another essential element: rules. What would happen if there weren't any rules for a game?

There would be confusion about the goal, how to achieve it, subgoals and their values, with some participants playing in unpredictable and unacceptable ways that sabotage collaboration, goal achievement, and ultimately, the game. Players would become increasingly irritated, frustrated, confused, intimidated, and angry. The solution is that players and officials reach an agreement about the game's common rules. But, as life doesn't come with an instruction manual, how do people achieve goals with some agreement of how to act?

Those within a community communicate and arrive at a consensus of widely accepted and encouraged rules and goals that evolve over time (e.g., language, gender roles, dating conventions, childrearing practices, driving rules, and socializing guidelines).[199] This common knowledge has another, more familiar, name: Common sense. It's something that people may take for granted and become frustrated or angry when others don't exhibit it. (Just reflect on how the question "Don't you have *any* common sense?" isn't a compliment.)

Now, liken a society to a restaurant and its collection of common sense to a restaurant's menu. No matter what a restaurant patron selects from the menu, it'll be acceptable to every employee. As individuals develop within a society, they select their goals and ways to realize them. Their choices can be based on numerous factors: environmental cues and feedback (e.g., living in a critical and chaotic household), bodily sensations (e.g., elevated heart rate, muscle tension), their interpretations of that data, and their education (e.g., others' direction and guidance).[200] Basically, each person contemplates various perceptions, rules, actions, and objectives, and then selects those most agreeable and appetizing, ignoring or discounting those deemed unpalatable. Whatever is selected from society's menu of common sense is regarded as normal, healthy, allowable, and, perhaps, commendable.

Yet, what about those choices that are "off the menu"?

This has notable relevance to neurotic anxiety. You see, an individual's decisions that deviate further from the predominant knowledge are often deemed incorrect, counterproductive, and/or as "mental illness." This reveals another way in which a person is tethered to society. *Psychology assesses an individual's movement and goals in comparison to others.*[201] In other words, a table of one at a restaurant stands out because it's adrift in a comparative sea of more populated tables. In the equation of an individual, there's always a social factor. While comparing a person's goals, thoughts, rules, and actions to society's common sense may seem like a simple and salubrious standardization, like agreed-upon time and distance measurements, how might it be problematic?

First, given that common sense evolves, it's a moving target, with some behavior entering or exiting the realm of acceptability depending on timing. Second, is common sense the same in Athens, the Australian Outback, or in an Amazonian clan? No. Different cultures maintain different truths and what's encouraged in one may be discouraged in another. (Even different news sources — conduits of facts — have diverse perspectives on the same event.[202]) And this gives you a glimpse of a larger problem. Squint your eyes a bit and you can see how even within a group, say a profession, religion, or political party, seemingly likeminded individuals have variations in their otherwise overlapping perceptions and rules. Narrow your focus some more and notice how parents and teenagers or contrasting siblings can hold different beliefs and values. Amazingly, while there can be overlap among rules and perceptions, *each person has a unique perception of reality*. Knowing this, what telling conclusion do you reach?

Common sense isn't especially common. However, does this mean that people always need to strive toward the popular to be healthy?

Well, think about how stereotypes, myths, superstitions, old wives' tales, some traditions, uninformed beliefs, various religions and political systems, improper medical treatments, and some family values and customs, demonstrate how unhealthy beliefs may be taken as common sense and encouraged when the majority in a society, group, or subgroup endorses them. *Just because certain thoughts and actions are in accord with common sense, doesn't mean they're healthy.* Conversely, reflect on the contributions of Darwin, Galileo, Stanton, and Leonardo, and realize that a unique selection of rules, values, and perceptions that initially disagree with common sense and are disparaged, can eventually gain acceptance and propel humanity forward.

Revealing Social Influences

Given the preceding you might insist that a person's thoughts, emotions, and actions should be assessed independent of the social context. Yet, what does the following suggest about an individual's functioning within the social surroundings?

- Observing another person's hostility may make an individual prone to be aggressive.[203]

- People are inclined to obey authority figures.[204]

- Parental encouragement or discouragement influences whether infants crawl across a glass platform where it appears to the infants as though any forward movement would incur a dangerous fall. This substantiates how social referencing (looking to others for guidance) may overrule individual decisions even those matters that are seemingly hazardous.[205]

- Familial factors such as parental encouragement or discouragement can influence goal selection.[206] (For example, consider how athletics, academics, and particular careers can influence income, health, status, and the ability to marry and have children.)

- Individuals may characterize themselves by how others perceive them (Looking-Glass Self).[207]

- A person may tend to conform to the group consensus (Groupthink).[208]

- When individuals were presented with three lines of clearly different lengths, approximately one-third of persons wrongly identified one line as longer to conform to others' statements (accomplices instructed to give the wrong answer), or because they doubted their faculties based on others' (intentionally inaccurate) responses.[209]

- Widowed, single, and divorced individuals have higher suicide rates than married persons.[210]

- Childfree individuals have higher suicide rates than those who are parents.[211]

- News about suicides may influence others to carry out "copycat suicides."[212]

- Conflict with parents is an adolescent suicide risk factor.[213]

- Having fewer social connections is linked to a shorter life span and increased vulnerability to an array of infectious diseases.[214]

- Isolation from a significant other is associated with decreased immune functioning.[215]

- Lonely individuals have meager immune systems.[216]

- Social stressors may have a more harmful effect on immune functioning than non-interpersonal stressors.[217]

- A spouse's death may be the most distressing event in an individual's life.[218] In fact, six of the top ten stressors have a social component (the remainder are: divorce, separation, death of a close family member, marriage, marital reconciliation).

- Human touch and social contact can stimulate the release of the hormone oxytocin, which can lower stress and promote healing.[219]

- Divorce can raise the risk of cancer, diabetes, and heart disease.[220]

- Hearing her baby cry — or even thinking about it — may make a breastfeeding mother lactate.[221]

- Newborn infants mimic others' facial expressions — even within their first hour of life.[222]

- Anticipation of sex can stimulate men's beard growth.[223]

- The socially-related variables of shame or embarrassment can produce blushing.[224]

- The inclusion of a laugh track on television comedies is to persuade the individual watching to laugh (like those in the "audience").[225]

- Low quality or lack of social relationships can impact the life span to a degree similar to factors such as obesity, cigarette smoking, hypertension, and physical inactivity.[226]

- Low job status is linked to greater likelihood of heart attack than high job status.[227]

- Job status is a better predictor of a heart attack than obesity, smoking, or high blood pressure.[228]

- The encompassing culture shapes individuals' self-concepts.[229] For example, people in Eastern cultures describe themselves in more social terms seeing themselves as part of the group while those in Western cultures have more individualistic memories and definitions.

- Augmented social support has been associated with a reduced cardiovascular stress response.[230]

- How a person supports a spouse (positive or ambivalent [both helpful and upsetting]) influences *both* individuals' risk of heart disease with coronary-artery calcification, with more supportive behaviors correlated to higher cardiovascular health and ambivalence associated with more calcification.[231]

Social surroundings can be stealthily and strongly persuasive.[232] Indeed, others can impact an individual right down to the microscopic level. (There's an intriguing peripheral note: No human pheromones have been identified to date and research is in its infancy and controversial.[233] However, studies suggest one or more human odor neurochemicals may provide a social communication function. For example, human odors may influence menstrual cycle timing synchronization for women who live together,[234] assist newborns in identifying their nursing mothers,[235] are associated with increased sexual intercourse for men and women,[236] influence perception and impressions,[237] improve women's mood,[238] and reduce tension and nervousness in women.[239] While in need of more research — and noting that bathing and scented products minimize or neutralize possible influence and outcomes — these curious findings indirectly add more testimony to the social aspect of human functioning.)

Life is replete with clues that reveal a pattern: single neurons talk with each other and cooperate toward a goal, bodily organs collaborate, individuals agree to achieve personal and societal aims, and the Internet mirrors on a global scale what you already learned on the microscopic one: pooled resources and quick communication among various individual factors can symbiotically attain diverse objectives.

While some view humanity as comprised of distinct and disconnected individuals who are perceived as a group only when observed at a distance, a person is as indivisible from society as goals, emotions, thoughts, actions, and neuronal functioning are entwined. *Given the social influences on functioning, a person can only be fully comprehended when seen in relation to others.* For that reason, the word "individual" may be insufficient. A person is never simply an individual, but rather is a societal individual.

Bonding

Humans are not the strongest, largest, or fastest animals on the planet, nor do we have innate camouflage, rugged exoskeletons, deeply penetrating sharp teeth or claws, secrete venom, or fly, and we're delicately dependent on others. So what are the advantageous characteristics that enabled humanity's continued existence as well as ruling species status?

Sure, there's the ability to adapt to various environments that's associated with the relative lack of preprogrammed behavior. There's also creativity and self-determination that allow an abundance of approaches to life's challenges rather than just a mindless replication of historical or genetic solutions. In addition, there's a remarkably adaptive, comprehensive, and unhesitating immune system. While you may conclude that a complex and powerful brain wins first place, it merely may be the runner-up. Still guessing? Well, a hint lies in the many forms of communication (e.g., speech, touch, eye contact, tone of voice, facial expressions, art, E-mail, various online forums, and texting). Consider how their numbers, as well as frequency of use, attest to the significance of social interaction and cooperation. Odds are, it's the social aspect of human functioning that best enables species survival and dominance. Ah, but Mother Nature has a problem on her hands. While communication allows interaction among individuals, what crucial element acts as the glue that fortifies those vital social bonds?

Well, study parents' patient and reassuring affection, friends' dedicated and sacrificing camaraderie, compassionate caretakers' sympathy and resilience, and lovers' harmonious and exhilarating connection. Each illustrates how emotion — and specifically, love — intertwines individuals with invisible, yet palpable sensations of connection and commitment. In fact, for those in an intimate relationship, love augments dedication and reduces the probability of thinking about appealing others.[240] *Love can be the intoxicating social adhesive that multiplies the likelihood that an individual and, by extension, humanity survives and thrives.*

Love Lost

Please take a moment to recall a specific time in your life when you were happiest and most at peace. After you have that firmly in mind, recollect a time or experience when you were the most hurt, depressed, afraid, or inconsolable. Your incisive answers may expose the heart of human functioning and, by extension, radiate an illuminating x-ray into neurotic anxiety.

During your happiest and most peaceful experience did you feel appreciated and connected with others? Obversely, was your most troubling time associated with failure, rejection, ridicule, or abandonment? If so, what characteristic do pleasant and unpleasant recollections share?

People's happiest and most peaceful memories, as well as their most distressing remembrances, are often associated with a social factor. Now, consider what the following facts imply about social functioning:

1. Physical pain can signal bodily distress and damage.

2. Pain intensity usually escalates in accord with injury severity.

3. Those body parts with greater importance to survival and thriving often experience greater sensitivity and pain (e.g., heart, eyes, teeth, breasts, testicles).

4. Social pain and physical pain are expressed in the same brain regions.[241]

5. The brain reduces social rejection pain like it does physical pain, by releasing endogenous opiates.[242] Likewise, medication for physical pain may lessen pain from social rejection.[243]

6. Looking at a loved one may reduce the experience of physical pain and love activates the same areas of the brain as cocaine and morphine.[244]

7. Endogenous opiates reward social acceptance.[245]

Is it possible that similar to how physical pain's magnitude frequently reflects injury severity and body part importance to survival, could the intensity of psychological joy and distress related to social experiences and connections whisper their importance on people's ability to survive and thrive?

Perhaps, but there's something else to examine that may be even more revealing. First, think of an intense physical pain you've endured in the past, say a broken bone, kidney stone, dislocated knee, or childbirth. Now recall an event or condition when you experienced agonizing psychological pain, such as the unexpected and undesired end of an impassioned relationship. After reflecting upon those experiences, answer the following:

Can you more readily and intensely re-experience the psychological pain than re-feel the physical pain? Have you periodically experienced unnerving reminders of that which is related to the psychological anguish more than that which caused the physical agony? If so, could this hint at the importance of psychological and social factors that guide thought, emotions, and behavior?

Now contemplate how as science becomes more proficient in addressing and explaining various physical illnesses and people are better able to obtain sustenance, clothing, and shelter, might social stressors supersede physical ones or at least magnify their respective proportion?[246]

As Freud wrote, "It is that we are never so defenceless [sic] against suffering as when we love, never so helplessly unhappy as when we have lost our loved object or its love."[247] Simply, love's rapture can exhilarate as well as protect people from life's pain, whereas rejection, ridicule, abandonment, and failure are associated with insufferable and lingering torment. (For instance, no matter how many years ago it occurred, often people can swiftly recall the cherished person who broke their heart.) Couple this with the necessity of social interdependence and you quickly conclude that people are, profoundly and inescapably, social beings. *Without friendships, alliances, and relationships, people can imperil their survival and experience excruciating, protracted psychological and physical pain that they try to avoid — especially if previously experienced.* Knowing this, how might anxiety be related to success and acceptance, as well as associated with failure, rejection, ridicule, or abandonment?

Chapter 6: Life Style

Consider how through communication and consensus, each society or culture creates and espouses common customs, rules, and laws. And, within the larger group exist divisions, say particular religious or political factions, that have additional subsets of guidelines and edicts that prescribe specific tenets that augment, create distinct conventions, or are incongruous with, the mainstream canons (e.g., distinctive attire and presentation, being pro-life in a pro-choice community). While these are more specific, they're insufficiently precise and distinct for an individual. So, what are the most fundamental rules of all?

Life Style Equals Personality

Revisiting the parallel between games and humanity can reveal people's most elemental rules of perception, thought, emotion, and action. While games' structure and implementation demonstrate the importance of goal orientation and social cooperation (matters essential to humankind), what's *the* defining feature of any game?

Within a game's general rules, each player must devise strategies (plans) and employ tactics (actions) believed to be the most effective means to the ultimate goal: victory. However, the dynamic between and among players requires various strategies and tactics throughout gameplay. In other words, the initial strategy (and related action) changes depending what another participant does or in anticipation of predicted plays. But there's something to note: Strategies are *articles of faith.* Just because a player believes them to be accurate and that they'll enable goal achievement, doesn't guarantee success. Nevertheless, individual strategies are the most defining characteristic of gaming as they guide action and determine goal achievement within a social interaction.

Note that when describing neurotic anxiety as personality based, it's necessary to define personality. Simply, it's one's style of living — each person's cognitive collection of rules, perceptions, and goals — that's used to make sense of life and act within it. The term "life style" is equivalent to the term personality, and has four components.[248]

• Self-concept: This is people's perception of who they are and who they are not. For example, "I'm a driven person" or "I'm not someone who relies on others."

- Self-ideal: This is people's belief of what they should be or do to be significant. For instance, "To be a good parent I should go over my children's homework with them and make certain they eat healthily" or "I should go back to school to get an advanced degree."

- *Weltbild:* This is people's respective impressions of everything external to themselves, positive or negative (e.g., "Life is a competition" or "People are judgmental"). This variable also encompasses others' expectations of them. The *Weltbild* can also be divided among gender lines, such as "Men are aggressive, but otherwise emotionally distant" and "Women are compassionate and social."

- Ethical convictions: These are moral guidelines that prescribe appropriate behavior, for instance, "Be patient and pleasant." These convictions do not necessarily mirror those of the surrounding society.

Still, life style and personality are broad-stroke terms — the box of crayons, rather than the specific hues of the colored wax sticks within. It's the life style *convictions* that are the most fundamental rules. They uniquely draw the defining lines of perception, thought, action, and emotion, which comprise and color each person's personality, or life style. *Life style convictions define how people move from an inferior position to one of significance (as they perceive it and within their environment).*[249] In a way, you may think of them as a personal and unique microcosm of philosophy, religion, or politics, which have certain perceptions, rules, and goals. Perhaps another analogy, that between computer code and life style convictions, can illustrate life style convictions' importance and persuasiveness.

Consider how computer code dictates a device's reality, presentation, as well as allowed or prohibited actions for the device and, by extension, the user. Comparably, life style convictions guide goal selection, shape cognition, perception, behavior, emotion, and ethics, as well as define reality. They determine who people are, what they like, what they do, how many and what types of friends they have, their careers, their relationships, etc. In short, they are each person's unique rules that legislate how to perceive life and progress from a felt minus to a fictional plus in the life tasks.

Given the areas of life encountered, and even those contemplated, yet never experienced (e.g., "What would I do if my spouse cheated on me?"), all the possible goals selected, modified, or discarded, you soon realize that *people have countless convictions.* Some are general, e.g., "I need to be in control," while others are more specific. These individually chosen rules for living can be socially influenced, and are used to comprehend the world and attain objectives within it. People hold and implement convictions they believe are accurate and effective, *even if they're disastrous.*[250]

Now, contemplate how some actions or conditions may be associated with anxiety for one person (e.g., being alone, public speaking, bankruptcy, flying, heights, the unknown, intimacy, failure, rejection), yet others handily deal with these situations (perhaps seek some) and do not experience anxiety. And as an extreme illustration, consider how a coroner can see, touch, and cut open dead bodies daily, yet not experience anxiety or other psychological symptoms. As the same event does not guarantee identical outcomes, you can see how the causal mindset of symptoms can be insufficient. *Given people's personality differences, there are few inherently or universally anxiety provoking things; rather it's how people's life style convictions influence how they think, feel, and act.* Each person conceives of, and interprets reality, through a unique, personality-defined lens. Though your grasp of neurotic anxiety hinges on knowing this, you've just opened the door to yet another mystery: What defining life style convictions are associated with generalized anxiety?

Chapter 7: The Anxiety Code

People are obligated to address the life tasks — those areas of life that don't have innate answers (e.g., work, social, and intimacy). This requires some conception of themselves, others, and the world. Although born in an inferior position, devoid of virtually all understanding and experience, through social interaction, guidance, influence, and individual choice, people accumulate innumerable life style convictions that constitute their personalities. These increasingly comprehensive rules prescribe their beliefs, actions, emotions, ethics, cognitions, and goals. Consequently, to decipher neurotic anxiety you must know the distinguishing convictions associated with symptom development. Yet, how can there be specific convictions common to individuals who...?

- Enjoy various hobbies.
- Live in urban or rural areas.
- Have attained various levels of education.
- Have diverse religious affiliations or none at all.
- Have heterogeneous careers or are unemployed.
- Live in distinctive countries throughout the world.
- Have countless (and often subtly shifting) convictions.
- Are affiliated with different political parties or are apolitical.
- Are married, divorced, separated, widowed, or never married.

Humanity's polychromatic composition with numerous, detailed, influential, and idiosyncratic personalities among individuals makes any attempt to determine telltale life style convictions about a complex psychological condition seemingly impossible.

The Quest for Common Convictions

When you buy a book or song from Amazon.com or the iTunes Store, why are you presented with other items that you might be interested in purchasing?

In accord with human goal orientation, it's best to determine what objectives are involved. Sure, your aim as a consumer is to have that song or book, but note that's only half the story. What's the vendors' desire?

Simply, it's to get you to buy…*more.*

Yet, to achieve this merchants are compelled to determine what you'd like to own and mustn't offer you offbeat or offensive things. If they had your life style convictions, or even your recent purchase history, they'd have an idea of your interests — a running start that would assist them in surmounting a relatively large obstacle. However, if these vendors have little or no data about you, what could they use to show you tempting items in harmony with your interests?

Other customers' purchase histories. But, as most people are decidedly different from you, that information appears unrelated and useless. Thankfully, comprehension comes from understanding that trends develop with a large enough data set (a.k.a. data mining[251]).

People have distinct and telling tendencies, and preference patterns emerge with a sizable sample of individuals. To maximize sales, merchants use the power of trends and associate shoppers' common convictions to predict what you're likely to buy. So, if you're interested in technological thrillers by a particular author on Amazon.com or are sampling a Chicago blues song from a specific artist on the iTunes Store, then the purchase history data of other shoppers who bought that book or song as well as other publications and music can now be used as a reference through the practice known as collaborative filtering.[252] The vendors predict that you have comparable interests with those who purchased the same item, and consequently present you with items others bought. Therefore, just because merchants do not know all of your specific life style convictions, they may not need to. Correspondingly, comprehending generalized anxiety disorder doesn't require knowing every life style conviction among all symptomatic people (or even one person); that would be an impossible task. However, might identifiable and relevant patterns be spotted in the densely-populated city of convictions?

Well, think about how although DNA is profoundly intricate and massively influential, its recipe contains four crucial ingredients (adenine, cytosine, guanine, and thymine), albeit in astoundingly long chains.[253] Similarly, while the compendium of life style convictions is mind-bogglingly complex, there's a recognizable subset of three that are relevant to neurotic anxiety.[254] For the sake of readability, I've nicknamed these convictions the Anxiety Code.

The Need to be Driven

Humanity's goal-orientation requires that people set objectives they believe will enable them to survive, thrive, and enjoy life; however, having intentions isn't enough. *Achieving goals requires the drive to attain them.*

How is success measured? First, experience or other intangibles can be viewed as aims (e.g., go on a luxury cruise, become educated). Second, routine tasks (e.g., walking) may be deemed inconsequential unless a challenge exists that makes goal achievement difficult (e.g., after a stroke, recent surgery). Third, attained objectives can have a cumulative effect (e.g., graduating high school, university, graduate school, post-doctoral training). *The number and/or difficulty of goals achieved are deemed identifiable measures of success.* So what does this have to do with ambition and generalized anxiety?

Everything else being equal, people can attain more goals than others and/or more challenging ones, solely based on their amount of drive. Successes can be reinforcing and increase a sense of competency. Drive can enable things such as better relationships, acceptance, improved status, dedicated athleticism, and higher income. Note that while ambition can be a good and healthy thing, it's problematic when it becomes excessive and lessens people's quality of life. *Neurotically anxious individuals believe they must be driven.*[255]

The Need to be in Control

There's more to success than an abundance of drive. After all, directionless energy is random and potentially dangerous, like a rudderless speedboat set at full throttle. People need to control what they say, think, and do to achieve goals. Although there are times when control can safely extend beyond themselves (e.g., responsible parents need to control what their toddlers eat), *people should only attempt to control those things that apply to them.* Healthy boundaries are good and necessary (hint: this is particularly challenging for some). However, there's a common misperception about control. Just think about when people say, "I've got the goal to exercise more this year." Is exercise the actual objective?

Nope. Exercise isn't an endpoint or a conclusion; it's a way to achieve aspirations, such as weight loss, better physical fitness, longevity, or winning a race. People attempt to control various events or conditions to attain a primary goal, for example, health, safety, financial security, peace of mind, or acceptance. When individuals want control, what they actually want is what the control allows them. *Control isn't a goal, but a means to an end.*

Control has striking relevance to anxiety. You can imagine how anxiety might be generated if you were unexpectedly free-falling from an airplane, if someone were shooting at you, or a lion were chasing you across a savanna. It's related to the fight or flight mechanism.[256] *Anxiety can be present when things are going out of control.* It can marshal physical and cognitive faculties, energize muscles, speed responses, and focus attention — all in a concerted attempt among bodily constituents (read: unity of the personality) to control a situation that's going out of control and achieve a goal.

Now envision walking through a war-torn city, with hidden insurgents planning to detonate a bomb, start a violent riot, or engage in some other behavior that would immediately imperil your life. Vigilance, increased blood pressure, and associated readiness to action as well as accelerated cognition and planning may increase the probability of remaining alive. *Even when things are calm, people may experience anxiety when they believe things will go out of control.* With that in mind, note that neurotically anxious persons are often "waiting for the other shoe to drop."

Though anxiety as well as having control can be healthy and beneficial, there's a difference between being in control (say, when driving a car) and being controlling (perhaps a micromanaging boss, intrusive parent, a know-it-all coworker, or nosy neighbor, who makes demands and gives unrequested directions). *Neurotically anxious individuals have an excessive desire to be in control.*[257] They can attempt (or desire) to control themselves (to an detrimental degree), others (e.g., what they do, think), the world, chance, etc. They draw unhealthy boundaries as they attempt to control those arenas in which they have no jurisdiction (e.g., adult children's lives, what coworkers, friends, and neighbors do).

The Need to be Good, Perfect, Right

Aren't children's formative years often about teaching them to be good (e.g., fair minded, moral, considerate), perfect (e.g., do something correctly), and right (e.g., be factually accurate)?

As people develop and mature they are obligated to find or create solutions for life's intensifying obligations.[258] They may acquire and implement life style convictions of being driven, being in control, and being good, perfect, right, to address those challenges. Essentially, this process instills laudable personality characteristics that may enable effective and efficient goal attainment in various areas of functioning, such as good health, better relationships, greater status, stronger friendships, and employment longevity. Moreover, these convictions may prevent pronounced unpleasantries that can otherwise appear, such as poor health, failure, divorce, alienation, conflict, incarceration, shame, and poverty. The guidelines of being good, perfect, right, not only overlap, but also can lead into one another. For instance, one can wish to be so good as to be perfect or desire to do things perfectly. *Those with generalized anxiety believe that they must be good, perfect, right.*[259] This can apply to one area or many. An intense or absolute tenacity to this conviction is related to symptom generation.

Code Commonalities

What do DNA, computer code, and the life style convictions have in common?

First, small components comprise complex things. DNA's intricate recipe has four primary ingredients. Individual lines of computer code constitute elaborate operating environments and applications on computers, phones, and tablets. Life style convictions are the basic elements of each person's personality.

Second, aggregated constituents can be incredibly influential. DNA commandingly guides countless bodily functions and constructions, impacts health, and shapes or dictates physical characteristics. Computer code establishes the reality of a virtual world, how things look, sound, and function, as well as what you can and cannot do. Life style convictions define reality and how to act, think, perceive, and feel, as well as influence goal selection. DNA, computer code, and the Anxiety Code provide goal-attaining rules.

Third, reflect on how a computer's central processing unit (CPU) is unknowing of the quality of the computer code it executes, and how — without testing — people are unaware of their DNA's threats to well-being. Yet, each may be followed dutifully, and this unmindful adherence to their respective codes can be devastating. For instance, harmful DNA code can lead to Huntington's disease, Down's syndrome, Hemophilia, Tay-Sachs disease, Celiac disease, or Sickle-cell anemia.[260] Likewise, a CPU following inaccurate code leads to hangs, crashes, and freezes.[261] Moreover, given its mindless execution, a computer can run a virus as easily as a word processing application. Likewise, people may be unaware of their convictions' totalitarian role and follow them unquestioned — even when they lead to anxiety.

Given people's countless convictions, how can just three poison a range of functioning?

Well, just like a fragment of DNA can cause disease and a few lines of computer code can halt functioning or make an application a virus, *merely a snippet of a person's entire array of life style convictions can lead to symptom development.* That's why people of various personalities, professions, places, pastimes, etc., can maintain the Anxiety Code, and why those convictions are so influential and persistent. But there's another factor to consider.

If you sprained your ankle, you might attempt to avoid pain by putting more weight on your other foot. Yet, by disproportionally distributing your weight you misalign your spine and strain associated muscles. Over time, this can precipitate back pain, neck pain, and headaches. The intensifying agony may generate progressive irritability, and others may disengage from you or become conflictual. So what does this have to do with neurotic anxiety?

In the example, you faced a simple challenge: How to minimize or avoid the pain of a sprained ankle. Your solution of compensating for a sensitive and weakened ankle by shifting your weight had unintended consequences. It aggravated the situation and caused physical, psychological, and social problems. Evidently, your tactic was only a temporary and partial solution. Likewise, when ill-suited and inflexible life style convictions are employed to address life's challenges, personal, physical, psychological, as well as social distress can ensue. Neurotic individuals use the Anxiety Code in innumerable ways to achieve significance; however, they may generate symptoms and aggravate matters (e.g., avoid people out of fear of rejection, be so industrious and controlling that they alienate friends and family members).

Personality and Psychology

Regrettably, some people inappropriately link neurosis or "mental illness" with a deficit of cognitive capacity or processing speed. On the contrary, those with generalized anxiety can be impressively quick-witted and exceptionally intelligent. Nevertheless, some individuals persist in the inaccurate belief that there's an inborn and immutable lack of capacity or cleverness that must be counteracted, say by medication, and that personality-based symptoms are lifelong. Thankfully, returning to the computer analogy may helpfully and reassuringly clarify the issue.

Mistakenly perceiving limited brain capability as causing neurotic anxiety makes it — to use a computer term — a hardware problem. Fortunately, a clue points the way to greater understanding: There are eight types of intelligence: logical-mathematical, linguistic, spatial, bodily-kinesthetic, musical, naturalist, interpersonal, and intrapersonal.[262] Nobody functions on the top tier of all of them. So rather than an innate and unalterable physical or biochemical flaw within the brain, you may wish to consider neurotic anxiety symptoms as related to areas of awareness; specifically, knowledge of the life style convictions and how to make them more flexible and appropriate.

With that in mind, liken a computer's central processing unit (CPU) to a person's brain. Next, equate computer code to an individual's life style convictions. Accordingly, you can see that regardless of how powerful the CPU is, if the computer code is inefficient and/or ineffective then problems arise. Likewise, no matter how mighty a person's brain, if the life style convictions (the rules that constitute personality) are insufficiently flexible or ill-suited, then symptoms can develop. This optimistically parallels generalized anxiety to a correctable software problem, with therapy that addresses life style convictions somewhat akin to a software update that rewrites and debugs problematic computer code.

Shamelessly overextending this metaphor, perhaps most interesting is how people are both the programmers as well as the entities that run the code, as they can select the life style convictions they employ — even if it occasionally takes outside guidance to identify and encourage them. The analogy is not to have you view people as computers, but to quickly demonstrate a concept.

Though you now know what life style convictions are and their importance in neurotic anxiety, you face another question: How are they related to symptom generation?

Chapter 8: Problematic Convictions

Although you know the life style convictions linked to neurotic anxiety, it's also necessary to comprehend how personality factors, among other things, are related to symptom generation.

Complementary and Clashing

Individuals act in accord with what's known as their private logic (their unique set of goals and reasoning).[263] And, the more their collage of desires and rationale overlaps their respective community's common sense, the healthier or "more normal" they're viewed. However, each person's perspective has innate errors — flaws in the lens — with respective distortions, weaknesses, and biases. Consequently, there cannot be total perfection of thought, only various imperfections (albeit some ways of thinking are incredibly more perceptive, accurate, and healthy than others). *The number of understandings of life is equal to the number of people, with each having inherent mistakes — a margin of error — as there isn't just one right way, or totally wrong way, of living.*[264]

Neurotically anxious persons may attempt to date common sense while being married to their private logic. They fearfully refuse to divorce their personal beliefs while they pursue approval (or avoid rejection and ridicule) by vainly complying with common sense — a mask that cosmetically covers unacceptable blemishes. However, *attempting to satisfy both creates tension and elicits symptoms.*[265]

So, how else might life style convictions clash and generate symptoms?

Just like each person has inherent mistakes in conceptions and rules, each has particular strengths, which allows for a mosaic of contributions. Contemplate careers that you deem gross, unnerving, conflictual, or too dangerous, yet others eagerly pursue. Think about how a company can have artists, engineers, accountants, lawyers, and secretaries, who may see the world and act within it in vastly different ways, but each employee's distinct input enables a comprehensive team that addresses a range of challenges which facilitates the company's ability to survive and thrive in the marketplace.

In life, group communication, reasoning, and consensus can smooth away individual imperfections, culling the cognitive and behavioral herd of ideas and actions, leaving only strong ideas to survive and multiply. A multitude of perspectives leads to a more comprehensive understanding of reality and provides various solutions to life's challenges.[266] One person's strength can negate another's weakness. An innovative idea that's outside of common sense, but which withstands intense scrutiny can make civilizations and individuals stronger, more resilient and accepted, and catapults humanity forward. *Dissimilar personalities can strengthen societies and individuals* — just like how genetic mutations are deviations from perfect replication, but may allow adaptation and evolution. This unearths a seemingly paradoxical conclusion: There's perfection in imperfection. Yet, when you examine those who most annoy you, what is it about them that's so irritating?

Odds are the frustration, irritation, anger, or anxiety you feel is due to nothing more than how they live differently than you; they see the world in ways you do not. Simply, it's the disparities in respective goals and life style convictions that don't reflect what you hold dear and as realistic, that gets on your nerves. ("Hell is — other people!" as Sartre wrote.[267])

These dissimilarities often do not exist in factual and easily-verified matters (e.g., how many miles there are between Chicago and London). Conflictual topics usually have a cloudy and subjective area of right or wrong, good or bad (e.g., childrearing practices, music, politics, religions, art, movies, best tasting pizza, cultures, the most advantageous way to load a dishwasher — or even hang the toilet paper roll [a surprisingly common niggle among couples]).

Also, anxiety may arise when those who need to be in control, good, perfect, right, and driven, interact with others who do not hold the same perspectives and values. For example, how might those who are driven and need to be right act with a spouse who's easygoing and uninformed? Or, consider how an overprotective parent may angrily reject the other's seemingly nonchalant parenting style and become anxious about their child's well-being when under the other parent's care. Interestingly, even people who each hold the Anxiety Code can disagree where and how to be driven, good, etc. *Differences in life style convictions among people can lead to personality clashes and symptoms.* Knowing that, what might happen when others point out how a neurotic individual violated personal rules (e.g., a person who despises bullies is called out for bullying others into compliance, or an individual who champions the underdog is identified as exploiting someone or an organization [say, leaving work early])?

People can develop symptoms (e.g., uncertainty, embarrassment, anxiety, self-directed anger) *when they become conscious that they act differently from how they perceive themselves* (e.g., "I'm a strong person and I'm upset that I didn't defend myself from that insult [shady salesperson, etc.]," or when others point out hypocrisy). Yet, how can people violate their omnipotent life style convictions?

Given the primacy of goal orientation and the unity of the personality, people can be completely unaware of their violations on their way to reaching a goal. For instance, individuals can be unmindful of how many drinks they've had on their way to intoxication, forget to go to a meeting when something sexier waits, fail to recall being on a diet when they order dessert, or overlook the times they worried needlessly when they want to control some event.

Progressive Deviation

Imagine a clock that loses a second of accuracy per hour. Such inexact execution appears minute and undetectable on the face of it, but in one year that clock is, perhaps alarmingly, inaccurate by more than two hours. One solution is to periodically adjust the clock as it starts to noticeably deviate from the correct time. So how might this be an analog to private logic, common sense, and symptom development?

As common sense is what a society deems accurate and healthy, and private logic can be different from common sense, it should only take some feedback to correct illogical and unhealthy thoughts and rules — as if resetting a clock. Ah, but what's the catch?

Like the clock, a number of tiny deviations in life style convictions can occur virtually imperceptibly over time. Accordingly, people may not recognize their convictions are gradually less efficient, effective, or realistic. Such subtle shifts and resultant symptoms may give individuals the misperception their anxiety is innate, as they see themselves as the same people they've always been. *There can be nearly invisible, insidious movement from common sense to unhealthy private logic. This is especially likely when people maintain the same environment, friends, and routines that do not challenge their convictions.*

Strong and Resilient

Life style convictions define reality and influence how, indeed *if*, things are perceived, as they filter what's valued, devalued, and ignored. So, how can this sustain and strengthen people's perceptions and rules for living?

Consider those who believe that dutifully coming into work an hour early will ensure job longevity. They may fortify their perception with the fact that they're still employed (an example of confirmation bias). Obversely, they may believe that employees who arrive on time or even slightly late will soon be unemployed. Now reflect on countless similar behavior, such as those who don't notice when their superstitions don't come to fruition, rationalized or forgotten unfulfilled prayers, or parents who never see when their children misbehave. Individuals may be persistently unwilling to test their belief systems or accept feedback that's contrary to their perspectives and rules. *People can reinforce and perpetuate their life style convictions when they perceive and prize only that which is in accord with them.*

So, how strong can life style convictions become?

First, please keep in mind that life style convictions are different from behavioral rules (e.g., what day to leave the garbage by the curb), as those rules can be changed willingly and with little or no tension. Second, think about those who religiously engage in superstitions, rituals, and compulsions, such as eating the same foods in the same sequence every day or having a morning routine that must go in a specific order. Even with frail and incorrect logic, they can deem their beliefs rational, hearty, and healthy. Consequently, they may not question them, yet feel compelled to engage in certain behaviors and find it incredibly difficult to alter or forgo them, perhaps fearing that something dreadful will occur. (Even hypnosis can be powerless to get people to relinquish their goals or violate their rules for living.[268] For example, I believe it's safe to say — as an extreme example — hypnosis couldn't make you to rob a bank or kill a child.) Knowing that, what's occurring in the following?

• You're in someone else's home and their different eating or childrearing conventions make you feel uncomfortable or disapproving.

• Your schedule is changed and you feel out of sync or confused.

• You're in a different country and are startled by how its residents have unusual customs or "do things the wrong way."

• You're discussing a particular topic with people of a different religious or political affiliation and perceive them as misinformed, ignorant, or obstinate.

Well, think about when you're in a foreign country. The overriding customs are that nation's well-entrenched and defended common sense. What the local residents see, think, feel, and do are logical and realistic to them, but may appear ill-conceived, wrong, or bad to you. Yet, maybe in their eyes it's you who's the odd or unenlightened one. While the above examples may serve as an illustration of how unshakeable others are to their life style convictions, *it can also serve as evidence of how tenacious you are to yours.* As an example, does it feel a bit strange when you sit in a different seat at your kitchen table? It's just a simple rule; yet stubborn and so invisible that you never question it.

As life style convictions define each person's unique reality, some individuals may become mindful of how strongly and stealthily they clutch their convictions only when facing contrasting ones. This is akin to how people are often unaware that they speak with an accent (after all it's "normal" to them and they learned it early on) until they go someplace else (where they readily and distinctly hear others' accent) and somebody points out theirs.

Comparable to how people stay in their hometown that has miserable weather, a high crime rate, pollution, prohibitive taxes, an unexciting venue, and limited growth, because of its familiarity — along with the unpredictability associated with moving to a new (but better) location — people may stick with inefficient or ineffective life style convictions. Inflexible tenacity to one's convictions is a principal and defining attribute of neurotic anxiety.[269] *Perseverance with unrealistic and unhealthy convictions increases the likelihood of symptom development.*

Now, imagine you have to defuse a ticking time bomb. Fortunately, you have proven, detailed directions and follow them meticulously. As you read the final instruction, "Cut the red wire," you anticipate the timer halting its insidious progression. You surgically descend the wire cutter into the bomb's intestines and authoritatively sever the wire with a distinctive snap. You experience peace…until you see the timer *accelerate* its countdown. Anxiety and confusion explode. You rapidly review the directions and realize that although you've followed them precisely, you failed. Worse, you've made the situation unimaginably more grave. Something bad is going to happen shortly, you're partially responsible, yet powerless and don't know what to do. Although this is an extreme and improbable illustration, it can show how anxiety can arise when things don't go as expected (a goal wasn't achieved) despite following previously successful guidelines, and a situation gets out of control, unspeakably dangerous, and with little to no idea of what else to do.

Those with generalized anxiety can be stellar human beings, resourceful, kind, industrious, athletic, and successful in many arenas by adhering to the Anxiety

Code. However, unsuitable life style convictions can lead to anxiety when they prohibit goal achievement — even if they've been previously effective. This can be seen in statements similar to, "I've done everything right. I've worked hard. And, I've been a good employee (spouse, friend, child, sibling, etc.), but I still failed!" *Anxiety can erupt when people are unable to attain their goal and don't know what to do next.* Worse, symptoms can mushroom when people don't have an auxiliary plan or are unreceptive to feedback.

Problems with the Need to be Driven

"Drivers" are the "workaholics" of the world.[270] Achievements (in whatever form) are their goal.[271] They may be continuously busy in some task, chore, or plan. Free time is their enemy.[272] They frequently have a torturous time remaining still, slowing down, or relaxing. Even when trying to rest, their minds anxiously race thinking about what they have to do in the next hour, day, week, year, or beyond. They may have impressive persistence and endure various trials and setbacks to achieve their goals; and their success fortifies their drive. They can fear losing value, prestige, or self-esteem if they're idle, and worry others will overtake their accomplishments. Anxiety can be related to their idealistic expectations and may fuel their actions. For instance, patients may fervently research their symptoms, prompt their healthcare providers for particular interventions or medication, and set unrealistically ambitious treatment deadlines that can lead to anxiety when they misperceive themselves as not progressing fast enough in therapy.

Problems with the Need to be in Control

Those who need to be in control may tremendously fear one or more of the following:

1. *The loss of physical control.*[273] For instance, they fear paralysis, being physically restrained (e.g., in a claustrophobic MRI machine, being bear hugged), forced to time their step onto an escalator, in a vehicle on a long bridge or thruway and unable to exit at will, stuck in a meeting, or on an airplane they cannot leave. Moreover, they can resent obligations and rules, and rebel against authority figures who urge or corral them into particular action or inaction — even if appropriate (e.g., when caringly told to drive slow during a harsh winter storm).

2. *The loss of psychological control.*[274] They can become anxious about things such as succumbing to dementia or irrationality, as well as dread losing control of their emotions, say by getting angry, panicking, or crying profusely and unrelentingly.

3. *The loss of control of how others perceive them.*[275] Those who need to be in control can worry that others are endlessly judgmental. Accordingly, they anxiously monitor and filter their presentation to control others' perceptions and assessments.

4. *The ultimate loss of control: Death.*[276] Some take unnecessarily varied or forceful and persistent action to protect against illness and harm (e.g., vigilance for threats, overprotective) and experience needless concern about danger. Also, they may be acutely sensitive to when death would be due to their lack of control (e.g., too close to a dangerous edge where one unanticipated slip leads to a catastrophic free fall that's due to their own error). While some accept the inevitability of death, they fear the *process* of dying — being forced to powerlessly witness their irreversible demise.

While none are enjoyable, it's the enormous strength and consistency of people's response and preemptive action that reveals the severity of their need to be in control. They habitually seek or demand control beyond what's possible, likely, or healthy, and determinedly evade or escape situations which risk losing control or being controlled. (For instance, some resolutely avoid using alcohol and drugs, or even prohibit themselves from experiencing multiple orgasms, for fear of losing control.) While this may limit failure, rejection, ridicule, and abandonment, it can progressively erode self-esteem and make avoidance, as well as anxiety, increasingly probable. Moreover, when neurotically anxious persons perceive themselves as incapable of success, they may fear losing control, and for that reason avoid particular challenges.[277]

People may control in ways they don't perceive as controlling (e.g., reframing their intrusive, micromanaging efforts as being a good parent or attentive spouse). Indeed, the need to be in control can take a particular toll on relationships. For instance, a controlling spouse immediately imperils the co-captain status of the relationship team, relegating the other to an inferior role with less responsibility, autonomy, and influence. (Consider the spouse who doesn't want the other to have the TV remote control even if they're watching the same program and the channel and volume aren't going to be changed.)

Some control vulnerability (and the risk of being seen as unacceptably weak) in their relationships by deeming healthy actions as unacceptable (e.g., not saying "I love you" — or more daringly, "I adore you" — to a cherished spouse). But it doesn't stop there, as the desire for control can bleed beyond its borders. With that in mind, what's related to an immense craving for control?

Here's a clue: Those who need to be in control may dutifully observe anniversaries, have the same weekly plans, and maintain specific practices. (As alluded to earlier, some may acquire Obsessive-compulsive personality disorder-like symptoms of observing routines, orderliness, need for power over their environment, etc.) Even when things are going as predicted and under control, they can be watchful for anything that *may* go out of control (e.g., "Sure, the kids are healthy and everything's fine, but there's always something you have to worry about. You never know what bad things are going to happen!"). They may gravitate to the news, weather report, or stock market ticker to be continually aware and alert, and avoid any ill surprise. After all, how could people have control without being able to anticipate what will happen next? Sometimes, they choose predictability over betterment, say by remaining in the same, unsurprising and unfulfilling, yet difficult relationship or dreary job. *Those with generalized anxiety can have a strong desire for stability and predictability; the close cousins to the need for control.*

Have you ever followed the financial market and have been surprised when a corporation's stock price has increased in value after the company has received a legal judgment against them? Although you may believe that a loss would make their stock plummet, when you realize that the market detests uncertainty, even a negative judgment is preferred because it provides clarity.[278] Likewise, neurotically anxious people may seek information — even when it's bad news — because certainty may enable stability and planning, whereas uncertainty does not.

Those who need to be in control can have difficulty accepting people (or things) as they are and may goad or cajole them to change. However, this is like going into an art gallery and repainting artists' work to be the way the controller wants them, instead of accepting the artists' vision.

Problems with the Need to be Good, Perfect, Right

Good is a subjective and inconsistent term, as each person crafts a unique definition with the prevailing culture or subculture perhaps influencing the conception. For instance, a street preacher may believe that it's good to sermonize, but others can find it annoying, inaccurate, misogynistic, and disparaging. Also, as people cannot be universally good in everything they do, they select where and with whom to be good (e.g., good to their children, but not their spouse). They can even engage in acts of goodness that are incompatible with other actions, say while volunteering for the underprivileged, they casually drive past a person whose car has a flat tire.

As powerfully as people strive to be good, they may fearfully avoid being bad with equal determination. This fuels attempts to be good or, at the very least, engage in image management to avoid exposing what may jeopardize their self-esteem, acceptance, status, or way of living.

For some, being good includes being a "people pleaser," by going to impressive heights in care, attention, fidelity, duty, compassion, sacrifice, and the like. Think about the submissive student who does an outstanding job at school to please parents, or a lover who continually showers the other with gifts, attentive sex, and flexibility. Perhaps unsurprisingly, those being pleased may not question people pleasers' behavior because everything is going so well and in their favor. For that reason, it's less likely others will deem pleasing behavior as unhealthy and give corrective feedback. Sadly, when others don't reciprocate such saintly kindness, people pleasers may worry about acceptance, fairness, and commitment.

Those with generalized anxiety may seek perfection universally, in one specific area, or in a handful of prized arenas. By definition, perfectionism requires that one is driven, in control, and wants to do the right thing, but with an interesting binary stipulation: it's either perfect or wrong. There isn't a gray area or permission to do something merely adequately. Accordingly, after an inevitable less than ideal thought, emotion, or action, perfectionists may…

• Be convinced they can never be consistently good or right.

• Dwell on the possible long-term personal and social negative repercussions.

• Expend more time and energy trying to rectify the past, rather than adapt to it.

• Ruminate on how they're irrefutable failures for falling short of their standards.

• Be continually repentant and ceaselessly apologize for their thoughts, emotions, and behavior.

- Believe they're terrible people who are going to "burn in hell" or doomed to some other irretrievable situation.

- Lose their sense of identification, competency, or superiority, believing that they're just average and "as bad as everyone else."

- Engage in self-flagellation, relive and reprimand themselves for some misdeed that occurred days, weeks, months, or even decades ago.

- Believe their imperfection is permanent, feeling eternally tarnished and never able to fully polish and regain their sterling reputation or standard, and no longer feel above reproach.

Perfectionists are prone to say, "If you want it done right, you have to do it yourself!" This may lead them to distrust others and endlessly search for imperfections to either correct them or point out others' errors. It also authorizes them to take control. They often feel perpetually judged, by others, themselves, or both, which can generate symptoms. And given neurotic anxiety's large overlap in convictions with those of neurotic depression, some of the same difficulties exist. For instance, deciding the better of two good choices.[279] Consequently, they may worry about what decision to make, perhaps to the point of immobilizing themselves.

To maintain a perfect image they may…

• Avoid challenges and opportunities in which perfection is impossible, improbable, or uncertain. Only pursue endeavors they can do flawlessly and in which success is guaranteed.

• Define perfection in a way they cannot be deemed imperfect.

• Limit interactions and exposure to only those who do not pose an intellectual, emotional, or physical challenge.

Regrettably, these stipulations and concessions can be maddeningly confining and needlessly lead to an unsatisfying and anxiety-filled life. After all, does excellence require perfection?

Last, those with generalized anxiety believe they *must* be right. They may have symptoms associated with, for example, the fear of being wrong, or when in conflict with others who believe *they're* right, or when facing gray (rather than right or wrong) questions and decisions with an unpredictable outcome.

So, what might happen when being good, perfect, right isn't acknowledged or valued?

Although some continue to abide by their conviction, perhaps merely out of the fear of being bad, imperfect, or incorrect, others may suffer in silence for the greater good such as the marriage, the children, or employer, which unfortunately can perpetuate symptoms. And, perhaps most interesting, overwhelming symptoms may arise and overrule fulfilling those self-stipulated mandates. (Although seemingly impossible because it appears to violate life style convictions, it provides a clue about symptom purposefulness.)

Stoplight Conflict

While originally applied to neurotic depression, given the two identical life style convictions involved there's one disagreement between convictions that also applies to neurotic anxiety: the Stoplight conflict.[280] This can be briefly summarized as the conflict between being good and being in control. For example, imagine a spouse who's in a progressively painful, distant, conflictual, and irreversibly unfulfilling marriage. Does the person stay in the marriage to be good, but lose control of happiness in the process, or take control of a miserable situation by getting a divorce, but risk looking bad to (unsupportive) others?

You can see how picking one would violate the code of conduct and spur anxiety. Vacillating in indecision of which option is better is also problematic, as the concern remains unresolved. *Irreconcilable convictions can generate anxiety.*

Drive and Control Conflict

How could the need to be driven and the need to be in control clash?

Well, imagine a lonely person who's driven to be in a relationship, but fears vulnerability and rejection. Does the person relinquish protective control, yet risk emotional and psychological pain? Does the individual control harm by procrastinating and retreating from vulnerability, but violate the need to be driven? Last, indecision when selecting which conviction to disobey or change can also precipitate anxiety...and (hint) vice versa.

Drive and Good Conflict

People can healthily combine the need to be driven and the need to be good, such as those who eagerly volunteer to help others. However, when can these convictions conflict?

Envision a driven businessperson who also wants to be a good friend (or volunteer for the less fortunate, etc.). Does the person ambitiously climb the corporate ladder, working at all hours and on the weekends, but at the cost of being an absent friend? Does the individual be an exceedingly good friend who is supportive, available, and organizes parties, but dial back the drive associated with a stellar career? Or does the person remain uncertain about which conviction to violate?

Crisis and Personal Kryptonite

When you contemplate how particular events are associated with anxiety development, and that symptom duration and severity seem to be correlated to the magnitude of the stressor, it appears that there's a predictable and inseparable mechanical link between an external event or condition and anxiety. However, why is this untrue?

To explain symptom development in more human and less robotic ways, you must comprehend how the life style convictions are a unique and identifying fingerprint, that once discovered loosen the grip of determinist theory. Starting circuitously, think about how Indy cars are engineered to break apart in a way that safely dissipates energy to protect drivers in the event of a crash.[281] Now consider how although people may attribute an airplane accident to one incident or circumstance, say a miscommunication or faulty latch, there may be a number of preexisting issues that went unnoticed until that event or condition.[282] In both examples, everything can operate normally until an event appears, but preexisting elements explain why trouble occurred. So what relevance does this have to neurotic anxiety?

Well, as some people can be anxiety-free until a stressor arises, this can give the impression that the situation caused the symptoms. However, the event is only part of the equation — and not the most important one. Once you recognize the life style predates symptom development, you come to a telling conclusion: *the crisis situation is a challenge that one's life style is unable to adequately address.*[283] Life style convictions are the long-standing and often silent and unobservable factors that guide symptom development after colliding with life's requirements or experiences.[284] Simply, where and when anxiety arises is due to the characteristics of one's life style, rather than something inherent in the situation that's perceived as the cause. The paper tears along the pre-existing perforations, so to speak. However, does this mean that neurotic individuals have to endure a crisis to experience anxiety?

No. It's when people follow their convictions unwaveringly and unquestionably that anxiety is prone to arise — particularly when approaching an inescapable situation for which they're not prepared such as a new job, marriage, socializing, or parenthood.[285] In fact, just the thought of an upcoming challenge can be formidable — like those who get stressed on a peaceful Sunday night because they're thinking about returning to a dreadful job in a handful of hours. People think about future events and how to address them, and when a task appears intimidating, anxiety can serve as a warning function and can escalate to meet a challenge.[286] Sometimes anxiety fuels successful action and is reinforced, or anxiety can prompt retreat from life's trials wherein failure is seen as likely or inevitable.

Next, how can someone can be a hardworking employee, an involved volunteer who champions the underprivileged, and regularly solve a flurry of problems without complaint, but become symptomatic when facing a single, and relatively boring task, such as drive on the thruway or sit in a plane on the way to a vacation?

Innumerable life style convictions can create a unique cognitive structure with such lock-and-key specificity that symptoms may arise in the face of a distinct stressor. This is why people can handle a stressor in one arena, but develop symptoms when faced with one of equal proportion in a different area. *It's not the number of responsibilities that generate neurosis, but rather one's character that's a more accurate predictor of neurotic development.*[287] In other words, an individual can be bulletproof to a barrage of stressors, yet fall prey to symptoms when the life style convictions are unable to address a challenge of a specific caliber. This hints at a related issue. Have you ever considered why, for instance, some people become stressed when parenting, while others aren't, but they experience anxiety while doing something else?

Simply, *unique convictions can account for symptom variation among individuals as they interpret, approach, and react differently to the same stressor.*

Last, why might anxiety arise rather than other psychological symptoms, such as depression, delusions, or voyeurism?

As long as the life style convictions prescribe certain behavior that anxiety can enable — including immobility — then you can see the link between the life style convictions (as well as the goal) and anxiety. For instance, consider how anxiety can be like a double shot of espresso that gets people moving, whereas other symptoms may not fulfill the same purpose.

To explain symptom development, direction, duration, and severity, it's necessary to inspect the relationship between mindset and stressor rather than lay blame on a crisis. Though neurotically anxious individuals may use their convictions to address the life tasks and enjoy many successes, they must realize *that which makes them great, can be that which works the greatest against them.* For instance, although drive or perfectionism can be employed to achieve tremendous accomplishments, they can also can lead to numerous issues, such as sleeplessness, bruxism, difficulty concentrating, an inability to attend to what's occurring in the moment, chest pain, being critical, conflict, alienation, and gastrointestinal problems.

Although anxiety symptoms can be problematic, can there be positive aspects?

Well, consider how at an early age you learned to identify the physical symptoms related to when you were tired, hungry, thirsty, too hot or cold, if you ate too much, needed to go to the restroom, were sick and going to vomit, among other states. Eventually, you became proficient in reading and responding to the symptoms: you may have gone to bed, foraged for food, got a glass of milk, taken off a winter coat or put on a sweater, stopped eating, or made a beeline for the bathroom. So, what does this reveal about physical symptoms?

First, symptoms can alert people when something is wrong. Second, when interpreted correctly, they can prompt individuals to act in a way that would alleviate them. Third, symptoms can teach people how to predict problems and take preventive action (e.g., drink water before exercising, bring a jacket when leaving home in case the weather cools, avoid certain foods, or go to the bathroom before a long road trip).

Relatedly, those with generalized anxiety may believe that for their symptoms to disappear others (e.g., children, parents, spouse) — or the world — must change. Yet, why is this incorrect?

Start by reflecting on how psychological symptoms can mirror physical ones. Neurotic anxiety can be the emergency flare that draws attention to when something is wrong (e.g., inefficient or ineffective life style convictions), thereby be part of a feedback mechanism. Accurately interpreting symptoms can empower and prompt people to act in ways that would reduce symptoms, say by altering their problematic convictions. Knowing this, the answer to the preceding question appears: *The person with the symptoms is the one who must change.* In addition, symptoms can teach neurotic individuals how to forecast problems and take preventive action (e.g., "I was needlessly worried that last time I was in a meeting. Everyone warmly accepted and encouraged me. This time I need to graciously receive feedback, not take things personally, and reduce my attempts at control"). So why might neurotic individuals believe that others or the world must change? Though it could be just a simple misperception, it may be more productive to investigate how it's a clue that reveals symptom purposefulness.

Knowing how problematic life style convictions have a fundamental role in symptom development can be enlightening and useful. Yet, your comprehension of neurotic anxiety remains incomplete. Further understanding requires recognizing the persuasive influences that foster the Anxiety Code.

Chapter 9: Influential Factors

Life style convictions can be the basis of generalized anxiety. Accordingly, the ability to comprehend — as well as prevent, reduce, and end — symptoms may flourish with the knowledge of which environments and conditions are the fertile soil that allow anxiety-prone mindsets to take root. Knowing that, which factors can be conducive for cultivating problematic convictions?

Blank Slate and Taking Cues

Imagine parachuting into a foreign land, unfamiliar with the language and customs. You have no personal contacts and only rudimentary communication consisting mainly of pointing and facial expressions. You're unacquainted with the cultural logic and linguistics, spatial orientation (where things are and how to get to them), acceptable physical movements (e.g., greetings, posturing, proximity to others), who the locals are, their goals, or how to treat them, and so forth. Also, you have no money, shelter, or sustenance, and only the clothes on your back. So how do you figure out what's going on and determine ways to reach your goals (e.g., food, refuge)?

You would have to identify and contemplate clues based on your observations and bodily senses. With that in mind, consider how infants disadvantageously enter the world bankrupt of knowledge. At birth, children can develop in any direction; however, bodily impressions and sensations as well as environmental data, education, and ultimately their interpretation, influence the chosen trajectory.[288]

Now, think about how innate compositions such as biological variations (e.g., allergies, differences in sight, hearing, primary sexual characteristics) can shape understanding and interpretation of self (e.g., being self-conscious, feeling inferior or superior), others (e.g., judgmental, accepting, intelligent, foolish), and the world (e.g., unfair, unpredictable). Also, reflect on how, for example, those who have physical weaknesses or medical liabilities may be dissuaded from certain pursuits while others are encouraged, or children may choose activities and areas to pursue and avoid based upon their physical and physiological strengths and limitations. These factors can foster certain perceptions, rules for action, and abilities. *Children's corporeal constitutions, constructions, and capabilities along with the social world can shape their personalities.*[289]

Please note that *biological factors, physical handicaps or childhood illness do not cause neuroses, but rather it's how people perceive their physical builds and functioning that's crucial.*[290] In fact, those with neurotic anxiety can find their strengths and skills, and may reframe their physiques, illnesses and challenges, in ways that allow achieving various healthy and socially-beneficial goals (e.g., determination, responsiveness, and compassion).

Individual Differences in Perception

Despite distinct genetic and social similarities between you and your siblings, such as being raised in the same house, playing identical games, attending the same school, sharing neighbors, and having virtually indistinguishable rules in your home, school, and other places, odds are that you don't have an identical perspective, mindset, or goals. Now, extrapolate this to neurotic anxiety to explain why some siblings develop symptoms while others don't.

When symptoms, and even different behavior among siblings, show up in early development it's easy and tempting to assign biological or genetic causes — after all, temperament differences can exist. Yet, contemplate how children can read their environments before they develop strong language ability and demonstrate individual choice. (Indeed, parents often tell me how they mistakenly expected their second child to act like the first one, say respond the same way to parenting, failure, or a broken toy.)

Children hypothesize, rightly or wrongly, how to act within particular environments and adjust their behavior accordingly. In fact, throughout life people view reality through their respective personalities and act according to their perceptions. *Even identical situations can lead to differences in thought and action, as idiosyncratic characteristics are inseparably interwoven with the experience.*[291]

It only takes small deviations in perception to lead to distinctively different behavior and outcomes. For instance, what one person views as personal failure, another perceives as bad luck, while a third sees others as responsible, and a fourth takes it as a learning experience.

Adaptation

Part of Darwinian theory is that those species that adapt to their environment in ways that increase the likelihood of surviving and thriving will persist and flourish, while those that do not fail to survive and thrive.[292] With that in mind, examine how babies' babbling produces all of the sounds in every language around the globe, but they only retain those that are productive and socially reinforced.[293] Similarly, trying and retaining perceptions and goal-achieving actions are universal — just consider those who pick the best route to get to work swiftly or when to go grocery shopping to avoid cumbersome and claustrophobic crowds. These examples collectively, yet indirectly, introduce a mechanism that applies to neurotic development. For example, imagine those growing up in stormy households where situations and moods worsen rapidly with little or no warning or provocation. Soon safety, predictability, and calm become priorities. However, if family members remain unpredictable and conflictual, what life style convictions might bloom to adapt to such environments?

A belief may develop that thunderous chaos can roll in at any time. The resultant anxiety can fuel protective vigilance for and sensitivity to others' word choice, body language, behavior, or tone of voice. This assists in reading and forecasting their mood, mindset, and impending action, as well as enable quick cognition and trigger swift responses. Some individuals become guarded and escape to a sanctuary of solitude or safety (e.g., bedroom, locked bathroom, playground, library, school, neighbor's home). Others may be so good, perhaps even ideal (e.g., doing chores voluntarily or performing well academically) that they preempt punishment, criticism, or chaos. There are those who develop a sense of humor, cuteness, or diplomacy, because those characteristics can reduce tension and foster peace. Yet, others might unscrupulously sacrifice a sibling to bait and misdirect parental attention and criticism, say by pointing out a bad report card or some other anger-provoking behavior. *Neurotic individuals try various paths and maneuvers in life, and those methods that work to achieve a goal will be retained and used later.*[294]

Rather than merely view some biological or genetic component as causing neuroses, *it can be extremely helpful to view neurotic symptoms as a maturational process.*[295] Comprehending generalized anxiety as related to acquired convictions to (imperfectly) adapt to life's challenges enables a more positive and flexible approach to understanding and treating it.

Parental Influence

Some parents believe their slightest error will bring their children cataclysmic and irreversible harm. Others believe they have little or no influence on their children's development, assuming their children will do as they please and that countless other persuasive factors such as friends, television, movies, books, and the Internet exert more control.

The truth resides somewhere in-between.

Neglecting, Rejecting, Spoiling, Pitying

Children can anticipate and expect their parents' unconditional and inexhaustible love (yet reasonably allow for episodes of disappointment, frustration, or anger). So what might children conclude when their parents routinely neglect their physical, social, or psychological needs?

They may view themselves as sadly unworthy of primary others' affection. This can be heart wrenching. Especially so when they see their parents cherish preferred siblings, or how other parents lovingly tend to their kids. Some believe that no matter what they do, they're unable to attract vital attention and nurturing acceptance. *Parental neglect may lead children to deem themselves inferior and unlovable.* Also, consider how demanding, neglectful, or chaotic parents may directly or indirectly foster people pleasing children who hopefully and painstakingly attempt to earn parental notice or affection.

Imagine witnessing a child's panic after unexpectedly losing a parent in a crowd. The child immediately feels hopelessly forfeited, in an uncontrollable free fall, and terrified of what might happen in an intimidating world. Additional feelings of self-blame for being distracted, inattentive, or bad believed to have severed the connection, can intensify dread and panic. Now keep this in mind when reflecting on how parents may reject their children.

Rejection implies a child had a close parental connection, or at least the budding opportunity for one, but through the exposure of some fault or misbehavior has lost that relationship (e.g., underperforming academically, athletically, or socially, or for biological or physical factors such as weight, intelligence, appearance). *Rejected children might believe that through their error or innate inadequacy they caused a severe and irreparable rupture in the parent-child bond, despairingly losing all that's important to them. They may endlessly try to be accepted or become fiercely independent as a way to avoid being hurt again.*

Parents often protect their children by swiftly taking necessary and beneficial action, say soothe their children after a nightmare or iron out social discord. Though childhood is a phase of life wherein adults tackle their kids' obligations, as children develop they must find solutions for the increasing responsibilities they face.[296] They meet stressors of escalating intensity and with each new challenge kids may needlessly, but naturally, experience apprehension or anxiety, or think, "This is difficult and I don't want to do it." Times like these require parental guidance and encouragement to overcome worry and prompt healthy and successful action that builds skills and self-esteem. Yet, what are the associated difficulties?

Some parents consider childhood a cherished, incomparable, and irreplaceable time in which their children shouldn't be deprived of anything or stressed under any circumstances (perhaps including even moderate challenges).[297] They may spoil their children, not for the children's well-being, but rather because they have immense difficulty witnessing their children pained in any way.[298] Accordingly, they overprotect their kids from stressors. Many metaphorically run behind their children with a pillow in case they fall, never allowing their kids to face, and learn how to deal with, failure.

Some parents misperceive the appropriateness of a challenge and step in too soon for something their children could accomplish successfully. Others may take over chores, grant a reprieve from them, or allow privileges unlikely to exist elsewhere. Just consider how parents who cave in to their children's anxiety and save them from homework or some other obligation, may merely reinforce anxiety and increase its likelihood. This practice can continue until the children are well into adulthood. Indeed, some people in their 20s, 30s, 40s, or older may needlessly and unhealthily live with enabling parents. *That which parents respond to, as well as their values, attitudes, and perceptions, can influence their children's symptom presentation.*

Learning and proficiency require experiencing loss, effort, failure, and collaboration that permissive and overprotective parents prohibit their children from experiencing. *Pampered children may not suffer challenges well, preferring protection and security; however, life can require adjustments that are (often incorrectly) deemed unachievable.*[299]

Although attending to children, encouraging them, making them feel special, and attending to their triumphs, as well as their attempts at success can be beneficial, some parents spoil their children when they do what the parents espouse as the right thing, such as being pleasant and thoughtful, earning good grades, or doing their chores voluntarily and well. There are also parents who have the "As long as the villagers are happy, they won't revolt" mindset and routinely pamper their children as a way to preempt disagreeable behavior. Additionally, parents who wish to end conflict or an embarrassing and disruptive scene may reflexively surrender and appease their children's demands or misbehavior (e.g., needless panic, arguing, temper tantrums). This may allow a temporary truce, but ultimately prolong the battle. (Insightfully, many shops are savvy to such childhood combative tactics and create, for example, candy-free register aisles to avert familial fights.)

Children don't like to fail or be put out. Consequently, they may cry, whine, beg, charm, persuade, pester, and engage in a number of different activities to get others to indulge them. When spoiled children confront a challenge, a quick complaint or raining of tears, or some other distress signal calls caretakers in to extinguish the threat. Children gradually gather that anxiety summons protective parents (or those who yearn for peace) who readily dispatch the worry. Kids can create situations that increase the likelihood of pampering.[300] Likewise, parents can inadvertently train their children to use fear as a means of control.[301] *To avoid facing stressful, but appropriate challenges, children may needlessly exhibit anxiety to call parents into action.*

Pampering can teach kids the following:

• Impatience.

• That social cooperation isn't important or essential.

• To be resistant to guidance, or corrective feedback when they fail.

• That arguing, being anxious, or creating a scene can get them what they want.

• That doing the right thing, being driven, or being good, should always garner admiration and special treatment.

• That everybody should always acknowledge and praise their smallest efforts or good intentions — even if no progress occurs.

• That they should get whatever they want, that their wants supersede others' needs or wants, and that others should always cater to their whims (perhaps regardless of cost).

Children may not learn how to follow rules or cooperate with others — things that are required when they're away from the family who spoiled them.[302] Pampering parents don't bolster their kids' self-esteem or ability to self-soothe and persevere in times of failure or not getting what they want. In this way, pampering can be like a protective leg cast that's been left on too long. It can weaken the muscles necessary to stand on one's own. Consequently, kids may experience anger, frustration and friction-filled interactions, as well as anxiety when they transition to situations where others do not indulge them. These emotions can reveal the difference between (home learned) expectations and (outside world) reality. *Pampered children are ill-prepared for life and as adults may experience neurotic symptoms when facing various demands.*

Kids look up to their parents as seasoned authorities who give knowledgeable advice. With that in mind, what impressions may children develop when parents state the following?

"I'm sorry it looks like you'll never get it. You'll need some help with that."

"I shouldn't have given you that chore. I thought it might be too much for you."

"I'm very concerned about your future because you've made so many mistakes."

Parental pity can lead kids to perceive themselves as hopelessly inadequate. This can be encapsulated by the statement, "If my own parents — the people who know me longer and better than anyone else and who should love me unconditionally — think I'm inferior, then I must be!" Children may adopt their parents' lower standards and convince themselves they'll certainly fail. They subsequently may become unwilling to take chances at success and growth. (Regrettably, parents with a limited or nonexistent social life or intimate relationships who want to avoid loneliness, or wish to have long-term affiliation with their kids, may pity them, which undermines their self-confidence and makes them reliant, say financially, socially, or for guidance, thereby unlikely to stray.) Parental pity erodes kids' self-esteem, cooperation, and healthy coping mechanisms. Those who view themselves as incompetent may avoid interaction, seek special allowances, have a sense of entitlement, and increase their dependence on others.

The ways in which parents and caretakers interact with children may shape the development of a neurotic life style. *Neglecting, rejecting, spoiling, and pitying them are four fundamental ways of mishandling children.*[303]

Inadequate Preparation

Neuroses reveal inadequacies in life preparation.[304] With that in mind, consider how parents may poorly educate their children to meet life's demands. First, they may instill the potentially-beneficial Anxiety Code convictions to an unhealthy degree. Parents may reinforce these convictions or yell and harshly punish when their kids deviate from them. However, rigid adherence is ultimately unsuitable, as life requires cognitive flexibility. Second, opposite to indulgent parents, some expose their children to challenges that are well beyond their ability, or with insufficient training, which regularly ends in confidence-eroding failure. Children may learn to anxiously avoid future opportunities that might otherwise build competency.

Blame and Criticism

Unfortunately, some parents blame and criticize their kids. First, consider parents who want to control their children. For example, they may use cruel words to change the way their daughters dress, or blame their sons' lack of friends on how they don't follow sports, to prod more stereotypically masculine pursuits. Even when parents have the best intentions and their goals are praiseworthy, say to get their children to study, parents may use harsh and discouraging words (e.g., call them lazy or stupid) when their children aren't doing what the parents want. While this may be a reflection of parental frustration and expose poor parenting skills, there's something else to note. *Parents may criticize and blame to gain compliance.*

Second, think about those who find out that parenthood isn't as peaceful, joyful, cooperative, or inexpensive as expected, then blame and criticize their kids as if those mistaken anticipations were their children's fault. Also, there are unplanned, unwilling, and aggravated parents who blame their kids for changing their life plans. Last, consider those who expect their three-year-olds to act like adults, then get upset when their kids act their age. *Parents' unrealistic expectations may make them prone to criticizing and blaming their children.*

So, how might blame and criticism play a role in developing neuroses?

First, when parents focus on and scold undesirable behavior, these negative interactions may preclude them from attending to and reinforcing their children's healthy and sensible activity. Blame, disapproval, and criticism can also occur silently as when parents scowl, frown, grimace, and refrain from acknowledging, supporting, or complimenting their children's actions and interests. Consequently, kids may anxiously avoid their unpalatable parents who erode their self-confidence and regularly create unsavory exchanges. Reprimands and critical statements of children's behavior are likely to develop and reinforce defiance.[305] (Similarly, spanking can be counterproductive and produce aggression, antisocial behavior, and mental health problems.[306]) Although criticism and blame might (at most) get short-term compliance, they can breed long term rebellion and distance, torpedo self-confidence, and lead to conflict and estrangement.

Second, children's innate curiosity as well as drive to experiment and learn, allow them to persevere through failure and arrive at success. However, parental discouragement erodes the interest that stimulates advancement toward goals.[307] Blame can concretize children's perception that they're inferior and correct in doubting themselves, lessening self-esteem that would otherwise fortify attempts at success and help weather failure.[308]

Third, when parents criticize to goad their kids into particular action (e.g., "You're so lazy! Why didn't you take out the garbage like I told you? I want it done now!"), and the children delay a bit more, but in due course comply before the parents criticize again, a problematic dynamic occurs. First, as the kids eventually do the chore, they ultimately reinforce the parents' criticism. Second, the time between censures liberates the children from blame and criticism. This reduction of tension can reinforce their passive-aggressive delay. This is known as the negative reinforcement trap.[309]

Fourth, when children learn to readily comply with what others' want or preemptively do so to avoid criticism and blame, might they become unhealthily compliant in their adult relationships? Relatedly, how can they fully experience love and acceptance which requires vulnerability if they're constantly guarded against criticism and blame?

Fifth, neurotic vanity or extreme self-consciousness may develop as a way to avoid future criticism.

Parents Role Model Behavior

You probably replicate many things your parents do or did, such as celebrate the same holidays, speak the same language, as well as other similarities — but with some variation. You may replicate one parent more than another, or have a fair mixture of both parents' characteristics, just as you do genetically. This is understandable and largely inevitable. There are countless similarities between you and your parents, even if you do not see it...*or wish to*. (Often, patients identify a thought process or action they despise in their parents [e.g., being critical, too rigid], yet do the same — utterly unaware they're doing it.)

Remember that dramatic experiences often may be remembered due to the connection between emotion and memory.[310] Now add in how imitation begins shortly after being born.[311] (Another fact that underscores that people are hardwired to be social.) Furthermore, when children approach novel situations they curiously look at how others react for cues of how to behave, and those actions that bring the children closer to their goals are reinforced over time and shape their adult personality.[312]

As observation is one of the primary, efficient, and effective means of learning, it's no surprise that kids observe their parents' coping skills in pedestrian, novel, or stressful situations. Now, envision those parents who become anxious about things such as financial stability and paying bills, view life in binary terms (e.g., good/bad, right/wrong) with no gradations, demonstrate rigidity and anxiety when situations change, express jubilation and radiant pride when proven right, or are driven, exacting perfectionists who suffer through sleepless nights, always thinking several steps ahead, never fully present in interactions, or constantly worried and unable to enjoy the moment. *Neurotic parents can role model neurotic behavior, and children are particularly prone to imitating caregivers when those experiences are prominent or dramatic.*[313] Consequently, kids may replicate how their parents handle life's stressors. While there isn't an exact imitation of parental actions, there can be a general tendency that's assumed, and children may pick up and uniquely fine-tune those actions and ways of thinking. *Neurotic parents may insufficiently or inappropriately train their kids for coping with life's challenges.*[314]

Parents Role Model Behavior Their Children Oppose

How might parents who engage in behavior that's *opposite* to what the Anxiety Code mandates, kindle neurotic anxiety in their kids?

Well, imagine children embarrassed or horrified by parents who they perceive as lazy, mean, selfish, wrong, or intemperate (e.g., consuming too much, emotionally volatile), who struggled to pay bills, presented poorly, or often put the family in crisis. Those kids witness actions and attitudes they deplore and intensely strive to avoid replicating. Accordingly, they resolutely think and act in complete contrast to their parents as a way to achieve goals their parents' attiudes and actions jeopardized or denied. This may take the form of an (often unspoken) oath similar to, "I swear that when I grow up I'll never _____." *Parents may role model behavior and life style convictions their children forcefully reject in a way that instills the Anxiety Code.*

Parents Unaware of Their Role

Family interaction, instruction, and observation are pivotal in children's accommodation of roles and rules of perception, communication, and action. Essentially, the family is the child's training ground for how to address social challenges.[315] Although sibling interactions are important and influential, kids are most likely to observe, receive instruction, and learn from their parents in countless ways, directly and indirectly. (For instance, chances are that you've seen children or young adults parrot their parents' political points of view, fire off repeated religious canons, or mindlessly photocopy some parental perspective without any independent thought or inspection.)

Parents impart what's valued and productive, set rules and goals, attend to, encourage, and reinforce particular actions and thoughts, as well as ignore, discourage, and punish others — even parental withdrawal, absence, and silence can communicate volumes. Parents can shape their kids' personality characteristics that may become entrenched over time. Children cherish their parents and may eagerly please them and seek acceptance...unless the parents alienate them. *Although individual choice may be the ultimate legislative authority of life style convictions, parents may sway their children's rules.*

Sometimes generalized anxiety may be explained as an early-learned phenomenon. *Childhood anxiety and problematic conduct can imperceptibly grow into adult neurosis.*[316] Viewing neurotic symptom development as a maturational process makes it easier to comprehend parents' role in symptom formation. Yet, some parents do not wish to be seen as inadequate and refuse responsibility for their parenting failures — or even the thought of it. So, how might they protectively perceive themselves as good parents?

Those who wish to avoid the connection between their flawed childrearing methods and their kids' unacceptable behavior are quick to underrate or reject their influence in the children's development.[317] For example, parents who regularly punish their child without any change in their kid's behavior do not consider how their parenting style is problematic, but prefer to blame the child for continuing to engage in undesirable behavior.[318] (While individual choice is the ultimate determinant of behavior, children may unconsciously adopt or mirror their parents' actions — say being controlling — but perhaps in a unique way, e.g., temper tantrums rather than echo their parents' threats.) Sometimes, parents who yell at their children are often shocked, frustrated, and angry that their children yell.

Parents may be anesthetically unconscious of how they role model objectionable behavior, and may paradoxically — and unproductively — increase their yelling to stop their kids from doing it.

Those parents who blame their children (while avoiding their own role) are quicker to criticize, threaten, and punish, which discourages their kids and perpetuates undesired behavior.[319] After all, criticism and punishment don't teach new behaviors. Sadly, some parents only comment on their children's negative behaviors. They believe that if their kids are acting appropriately, then there's no need to interrupt or say anything. For example, "If my kids did the right thing then I wouldn't *have* to criticize them." However, this starves children of nourishing encouragement as well as the acknowledgment of positive attributes and actions.

There are parents who self-righteously portray themselves as wise teachers and give themselves a hall pass to blame and criticize their children at will with the rationale of "showing them the right way" to think or act. By perceiving their children as incompetent or dunces, parents self-aggrandize and make themselves vital in their children's lives (e.g., "They need me to teach them how to do things correctly and be successful"). Unfortunately, such parents may be impervious to reason and preserve their parenting style, often pointing out when criticism and blame have worked previously, while remaining unaware of when it hasn't or the psychological toll on their children. *There are parents who protect their self-esteem by blaming their children instead of taking responsibility for undesirable situations and failures.*

So how else might parents obscure their role in their children's symptom development?

Well, imagine those who — without training or credentials — attempt to diagnose their children, and state something similar to the following, "My kid has an attention deficit disorder (or social phobia) and never listens to me (or stays in the bedroom all the time)." On the surface, this makes sense to them given the observed behavior. But what if you found out that the parents were acidly critical, indirectly disapproving, imperialistically intrusive, and tyrannically controlling, and that their child often focuses on other things rather well for extended periods, interacts and listens attentively to others, and regularly follows rules in various settings. Then what the parents thought was genetic or biological may be estrangement or the budding development of generalized anxiety associated with their parenting style. Yet if that were the case, then why would the parents impose such an innate and chronic diagnosis on their child?

By placing responsibility for unacceptable behavior on genetic or biological factors, parents can avoid accountability for their role in their children's behavior.[320] By viewing their children as genetically or biochemically flawed and beyond parental influence, parents safeguard their self-image, and are spared from examination and improving their parenting style. In fact, some parents immediately dismiss their role in symptom development and — as a corollary of their mindset — seek to medicate their children's symptoms.

Interestingly, when I ask parents about their ratio of positive interactions (e.g., encouragement, compliments) versus negative interactions (e.g., discouragement, criticism) with their kids, often the parents proudly state that they're "fair" — for every criticism, they make sure they say something nice. On the surface, this seems evenhanded, reasonable, and as good parenting. However, please note the following research findings on marriage. In what's known as the Gottman Stability Ratio, healthier marriages have (at least) a five-to-one ratio of positive-to-negative interactions.[321] It appears that people can withstand the one distasteful interaction if many other pleasant and praiseful ones buoy it. Perhaps, the healthy recipe for parent-child interactions similarly requires at least a five-to-one sugar-to-salt ratio.

Some people believe there's a singular, specific reason for the development of unhealthy life style convictions and related neurotic anxiety symptoms. In reality, there are many influential contributing factors that need to be properly defined and investigated. However, note that given the layers of learning over many years, subtle influences, the inexactness of human memory, as well as many other pertinent factors, focusing on past events may not be as therapeutically productive as focusing on current functioning.

Additionally, people may conceptualize neurotic anxiety symptoms, as well as neurotically anxious individuals, too simplistically and apply various inconsistent, blurred, and offhand definitions. This can be an injustice to symptomatic persons as well as impede comprehension, assessment, and treatment. Therefore, that which is defined as "neurotic" needs illumination and clarification.

Chapter 10: Neurotic Characteristics

Generalized anxiety symptoms can be, unsurprisingly, generalized. This may be due to the Anxiety Code's non-specific guidelines. For instance, to be driven or in control doesn't state exactly how to fulfill those stipulations and illustrates the difference between *modus vivendi* (a way of living) and *modus operandi* (a specfic way to do something). Also, even though you know that neuroses are equated to personality disorders, that's a vague portrait in need of more color and detail. For example, it's necessary to know that given the variety of different anxiety diagnoses, not all anxious persons are neurotic. Moreover, all neurotic features cannot apply to any one person; some are common, others pertain only to particular individuals. Perhaps most important, although you're aware of what anxiety looks and feels like, what are the defining brush strokes that illustrate *neurotic* characteristics?

Inferiority Feelings

Every person starts life in an inferior position. As infants and children develop they become increasingly aware of their general inability and dependence on others, which may stir up an insufferable sense of inadequacy.[322] In fact, people face challenges throughout life that can spawn inferiority feelings, to others or to an endeavor, but does this mean those feelings are inherently harmful?

Odds are, it's accurate to rate yourself as financially inferior to the mega-wealthy. Yet, you may not experience anything adverse — say feeling insufficient, or any other collateral damage — if those matters that don't interest you, or if you're secure and noncompetitive. Objective inferiority is common, can be a correct assessment, and doesn't have to generate symptoms. *People's attitude toward their inferiorities is a more accurate predictor of whether symptoms develop.*[323] They can adapt to challenges without feeling inadequate. For instance, they may reframe failure at a task in such a way as to bolster confidence by no longer defining success as task mastery, but rather as being triumphant in summoning their courage and facing their fears, "Well, at least I tried!" In other words, it isn't whether one strikes out or hits a home run, but rather if the person has the courage to get off the bench, approach the plate, and swing for the fences in front of a sea of spectators. *Individuals define themselves by the meaning they assign to their experiences and situations.*[324] Therefore, people who have a genuine, unresolvable objective inferiority (e.g., physical, financial, cognitive) aren't inescapably bound to have anxiety.

Conversely, even if neurotic persons wholeheartedly believe they're inferior and ineffective, doesn't mean they are.[325] Indeed, genuine competence or significance doesn't guarantee that people are free from inferiority feelings. Those with generalized anxiety who excel and are legitimately superior in valued areas may nevertheless perceive themselves as inferior. It's people's subjective perception that's decisive. (I've often heard remarkably intelligent patients with low self-esteem demonstrate difficulty acknowledging their intellect. For instance, they may state, "I'm not dumb," rather than "I'm smart." A subtle, but telling, difference.)

Life is replete with chores, challenges, and circumstances. Some can be injurious, dangerous, or life threatening; for example, skiing a double black diamond slope or lifting something heavy and unwieldy. People have two obligations in such circumstances. First, assess perilousness. Second, evaluate their ability to achieve their goal. If they correctly judge themselves unable to successfully complete the task, they can decline pursuing it and avoid failure and other adverse outcomes. *Health and survival can be maintained when inferiority feelings are accurate and acted upon appropriately.*

Now envision a group of children swimming with one exception who sits poolside, unknowing of how to swim and feeling profoundly and desperately inferior to those in the pool. While it's normal and natural to have inferiority feelings about undeveloped skills, what vital things does the child's lack of knowledge imperil?

Self-esteem as well as social interaction and acceptance are threatened. But there's a crucial detail you need to know. *Inferiority feelings can be intolerable and produce pressure that prompts movement.*[326] Yet, in which direction?

The child has a choice of how to handle those painful inferiority feelings. Assume that the kid elects to ask for guidance on how to do the dog paddle, tread water, or some other action that will enable group participation and may protect acceptance. Ah, but what about self-esteem? Well, the child's desire to extinguish inferiority feelings may not only urge interaction, but also sustain countless attempts at learning how to swim and overcome fears and inabilities in an afternoon. This reveals an important detail about self-confidence. Demonstrating competency to others isn't enough; it's how individuals view themselves that's their reality. When the child learns how to swim there's proof of competency, which builds confidence and acceptance. Until that point, the most the child could have is a goal and the drive to attain it. Sometimes, more intense inferiority feelings kindle increased drive that stimulates persistent attempts in the face of failure and, perhaps, lifelong striving that practically assures success.

Relatedly, neurotically anxious individuals often assert they would do something *if only* they had the confidence to do it. Yet, why is this incorrect?

As people's self-esteem develops only after reaching a goal that proves proficiency to themselves, confidence without demonstrating ability is impossible, mistaken, or delusional. Therefore, the stipulation is a Catch-22. It prohibits effort that would allow them to achieve their desires and build confidence. However, note how this requirement of confidence before action unearths an intriguing fact — people can cite their inferiority feelings as rationale for action or inaction. *Inferiority feelings aren't necessarily detrimental to functioning; rather it's how individuals elect to manage them.*[327] Akin to the preceding, neurotic individuals' fear of failure, ridicule, rejection, or abandonment may be so severe that they want a guarantee of success before they try something. This is impossible...but think about what such paradoxes can allow.

Now, imagine parents who lament limited job mobility and access to various qualities of life, who unwaveringly and emphatically encourage their children's education to attain job security, increased income, status, among other things. *One person's inferiority feelings may lead to prompting others towards competency in a particular arena.* Yet, this can be problematic, say when it isn't their children's goal (e.g., those who failed at sports then fanatically goad their uninterested children to pursue their parents' broken dreams).

Consider how when people feel inferior...

• Concerned others may successfully encourage them to take action toward their goals.

• Compassionate people may take pity and fear the possible negative emotional and social impact of failure, and effectively dissuade individuals from trying.

• Some individuals choose to address or avoid areas of their perceived or actual inferiority, regardless of others' discouragement or encouragement.

• People determinedly select and rebelliously strive toward goals that are in direct opposition to others' discouragement, criticism, encouragement, or undue pressure.

While social influence can be important, it isn't an essential factor in addressing either objective inferiority or inferiority feelings. *Individual choice can trump social influence.*

Fortunately, inferiority feelings don't have to limit people needlessly or harmfully, but rather can indicate an area in need of growth — like a brutally-honest bathroom scale that shows undesirable digits, or a malnourished retirement account that hungrily begs for money. Neurotic persons endure inferiority feelings.[328] However, it's less important what thoughts and feelings individuals maintain, than what use they make out of them.[329] It's the progression and path between inferiority and significance that's particularly relevant in understanding neuroses.[330]

Inferiority Complex

When people believe their inferiority is immutable, and do not take action to improve their situation, they experience an inferiority complex.[331] Therefore, the distinction between common inferiority feelings and an inferiority complex is of scale rather than kind.[332]

An inferiority complex can be people's vocal and/or behavioral declaration of marked inadequacy that informs others to refrain from relying on them. It consists of a cognition (e.g., "I'm not good at _____.") and behavior (e.g., retreat, immobility). The development of inferiority feelings to an inferiority complex can go unnoticed and pervasively seep into a wide range of activities or a specific one. People may not vocalize their inferiority complex, and avoid areas in which they perceive themselves as inadequate to successfully address. Every person has inferiority feelings; however, the reason not everyone has an inferiority complex is that some marshal their energy and employ it in socially useful behavior.[333] However, does having an inferiority complex automatically imply that someone is neurotic?

No. Just consider how someone can say, "I have terrible balance and I'm extremely clumsy, so I can't help you fix your roof. Call a professional roofer." This is an acknowledgement and broadcast of a significant inferiority paired with a behavior (immobility). The truth was expressed, appropriate action was taken, and no one was injured or exploited. Inferiority feelings are common and don't make people neurotic, nor does having an inferiority complex.

So, what's the link between inferiority complexes and neuroses?

People may develop inferiority complexes when they misperceive their situations (actual or imagined) as inescapable and insurmountable, and surrender to them rather than mend or improve them.[334] Neuroses are intensified inferiority complexes.[335] *An inferiority complex is a prerequisite and a defining characteristic of neuroses.*

Fear of Exposure and Vanity

Given the need to protect their self-esteem, acceptance, and life style, neurotic individuals can be exceedingly motivated to hide their inferiorities.[336] For example, they may be anxiously aware of their appearance, carefully monitor what they say and intensely filter their presentation, ceaselessly worry about what others think, and react quickly when they fear they've said or done something unacceptable. Unfortunately, neurotic symptoms can become troublesome when they persist and lead to a restriction of social activity.[337] And indisputably, vanity prohibits the authentic interaction and vulnerability necessary to overcome anxiety as well as have healthy friendships and relationships.

Superiority Complex

Those with generalized anxiety may face an imprisoning situation of desperately wanting to be proficient and successful, but believing they're too inadequate to metaphorically climb the fence of competency and liberate themselves. So how might they attain a sense of significance in such confining circumstances?

They may airbrush their flaws and inadequacies out of awareness by becoming unconscious of them. However, this is merely the first step in their pursuit, as it doesn't grant a sense of competency. So what else might come into play?

Well, recall how inferiority feelings can be so objectionable that people are motivated to eliminate them by facing their fears and challenges and achieving impressive goals. Additionally, with more intense inferiority feelings, there's a greater drive to compensate for them. These clues reveal an interesting neurotic mechanism.

Immense inferiority feelings can initiate and sculpt the goal of superiority.[338] In fact, neurotic individuals can be motivated to go beyond feeling capable and on par with others, to feeling all-powerful.[339] They can develop a superiority complex, which is nothing more than camouflage and excessive compensation for their inferiority complex.[340]

For example, they may…

• Freely trumpet the benefits and brilliance of their actions or objectives.

• Excessively pride themselves on some distinction or attribute, say a skill, characteristic, accomplishment, or ability in a particular area of functioning or prized category.

• Narrow their focus to only those areas of their legitimate competency and superiority and emphatically express their greatness and simultaneously downplay possessions or realms of functioning in which they're merely average or altogether inferior.

• Be venomously critical of others. Some can be "arrogant, impertinent, conceited, and snobbish."[341]

• Be blissfully unaware of their mistakes, failures, and areas of inadequacy. Pride may preclude partial or total recognition of their failures.[342] Some state, for instance, they have expert intelligence and abilities but "don't test well," which suggests unfalsifiable superiority. Often, failure is forgotten, denied, or discourteously and inaccurately put on others, life, or on the invisible and intangible such as luck, chance, fate, or their god(s). In this way, Teflon-coated superiority prevails.

• Create and live by unique rules that only they can fulfill successfully, yet modify those rules when status and acceptance are jeopardized.

When neurotic persons intensely and repeatedly broadcast their superiority, they may persuade others into accepting and believing this advertised conception — even if it's completely false. Curiously, when might those with a superiority complex identify and own their mistakes?

While this may seem like a trick question, it isn't. They may, for example, state they've given others "too much credit" or "should have dumbed it down" so that others could understand, which indirectly self-elevates neurotic persons by defining others as inferior.

So what characteristic problem might those with a superiority complex face?

They may make unrealistic demands on themselves and others.[343] This increases the risk of failure and subsequent erosion of self-esteem and acceptance.

Also, note how unrealistic expectations of others doom them to failure. This may increase neurotic persons' sense of superiority — as well as their anxiety, frustration, annoyance, and anger.

Sensitivity

Examine how sensitivity of certain devices can productively enable quicker awareness and response (for instance, you want aviation radar, smoke detectors, home security systems, and medical tests to be sensitive enough to accurately detect problems as soon as possible). Likewise, people's sensitivity to possible threats can beneficially influence their physical movement and health before pain and problems have the opportunity to occur. For example, people can swiftly grasp the perilousness of a steep cliff and their fear judiciously prompts a profitable retreat. Correspondingly, insensitivity to possible or additional injury can be problematic.

Neurotic persons can fear exposing perceived or actual inadequacy and wish to avoid people, places, or circumstances they deem threatening. With that in mind, might sensitivity...?

• Facilitate rapid identification of threatening situations.

• Allow for safe negotiation of social hazards.

• Prompt and fuel retreat from those dangerous interactions or conditions.

• Get others to be compassionate and helpful, or persuade them to back off from pursuing a course of action.

• Initiate and assist quick recovery when neurotic individuals believe they've disclosed information or acted in a way that jeopardizes self-esteem and acceptance.

Sensitivity can protectively warn of distant threats or sudden danger, and prompt swift redemption if something that imperils acceptance, self-esteem, or life style, escapes. Moreover, with amplified inferiority feelings and/or risk of exposure, there's a corresponding escalation of vigilance, touchiness, and defensiveness. *Pride and sensitivity can play a significant part in neuroses.*[344] For example, sensitivity to social comparison can be extensive. Neurotic individuals can be extremely competitive and take things personally — even with trivial matters; for instance, needing to beat the car next to them to a lane merge or off the stop light; call their doctors by their first name, rather than their professional title to avoid feeling inferior to them; demand to sit at the head of the table, refuse to take the backseat when in a car, and so on.

Internal Struggles

Those with generalized anxiety may endlessly grapple with decisions, engage in an interminable tug-of-war of ideas and values, and act as if even the most trifling ones are indisputably momentous. They may perceive themselves as powerless, torn, and as victims.[345] This generates a persistently painful and unnerving state, which may prompt them to seek sanctuary in medication. Compassionate others often notice the internal conflicts and attempt to provide aid, limit their requests, commandeer decision-making, engage in damage control, or deploy whatever means necessary to penetrate and cease the problem. Even if an internal armistice is reached, it's often temporary or so devastating as to be nearly equivalent to defeat — a pyrrhic victory. In addition, neurotic individuals may be torn between two or more choices and unnervingly indecisive. While this can be due to conflicting life style convictions, might these internal struggles have a purpose?

Schadenfreude/Epicaricacy

What do measures of vision, height, weight, fitness, income, and intelligence have in common?

Each assesses an individual in comparison to social norms as a determinant of health, well-being, achievement, or functioning. While evaluating a person to a relevant group is a common and acceptable practice, *neurotic persons may be agonizingly aware they may be measured with a socially-defined yardstick.* After all, it only takes one person, say a sibling, coworker, or neighbor, to attain some goal (e.g., better home, higher income) that dramatically, and perhaps threateningly, alters the calibration of what's acceptable and comparatively lowers neurotic individuals. Moreover, given that others (the social background) may determine and reflect what's acceptable, it's an uncontrollable elastic gauge that's in constant flux (e.g., fads, home trends). *The social standard of worth can be frighteningly subjective, fleeting, and fickle.* Yet, what's the obverse to this measure of merit?

Neurotic persons may interpret accidents, failures, and adversities that befall successful others as a leveling of the playing field, or proof that life is fair and there's balance in the universe. They can view it as a lowering of the baseline that advantageously increases their relative worth. *Neurotic persons may take overt or covert delight out of others' misery, defeat, and misfortune.* For every apparently earnest, "I'm so sorry that your son didn't get accepted to medical school" or "You were an ideal couple, I'm shocked that he left you for another woman," there may be an inner smirk, satisfaction, or sense of relief from competition. Just consider the phrase "It's not enough that I should succeed, others should fail."[346] It highlights how some people want to be indisputably victorious in a social comparison.

Apathy

Neurotic persons genuinely and indisputably suffer with serrated symptoms that relentlessly saw away at them. Yet, why might some calmly make the following dismissive statements?

"I don't want to go on medication and become a zombie."

"I've always been this way. Besides, I don't believe in therapy."

"My symptoms are beyond the scope of treatment. I'll be all right."

"I'm sure it's genetic, so there is nothing I can do about it. Don't worry."

"It's my problem. I've had it for too long for anyone to fix it. I'll deal with it."

Those with generalized anxiety can be curiously serene in accepting their aggravating and antagonizing symptoms. Perhaps they've fought bravely, but have deemed their symptoms invincible and surrendered to them. Conceivably, to be good they accept their symptoms as to not burden others. There's even the possibility of learned helplessness.[347] They may endure their symptoms — even if escapable — under the depressing and disconcerting belief they're powerless to control their situation. Yet, without the interest or emotion to fuel action to address their symptoms, they sustain them. So, could it be that as exasperating, painful, and exhausting as symptoms are, might maintaining them allow some form of goal achievement? This may explain the otherwise puzzling and inexplicable apathy toward symptom reduction.

Extremism

The world is filled with variation, exceptions to the rule, approximations, imperfections, yet neurotic persons may see the world in binary terms (e.g., good/bad, black/white, right/wrong, all/nothing).[348] So why might they have such a noticeably incongruous digital perception in an analog world?

Recall that people can zero in on one or more thoughts or images that generate emotion. This can illuminate why those with generalized anxiety have laser-like focus of perception rather than a diffuse floodlight. With more concentrated attention — perhaps to the near or total exclusion of other thoughts — there's corresponding emotional intensity that either fuels extraordinary and resolute action or is so overwhelming as to ensure immobility.

Neurotic individuals may state they have "an addictive personality," then reference their tendency to become obsessed about something and compelled to engage in particular action. Additionally, they can have a "if it's worth doing, it's worth overdoing" mentality. There can be an assurance that they're in control or right when they exceed a task's requirements. Moreover, success at doing something perfectly, for example, can be addictive. *When neurotic persons experience thoughts, images, or recollections that create terror, adrenaline-saturated suspicion, exceptional pride, or some other immense emotion, their moods, mindsets, and motions correspondingly change as quickly and decisively as if attached to a light switch.*

Yet, what might be the social impact of such extremes?

People may overstate their symptoms. First, this underscores how serious they perceive their circumstances. Second, it communicates symptom severity to others— but maybe not merely for sharing information. For instance, imagine a neurotic person is asked why paperwork wasn't submitted on time, which ultimately cost the employer a hefty fine. There might be an instant flood of defensive and combative responses, claiming an impeccable job or blaming someone or something else. Or, perhaps an abrupt reversal and merciless self-rebuke, "I'm the worst employee ever! I should have been fired years ago!" Such extremism not only painfully abbreviates the world far too much, but also leads to intense mood and action, going from indisputable victor to the most abject failure. More important, how might others shift their stance in response to such nimble and incandescent pivots in conversation?

Perfectionism

Neurotic individuals may endeavor to do things flawlessly and/or demand perfection, and appreciation, from others.[349] While this is a prime example of neurotic extremism, what are the personal and social corollaries of perfectionism?

Consider how demanding error-free functioning from others instantly puts neurotic persons in a commanding position, with others inferior to them, pressured to fulfill an impossible decree or face an imposed verdict of inadequacy and negative judgment. In addition, when others don't do things perfectly, those with generalized anxiety may give themselves permission to take control and tell others what to do as well as evaluate their (imperfect) work.

For those who are driven, having perfection as the only acceptable outcome can fuel perpetual effort until things are done perfectly. Yet, what's a downside? When they stipulate perfection for themselves even their smallest flaws, mistakes, or variations may be deemed apocalyptic. By definition, perfectionism means that it's either perfect or it's wrong — a clear illustration of binary thinking. Such rules for living have a number of effects and repercussions. For instance, picture a perfectionist who imposed a strict financial regiment, scrupulously saving money to get ahead on mortgage payments. All is going well until the person, bored with the same routine of work, bland home-cooked meals, and boring TV shows, splurges on a night out on the town. How might that individual handle such a tiny infraction?

There's anxiety accompanied by scorching self-criticism and the belief that all is lost, "I can't even stick with simple financial planning without goofing it up. I'm a complete failure!" Ironically, even though you might expect that a perfectionist might try twice as hard to make up for the transgression, there are times when spending may increase with the belief, "Well, I've already ruined it. There's no sense trying to get ahead now!" After a flurry of spending, there's a corresponding increase of inferiority feelings, regret, and anxiety.

Neurotic perfectionism can be more taxing than non-neurotic perfectionism. It can foster markedly greater inferiority feelings because neurotic perfectionists set the bar so high that they feel proportionately inferior when they fail to attain their goals.[350]

Literalism

Those with generalized anxiety can take words and ideas literally.[351] For instance, before heading out to the store one spouse asks the other, "Do you need any tea?" "No," is the reply. However, upon returning home the question, "Did you buy my tea?" is met with a perplexed, "No, you told me not to." This leads to a literalist argument:

"First, I never said *not* to get tea. Second, you know I drink tea every day. Third, we are out of tea."

"That's why I asked if you wanted any tea."

"No, wrong again. You specifically asked, 'Do you *need* any tea?' and that's wrong for two reasons. One, I don't *need* tea. The human body can function without it. Second, it isn't just '*any*' tea that I drink. You know I've enjoyed the same brand of Earl Grey for 20 years!"

Literalism can frustrate all involved. For those who detest a gray world, the stringent use of language can provide predictability, simplification, and clarity. In addition, literalism can elevate neurotic persons as they're right in the absolutist sense, while prompting those proven wrong to make amends or engage in some other conciliatory behavior. Also, note how literalism can allow beneficial outcomes, say when stringently following healthy rules and regulations and avoiding harmful shortcuts (e.g., strictly follow infection-control protocol in food service or medicine).

Dogmatism

When those with generalized anxiety face challenges their life style convictions are unable to satisfy, they can learn new information and acquire better and healthier skills. However, this comes with an unappetizing dessert. It requires challenging and changing their entrenched convictions and exposing ignorance and inability in a rather taxing and occasionally unsettling process. With this in mind, consider how neurotic individuals may have absolute confidence in their belief and feelings.[352] They obediently abide by their characteristic rules they believe ensure success and goal attainment.[353] In this way, they get to avoid challenging their worldview and rules, but this strengthens their cognitive rigidity, counterproductively maintaining or amplifying symptoms. Cognitive rigidity can be like a football team using the same play repeatedly even though it seldom, if ever, works. Sometimes, a neurotic individual will label cognitive inflexibility and proneness for routines as being a "Creature of habit." This label is a bit easier on self-esteem and may protect acceptance and status.

When discussing life style convictions it may be helpful to compare them to familiar and non-neurotic domains, such as politics, philosophy, or religion, as each creates a person's reality, prompts certain actions, and may be defended vigorously. For example, consider religious individuals who believe that praying for those who are ill may make them healthier even when research demonstrates it's more likely to have no effect or make ailing individuals sicker.[354] Yet, how likely are they to renounce or discontinue prayer? It's a matter of faith. Equally, some believe their political stance is the best. However, when confronted with facts that highlight flaws and costly mistakes, they may rationalize the results and continue believing their political party is superior.

When neurotic persons unwaveringly believe their logic is realistic and effective, they can become impervious to external influences.[355] *Neurotic dogmatism can concretize private logic and may worsen an unhealthy situation, however, by contorting perceptions it erases awareness of inferiority.* This can exasperate and estrange others as well as create obstacles for psychological treatment. However, can neurotic dogmatism have an upside?

Even though it may generate symptoms, examine how the dogmatic need to be good, for instance, mandates impassioned determination to follow through on good acts, say complete a job, provide for others, or tirelessly defend powerless victims.

Emotionalism

Neurotic persons can experience emotions intensely.[356] It doesn't matter if it's the exhilaration of success, the agony of defeat, the panic of a loss of control, the terror of rejection, or anything else. Just like uninterested individuals don't take action, strong emotions are in accord with dogmatic thoughts, determined action, or paralyzing inaction. Emotional shifts and mood volatility can destabilize relationships, annoy and perplex those with generalized anxiety as well as others. However, emotionalism can also energize socially-beneficial actions, such as the passionate pursuit of humanitarian causes.

Present-ism

Neurotic persons may exaggerate slight aches and stresses as well as gauge pleasures as merely adequate.[357] Perhaps they're under undue stress and their nerves are frayed, therefore unable to get as much pleasure out of life, and experience physical, emotional, and cognitive strains to a greater degree. Think of this as akin to being unable to enjoy an otherwise pleasurable walk in a park because you overexerted yourself at the gym the previous day. However, when you think of sensitivity and dullness it's helpful to consider what movement they allow or prohibit. Also, it's necessary to see the association among thoughts, emotions, and actions, and how intensity of one can magnify another.

The maxim "I want what I want when I want it," may best illustrate Present-ism, which has three constituents: Impatience, Intolerance, and Domineeringness.[358]

Impatience

Being impatient is a characteristic of inferiority feelings that leads to a state of intensified emotion.[359] In other words, those who feel inadequate may be prone to be impatient and become frustrated when they cannot do something as quickly as they want. They can be immensely resistant to accommodate others' pace or time.[360] Uncontrollable things such as ill-timed traffic lights, or people who don't move at the preferred rate of speed, can generate anger and anxiety. Intense inferiority feelings, increased emotions, and impatience can lead to certain behaviors. Indeed, neurotic persons can be unpredictable and clearly establish their impatience.[361] You can imagine how even something as subtle as a loud sigh or foot tapping can send ripples through the social pond — which might provoke certain action from others. When it leads them to get their work done or prompts others to take action, those with generalized anxiety may upend an old phrase and think, "Impatience is a virtue."

Intolerance

Neurotic persons may be notably intolerant. Their frustration, annoyance, and anger, can sever social ties, flout obligations, and disrupt situations to either get their way or dismiss what they cannot attain.[362] Others may alter their actions or desires to avoid hostility (e.g., partygoers who forgo bringing their children because of one person's intolerance, the spouse who refrains from talking to anyone of the other sex). Intolerance can allow for a quick exit from situations (e.g., "I can't take this job [or marriage, party, movie] anymore!"). Also, intolerance of anything not in accord with the Anxiety Code (e.g., meanness, imperfection) can enforce personal or social compliance.

Domineeringness

When neurotic individuals are controlling, overbearing, or conceited they can corral others to take action that provides instant gratification.[363] This is unsurprising. After all, being bossy or a bully can get others to engage in particular action (e.g., chores, back down from an argument). If this interactional pattern is maintained others may preemptively act in accord with anticipated demands as a way to avoid the otherwise inevitable outburst or caustic remark, which reinforces domineeringness. For instance, "While I'd like to go out for a coffee (or join the gym, bring cookies home), I'm sure that my spouse would have a fit, and I'd rather not deal with it."

Disproportionalism

Neurotic persons may instantly want some object or action and willfully pay an exorbitant price (e.g., financially, socially, emotionally, physically, medically, behaviorally) — even a penalty — for such an indulgence.[364] For example, without permission or communication to their prescriber, they may double their medication to reduce symptoms quicker. They may be completely unaware of, or apathetic to, realistic time requirements, people's needs and rights, or a sense of fairness. Yet, when others engage in those actions, those with generalized anxiety may label such acts as brazen unfairness, stupidity, ignorance, etc., which may generate a disproportionate amount of outrage and quest for retribution. They may take small, incidental infractions personally and become furious or alarmed. When neurotic individuals experience emotions and thoughts disproportionate to circumstances, might they enable particular goal-achieving action that may be otherwise unjustifiable?

Serving Two Masters

Envision being in a country and unwilling to engage in its unfamiliar and uncomfortable customs, yet violation of such traditions and conventions risks creating a scene, embarrassment, or insulting others. Might you comply only to the degree that avoids concern or conflict, thereby retain as much of your value system and behavioral habits as possible?

With this in mind, think about how neurotic individuals may maintain private logic that's different from common knowledge. However, to preserve acceptance they may avoid appearing odd or unconventional by attempting to fulfill real (social) and imaginary (private logic) obligations.[365] They try to juggle private logic with common sense to have the best of both worlds. They may anxiously strive to fit in socially, while acting in agreement with their private logic as much as possible. In other words, they can play along or appear to adhere to social rules. However, they prefer to take an individualized goal of achievement, and gauge their accomplishments from within their private logic.[366] This may occur in situations in which their life style is potentially imperiled. For example, they might state they have a cold and don't want to get the other person sick to avoid hugging or being physically close to others. Or, they may anxiously avoid taking a lunch break at work, say by stating they have much work to do, because they want to see themselves as driven, don't want to make small talk, or don't want others to think they're lazy. Anxiety increases as neurotic logic has more frequent or in-depth discord with the environment and the opportunities for failure escalate.[367]

Chapter 11: Symptom Purposefulness?

Anxiety can hopscotch from feelings of pressure to tension to dread to fear. It can attack with little to no forewarning or apparent provocation, and routinely leave its victims unnervingly unable to forecast symptom appearance, severity, or duration. While the causal perspective proposes that some event or condition precipitates generalized anxiety, could that be only half the picture?

Well, contemplate how biological symptoms such as fever, sweating, vomiting, and diarrhea are painful, unwanted, disruptive, and potentially embarrassing. You can see how each is caused, for example, by infection, by a sweltering summer sun, after drinking too much alcohol, or eating spoiled or ill-prepared food. The medical cause and effect perspective accurately and soundly states that circumstances or behaviors cause symptoms that remedial action (e.g., take off a jacket), or medication, swiftly and effectively eliminate in an acceptable way. Yet, why is maintaining only that understanding a nearsighted injustice to the wonders of the human body?

Although an infection can cause a fever, body temperature above an optimum range can prompt perspiration, and vomiting and diarrhea can be natural results of ingesting what should have been left on the table, fuller comprehension requires examining what happens *after* symptoms occur.

As sweat evaporates it wicks away heat, lowering body temperature.[368] (It's also interesting how malodorous perspiration may keep other warm bodies that would worsen the problem coolly distant.) Fever may elevate body temperature that augments sleep and immune functioning.[369] And, if you follow vomiting and diarrhea to their natural conclusion, you can see how they (rather mercilessly and indelicately) rid the body of toxins.[370]

Now consider what happens when people experience a simple wound. Their bodies initiate a wave of wondrous, dutiful actions. Blood flow is redirected and platelets are funneled to the injury. This promotes clotting and prevents further blood loss. White blood cells race to the wound and consume harmful bacteria to eliminate or reduce the probability of infection. Dead tissue and cells are whisked away or are otherwise displaced. The bisected area may contract to assist healing speed and success. Newborn cells arise, tissue develops, and cells mend which aid in restoring previous structures and functions. The final act of this ensemble play is the creation of scar tissue and its eventual reduction or removal.[371] So, what might these processes reveal?

If you're uncertain, consider these accompanying corporeal clues:

- A blinking reflex that shields the eyes.[372]
- Faculties to assess hunger and initiate eating.[373]
- Mucus and pus evacuate harmful viruses and bacteria.[374]
- The gag response that averts choking and asphyxiation.[375]
- An infantile sucking response that prompts nutritional intake.[376]
- Thirst-detection mechanisms and systems that stimulate re-hydration.[377]

When you recognize these innate functions are automatically and unconsciously orchestrated to strive toward the goals of well-being and survival, you arrive at an irrefutable and captivating conclusion: *Symptoms can protect the body and aid survival and thriving.*

Now, what happens when people who've broken their leg try to move?

Their agony is the body's feedback mechanism that screams, "Stop! That area isn't strong enough for what you want to do and things will only get worse if you keep trying to move." In various situations, pain alerts sufferers to physical damage and can immobilize them, which prevents further injury. Ah, but what if action rather than immobility is needed?

Consider how pain also can be the starting pistol that prompts movement, such as flight to a medicine cabinet or hospital. So, although pain can be excruciating, the ability to perceive and respond to it is a necessary and remarkably healthy mechanism. Note that this applies to more than pain. Any physical symptom can provide feedback that people interpret (e.g., rash, limited mobility, sores, tooth grinding, trembling, ear ringing, sweating, cold hands, dry mouth, problems swallowing, difficulty breathing, diminished sexual performance). Fair enough, but what's the deciding factor that determines how people read symptoms?

At this point, the answer should be unsurprising — and you may be able to guess it purely out of reflex.

People's goals govern how they translate symptoms and the resultant, related behavior (e.g., immobility, retreat, movement toward something specific). For example, if they don't want to visit their doctor, they may dismiss pain as temporary or insignificant. *Also, note that symptoms may be the memorable signposts that guide future behavior (e.g., don't jump from unsafe heights, go easy on spicy food).* But there's another revealing element to consider.

So, why might sharp pains, for example, immediately provoke grievous yelps?

This is a curious connection between essentially different and seemingly unrelated systems of pain and vocalization. But given what's been discussed, you should be able to determine the answer nearly immediately.

First, the unity of the personality reveals how different bodily symptoms can work in tandem to reach a goal. Second, consider how communicating pain (e.g., crying, yelling, colorful exclamations of various sorts) can alert those nearby of the crisis, appeal for their assistance, or get them to stop what they're doing. Just think about how compassionate others help those who subtly groan from pain, say from attempting to lift a heavy object or even wrestling with a stubborn jar lid. In addition, reflect on how infectious physical symptoms (e.g., the flu, chicken pox, sexually transmitted infections) are transmissible. These facts uncloak a consequential conclusion. *An individual's symptoms can have a social component.*

How might you apply this comprehension of physical symptoms to neurotic anxiety?

Although various biological, genetic, psychological, and social factors may foster symptoms, review the points progressively developed since the first chapter and you'll arrive at an interesting and illuminating question.

• There are limitations in the medical cause and effect paradigm when it's applied to the assessment and treatment of psychological symptoms. For instance, an association between specific genes and generalized anxiety can be present — but not in the majority of cases. Also, the correlation of characteristic neuronal activity and neurotransmitter levels (among other biological factors) with symptom presence exists, but doesn't prove symptom causation. Recall that memories are often imperfect, and may be more relevant to present functioning than past events. Moreover, insight doesn't assure symptom alleviation. Searching for symptom causes may be futile and counterproductive. Medically suppressing symptoms may be counter therapeutic at times. In addition, perceiving people exclusively as passive victims can limit understanding and treatment. Last, psychological symptoms can have a social function.

• People are goal-oriented beings who must inescapably select goals in those areas of life without biologically-innate answers.

• Individuals can focus their attention to generate emotions that fuel goal-achieving behavior.

• Thoughts, emotions, actions, and various body systems work consistently and harmoniously toward goals, consciously and unconsciously.

• Individuals are group constituents, with interaction, cooperation, subjective measurement, as well as acceptance and rejection being powerful social factors in human functioning.

• People's library of individually chosen and socially influenced life style convictions — their personalities — define their respective realities by shaping perception, emotion, behavior, thought, and goal selection.

• Unsuitable or conflictual life style convictions, low self-esteem and fear of rejection, ridicule, failure and abandonment may prohibit goal achievement and precipitate anxiety.

• Biological symptoms can be an active, purposeful means of surviving and thriving, and have a social component.

With this in mind, could generalized anxiety be akin to some biological symptoms?

Well, just imagine those children terrified by a nonexistent monster under their beds, and experience muscle tension, increased heart rate, racing thoughts, vigilance, among other anxiety-related symptoms. Though the monster is a figment of their imagination, consider the psychological, physical, and physiological symptoms that arise as well as the vital details.

First, anxiety can be based on a misperception. Second, those symptoms cannot be caused or due to past events because there isn't — and has never been — a monster underneath the bed. So why do those children experience anxiety? Simply, their bodies are preparing for confrontation if those imagined creatures were to savagely pounce. If this example is opaque, perhaps another may help.

Envision that you're driving well above the speed limit, and as you rounded a bend a police officer was lying in wait for speeders such as yourself. You're caught and eventually pay an excruciating fine. So what might happen the next time you drive down that road?

As you approach the bend, it's likely that an image of the police car pops into your head, your heart surges, and your right foot reflexively lifts off the accelerator. Interesting, but why does this occur even if there isn't an officer there? While you might be tempted to say that it's strictly due to the past, think about how that's untrue. It's helpful to examine your anxiety-related movement as well as the potential outcome of the anxiety. As long as your anxiety leads to you slowing down, you can see how it's an unconscious protective mechanism that protects you from getting another ticket.

But, wait a second. You may say that these examples aren't neurotic anxiety — and you'd be right. They're simple starting points that provide conclusions that can be readily and beneficially applied. By gently and indirectly presenting the first point, it's easier to learn what's extraordinary and enlightening.

Anxiety symptoms can face forward in time.[378]

To extend this conception to neurotic anxiety, it's a bit more complicated and not so mechanical (and will take the rest of the book to explain). Nevertheless, you deserve a break from all the questions and are entitled to a straightforward answer. *Those with generalized anxiety may unconsciously employ anxiety-producing thoughts and images to spur goal-attaining action or inaction.* This conception complements the causal paradigm, addresses its pitfalls and boundaries, and broadens understanding, assessment, as well as treatment.

Upon recognizing that anxiety is the result of an expectation of the future, analyzing behavior with respect to the past can be insufficient and deceiving.[379] This understanding naturally presents you with another question: If generalized anxiety can be used to achieve goals, what are they?

Chapter 12: Symptomatic Goals

In moderation, personality characteristics of drive, being in control, being good, doing things perfectly, and being right allow people to healthily and beneficially address the life tasks without developing anxiety. They may have robust and resilient friendships, rewarding and gainful employment, as well as happy and nourishing intimate relationships, all of which exhibit social interest and kindle the warm, invigorating, and reassuring feelings associated with recognition, validation, approval, allegiance, and success.

So where does anxiety enter the equation?

While people can experience anxiety when their convictions are inflexible or inadequate, you may be more curious about how anxiety can assist goal attainment. Start by examining the Yerkes-Dodson law.[380] It asserts that higher levels of anxiety can enable sustained effort on simple tasks, for instance, feverishly cleaning up the house before a big date, or consider factory workers who must pay attention and complete repetitive, but vital duties. In addition, it contends a relationship between arousal (low levels of anxiety) and goal achievement for challenging or intellectually difficult tasks. For example, it can assist concentration, say when you're doing a crossword puzzle or trying to determine the murderer in a mystery novel. Simply, anxiety can facilitate goal attainment. Fair enough, but where does *neurotic* anxiety fit?

Well, it's a persistent, but somewhat mild level of anxiety — say arousal and above, but falls short of intense anxiety, like that experienced during a panic attack. (Though, recall that neurotic anxiety may coexist with panic disorder, which explains why those with generalized anxiety may experience panic.) Now, reflect on how neurotic individuals attempt to reduce inferiority feelings and strive toward goals they believe grant significance.[381] Knowing this, might generalized anxiety enable people to fulfill their ambitions while abiding by the Anxiety Code?

Just take a moment to envision perennial Dean's List university students who — two days before an important exam — forcefully and inconsolably convince themselves they're going to fail it. Their perception initiates a flood of associated feared outcomes (e.g., "I'll be expelled," "My student loans will become due immediately," "I'll have to tell everyone I failed," "I won't be able to have the career I wanted," "My parents will be devastated and kick me out of the house,"

"People will see me as a loser and no one will marry me"). This appears illogical and detrimental, to say the least. However, not everything is as it appears.

At first, you might be tempted to say that the exam causes their anxiety, but does every student have symptoms? No, therefore blame cannot be fully attributed to that external factor. Next, you may suspect that something biologically innate in those symptomatic students generates anxiety. Yet, why is that untrue? Their otherwise dormant symptoms awaken only near the time of a test. If they were strictly genetic or biochemical in origin, might they be constantly present and not associated with changes in the external world?

So, without relying on inborn or external causes, why might symptoms develop given these sterling students' academic history wherein failure is nonexistent?

As their perception is so distant from the facts of previous performance, they seem to border on the delusional. Yet, that would be a grossly incorrect assumption. Resolving this riddle requires remembering the importance of goal orientation. So what's those students' goal? *They want to ace the exam.* Ah, but how? That's where the Anxiety Code comes into play — after all, it's their rulebook for solving life's problems. Accordingly, they believe to achieve their desire they must be driven, and be good students who give the right answers on their exam (perhaps be perfectly correct), which controls for failure as well as a host of related negative outcomes. Alas, there are a couple of challenges. In a distraction-filled setting (e.g., TV, phone, Internet, video games, socializing, and sex), they must not only prioritize studying, but also cram for extended periods.

Knowing what you do, you should be able to decipher why anxiety arises.

Here's a hint: Imagine driving to a vacation destination and your car had a flat tire. While you'd prefer to replace it with a full-size tire, you must use the smaller, temporary spare tire which addresses the problem, but in a substandard way (e.g., slower speed, worse handling, poorer braking). While you're able to achieve your goal of getting to your vacation spot, it's in a way that's less efficient or effective (e.g. harsh ride, it takes longer to get there, you have to take side roads instead of the thruway), and can have unintended consequences, such as fatigue and irritability. The spare tire is a solution, but an imperfect one.

Analogously, consider how students' painful and persistent fear of failing can emphasize the need to study. Worry about performance-jeopardizing distractions may lead them to turn off their TV and phone. Anxiety can rouse them out of bed and spur a trip to the library, power intense review and sustain all-night cramming sessions. In addition, these students can angrily distance those who attempt to sidetrack them from studying with goal-imperiling temptations (e.g., going to a bar for chicken wings and beer, dorm room romance). So, although anxiety is often viewed negatively, it can fuel the actions required to be in control, to be good, perfect, right, and sustain ample drive toward valuable and useful endeavors. While these symptoms aren't healthy or necessary, they're temporary — albeit likely recurrent. (Odds are, if these symptoms help attain a goal, they'll probably be employed repeatedly.) *Neurotic anxiety can enable people to achieve personally and socially beneficial aims, but at a cost of personal stress and/or social discord.*

Now examine other conditions in which anxiety is generated:

• Strict adherence to convictions (cognitive inflexibility).

• Being forced to prioritize one conviction above another.

• Conflicting convictions that impede movement toward an ambition.

• Ineffective or inappropriate convictions that prohibit goal achievement.

• Uncertainty of what to do after failing to achieve objectives may multiply symptoms.

• Attempting to simultaneously live by private logic as well as society's rules for living.

While you might say the solution is to adopt new life style convictions or at least modify the current ones, why isn't this as easy as it sounds?

First, those with low self-esteem can genuinely want to change, but are supremely reluctant to try, fearing failure and its personal and social ramifications. This is akin to those who shy away from asking out a desired other for fear of rejection and ridicule.

Second, when convictions have occasionally proven useful in attaining goals, they have been intermittently reinforced. This makes it particularly demanding to renounce or alter them — like financially-troubled gamblers who occasionally win, therefore feel compelled to keep at it.

Third, as life style convictions define each person's reality, discerning that they're problematic can be exceptionally challenging without someone else's perspective and feedback.

Fourth, discarding or modifying reality-defining convictions can scarily change one's conception of existence. Moreover, it initially risks making life less predictable as well as increases the probability of failure as individuals hone their newfound rules and related skills. As some people have tremendous difficulty surrendering their way of perceiving life, they may maintain unhealthy perceptions. They might deny and distort certain perceptions of reality like a funhouse mirror, rather than abandon predictability and stability, for example.

But wait a second.

After all the discussion about the primacy of goal orientation, the need for competency, and the desire for acceptance, why would people maintain life style convictions that prohibit or risk those things? Wouldn't ineffective convictions be selected out of the system? Aha! Might this be a flaw in logic that invalidates the theory and brings it tumbling down like a house of cards?

Well...*no*. But why not? Just consider a non-neurotic example where some people who dislike their poor health and body shape want to go to the gym to lose weight and be fit, but elect to avoid it because they don't want to be enslaved to an exercise regimen, experience the pain associated with exercise, or change their way of being which includes eating unhealthy food, watching TV endlessly, becoming immersed in video games for hours, or wandering the Internet aimlessly. Simply, they choose not to change to protect their life style.

Comparably, neurotic individuals may wish to avoid chaos, confrontation, (initial) failure, altering their perception of reality, awkward discomfort when trying new things, etc. Consequently, *they unconsciously maintain their life style convictions to achieve a superseding goal.* Yet, this can unsatisfyingly prohibit achieving a sense of significance.

So, how might those who live by the Anxiety Code and unable to achieve goals on the useful side of life — or feel they'll fail therefore don't take the necessary action — resolve the stalemate between uncompromising obedience to problematic convictions and their desire to achieve significance in the inescapable life tasks?

When neurotic persons believe they'll fail in certain life tasks, they attempt to attain subjective worth and significance.[382] But how? By operating within the Anxiety Code framework they unconsciously (or in the suburbs of consciousness) strive to attain those aims they believe will allow significance...*but on the socially useless side of life*.[383] In this way, they can maintain their life style convictions without relinquishing a sense of competency and worth. At first, this perspective appears misguided, mistaken, and malicious. After all, suffering persons often clearly and emphatically state they want to eliminate their symptoms and attempt to do so through various means. In addition, it appears to cruelly blame innocent victims. But as physical symptoms of medical origin reveal, sometimes symptoms can be rather ruthless, repellent, and — as contagious afflictions substantiate — socially detrimental. With this in mind, if neurotic anxiety can achieve objectives on the useless side of life, what are they?

Determining symptomatic goals can be challenging. Not only can they be subjective, but also inarticulable, as they're often unconsciously concealed from those who strive toward them.[384] (Indeed, patients are often in the dark as to why they do something until their psychologists identify the purpose and rationale of certain thoughts and actions.) Fortunately, an illuminating clue shines through what appears opaque: recall that childhood is a prime time of personality development and goal selection.

People begin cultivating their coping mechanisms in childhood, and power, attention, displays of inadequacy, and revenge are four exploitive or self-protecting childhood goals.[385] Such strivings are referred to as "goals of misbehavior" when applied to children's conduct, but are legitimately applicable to teenagers and adults as well.[386] Like the life style convictions, these goals are attempts to satisfy life's demands. Although such strivings may appear evil-intentioned, *neurotically anxious persons are authentically unaware (or perhaps only vaguely aware) of their motivation.* Their suffering is real and deserves compassionate and comprehensive care.

Power

As people acquire the ability to attain their goals, they develop a sense of confidence-building mastery. However, neurotic individuals may feel inferior and strive to liberate themselves from such a distressful state, yet find themselves unable or too intimidated; therefore, effectively powerless to do so. Nevertheless, their hunger for proficiency persists.

Power can exist in many forms. Those with generalized anxiety may use their symptoms to control others or themselves to address a situation. However, recall the neurotic characteristics of extremism and disproportionalism. Their striving for supremacy can be severe; *some people seek some form of omnipotence over the environment and those in it.*[387] Power can also include the ability to avoid or escape situations that jeopardize self-esteem, status, acceptance, or life style.

Attention

A sense of recognition, acceptance, serenity, purpose, value, as well as improved health — or a reduction in threats to it — reward and reinforce the essential activities of social interdependence, cooperation, and communication. Yet, what's the crucial prerequisite?

Attention. So how might those with generalized anxiety attract attention?

Neurotic individuals may seek attention, the prerequisite to acceptance, in accord with their life style convictions and in a way that validates their worldview. They can gain nourishing attention on the socially useful side of life by their kindness, intelligence, or industriousness, for example. Fair enough, but what about those who desire attention, but feel too inadequate or have ineffective life style convictions, and fear failure, rejection, ridicule, or abandonment?

Note how attention has two general directions, as this hints at a neurotic solution.

First, think about two individuals interacting, say about an idea, event, task, person, or thing, respectfully acknowledging each other and contemplating what's discussed. This is an example of two-way attention, as each person is reciprocally attending to the other.

Second, imagine parents attentively watching their infants slumber in their bassinets. The parents are dutifully surveilling the situation, and ready to act at a moment's notice. The children have their parents' attention, but they have no obligation to interact with them, they merely receive attention. This illustrates one-way attention. It refers to how a person may receive attention and service without any responsibility for reciprocation of attention, interest, or action.

Now, consider the phrases "There's no such thing as bad publicity…" and "…there is only one thing in the world worse than being talked about, and that is not being talked about."[388] They suggest that attention in any form is attention all the same. With that in mind, recognize that anxiety, fear, tension, frenetic movements, expressed concerns, and drama may draw unwarranted or unhealthy attention — even as an indirect result — with minimal or no risk of vulnerability or obligation to reciprocate attention. *Neurotically anxious individuals can use their symptoms to gain attention.*[389] Those who seek the spotlight can leave others in the shadows, blinded to them, except for the presence of an audience. Dramatic individuals may demand notice, applause, encouragement, or sympathy, and broadcast their thoughts online for the world to see.

Display of Inadequacy

Life has countless tasks, with some being virtually unavoidable. In addition, people routinely compete with others for a specific goal, say by applying for a job that has scores of candidates, pitting themselves against a successful sibling, or vying for the affections of a beloved other. Moreover, an individual can be compared to others or judged by some socially-based barometer (e.g., comparative income, house size). However, this can be particularly problematic for neurotic persons who desire significance, yet perceive themselves as inadequate, with failure, ridicule, rejection, and abandonment appearing imminent and inevitable. So how might they address a seemingly unwinnable, yet mandatory situation, in a way that achieves significance with little or no threat to acceptance?

Well, think about how golfers of appreciably different skill compete in a way that superior golfers do not routinely trounce the less practiced or talented. They implement what's known as a handicap. Each hole has a number known as par, which is the average number of strokes a skilled player needs on average to get the golf ball from the tee to the hole. As less proficient golfers aren't as powerful or accurate as first-class players, they need more swings of the club to accomplish the same task. The handicap number is the average number of strokes those individuals exceed par. That number is deducted from their total to level the playing field between them and more skillful golfers. So, if you regularly shoot par and your friend is usually 15 strokes above par, then your friend is able to subtract 15 strokes from the total. This enables you and your friend to compete in a fair way. Knowing this, why might neurotic persons freely publicize their symptoms and limitations?

For example,

• Unrelenting self-critical statements.

• Quickly forfeit pursuing a particular goal.

• Fail tasks that are well within their ability.

• Exhibit anxiety, tears, and frustration when something needs to be done.

Although appearing to imperil self-esteem, status, and acceptance, comprehension comes from viewing those symptoms in an environment populated with compassionate individuals.

For example,

• Might others lower their expectations?

• Are trivial accomplishments viewed as more significant?

• Can severe anxiety permit individuals to disengage from a challenge in complete discouragement, thereby enabling retreat before failure has the opportunity to occur?

• Might others balance neurotic individuals' self-directed criticisms with a series of compliments or soothing statements, (e.g., "You're a good person and intelligent. I'm sure plenty of people would want to date you")?

Displays of inadequacy may require the presence of an audience who react in a way neurotic individuals desire. Anxiety can equalize people by redefining success and productivity, assist in the evasion of responsibility, and can subjugate others. After all, severe and debilitating symptoms can declare, "I'm inferior to the requirements of this task and I need your help."

Displays of inadequacy may prove to neurotic individuals why they should give up on a challenge or grant themselves greater leeway or special privileges (e.g., lower others' expectations or demands), and their distress legitimizes their retreat or requests.[390]

Revenge

Given the importance of goal orientation, self-esteem, and acceptance, when neurotic persons fail to achieve their goals — say unable to secure or maintain employment or a relationship —such outcomes may require explanation. Yet, think about how difficult this can be. Self-blame requires recognizing and revealing inadequacy. However, such unsavory thoughts threaten self-esteem, acceptance, and their way of living, therefore may become unconscious. Also, admitting failure requires a review and revision to life style convictions to avoid future failure. Yet, as they define reality and have been helpful in attaining goals previously, it may be exceedingly difficult to discern their role in failure. Therefore, they may remain unexamined and unimproved. So how might those with generalized anxiety explain their failure while maintaining their convictions?

They may depict life as unfair and others as thoughtless or hateful victimizers; for example, an unscrupulous company, critical employer, deceitful neighbor, promiscuous coworker, undermining spouse, or disloyal friend who exploited, duped, mistreated, or seduced them against their will. Though this may appear illogical, clarity comes from identifying goals. So what benefits might those conceptions allow?

• Others are made responsible for neurotic persons' failure and missteps.

• Neurotic individuals can perceive themselves as innocent victims, which makes them blameless for failure and minimizes risk to self-worth and acceptance.

• They are liberated from reviewing, altering, or renouncing their problematic convictions.

• They can deem themselves morally superior to those characterized as abusive, exploitive, neglectful, and backstabbing.

• When they persevere in the face of life's injustices and others' mistreatment, they vitalize and sustain an honorable image of fortitude and resilience.

• Others may be more sympathetic and recalibrate expectations or allow special provisions.

So, what does this have to do with revenge?

Well, examine how when oppressive regimes or police tyranny arises, people may engage in acts of reprisal that expresses their frustration, can be attempts to right a wrong, and perhaps reduces the power of those regarded as harmful or exploitive. When neurotic persons have difficulty accepting their role in failure or changing their life style convictions, they may protectively portray others as accountable. But it doesn't end there. They may be compelled or morally obligated by a sense of justice and need to be good — as well as the desire to defend their honor and principles — to right a perceived wrong. Interestingly, this can strengthen the belief that they're victims. Yet, as expressing anger directly and regularly imperils acceptance and self-image, what might be the neurotic solution?

Those with generalized anxiety may feel powerless to achieve their aims in life and so demotivated that symptoms arise, and their frustration may manifest itself in unsocial ways. In fact, discouraged individuals who sustain the belief that there isn't an avenue of productively addressing a challenge may wield symptoms to angrily retaliate.[391] Just consider how symptoms can negatively impact others, say by being too frazzled for sex, or so fearful that others' movement is restricted (e.g., not go to particular places or speak with certain persons). Though initially seen as unintended collateral damage, unconsciously employed symptoms can indirectly harm others emotionally, financially, socially, or in some other way. Such acts state, "You really hurt me and I'm going to hurt you back!" Symptomatic revenge can be an aggressive weapon.[392] This underscores the interpersonal element in neurotic activity. The combination of unconscious execution (the how and why they retaliate) and oblique nature obscures symptom purpose and means, which protects self-esteem, acceptance, and life style. Furthermore, unconscious symptom use evades emotions and thoughts, such as guilt feelings or moral rules, which would prohibit retaliation. Symptomatic revenge may also be direct and obvious — even used against the innocent — but in ways that protect self-esteem and allow goal achievement. For instance, if a neurotic person's spouse urges a reasonable spending limit, by defining the spouse as controlling and unfair, the anxious individual can legitimize spending.

Goal Origins

People have attempted to control their environment to attain their objectives since the embryonic stages of humankind. Initially, they used rocks, sticks, sharp stones, and other rudimentary tools as the means to build shelter, kill animals, start a fire, or achieve some other intent. Over time the goals, as well as the tools to accomplish them, became vastly more complicated. Just consider how attaining complex, collective aims such as education, building a hospital, and commerce, underscore the necessity and value of social interdependence and how people live in a social world as well as a physical one.

Every infant is born into an inferior position in life — unknowing of how to address the inescapable life tasks. People strive to reduce or eliminate unwanted and unnerving inferiority feelings by adopting healthy and productive life style convictions and achieving valued goals that enable a sense of significance and allow authentic connections with others.

When individuals hold the Anxiety Code convictions flexibly (e.g., sometimes be in control), they can function well and attain various healthy desires without developing symptoms. However, anxiety can arise under different conditions. First, people can experience symptoms when they have inadequate or inflexible life style convictions that are unable to sufficiently address life's challenges. Simply, they do not know how to achieve their desires. Second, anxiety can arise when people clutch their convictions too tightly, or sustain them even if they lead to disastrous conclusions. Dogmatic allegiance to their way of thinking prohibits them from flexibly adapting to situational needs. They believe their conceptions are true and correct, yet are unsuccessful.

Nevertheless, the life tasks remain.

Whether people acquired or were taught inappropriate convictions and harmful goals, or are so discouraged that they forgo pursuing beneficial objectives and develop unhealthy ones, they may employ symptoms to achieve goals on the useless side of life. This understanding, as you might imagine, can meet icy and intense resistance as people may interpret it as insensitive, malicious, and as blaming the victim. After all, there's a tendency for people to perceive and comprehend symptoms as caused, rather than as a means of goal achievement. This can make for a glacial pace of adoption.

Fortunately, there's a precedent that proves symptom purposefulness. There are numerous biological defenses that distress and pain the sufferer as well as adversely impact others, but ultimately aid the ability to survive and thrive. Recognizing this allows you to see the analogous psychological mechanisms that safeguard people's self-esteem, acceptance, and life style. For this reason, it's important to note that symptoms can be self-serving, even when those with generalized anxiety perceive them as caused and criminally counterproductive.

Some neurotic persons may avoid accountability and responsibility and act in self-interested ways.[393] For example, symptoms may arise as an obstacle that simultaneously prohibits addressing the life tasks in a customary way that risks defeat, and can allow neurotic individuals to occlude their inferiority and grant a sense of safety.[394] They can unconsciously select symptoms as the lesser of two evils, as opposed to enduring the anguish and torment they believe would result if their inferiority were revealed.[395] In this way, anxiety symptoms provide a wedge between them and the life tasks as a way to protect self-esteem in the face of failure.[396] So, while neurotic individuals do suffer, they may (unconsciously) prefer their current distress to what they imagine would be a more significant amount if they were to attempt to achieve their goal and fail.[397] (Indeed, patients often state that failure is their biggest fear.)

When life's obligations and responsibilities appear so overwhelming that neurotic persons experience an interminable sense of imminent failure and unmasking their (perceived or actual) inferiority, they're less impacted by a psychological disorder, per se, than they employ symptoms to remain safe.[398] Ultimately, as distressing and insufferable as those emotions and physical manifestations can be, they can serve a purpose.[399] However, as goal achievement requires action or inaction, you face an intriguing question: What types of movement does anxiety enable?

Chapter 13: Movement Types

Think about how other than by chance or coincidence, people achieve their aims either by action (e.g., applying for a job) or inaction (e.g., maintain acceptance by refraining from status-jeopardizing behavior). *Goals and movement (as a category) are inseparably and necessarily intertwined.* Therefore, comprehending what objectives neurotic symptoms can attain requires assessing anxiety-enabled or prohibited movement and other related factors such as,

- What action is taken?
- How often is the action taken?
- What path does the action take?
- When does anxiety lead to immobility?
- Does it matter who is present or absent?
- Does action or inaction change depending on time of day or location?
- How forceful is the action or how resistant is the person to taking action?

Each person has a unique law of movement that has direction and goals, and life must be considered regarding these.[400] Accordingly, the field of psychology may increase understanding and treatment by focusing on people's objectives that stimulate or prohibit movement in a given direction.[401] In other words, people — and their symptoms — are much more comprehensible once you factor in how their desires shape their movement.

Physical Movement

Imagine a man opens his refrigerator and sees chocolate cake. He gazes at it then abruptly grabs his stomach and jiggles it. He sighs, scowls, and slumps, then resolutely closes the refrigerator door. He puts on his sneakers, opens the front door, peers at the gunmetal gray clouds barreling overhead as he closes the door behind him. He starts jogging as it begins to rain.

So might the man's physical movement express the following?

- He's hungry.

• He finds the cake appetizing and tempting.

• He considers himself overweight.

• He is unhappy with his weight (finds it to be an inferior state).

• He has the goal to lose weight (a state that is superior to his current one).

• He has a means of losing weight.

• He values weight loss more than having cake.

• He (begrudgingly) prefers running at that moment above virtually any other activity (e.g., lifting weights, eating a healthy meal, watching TV, going to sleep).

• He pursues his goal in the face of (at least) moderate obstacles and distractions.

Now, envision a married individual who regularly and solemnly expresses the virtues of marital fidelity, pridefully declares devotion, and gushes poetically about the narcotic properties of wedded bliss, yet who nakedly fawns over and habitually touches a coworker. *Physical movement can reveal people's inner states (goals, interests, values, rationale, emotions, and capacities) — even if they're in direct contradiction to what they say or how they see themselves.*

Although some individuals classify neurotic symptoms like reflexes — instigated, involuntary, inborn, unpredictable, uncontrollable, and ultimately unalterable, is that an accurate analogy?

Well, consider how reflexes are often quick and simple physical responses to specific physical actions (e.g., a knee tap triggers a leg extension, a puff of air on your eye causes you to blink). How might this allow you to conclude that anxiety-generated movements aren't as reflexive as perceived?

While a knee tap reflex is the same no matter who's present, think about when people's anxiety varies due to changes in the social environment. Environmental assessment and related cognition must occur. This weakens the argument that symptoms are merely a reflex. But you may say, "Perhaps it's a different type of reflex — a non-physical one, wherein psychosocial conditions spark specific, unalterable psychological reflexes." Yet, if that's the case, when anxiety provokes and empowers movement why is it one action rather than another?

Consider how physical reflexes are universal (or close to it) as people have the same responses, e.g., blinking, leg extensions, and recoiling from scalding surfaces. However, sometimes anxiety urges retreat, yet at other times movement toward a place or person. For example, hospital-related anxiety may prompt avoidance until worry about symptoms becomes so severe that it powerfully persuades a hospital visit, or consider how some people are so worried about bankruptcy they work two jobs, while others' equally-intense anxiety acts as a symptomatic stranglehold that restrains them from seeking employment). Anxiety isn't as reflexive or mechanical as it first appears. Anxiety-fueled behavior has direction, which reveals cognition. It's employed selectively — though unconsciously — to achieve particular outcomes in certain situations in accord with an individual's personality.

Goal direction requires forethought; the mind selects objectives for the physical actions to attain, which is an attempt to influence the environment.[402] *Anxiety can fuel goal-achieving behavior in a specific direction, and for that to occur it must be chosen, albeit perhaps so swiftly and imperceptibly as to appear as a thoughtless reflex.*

Now, examine how reflexes are simple actions (e.g., blinking, sneezing, iris dilation or constriction, arm retraction). Conversely, can you think of any elaborate physical movement that — even though may appear reflexive — isn't learned?

While many intricate behaviors are executed as if a reflex, say playing a piano concerto, they're learned complex behaviors that have become virtually and seemingly automatic. So what implication might this have for neurotic anxiety?

As anxiety can initiate and sustain complex, directed, goal-achieving actions, the conception of anxiety-fueled behaviors as mere reflexes — even if they appear that way — is discounted. This doesn't mean that those with generalized anxiety are conscious of their symptoms' purpose or aware their anxiety-fueled action has direction. For instance, they may be unmindful of when they get defensive, retreat, or symptomatically spur themselves into completing a task, which makes the purpose or direction invisible or opaque. Goal-oriented movement (or immobility) can reveal cognition and emotion.[403] Therefore, thought and emotions can have objectives, *even if neurotic individuals are unable to articulate them.*[404] They must select their goals as well as those movements they believe will attain them, although they may be utterly unaware of doing so.

Now, think about how the quickest escape from a burning building is the most direct path to a door or window. *Efficiency of goal-achieving movement can be a crucial component in addressing life's challenges.* Extending this example, if people decided to stay in a room and close the door behind them with the hope of the fire extinguishing itself, it could be a lethal mistake. *Effectiveness of goal selection and lines of movement is vital.*

It's important to consider not only what people are moving towards, but also that from which they move away. For instance, the spouse who dutifully goes grocery shopping appears altruistic. Ah, but what if it's merely an escape from a house with three screaming, unruly toddlers? Then, chances are that you arrive at a different conclusion.

Although neurotic symptoms and related movement may appear incomprehensible, clues are in plain sight. While people are prone to work from the information others tell them, they may become curious, frustrated, anxious, or angry when others don't act in accord with their stated intentions. For instance, a spouse or family member soulfully states a desire to spend more time together, but revealingly dismisses every opportunity, or is distracted and divides that time among other things, say inalienably engrossed in the phone, computer, or TV.

All psychic life can be interpreted in terms of movement.[405]

Accordingly, if symptoms appear indecipherable, it's best to focus on simple, uncluttered movement or immobility as that may allow comprehension of goals, thoughts, and feelings.[406] It's essential to examine where neurotic persons feel unable to satisfactorily address a challenge and determine two vital points: where they're moving away from and where they're heading.[407] For instance, some people energetically work overtime and state they want to get married, but not exert any effort to date. Others may experience paralyzing anxiety that prohibits finding a job, but are enthusiastically and irresistibly social. Demystifying people requires recognizing that movement reveals their objectives. (To augment patients' understanding of theirs or others' inconsistent statements and behavior, I suggest they interpret physical actions as if they were watching a movie with the sound muted.) *Assessing physical movement can clarify intentions and may be the world's best lie detector.* For instance, if your coworkers tell you they're on a diet, but the following day you see them walk into a pastry shop...

Psychological Movement

If you failed to achieve a desire, fell short of others' expectations, were criticized, or had your heart broken, you may subsequently feel sad, miserable, tense, inadequate, frustrated, lonely, or other unpleasant states. These experiences are psychological movements toward a felt minus.[408] So just as there can be physical movement, people can experience psychological movement. Now think about how you may feel after completing a difficult chore, receiving recognition and acceptance, winning the lottery, or attaining a sought-after achievement. Progression from an inferior position to one of significance is psychological movement away from a felt minus and towards a fictional plus.[409]

But why are the words *felt* and *fictional* used?

Due to the variation of people's values, each person's assessment of what's desirable is subjective. *People can have different experiences of the same behavior.* For instance, someone might feel bad for not donating money to charity, yet someone else might feel satisfied for not "wasting" money. Also, it doesn't require an epic achievement or loss to feel good or bad. *That which spurs psychological movement can be of any magnitude* (e.g., getting married, a typo). *To understand neurotic anxiety you must recognize the subjectivity of an individual's value system that determines whether a fictional plus or a felt minus is experienced as well as what personal values influence psychological movement.*

Comprehending psychological movement also requires an appreciation that an individual exists in a social world. Knowing this, what relationship might be found between a person's value system and the social environment that could influence the experience of a fictional plus or felt minus?

Start with an agreement between an individual's values and the encompassing community's values. So, for instance, when you voluntarily and happily do thing such as go to work or do a favor for someone, your values and behavior echoes what the general public accepts, encourages, and cherishes. However, is an agreement between an individual's goals and values with society's the determining factor whether the behavior is healthy?

Consider how an individual's exploitive and harmful actions may be accepted — even prodded and praised — if a significant percentage of an individual's community values it (e.g., law-enforced segregation, denying rights to particular populations), or if a subculture such as a gang, sect, or family highly regard those actions (e.g., theft, discrimination). *The agreement in values between an individual and the community doesn't guarantee that an action or inaction is healthy.* But does that prohibit a person from experiencing a fictional plus?

No. People can enjoy a fictional plus because they're doing what they value. Additional recognition and applause (albeit from audiences that cheer and cherish unhealthy behavior) may boost those positive feelings.

Agreement between an individual's values and that of the larger community isn't necessary to experience a fictional plus or a felt minus. For example, people may shoplift, live off their relatives, or cheat on their spouses and feel entitled and good about it — even though they may effectively prohibit themselves from receiving others' support or acceptance, and what they're doing is detrimental to others. Note that acting in a way that isn't socially sanctioned doesn't necessarily mean the behavior is a desire to exploit others. For example, you may have driven your car well above the speed limit on an unpopulated road not to brazenly break the law, but rather as a way to courteously arrive on time to an appointment or simply because it was a beautiful day, the roads were unoccupied, and the drive was exhilarating. *People may experience a fictional plus when they do what they value* (e.g., a conscientious objector, women's right advocator), *even if their community finds it unacceptable.*

What might you conclude when people work insufferable, but socially beneficial, jobs? For instance, those who reluctantly do community service because it's court mandated and enforced with significant negative consequences for noncompliance. *It's a person's conception and valuation of a fictional plus or a felt minus that defines psychological movement. Therefore, individuals can experience a fictional plus even when acting in self-serving, yet possibly socially detrimental ways, or experience a felt minus when they act in socially useful ways.*

So why might the body have the capacity for experiencing a fictional plus and felt minus?

Reflect on how physical pain or pleasure can provide feedback that lets you know what's healthy or unhealthy. But what else do they allow? Interestingly, the feedback isn't only for the activity at the moment, but also to increase or decrease the likelihood of engaging in that action again. So the pleasure experienced from eating, drinking, and having sex, not only is immediately enjoyable, but also prompts you to engage in those actions repeatedly into the future. Conversely, falling, lifting something that's too heavy, painful vomiting after consuming spoiled food, gets you to stop what you're doing and reduces the probability of doing it again.

Likewise, experiencing a fictional plus or felt minus can be a feedback mechanism that reinforces or punishes behavior. Simply, those feelings inform individuals if their actions are productively in accord with their goal. *Whether the actions are healthy is virtually irrelevant, as it's one's subjective life style convictions that define the value.* And just like there can be a correlation between the amount of physical pain and bodily damage, the searing emotional pain and jarring cognitive distress people experience from rejection, ridicule, abandonment, and failure reflect the importance of acceptance as well as goal achievement. (If you're in doubt, recall the most insufferable time in your life and your willingness to re-experience it — or the lengths you've gone to avoid it.)

While you can easily conceive of a fictional plus and a felt minus as movement up and down, can there be psychological movement that's toward and away?

Of course. Just contemplate how those who fall in love progressively grow closer to each other emotionally and cognitively as they embrace some of their significant other's life style convictions (e.g., adopting new holiday practices, pastimes, interests, memes). Or, consider those friends who experience a falling out and sever communication, generate animosity, and reflect on their previous bond with suspicion and disgust. Spurned lovers may become defensive, wary, caustic, and erect impenetrable walls that occlude sight and sound. *People can experience psychological movement toward and away from others.* However, does the same apply to inanimate objects?

When you think about your favorite movie or book, what do you like about it?

Odds are these inanimate objects mirror treasured beliefs and fortify your convictions. Perhaps they provide guidance or a sense of clarity that amplifies your sensation of a fictional plus, like movie theater patrons who cheer when the villain gets caught. People may come to appreciate and hold dear particular philosophies, books, or movies. On the other hand, people may bristle and become irate when they're exposed to material that contradicts their beliefs. All you have to do is examine the fervent and raucous debates associated with political and religious differences. And, people may experience numbness or neutrality (neither a fictional plus or a felt minus) when they engage in, or refrain from, activity of which they're uninterested. *People may move psychologically closer to, or away from, inanimate objects.*

People with generalized anxiety may experience fictional pluses and avoid felt minuses by cherishing and living by their life style convictions in socially beneficial ways, say with anxiety-fueled efforts enabling an impressive career, a spotless home, dedicated friendships, or corpulent bank account. However, note that although people may feel psychologically close to someone, something, or some belief, doesn't mean that it's healthy or socially beneficial. (This is akin to how people often derive enjoyment from seductive things that risk harm, such as drugs, gambling, flirting, high-fat foods, dangerous individuals, and sugary treats.)

Neurotic individuals may resolutely maintain their convictions while striving to attain fictional pluses and/or avoid felt minuses.

Self-elevation

Those with generalized anxiety may elevate themselves. For example, do what they value and believe is correct and experience a fictional plus, by adhering to the Anxiety Code and achieving various aims on the useful or useless side of life. But there's something else to consider. Imagine how those who stick to their diets when plied with sweets may experience satisfaction for not giving in to temptation. Similarly, neurotic persons may take pleasure and self-elevate by demonstrating fidelity to their life style convictions — even when they're inappropriate or ineffective.

Depreciating Others

Neurotic individuals have a tendency to depreciate and accuse significant others more than non-neurotic people do.[410] However, why might they do this when it imperils acceptance and the need to be good?

When those with generalized anxiety believe they're powerless to change their lives or fear trying, they may seek fictional plusses and achieve them by shifting the evaluation of others and things. Discouraged persons can take on a superior position over others through depreciation, which can justify avoiding situations or people that imperil status or self-esteem.[411] For instance, imagine someone stating, "An Ivy League education is overrated! Only rich, eggheaded losers who need to prove something to themselves go there." Yet, what might you think when you find out that person wants to go to an Ivy League university, but fears either a rejected application or failing if accepted?

Neurotically anxious persons can disparage people, places, things, events, etc. to create distance they deem safe, among other self-benefitting outcomes. As significant others and family members are the most available and prominent people around, they may be the biggest criticism targets. Moreover, family bonds, marital vows, and financial liabilities may act like invisible chains that keep those criticized individuals nearby when they might otherwise escape.

Self-depreciation

Why might neurotic individuals dwell on their flaws and failures, ridicule themselves, and underrate their abilities and characteristics to the point of generating a felt minus?

This self-depreciation seems inscrutable and counterproductive. However, one of psychology's greatest attractions is that there are always plenty of mysteries to solve. Perhaps it's best to start with an indirect analogy. Why might people aim a gun at their healthy foot and pull the trigger?

For some, this may be an attempt to avoid being conscripted into military service and sent off to war. In this way, a small injury is the price paid to avoid the possibility of a much larger one: death. From this perspective, one can see the reasoning and purposefulness of the otherwise unfathomable self-harm. This hints at one aspect of neurotic self-depreciation.

While it could be that low self-esteem makes it difficult for people to recognize their genuine skills and beneficial characteristics, as well as make them prone to denigrate themselves, there's more to consider.

They may wish to avoid any situation that risks failure, ridicule, rejection, and abandonment. Dwelling on their flaws and failures allows them to generate a felt minus and related anxiety that enables protective retreat. Similarly, those who underrate themselves and discount their successes on the useful side of life (e.g., "It's not a big deal, anyone could have done that"), prohibit themselves from trying anything greater and avoid those things in which they could achieve a greater sense of significance and a fictional plus.

Now, keeping in mind the social aspects of neurotic symptoms, how might you interpret, "I'm a terrible parent! I never learned the proper way to raise children," when stated in front of the grandparents?

Self-rebuke and inward-directed torture can be self-enhancing as they depreciate the environment, friends, and family.[412] Exaggerated statements (e.g., "I was never good enough," "I'm always wrong") may highlight others' unrealistic demands, callousness, and selfishness, and prompt reassurance, encouragement, as well as persuade others to give neurotic persons a pass on responsibilities. Yet, this seems one-sided and a bit critical. So, how might self-depreciation arise to achieve goals on the useful side of life?

When neurotic individuals think poorly of themselves and generate a felt minus, they desire to reduce or eliminate such unpleasantness. Given their life style convictions, they may attempt to do so by working harder, being more attentive, being nicer, being more determined, etc., which may allow a sense of significance, closeness to others, and so forth.

Movement in the Social Hierarchy

An individual's movement can also be assessed within the social context. You can see, for example, how making the news for committing a crime may lower one on the social totem pole, whereas saving a child from a burning building may elevate status and increase acceptance. In fact, given that an individual may assess self-worth by cultural or subcultural standards, that person may attain a sense of significance and lauded in one arena and a sense of incompetency and disparaged in another. For instance, stockholders may commend a greedy titan of industry for building the business and raising the stock price, whereas others (e.g., laid-off employees, consumers who have to pay more) view that person as deplorable. Knowing this, what types of movement exist in the social hierarchy?

Self-elevation

Those with generalized anxiety may view their symptoms as a noble burden that shows their fortitude, which elevates them above symptomatic others who medicate their symptoms into submission. Or consider how some can employ anxiety-fueled actions (e.g., dedicated exercise, working two jobs, compassionate worry about others' well-being) to achieve things family or friends do not. In fact, there are many ways in which people may use symptoms to elevate themselves in the social environment.

Status Quo

Neurotic individuals may want to "fly under the radar," never singled out on either end of the scale (e.g., avoid attention for being stellar employees or stragglers). So while somewhat deprived of opportunities for stratospheric fictional plusses, they avoid subterranean felt minuses. Think of this as akin to those who don't gamble. While they don't win the lottery or at the gaming table, they don't lose anything either, and may take satisfaction in their financial security and stability. Neurotically anxious persons may avoid jeopardizing their status and self-esteem by maintaining the status quo, which protects their life style. However, life regularly and indifferently upsets schedules, demands, functioning, etc.

Lower Others

As status is measured against a subjective and fluid yardstick that changes from generation-to-generation, topic-to-topic, society-to-society, and person-to-person, those with generalized anxiety may maintain or elevate their status and self-esteem relative to others by discounting others' accomplishments or characteristics. (I often see this within families. Criticizing siblings or parents is common. However, I see it most frequently with couples where one person routinely picks on the other's flaws and mistakes and expresses doubts of improvement, which can be an attempt to avoid examination, accountability, and the need to address fears and change convictions).

Lower Self

While lowering oneself in the social hierarchy appears counterproductive, might doing so…

• Get others to make fewer, and perhaps less demanding, requests?

• Allow small accomplishments to appear significant and gain praise?

• Permit withdrawal from additional challenges that risk lowering status?

Symptoms can enable physical, psychological, and social movement. And, as movement can reveal thoughts, emotions, and goals, comprehending various types is necessary to grasp neurotic anxiety's construction, manifestations, and functions.

Chapter 14: Neurotic Symptom Functions

While you've had fleeting glimpses of how neurotic anxiety symptoms can enable various types of movement (physical, psychological, social) that achieves goals on either the useful or useless side of life, it's best to introduce the general ways in which they function:

• Anxiety

• Safeguarding through Aggression: Depreciation through idealization and solicitude, Accusation, Self-accusation and guilt

• Safeguarding through Distance: Moving backward, Standing Still, Hesitation and Back-and-Forth, Construction of Obstacles

• Exclusion tendency[413]

Safeguards and Excuses

You can consider *safeguards* as unconscious attempts to defend self-esteem, acceptance, and the life style and *excuses* as serving a conscious function; for example, those with generalized anxiety may unconsciously generate symptoms to the point where they become legitimate obstacles of which they are consciously aware and provide an excuse or rationale.[414] For instance, "I'm worried that they'll think I'm lazy and laugh at me because I haven't worked for so long. I couldn't face applying for a job." The worry about scorn provides an excuse that enables immobility that prohibits employment as well as reduces the possibility of ridicule, rejection, abandonment, and failure. Excuses can also be used to explain undesirable outcomes (e.g., "I was too anxious to study properly").

When neurotic persons face demands that are seemingly unachievable or daunting, they may nurture symptoms to the extent where they're judged to be legitimate impediments.[415] They then can change their focus from the threatening demand to their symptoms.[416] For instance, some say they want to address their symptoms before they try something (e.g., dating, working, socializing). Indeed, people often use the phrase, "They say you have to be okay with yourself before you start dating." However, is this statement accurate or possibly an excuse to authorize veiled safeguarding?

Well, if that proposed stipulation were true, then dating would rarely occur as most people can readily list their flaws and faults and often don't fully accept themselves. In fact, as people know what skills and attributes they lack but desire, they regularly seek those who have those compensating characteristics and abilities (e.g., good with finances, socially adept, height, eye color), or consider how people can say that engaging in those otherwise prohibited endeavors would help them overcome their symptoms (e.g., "Being in a relationship would allow me to practice how to reduce my unhealthy desire for control and become vulnerable"). In other words, people can use anxiety to evade threatening challenges as well as portray symptom resolution as the healthy and acceptable priority — like staying home with an ill newborn takes precedence over going to a party. This provides a safeguarding function. Neurotic persons may be entirely unaware of the association between their anxiety and the situation they want to avoid (control, create, etc.).[417] While they must be conscious of the excuse (otherwise they couldn't use it), why must they be unconscious, or nearly so, of their symptoms' safeguarding function?

They couldn't protect their self-esteem, acceptance, status, and life style if they were completely aware they were using their symptoms to achieve a goal. Cognitively blindfolding themselves in this way allows them to avoid the sobering responsibility for changing convictions, facing fears, etc. This enables continued symptom use, unimpeded and without perceiving the violation of their need to be good or driven, for example.

So what might be another way to determine how symptoms are being used as an excuse?

Envision symptoms employed to avoid a picnic (where there's small talk and possible judgment that an individual wishes to avoid), but later an unexpected torrential rain rolls in. The inclement weather is a suitable and less threatening excuse than symptoms that enables evading the picnic. When legitimate reasons arise that allow task evasion, neurotic symptoms may disappear.[418] If symptoms evaporate when a demand is rescinded or challenge is avoided, then the symptoms may have been a protective excuse. But excuses aren't always used to avoid matters or employed on the useless side of life. Knowing that, how might neurotically anxious parents symptomatically assist their children who seek acceptance into a sought-after university?

They may brew fears that the competition for entry is intimidating and that others have a better chance or unfair advantage (e.g., their relatives attended the school, their families made a sizable donation). Moreover, they wholeheartedly believe their children's immediate and correct actions are essential for acceptance. This skewing of perception may stoke anxiety, which energizes them to prompt their children to write their application and review their children's submission. Last, the parents' quest to eliminate symptoms such as insufferable tension, headaches, poor appetite, and sleeplessness may be the excuse that legitimizes and enables anxiety-fueled movement (e.g., "I'm not going to be able to rest until this is done! I can't stand to lose another night's sleep!"). They may be unaware of how their drive, need to be good, perfect, right, and desire for control are related to their symptoms. Consequently, they attribute their symptoms to the process of application, the importance of the decision, their altruistic love for their children, and the uncertainty of the outcome. The symptoms help control the situation to achieve a goal, fortify their life style convictions (e.g. demonstrate drive and goodness), and benefit their children. Although their intentions are good and the result may be favorable, their excessive and unnecessary worry is what makes it unhealthy. *Those with generalized anxiety may develop symptoms and use excuses to do things that enable socially-beneficial goals.*

Anxiety

Some people set their clocks five or ten minutes ahead as a way to generate enough tension to get them to work on time. While this isn't necessarily a neurotic tactic, it demonstrates how people can create unnerving stress or anxiety to motivate themselves. Just consider how a driven employee who's needlessly concerned about getting fired if a project isn't completed on time can fear the ensuing financial, social, and occupational consequences to the point where anxiety acts like the body's internal coffee machine that energizes and motivates working through the night, has positive outcomes, and enables the avoidance of failure and unemployment.

Now, imagine being a museum curator in charge of protecting priceless, irreplaceable antiques that recently were the target of an unsuccessful theft. Hiring a lethargic or lackadaisical security guard could be costly and dangerous. Rather, you would recruit an eagle-eyed sentry, vigilant of suspicious behavior or conditions, who responds quickly and forcefully at the slightest hint of a threat. Similarly, neurotic persons want to protect themselves and be able to swiftly recover if put in psychologically or socially threatening situations. Being alert for threats and acting rapidly when things go out of control — or are about to — is required, and anxiety can energize vigilance and prompt action.

Also, consider how anxiety can beneficially fuel action to move toward a challenge (e.g., "I'm running late to work! I've got to go now!"). As well, it can assist following through on tasks that might otherwise be insurmountable or unsustainable. Indeed, people can generate anxiety that empowers continued effort beyond their normal range.

Even though neurotic anxiety can protect self-esteem, acceptance, status, and the life style by enabling goal attainment on the useful side of life, there are a number of downsides. For instance, anxiety can be overused. People may attend to conceivable perils with a bias to worry about those things that often aren't genuine threats, as a way to err on the side of caution to ensure safety ("better safe than sorry"), with difficulties arising when they become excessively sensitive and believe they're ill-equipped to address matters successfully.[419] In other words, neurotic persons may experience "false positives," and needlessly generate anxiety, which may erode their self-confidence and skill set. (Interestingly, when I ask patients how often their worries materialize, they usually say "Never," or a response close to it.)

Though this unwarranted perpetuation of anxiety risks giving the impression of it being an irrepressible genetic or biochemical creation, perhaps a more satisfying and suitable answer comes from viewing the benefit. To control for undesirable outcomes, neurotic individuals may think about every conceivable one that could possibly — though not probably — occur. While this could make them tremendous disaster planners, note that they can perpetuate their anxiety when they believe that it's because of their worry that nothing bad happened. Yet, like superstitions, it's habit-forming and unhealthily feeds their desire for control.

Anxiety can also effectively blockade behavior, which allows neurotic persons to avoid trials without revealing to themselves a sense of inferiority.[420] The anxiety is seen as the obstacle with the belief that success would occur if it weren't for the symptoms. Regrettably, people can magnify symptoms when they evade situations where they could demonstrate competency. Consequently, anxiety can counterproductively narrow areas of functioning, splinter social bonds, and erode self-esteem as well as jeopardize status and life style.

Anxiety fuels behaviors such as vigilance and readiness for action, as well as reveals the amount of fear associated with life's dangers, therefore can initiate caution, immobilization, and withdrawal.[421]

While generalized anxiety disorder is defined by relatively low-level symptoms, recall that a second diagnosis of panic disorder can coexist with it. Therefore, it may be helpful to briefly investigate the sibling relationship among neurotic anxiety, being panicky, and panic attacks.

People with generalized anxiety may have moments in which their symptoms are amplified and they become panicky. However, just like a brother and sister, panic attacks are categorically different from generalized anxiety. While they're related, have similar characteristics, and can coexist, they're essentially unique.

Interestingly, as people differ in symptoms as well as how they perceive them, there's no universal description of a panic attack; yet they can be roughly described as sudden intense anxiety that peaks quickly, with physical symptoms and dread of undesirable consequences.[422]

Applying what you know about neurotic anxiety, why might intense fear and panic *not* arise during a crisis?

Although people often believe that highly-stressful situations always spark panic, what they fail to take into account is the primacy of goal orientation. For instance, if a house is on fire its occupants do not have immobilizing fear, they quickly run outside. Even under more complicated and stressful circumstances anxiety doesn't necessarily paralyze people's movement. For example, imagine parents who wake to a fire in the bedroom hallway. Does fear of agonizing injury or death arrest their movement? No, they run through the flames to their children's rooms and bring them to safety along with the family pet. Granted, this isn't generalized anxiety. It's merely an example to illustrate a point. While immobilizing fear or panic may set in afterward upon reflection of the danger, when a vital goal needs to be achieved, anxiety, fear, and panic might delay, but not necessarily prohibit, attaining it. This has particular relevance for neurotic anxiety, as when symptoms appear can be revealing.

Incapacitating fear or panic may not be experienced during a crisis as individuals must address the circumstance, but can arise before or after; when they believe they cannot successfully tackle a challenge they may paralyze themselves with fear and render themselves immobile.[423] Equally, fear and panic may allow tremendous — albeit frantic and possibly inefficient — effort on the useful side of life, say rushing to a hospital for immediate care. Stated differently, to achieve particular outcomes people may unconsciously generate high anxiety and panic.

Anger

It's normal and healthy to experience the full emotional spectrum — including anger. It's the duration, severity, and frequency, as well as how much it erodes people's quality of life and jeopardizes social interactions, that indicate when anger becomes unhealthy. Indeed, those with generalized anxiety can be particularly prone to experience frustration, exasperation, irritability, moodiness, annoyance, disgust, as well as be quick to anger and slow to cool down. So why might such symptoms arise?

Well, reflect on how people are happy or content when life goes as expected or desired. Knowing this, why would they become frustrated, upset, angry, or furious when things aren't going as expected or they're not getting what they want?

Recollect how neurotically anxious persons may endlessly examine and assess what are the best thoughts, emotions, and actions for various situations, attempt to almost clairvoyantly foresee diverse possibilities and outcomes, as well as divine the most advantageous way to approach or react to them. Ultimately, they can compile detailed and comprehensive rules of what's good, perfect, right, with anxiety fueling exhaustive investigation and analysis. And, after considerable thought and judgment they may have strong emotions associated with their conclusion. For instance, there may be an instant and negative association with things such as bad manners, errors, or ignorance, and/or positive emotions connected with hard work, perfectionism, kindness, organization, and follow through. An interesting corollary is that because they have deliberated so thoroughly, and have attached deep and intense emotional value to their conclusion, *they may be particularly resolute and impervious to argument.* Fair enough, but what does this have to do with irritability and anger?

For those who maintain a detailed rulebook of which they're certain (or nearly so) of its correctness and have assigned significant emotional value, does this mean that life will go as expected, that others will act the way they "should," or even that neurotic individuals will always abide by their own rules and fulfill their self-imposed expectations?

Absolutely not...*and this is when various forms of anger may arise.*

As neurotic persons may be cognitively rigid and determinedly maintain their private logic, they may have an exceedingly difficult time adapting to people or situation — or even their previous acts or ways of thinking. This extends, and perhaps intensifies, anger when their tenacity to their perceptions and rules maintains the distance between the way they think and reality. While this explains how anger can be the effect of a cause, what might be its purposes?

Perhaps you're best served by considering how others respond to anger. Could they back off, comply, or might neurotic persons employ anger as a way to maintain their life style? (Just think about those who become angry or hurtful when their politics, rationale, or religion is challenged.) In addition, consider what movement anger allows.

Most neuroses have camouflaged aggressive or vindictive elements.[424] Additionally, anxiety may lead to aggression.[425] Heightened system arousal may warm the body to fiery anger and act as an accelerant. As the body has a capacity for anger, it's useful to consider possible purposes. With that in mind, reflect on how anger can...

• Arise due to unrealistic — even if good — expectations (e.g., "I'm furious that my parents [children, friends, etc.] don't visit more often").

• Be generated as a means to get others to comply (e.g., "You're making me upset. Do your homework!"). This includes retaliation for a perceived injustice used to prevent later infractions. For instance, "I'm livid that you didn't tell me you were going on vacation," while this is about a past behavior, look at what it implies for the future: "Always tell me when you're going away."

• Give license to leave a situation or create distance ("I'm so angry about what goes on here that I'm looking for another job," "I'm livid about the way this marriage is going and I want a divorce," "Don't bother me, I'm still upset with you").

Although anger seems unlikely as it ostensibly conflicts with the need to be good, recall how people can be unaware of the link between their emotions and their goal, how they unconsciously build up and employ anger, and how they can rationalize and stimulate it, say by misperceiving others, genetics, or biochemistry as responsible, or by defining their anger as necessary to achieve a greater good.

Safeguarding Through Aggression

There are three divisions of safeguarding through aggression:

• Depreciation — False Valuations (Idealization and Solicitude)

• Accusation

• Self-accusation and Guilt feeling

Depreciation — False Valuations occurs when neurotic individuals are unaware of their inadequacy and amplify their self-esteem by devaluing someone or something else.[426]

Depreciation — False Valuations: Idealization

Neurotic persons may, for example, idolize a doctor, spouse, or child. Given their sensitivity to comparison, elevating others appears to threaten their self-worth and acceptance; however, the following may illustrate the purpose: "You're the *best* personal trainer I've seen. I'm sure you'll get me in shape in no time." Yet, what might happen if that doesn't occur promptly or at all?

The deified trainer falls from the perch of perfection and can be crucified. Elevating people in this way can prompt them to attempt to live up to the expectation. It also can be a way to disparage and belittle them through direct or oblique criticism and disappointment. For instance, "You're not as good as I hoped and I'm disillusioned (even though it was the neurotic person who created the illusion). I shouldn't have expected so much. You're only human after all." In this way, it's the trainer who's the failure. *Idealization is when individuals judge others in comparison to an ideal they may not, or are unlikely to, achieve or approach.*[427]

Idealization can be employed to devalue a place, time, event, practice, or other construct such as politics or economics to elevate self-esteem, as well as allow movement or immobility. Dramatic evaluation shifts can get others off-balance and unprepared for the attitude and behavior change.

Depreciation — False Valuations: Solicitude

What might you conclude if you heard grandparents tell their adult children the following?

"We're worried about your kids. Are you sure they're doing okay? You should double check their homework and make certain they're not associating with the wrong people. We'll be glad to keep an eye on them to ensure that everything is fine. You're relatively new to parenting and haven't always made great decisions. Just call us and we'll gladly come over immediately to help you out."

When people concern themselves with others' (in)abilities, give (usually unsolicited) advice, check in on them, don't give people responsibilities for fear of incompetency, and endlessly agonize about numerous and varied perils and hazards, *they employ concern as a means to make rules for others, and as a way to be critical.*[428]

Worry can be used to fortify self-esteem as people portray themselves as compassionately and selflessly concerned about others' welfare.[429] Individuals generate anxiety and engage in solicitude, which can appear as socially acceptable and legitimate care, but bewilders, discourages, undermines, and critiques others, and therefore is aggression under the guise of social interest. Moreover, neurotic persons may depreciate others by attributing lofty ideals to themselves and unambitious ones to others.[430] For example, attempting to demonstrate higher morals by being concerned about a situation or condition when others aren't.

Accusation

How might those with generalized anxiety explain things such as unemployment, loneliness, or incomplete projects in a way that safeguards their self-esteem, acceptance, status, and life style?

They may limit or eliminate their accountability by accusing others and portraying them as responsible for failure, symptoms, economic hardship, loneliness, or virtually anything else.[431] The targets of allegations are frequently family members, as well as a boss, coworker, neighbor, or society.[432] Or, they can blame their genes, biology, neurotransmitters, physiology or intangible entities such as fate, the stars, or their god(s). Public accusations allow neurotic persons to avoid being the center of attention (which may garner unwanted evaluation) and can keep attention on others, making them the focus of derision.[433] *Accusations are an aggressive act, and can be concealed in neurosis.*[434] Accusing others, say by making allegations of poor effort, dubious merit, or suspicious intent may allow those with generalized anxiety a sense of significance or superiority as well as rationalize and fortify the exercise of vigilance and control.

Self-accusation and Guilt Feeling

People often use the word "guilty" inappropriately when they experience guilt feelings. For example, "I feel guilty about not going home directly from work." To clarify the difference, after deliberating evidence, judges and juries may find a defendant guilty of a crime. This is fundamentally different from having guilt *feelings*. Whereas guilt is objective, guilt feelings are subjective, and may arise when people violate their ethical convictions — a moral/ethical inferiority feeling.[435]

It's a sense of "Morally, I should have, but didn't and for that reason I feel bad." Guilt feelings are sensations, essentially self-condemnations. They may be communicated to others or harbored silently. Just like there can be an objective inferiority (e.g., less income compared to others) and subjective inferiority feelings (e.g., "I feel ugly next to them"), people have objective guilt and subjective guilt feelings.

Sometimes neurotic persons may not express their guilt feelings and self-accusations believing they would waste others' time, burden them, or that others would view them as bad or unacceptable. However, guilt complexes can publicize guilt to the world.[436] They are a combination of self-accusation and repentance, which is an attempt for superiority on the useless side of life.[437] For instance, people may broadcast their guilt feelings to flaunt their compassion and morals as well as pull in others for support.

Paradoxically, symptoms can safeguard precisely what they seem to imperil. For example, when those with generalized anxiety accuse themselves, it doesn't appear to be an aggressive act toward others; therefore, it's less likely to raise others' anger, suspicion, defenses, and condemnation. Self-accusation can be so effective for the reason that it's seemingly an act of inward aggression, a lowering of self-esteem rather than the safeguarding of it.[438] For instance, "I'm a terrible spouse and I did an awful job of helping you prepare for that test you failed. I used too many scholarly words! I feel dreadful for that." Self-rebuke is used as a backhanded reference to the spouse's lack of effort and intelligence.

Guilt feelings and self-accusation can indirectly safeguard neurotic persons through self-torture and disapproval of the surroundings.[439]

Safeguarding Through Distance
Moving Backward

When you think of those who push the limits of their abilities you may also recall those who were injured or killed by imprudently pushing themselves beyond their abilities. Identifying and retreating from that which dangerously exceeds one's capability is irrefutably advantageous. However, those with generalized anxiety may back away from challenges they could accomplish, choosing to stick with what's familiar and unthreatening. (A rationale underscored by Shakespeare's *Hamlet* "…and makes us rather bear the ills we have than fly to others that we know not of."[440]) They may view forward movement as terrifying, therefore intently focus on those thoughts and emotions that result in retreat, which provides relief from the threat and protects self-esteem.[441] (Interestingly, when symptoms appear to give the impression of moving forward, say applying for a job, such movement may also be identified as moving backward from something, e.g., financial worries.)

Neurotic persons may generate and augment symptoms such as exhaustion, migraines, lack of appetite, or anxiety that enable withdraw, thereby minimizing the likelihood of exposing (perceived or real) inferiority.[442] The desire to move backwards may also explain the co-occurring presence of depression with neurotic anxiety. For example, depressive symptoms that drain the energy to approach those endeavors which risk failure, ridicule, rejection, or abandonment. Or, as driven individuals set high standards, they might experience depression when they fail to attain their ambitious goals. *Depressive symptoms can allow a retreat from a challenge or a break that allows time to think and take a different approach.* Sometimes, when people get knocked down they stay down for a bit, quickly assess their state, and recuperate for a moment before they get back on their feet and return to the fight. Depressive symptoms can allow parallel actions.

So what might be the ultimate symptomatic move backward?

When neurotic persons believe that they're overwhelmingly challenged, they may engage in suicidal ideation, suicide attempts, and suicide.[443] Neurotic anxiety is significantly correlated with suicidal ideation (thoughts and planning); however, those diagnosed *only* with generalized anxiety have a low risk of suicide attempts.[444] It is vital to note that *comorbidity with another mental disorder significantly elevates the likelihood of suicide attempts.*[445] Of course, these symptoms require immediate attention, meticulous investigation, and unreserved care.

Standing Still

It's easy to understand how a broken back or leg, or some other physical medical issue can immobilize people. Although psychological symptoms aren't as tangible or visible as physical symptoms, *they may prevent movement just as much.*[446]

Neurotic symptoms can bring people to a standstill, precluding them from engaging in activity even that which they state they wish to do (e.g., date, find employment). Although this appears to negate the assertion that people move toward their goals, how else might you interpret their symptoms?

To maintain acceptance and self-esteem, people may profess a socially acceptable goal (something they "should" do, but don't want to), or a genuine one (but are afraid of failing), yet their symptoms stop their participation or progress. Immobilizing symptoms such as sluggishness, disinterest, or faulty memory can thwart movement toward threatening tests and situations.[447]

When else might symptoms create a standstill?

Well, imagine neurotic persons who want to get the perfect job or marry their perfect match. They may be unable to determine *the* right choice and their anxiety becomes an insurmountable obstacle that creates a standstill. They don't know which choice is correct and anxiety prohibits applying for any job or dating. Ultimately, such "analysis paralysis" allows the evasion of possibility of making the wrong decision — something essential for those who need to be right. Such conflicts can be of various forms, but are chosen (unconsciously or on the periphery of consciousness).[448] *Neurotic persons can instigate and magnify symptoms to the point where they are perceived as insurmountable and legitimate obstacles, which they may take refuge.*[449] (Please do not underestimate the word "legitimate." Their symptoms and related stipulations [e.g., "I can't date until _____"] are as real to neurotic individuals as anything could possibly be. It is their reality, and they respond accordingly.) The desire for immobility can be so intense that *symptoms can become obstacles when no other barrier exists.*

An anxiety-based standstill can also occur on the useful side of life, as when people stop themselves from engaging in behavior that's detrimental. It can be symptomatic when their barometer is miscalibrated (e.g., having anxiety when thinking about slightly breaking the speed limit, or anxious about arriving on time when they usually arrive well ahead of time) or when it interferes with their quality of life. For instance, they can just avoid unhealthy behavior without experiencing anxiety. However, the anxiety may justify to others why no movement can be made — especially when others engage in that behavior, say drinking too much alcohol, leaving work early, etc.

Hesitation and Back-and-Forth

Neurotic persons may experience the ebb and flow of anxiety that cripples and coaxes movement. They may discard completed work, abandon a project, get involved in distractions at the cost of attending to the stated priority, postpone decision making, or be inundated with symptoms until it's too late to take action.[450] In addition, they may generate symptoms and attempt to overcome them, but are unsuccessful. So how might you explain this?

Symptoms can enable hesitation and back-and-forth movement that distance neurotic persons from challenges.[451] Anxiety may promote action, immobility, or enable retreat. Also, depressive symptoms can reduce energy to the point of arresting activity. Neurotically anxious persons can act "as if" they were engaging in some valid action, but may be merely wasting time.[452] In this way, they display good intentions and may take action in accord with their stated goal, but avoid completing their work. This can avoid being judged or facing something (e.g., another project) they want to avoid.

Construction of Obstacles

How do you explain why some individuals with generalized anxiety industriously achieve numerous objectives despite being burdened with harsh, punishing symptoms?

Well, consider how running a marathon is an impressive achievement; however, doing so while wearing a 50-pound backpack would be extraordinary. High achievers may experience greater self-esteem and garner more accolades by attaining goals while weighed down with symptoms. *Some neurotic persons feel even more competent or superior by overcoming their symptoms.*[453]

So how might creating and surmounting symptomatic obstacles function in a social environment? First, being successful with symptoms can minimize symptom-free persons' achievements. Second, neurotic individuals can use overcoming their symptoms, or success while symptomatic, to control others. For instance, "I'm sure you can date, (make dinner every night, raise kids, work, etc.). If I could do it with overwhelming anxiety, I'm certain you can do it without symptoms burdening you."

Now examine those who wonder aloud, "If only I didn't have these symptoms holding me back, I could see my true abilities and have even greater accomplishments." *When high-achieving neurotic individuals depict their symptoms as obstructions to further successes they augment their self-esteem and status (without proof of ability).*[454]

Exclusion Tendency

Picture going to Las Vegas and attempting to determine what games are most likely to have you return home with more money; playing those believed more profitable while avoiding those deemed riskier. In addition, you might vary your bets or participation on other factors (e.g., odds, number of players). Simply, movement doesn't have to be binary in either you gamble or don't. Your participation fluctuates based on a number of variables to achieve your goal. Now, how might you extrapolate this to generalized anxiety?

Neurotic persons may use their symptoms to operate solely within those areas they're able to control (at least to some degree) and exclude some arena of functioning, magnifying their feelings of competency by acting in chosen arenas in which success is mostly ensured, and restricting their activity with others so that there's much less likelihood of having their (actual or alleged) inferiorities seen and evade perceived threats.[455] This narrowed path of approach is an attempt to get the most payoff and least probability of loss. In fact, they may do extremely well in one area even as they fail at others.[456] For example, they can be excellent friends, but unfeeling spouses, or they can be tremendous employees, yet absent parents.

Neurotic symptoms can function as imperfect solutions to life's demands and can protect individuals' self-esteem, acceptance, status, and life style by achieving various goals, but with a penalty to themselves or others. Symptoms, excuses, lies, placing the blame on others, avoidance of responsibilities, can be attempts to hide neurotic persons' perceived inferiority while taking advantage of others' social interest.[457] They may employ symptoms as a way to solve their problems, to protect themselves, at the cost of common welfare, and would feel exposed if their symptoms were to cease to be.[458] Anxiety may also be a means of not violating life style convictions, as well as a result of having unsuitable convictions. Last, keep in mind that generalized anxiety symptoms can be used to achieve goals on the useful side of life, but often at a personal, and perhaps social, cost such as tension, sleeplessness, and physical symptoms.

Chapter 15: Symptom Variation

Psychic tension manifests itself differently among people.[459] Accordingly, generalized anxiety symptoms can vary in duration, frequency, appearance, severity, timing, and type. So, why is there such inconsistent and wide-ranging symptom presentation?

Conflicts and Compromises

How could conflict among or between life style convictions generate anxiety and account for symptom variation?

Neurotic persons may be put in a position of determining which conviction to prioritize or obey (e.g., be good or in control). Consider the woman who suffers through an intolerable marriage and faces two options. She can be the conflict-avoiding "good wife" by allowing her exacting and inconsiderate husband to make nearly every decision and acquiesce to his demands (everything from the TV remote control to how money is spent to vacation decisions to sex) and dodge a divorce that she deems not only shameful and immoral, but also as being a bad mother to her children. However, in her decision to be good, she loses control of her happiness and autonomy as well as role models a poor marital relationship to her children. Or, she can take control of her situation and prompt marital therapy or pursue divorce, but does so with a fear of being seen as a failure in her marriage or as a bad mother, facing unpredictable and unproductive dating, etc. *Prioritization of life style convictions can influence anxiety production.*

Now, imagine a man who feels he must be a dedicated, driven professional as well as a good parent. He's supremely reluctant to make any compromise, but each pursuit requires significant time and energy. Anxiety may reflect the stress he puts himself under as well as a means to fuel attempts to avoid violating his life style convictions by striving to fulfill both demands. *When those with generalized anxiety seek to strictly obey two (or more) conflicting convictions the resultant political stalemate can shape symptom presentation.*

When neurotic persons state, "I've done everything right, but things still didn't go as planned! Now what?" or "I don't know how to handle this situation," they reveal how *inefficient or ineffective life style convictions can lead to and vary anxiety, based on the challenge faced.*

Illness, Handicaps, and Organ Inferiority

With awareness of the unity of the personality you can better grasp the physical manifestations of neurosis.[460] As you'll recall, the unity of the personality asserts that with no definitive boundary, the mind and body are reciprocally integrated, cooperative team members that harmoniously work toward the same goal. For that reason, psychological symptoms can become entwined with and piggyback preexisting physical concerns. *Bodily organs, to such extent as their functioning can be guided, can be influenced in accord with neurotic individuals' goals.*[461] For instance, people may develop migraines that sideline them from socializing they deem threatening.

Such "organ inferiorities" (as they were originally labeled) may shape which symptoms wake and when — possibly due to symptom familiarity or ease of production. For example, dwelling on particular thoughts can induce trembling, vomiting, headaches, increased heart rate, or sweating. One principal guideline for whether, and which, symptoms arise depends upon if they enable an escape from a challenge; with symptoms changing or ending when they're no longer efficient to maintain, unavailable, or impossible to continue.[462] Or, consider how anxiety may foster physical symptoms that prompt action on the useful side of life (e.g., an easily-aggravated nervous stomach that prevents illegal action, an achy back or stress headaches that continue until obligations or tasks are completed).

Preexisting physical ailments and limitations can shape symptom selection and production. Note that this process is unconscious (or perhaps on the hazy boundaries of consciousness), therefore different from malingering and factitious disorders, and unlike conversion disorder where no neurological foundation exists. These symptoms are not evidence of willful maliciousness, but rather a means of safeguarding self-esteem, acceptance, status, and life style.

Those with generalized anxiety may communicate their organ inferiority actively (e.g., telling people directly or through demonstration) or passively (e.g., informing others only when asked, faint verbalizations, subtle actions). Given the unconscious characteristic of physical symptom development, how might neurotic persons interpret them, especially long-term ones?

They may believe and profess that their symptoms must be physically based and therefore out of their control, which may efficiently and effectively evade any personal responsibility for change.[463]

Not only can psychologically-influenced physical symptoms allow for a retreat from a threatening challenge, they can also enable movement toward some desired activity (e.g., "Sex always cures my migraines") or positive result (e.g., "My back is killing me, but it always goes away when I get my chores done"). *When organ inferiorities aren't present, those areas that psychological tension most influences can be the first to develop physical symptoms.*[464]

Values, Perceptions, and Attitudes

What might you determine from the following?

• Symptoms appear, disappear, or vary in appearance when particular others are nearby.

• Symptoms change depending on the tasks presented (e.g., traveling, going to work, project due, upcoming exam, socializing, parenting).

• People who resolutely refrain from chaos or conflict, yet furiously defend and advocate for the poor, animal protection, children's rights, or environmental conservation.

How people view themselves (e.g., adequate or inadequate), perceive others (e.g., those less driven or kind, more attractive or smarter), or concepts (e.g., childrearing, religion, politics, ethics) may guide symptom development and presentation. *Variation in people's values, perceptions, and attitudes can explain symptom differences. Likewise, symptoms and emotions can reveal morals and interests.*

How might this relate to those whose anxiety prohibits action toward their stated goals?

Perhaps certain activities (e.g., being employed, dating) aren't an individual's goals, but are stated because *others* value them, and proclaiming socially-admirable objectives may be an attempt to maintain acceptance, yet symptomatic prohibition safeguards neurotic persons from trying, following through, or sustaining action (e.g., dropping out of college due to symptom severity may reveal how a student's parents value education more than the student).

What might you determine when anxiety gains attention (e.g., sympathy) or avoids it (e.g., by allowing a retreat from others)?

The same symptoms, either within the individual or among people, may not reflect identical purposes. Consider how someone can anxiously get to a sought-after job interview early, but a comparable symptom level may prohibit visiting an insufferable relative.

Now think about how people from various backgrounds buy the same type of vehicle because they value its attributes (e.g., fuel economy, seating capacity) that fulfill particular requirements. What does this hint about similar symptoms among vastly disparate people?

Unconscious symptom selection in agreement with each person's life style may account for a virtually identical symptomatic presentation.[465]

Environmental Requirements

Neurotic symptoms may change depending on who's in the room. For instance, one friend may be more responsive to the stresses of parenting and take over or assist, whereas fear of rejection may prompt another friend to voluntarily act as matchmaker. Symptoms may arise with a compassionate spouse but be nonexistent in front of an inflexible supervisor, because they'll achieve a goal with one and not the other (or aggravate the situation). The addition of a newborn may give birth to fears about bankruptcy or the child's well-being that would precipitate enough anxiety to find a better (or second) job, or be more vigilant of household spending and safety. Symptoms may arise upon facing trivial chores or unnecessary requests (e.g., going to a party), which allows, for example, avoidance, but anxiety doesn't appear when tackling mandatory work (e.g., laundry, grocery shopping, employment). *Symptom differences may be due to environmental conditions that enabled or fostered the growth of particular neurotic symptoms.*[466] This includes parental influence that shapes children's neurotic development.

Assess and Hone

When people are introduced to a sport, they initially play with coarse and imprecise movements, a low ability to assess and employ the most advantageous tactic at the best time, and a lack of sophistication in understanding and playing the game. However, with dedicated practice, experience, and feedback as well as improvised or experimented exercise of various yet specific behaviors, there's increased skill. What clue does this provide about neurotic symptom variation?

Initial symptom application may be inappropriate, inefficient, and ineffective; however, over time there's rising proficiency of how, when, where, and with whom to use various symptoms, with those that are most effective (if not necessarily efficient) in achieving goals retained and employed later.[467] Ineffective symptoms wither, some become unavailable, those that are impossible to maintain are abandoned and, perhaps, later resurrected if believed to be effective. Some people can quickly weed out symptoms and cultivate new ones.[468]

Symptoms are effective for the reason that they're selected.[469] An unconscious, or virtually so, choosing of symptom type, strength, duration, and frequency employed to attain various objectives reveals a telling characteristic: neuroses are creative acts.[470] *Those with generalized anxiety may assess their environment, unconsciously select, evoke, and hone symptoms depending on a number of factors, gauge symptom effectiveness and discard ineffective ones.* This accounts for symptom variation as well as progressively automatic symptom implementation. If symptoms are developed in childhood, individuals have a decade or two of unconsciously refining their symptomatic presentation prior to adulthood and to the point where it becomes automatic, efficient, and increasingly prominent and effective in various environments. During childhood neurotic development can be so vague and unnoticed as to be effectively subterranean, below the surface of perception. Yet, symptoms can take root, rise and strengthen like a towering oak tree from an undistinguished acorn buried years prior.

Infinite Presentations

While determining the pivotal factors that account for inconsistent and wide-ranging symptom presentation may have appeared overwhelming and inscrutable, the answer is simple and consistent. First, there are innumerable personal, social, and environmental elements that bias a response, such as conflicting convictions, biological precursors, and parental influence. Second, after anxiety has been employed as a means to an end it can be used in various ways.[471] Third, which objectives are sought can account for symptom variation.[472] Ultimately, a Swiss Army Knife variation of symptoms may be necessary to attain various goals in diverse conditions.

Chapter 16: Strategies and Tactics

Some people believe that all neurotically anxious individuals are innocent victims of their minds, bodies, or circumstances. Indeed, generalized anxiety may arise as a consequence of organic influences, as well as be related to conflictual, inefficient, or ineffective life style convictions. But perhaps far more intriguing, is how it can fuel or freeze action to attain goals. However, the suggestion that symptoms can be purposeful risks appearing insensitive, cruel, and misguided. Fortunately, biological symptoms provide an illuminating precedent. They reveal harmonic action among bodily systems, and demonstrate how symptoms can be protective, purposeful, communally influenced as well as socially detrimental. With that in mind, you may also consider neurotic symptoms as the psychological siblings to the body's biologically-based defense mechanisms — but with a future-oriented ability to safeguard the vital variables of self-esteem, acceptance, status, and life style. Moreover, as each individual's personality defines reality, objectives, and how to think, feel, and act, it guides how and when symptoms wake and sleep. While people may believe that neurotic persons must be malicious to attain their aims symptomatically, that's simply untrue as symptoms are employed unconsciously, or nearly so, therefore not willfully unkind.

Given these elements you now face an extraordinary question: What strategies (plans) and tactics (behaviors) may be used to achieve goals?

Aim Low

Some individuals with generalized anxiety may be so industrious and perfectionistic that they multitask and achieve numerous and incredible feats, resolutely erasing each one off their To Do list and take a break only after they have depleted themselves of energy, completed their work, or don't have the ability to achieve the task at hand. Yet, why might others set unimpressively low standards or easily achieved goals (e.g., move only one storage box from a cluttered living room or wash one load of laundry when mountains exist)?

At first, this appears to be merely the repercussion of anxiety's debilitating nature; however, keep goal orientation in mind. You can readily and logically see how a person who hasn't been to the gym in a while might only bench press the bar, rather than put weights on it and risk injury. Similarly, *neurotically anxious persons may approach those less intimidating and more achievable tasks without any danger of failing.* This can bolster self-esteem, demonstrate effort, and allow collaboration with others, all of which maintains acceptance and can elevate status as well as confidence. They are assured of success, albeit a minor one.[473] Those with generalized anxiety may prefer a small triumph to a grand failure. In time, they accumulate these accomplishments without generating anxiety about failing and sullying their ostensibly perfect (but otherwise relatively unimpressive) success rate. However, what might be another benefit to setting undemanding goals?

Consider how if they were successful at more taxing challenges, they trigger the countdown on a ticking time bomb. Others may soon issue duties of equal or greater difficulty, fully expecting them to be accomplished. However, this is an unsustainable proposition that ultimately ends in failure. Anxiety can influence movement like a traffic light and dictate which responsibilities are undertaken and prohibited. In addition, easily achieved standards allow neurotic persons to remain in motion and maintain success, which gives the impression of noble intent and drive. Setting low standards suggest a fear of failure or success, or both — which indicates a desire to safeguard self-esteem (as well as acceptance, status, and life style).[474]

So, why might neurotically anxious persons set, yet fail, easily-achieved low standards?

When symptoms overwhelm attempts at even the simplest tasks, their severity is substantiated. But what else is validated? For those who perceive themselves as grossly inferior, failing at basic jobs testifies to themselves and others that they're ineffective. While this seems to devastate self-esteem and threaten status, what might be the purpose? It fortifies their logic, for instance, "I can't even do something so simple. That's what I get for trying! I'm not going to attempt that again!" Although appearing counterproductive and counterintuitive, might such a characterization protectively enable evasion from various future tasks that risk failure, as well as lower others' expectations and the likelihood of them issuing additional or more challenging responsibilities?

Subjugate Others

Imagine those married couples where one spouse perpetually worries about various aspects of life from the most trivial concerns to the metaphysical ones (e.g., running late, burglary, safety, bills, illness, death, afterlife). The attentive and compassionate spouse listens to each concern with saintly patience, explains away worries, reassures, and endlessly engages in assorted styles of soothing. Yet, why might the worries never stop, with new ones rising and old ones revisited, with logic and facts readily dismissed?

The solution comes from assessing how apprehension and panicky behavior influence others. For example, fears of an intruder (disease, infidelity, etc.) prompt a spouse to continually verify that matters are fine at all hours of the day and night. In addition, neurotic persons may interpret others' attentive actions as intoxicating proof of worth, affection, and care. *Anxiety can be employed to exert control and used to achieve various goals, such as power and attention.*[475] But as long as anxiety serves a purpose, any peace must be brief, and that's why anxious dwelling soon reappears and others' reassurance is swiftly disregarded.

Those with generalized anxiety may work up their worry to where they grant themselves license to give orders and offer unrequested advice (e.g., they may tell others how to parent "out of concern for the child") — perhaps akin to overzealous sports spectators issuing unrequested directives from the sidelines. Yet, they don't see such action as unhealthy boundary violation, but rather as altruism.

Why altruism? Because that's in accord with the need to be good and removes any barriers to foisting guidance upon others — indeed, once viewed as socially beneficial, neurotic individuals believe they *must* express themselves for others' sake. However, this can backfire when people rebel against such control and distance themselves. (When patients give unrequested suggestions then get upset others dismiss their counsel I suggest, "Unsolicited advice is unheeded advice." Neurotic individuals may identify healthier boundaries by asking themselves, "Do I own this problem?" or "Is the person asking for my advice?" In addition, it's beneficial to recognize that others may not follow advice — even if it's requested and sound — when it's not in accord with their goal.)

Now imagine a concerned parent worrying about an older teenage child going alone to a suburban shopping mall. That parent is pacing in the kitchen while an unfazed spouse casually eats a bowl of cereal, until the stressed parent blurts out: "How can you just sit there feeding yourself? You have no regard for our baby out alone with who-knows-what kind of people who roam the mall! Your indifference makes me sick! Lord knows what kind of pervert or kidnapper is stalking about!" Such worry allows not only a needless and hurtful accusation, but also may be an attempt to achieve self-elevation (e.g., worry may portray care and compassion), prompt action ("You better go to the mall and see if everything is okay"), and a superstitious effort to influence chance (e.g., "If I worry about it, then nothing bad will happen"). *Anxiety and fear fuel awareness for threats to self-esteem, can control others, and protect status.*[476]

Get Others to Invest In Them

Sunk cost (a.k.a. the Concorde effect) is when people make an investment it can be quite difficult for them to break free from it, even when it's improbable they'll receive a significant, if any, dividend.[477] For example, if a person believes a company will flourish exponentially and buys many shares of expensive stock, when that stock dwindles in value that person may continue to hold onto the belief that the company and the stock will do well — perhaps purchase more stock — as it continues to decrease in value. While this would be a shrewd tactic if the company were to regain its financial footing, imagine that the corporation was in an irreversible spiral to bankruptcy. So what clues does this provide about the possible relationship between neurotically anxious individuals and attentive, supportive, encouraging, and consoling others?

First, *dedicated persons may come to define themselves by the roles they've assumed.* This can bolster their emotional, psychological, and physical commitment and strengthen persistence. Second, reflect on how the variable intermittent reinforcement found in slot machines increases the likelihood that gamblers will persist in their gambling.[478] Simply, people are prone to continue behavior that's randomly and intermittently reinforced.[479] *When neurotic persons experience moments of confidence, peace, and demonstrate healthier actions, they may intermittently reinforce supportive others' efforts and hope for improved functioning.* Yet, how can this be problematic?

The Sunk cost effect can occur when supportive others invest considerable time and effort (perhaps greater than neurotic persons spend) in resolving symptoms or addressing obligations, but symptoms remain or worsen. However, rather than acknowledge their efforts were for naught or counterproductive, and change the situation or abandon their goal, these compassionate persons may continue their course of action, double their efforts to assist and alleviate symptoms, and *fortify their belief that their work will pay off* (especially if there are glimpses of symptom reduction) to justify their mindset and effort. Alas, this can erode neurotic persons' self-confidence, increase dependence, as well as multiply and perpetuate symptoms, including their fear of abandonment. Some neurotic persons interpret symptom recurrence not as they who failed, but rather as a reflection of their therapists', friends', and family's inadequacy.

Pleas for Assistance

People with generalized anxiety may be notably reluctant to ask for help directly, fearing that it indicates incompetency. Pair this with a desire to be social or fear of being alone, and contemplate what the following anxiety-permeated expressions invite.

"I want to ask out that cute accountant, but I'm uncertain where I stand."

"I'm worried that the ladder is too wobbly and that I'm going to fall off."

"I'm really edgy about bringing my car to the mechanic in that part of town."

Compassionate others may feel compelled to ease the anxiety by engaging in some act that pardons symptomatic individuals from stressful chores. *Symptoms can be an indirect means of summoning assistance without pleading.*[480]

Greatness Through Others' Sacrifice

Why might a neurotic person anxiously state the following?

"I *explicitly* told my children not to do anything for my retirement, but did they listen? No. They surprised me with the most ambitious party I've ever seen! They invited every person I have ever worked with, all my neighbors and family members. All took time out of their busy schedules and some came hundreds of miles! I'm worried my children overspent on me and they have their own bills to pay. I'm a humble person and they didn't need to lavish me with all of that attention and praise, and I'm sure they have better things to do with their time and money."

Commending others by stating how they go to great lengths to honor or do something (perhaps despite protests) can implicitly make the speaker appear good and valuable, among other praiseworthy characteristics (e.g., selflessly worry about others' financial ability and scheduling obligations, humble, grateful).

Restrict Others' Movement

What might the following reveal?

"The roads are far too icy and treacherous. I'm worried that you'll get into an accident. In fact, I was going to go out, but I changed my mind."

Worriers can elevate self-esteem when their apprehension permits them to be regarded as thoughtful, compassionate, and caring.[481] But there's something else to consider. What if the roads aren't dangerous?

Then maybe those statements are best understood as, "I want you to stay home," and possibly unveil a fear of loneliness or abandonment. Guilt feelings can give the appearance of compassion and interest (e.g., "I would feel awful if you had an accident. Stay until the weather eases up"). Pronounced worry of infidelity or others' intentions may lead a compassionate spouse to refrain from going to lunch (party, the gym, etc.). Or, consider how vacations can be limited in number and distance due to worries about finances, plane travel, or getting ill in another country where medical care is deemed substandard.

Why might neurotic persons express anxiety about their children's abilities?

For example, they may state, "I doubt you can manage your bills or keep an apartment in order. You've never been any good at those things." Such statements undermine their children's confidence and discourage them in ways that increase the likelihood of making them dependent and always within reach — a way to keep the umbilical cord attached long after what's healthy. Likewise, criticizing significant others can erode their self-esteem and get them to believe they couldn't get anyone better, which confines their movement and grants neurotic persons a sense of security. *Neurotic symptoms can restrict others' movement in numerous ways.*

Self-fulfilling Accusations

Those with generalized anxiety may feel inadequate to effectively address life's challenges and rely on dedicated others for things such as paying bills, shopping, chores, or childrearing. Yet, even with significant historical data that these individuals are devoted, the fear that others will leave can escalate to the point where neurotic persons falsely accuse others of abandonment or neglect (e.g., "You're going to leave me. I can tell," "You don't love me," "You're a selfish person"). When those dedicated caregivers reassure repeatedly, yet their statements are dismissed, they may increasingly tune out those expressed concerns due to their repetition or noxious character, and slip away, perhaps only briefly. Subsequently, neurotically anxious individuals may declare, "You see! You abandoned me. I was right about you!" Caring people who don't see themselves as selfish or mean may try even harder to please and become ensnared in a servile function. *Neurotic persons may worry that others may leave them, regularly express symptom severity that pulls for reassurance, and make accusations that keep caring, protective people nearby.* Those with generalized anxiety may make such black-and-white statements that — given the natural variability of human behavior — others may act as accused (e.g., they can't always be 100% attentive, may interrupt, look at another person). Neurotic persons then may use that as evidence that grants them permission to take control, insult, doubt, view themselves as the good one, etc.

Dogmatism

Neurotically anxious individuals may be dogmatic in their way of thinking, perceiving, and acting. Yet, why might they stubbornly maintain problematic and symptom-generating convictions? Although this appears illogical and counterproductive, consider the following:

- They never have to admit they're wrong.

- They may view anxiety as the cost of "doing it right."

- They avoid areas they fear would expose inadequacies.

- They can make swift decisions without much, if any, contemplation.

- They can generate pure and potent emotion that fuels intense behavior.

- They avoid being adrift in a vague and unnerving sea of gray indecision.

- They may convince themselves, and perhaps others, of the supremacy of their logic.

- They can ascribe their symptoms to something else (e.g., biochemical, genetic causes) rather than an indicator of their improper thought and action that require change.

Impatience

Those with generalized anxiety can be conspicuously impatient. While this can be a natural correlate of intense drive, greater comprehension comes from viewing such behavioral and emotional symptoms within a social context. For instance, how might people respond to someone who wears their emotions on their sleeve and is visually and/or audibly impatient — a tapping foot, an unnecessarily loud sigh, a terse response, rapid speech, a furrowed brow, a contorted face, or the demand for prompt action, perhaps with a not-so-veiled appended threat?

Compassionate people, those who want to avoid conflict or chaos, and those who wish to do a good job, for example, are particularly prone to being responsive to such impatient acts, complying readily, or caving into an array of requests — often with few or no objections or questions asked. Unfortunately, yielding to neurotic persons' impatience reinforces it. Impatient individuals may alienate friends and family as well as breed frustration and rebellion. For instance, children may defiantly drag their feet to madden impatient parents. Also, impatience can be a means of blaming others and permit movement or immobility, (e.g., "I can't wait for you to get dinner started. I'm out of here!"). Relatedly, those too impatient for the time required in therapy to acquire new ways of thinking and acting, can be irresistibly drawn to anxiolytic medications' alluring ability to suppress symptoms relatively quickly.

Binary Thinking

Neurotically anxious individuals may contemplate various scenarios, plan for many possible outcomes, distressingly deliberate about an event or course of action, weigh countless variables, replay scenes in their minds, endlessly process and evaluate from multiple points of view, and act as if life were a chess game with each move having critical importance. In addition, they can detest considering vague, nuanced matters and accordingly engage in binary thinking, insisting on right or wrong, good or bad conceptions and classifications. After much systematic thought, they come to a conclusion they may perceive as "the Truth" and of which they are unarguably certain. As you can imagine, anxiety can fuel such in-depth and nearly constant cognition. Yet, why *binary* thinking?

After all, it's exhausting, agonizing, and time consuming and, given the natural and necessary variation within life, it can be inappropriate and unsuitable...but keep in mind the Anxiety Code.

First, to be good, perfect, right, people with generalized anxiety may continually evaluate innumerable factors and build a massive, well-defined book of which actions are deemed good, how to do things perfectly, and what's right. This knowledge may maintain or increase self-esteem, acceptance, status, as well as goal achievement. There isn't "good enough," but rather "perfect or wrong." Such zero-sum criteria can lead them to be adverse to indistinct, uncertain areas of life, and avoid indistinct logic or outcomes.

Second, while uncertainty may lead to not taking any action for fear of being wrong and failing, those who need to be driven can intensely dislike inaction, perhaps feeling unproductive or lazy, hampered, or burdened with free time when they dwell on unnerving things. With that in mind, what does knowledge of right and wrong, good and bad, perfect and imperfect allow driven individuals?

It permits them to take control and strive full force toward a goal, free of guilt feelings and doubt. Binary thinking allows for irrepressible zeal and persistence in achieving objectives, even in the face of difficult challenges or fatigue. Additionally, when they inflexibly believe they know the right way to do something they often can persuade others to relinquish control.

Binary thinking clarifies choices, affords exceptional security in decisions (even if incorrect), intensifies emotions that fuel swift and sustained effort as well as blurs distractions, and enables control — *it also allows immobilizing-levels of emotion.* However, life is inexact and vague, and even when those with generalized anxiety are wrong they can be stubbornly impervious to different perspectives and conclusions. Unfortunately, anxiety can explosively mushroom when their thoughts are cloudy, mistaken, and they're resistant to other ways of thinking.

Glory Days

Neurotic persons may regularly recall and savor those times they were successful, swiftly and effortlessly reliving accurate and familiar recollections. These retold stories cast an image of competency that may maintain or bolster self-esteem, status, and acceptance, and fortify their drive to successfully push forward on some task. However, why might they polish and embellish anecdotes to the point of morphing pedestrian achievements into monumental feats?

Exaggeration may artificially bolster self-esteem and enable audience retention. In addition, a happy and elevating pleasure trip down memory lane may dead end with anxious dwelling on, for example, aging, where they are in the life span, and how they'll never resume that level of functioning. Anxiety may invite attention and reassurance or prohibit movement toward some challenge. In addition, as long as they speak about the past they can keep others, as well as themselves, from focusing on what they're not accomplishing today or tomorrow. On the other hand, those driven to accomplish something that might be difficult or above their current ability, may reflect on, and perhaps exaggerate, previous achievements to craft a self-image of competency that encourages forward movement toward the present challenge (e.g., "In high school, I ran the 100-yard dash faster than anyone. I should be able to get into shape fairly quickly after I join this running group").

Anger

Given that neurotically anxious individuals may frequently and exhaustively think about countless variables and outcomes and come to a steadfast conclusion, as well as maintain rulebooks with binary logic, why would they experience anger and what might it allow?

Unrealistic Expectations

Those with generalized anxiety may maintain a distinct logic, a drastic sense of right and wrong, and clear goals — *and unrealistically expect others to know and adhere to those parameters of thought and action as well as have the same objectives.* However, such an impossibility cannot end well. Even good and healthy expectations of others (e.g., be financially responsible, organized, thoughtful, reciprocate kindness) may be unrealistic for certain individuals or situations. (Indeed, I often see patients who are frustrated and upset because they anticipate their spouses, siblings, or friends to act differently than how they've acted for years.)

Neurotic persons may not take human variation into account and uniformly project their goals and rules onto everyone. For instance, statements such as, "You'd think that people wouldn't drive so fast in the rain (leave their shopping carts in the middle of the aisle, etc.)" doesn't factor in the variation of people's skill sets and how they think differently. Those with generalized anxiety may expect that everyone should have "common sense." But as you'll recall, common sense isn't as common as the label implies.

Even if neurotic individuals are factually correct and have healthy rules, as long as they have unrealistic expectations of themselves, others, and life (e.g., poorly-timed traffic lights, inopportune weather) they're prone to experiencing anger as well as its related cousins: frustration, irritation, exasperation, and moodiness. *Anger can be a feedback mechanism that communicates the difference between expectations and reality and should prompt an adjustment of expectations to reduce symptoms.* Also, consider how unrealistic expectations may merely be the kindling for the fiery anger that follows...

Compliance

While venting emotions can act as a pressure release valve that avoids building up anger and allows people to abide by the need to be good, why might anger remain and what may diminish it?

View an individual's irritation and anger within a social environment. Others might try to address the issue, reassure, fix the problem, or assist in some other way. For instance, they may clean the basement (stop gambling, refrain from talking to a coworker, etc.) after the spouse barks violently about it. In short, anger may allow satisfaction of the need to be in control by gaining compliance through force. *Threats, anger, and temper tantrums get others to comply.*[482] Apologies afterward may reinforce their symptoms' seemingly uncontrollable characteristic and fortifies the conception of goodness through recognition of, and compensation for, misbehavior. Note that neurotic persons' anger can frustrate, enrage, and alienate others who may eventually revolt. *Although anger may be used to gain control, it can create a self-defeating, antagonistic, and escalating spiral of anxiety and anger.*

Create Distance

Why might those with generalized anxiety get angry when their therapists prompt them to look at their role in, for instance, marital discord or parent-child alienation?

When neurotic persons do not wish to be held accountable (perhaps fearing change or the expression of inadequacy), yet unable to halt the inevitable examination of their role in problematic situations, they may become angry and give themselves license to leave the session or terminate treatment. *Neurotic persons may generate anger to justify distance and fuel an exit.* For example, think about people who want to leave their job. They may get increasingly angry about their boss or the long commute. Or, consider how those who feel too vulnerable in a relationship can enflame anger that energizes, and assists in rationalizing, breaking up.

Irritability

If your stomach were irritated you'd probably avoid consuming anything that could aggravate that delicate situation. Irritability significantly lowers the symptom development threshold. Similarly, *psychological irritability is a mild form of anger that enables people to rapidly accelerate anger or elicit rage when others incur the slightest infraction or when life disappoints.*

So what may irritability allow?

First, it can serve as a general warning to others to tread lightly and not do anything that would spark a volatile reaction. Second, irritability allows neurotic persons to keep themselves just below the flashpoint, allowing them to trigger anger quickly and forcefully. Third, protracted moodiness and being slow to cool down can prolong the reign of power, as well as extend it beyond its natural boundaries, allowing neurotic persons control *even when they're absent.* For example, "I want to stay out later, but it isn't worth the trouble. My spouse has been so grouchy that it would lead to a blow up."

Facilitate and Fortify Anger

When irritability doesn't get the anticipated response or the action it once did, what may neurotic persons do when they don't change their goals or life style convictions?

Well, consider the escalating fines of an overdue library book or how criminals may receive harsher fees and prison sentences with each subsequent conviction. When people don't alter their behavior with a certain amount of consequences there may be an increase in severity to facilitate change. Accordingly, if some irritation worked to achieve one or more goals, then in the face of diminishing returns (or no response) neurotic persons may roil their irritation to the boiling point of anger...but how?

They...

• Focus on and scrutinize what's going wrong.

• Follow their rules with greater fidelity and frequency.

• Foster increasingly unrealistic expectations (e.g., unreasonable demands, expect perfection).

• Fortify their perception of how correct they are (by comparison others are increasingly incorrect).

• Find the errors in others' logic or behavior, but disregard their legitimate points and sound rationale.

Conflict with the Need to be Good?

At this point you might say that anger undeniably violates the need to be good and imperils exactly that which neurotic symptoms protect: self-esteem, acceptance, status, and life style. Yet, considering that anger can be purposeful, it may be maintained. So how can those with generalized anxiety employ anger without violating their need to be good?

Unconscious Invisibility

Neurotic persons may be completely unaware of how, why, and when they stoke their anger. Therefore, as long as they are unconscious of its development, purpose, and execution they get to achieve their goals (e.g., compliance) without violating their need to be good (from their perspective).

Blame Biology, Medication, Others, Etc.

By attributing anger to genetics, biology, medication, disobedient children, insufferable coworkers, an intolerable job, etc., people liberate themselves from accountability for their moods and actions. Consequently, they don't violate their need to be good conviction, but rather (to them) it's their genetic constitution, hormones, medication side effects, "bad wiring," natural response to others, etc. that "made" them get angry.

Righteous Indignation

How might anger protect — or even elevate — self-image, acceptance, and status?

When neurotic persons portray themselves (or others) as the innocent victims of either life or mean-spirited people, they can classify their anger as "righteous indignation." This is deemed a "sinless" and morally-encouraged anger that doesn't violate the need to be good. Such relabeling grants them license to mete out justice as they unrepentantly reframe their anger and revenge as "balancing the scales," "righting a wrong," or "defending the underdog," which allows them to maintain, or hoist, their self-esteem, acceptance, or status as well as substantiate how others and life are unjust and inferior.

"Tough love"

Now contemplate constructions such as "tough love" and related rationalizations of anger such as, "Sure I yell and lose my temper. It teaches my kids what *not* to do. If they just did the right thing, then I wouldn't *have to* get upset!" or "I'm only doing this for your own good, to teach you properly, and because I love you and don't want you to do the wrong things in life!"

When neurotic persons frame their angry bullying in this way they depict themselves as selfless, moral guides or astute teachers who have others' best interests at heart and whose anger is necessary and beneficial. This allows a sense of significance in a way that doesn't deviate from the need to control and be good.

Increase Anger Over Time

Why might those with generalized anxiety experience a gradual growth of irritability and anger like a pebble in a shoe that ultimately becomes infuriating?

First, by keeping a lid on their anger they can be good and do the right thing (being piously patient and refrain from anger), and avoid conflict or chaos. Second, after giving ample evidence to themselves (and perhaps others) that they're trying to be good, they can grant themselves license to unload pent-up anger and blame others for ruthlessly antagonizing them — especially in the face of their patience (e.g., "I was trying to be good and let it go, but *you had to keep pushing it and make me angry!*").

Passive Aggression

Passive aggressive behavior, such as withdrawal and forgetting, may indirectly express anger without breaching the need to be good. For example, being too anxious to have sex can frustrate, punish, and control others in a way that protectively makes the symptoms accountable.

Criticize Through Compliments

Those who want to be good and avoid conflict may nonetheless strive to express anger or act out. Knowing this, why might a neurotic person compliment a friend's frugal spouse by saying, "It was immensely thoughtful and generous of you to give your son the boat he wanted"? It highlights the bias of the spouse who regularly denies even the smallest expenditures to the friend. *Compliments can be used as a form of criticism that doesn't overtly violate the need to be good.*

Seethe with Anger

Although anger can be used to gain compliance, refraining from displaying anger can control for things such as getting fired, divorce, conflict, chaos, or embarrassment. Those who need to be good, and more expressly people pleasers, may suppress their anger for significant periods.[483] Consequently, neurotic persons may merely seethe with anger as a way to control situations and others' perceptions.

Depression

Why might those with generalized anxiety experience bouts of depression? Although depression appears to be the brake pedal to anxiety's accelerator, to realize why it can arise please take a moment to list defining depressive characteristics and symptoms. Now, consider how the following may illuminate the solution.

Think about how if you wanted to turn off a desk lamp you may simply flip a switch or pull the plug from the outlet. But what if the light didn't have a switch and were hardwired into the house? You'd have to go to the electric distribution board and flip the switch of the relevant circuit breaker. While this turns off the lamp, it also interrupts power to many outlets, rendering various other electrical devices impotent. Fair enough, but what does this have to do with generalized anxiety?

Neurotic individuals may want to avoid anger that creates undesirable conflict or chaos, violates the need to be good, imperils self-esteem, acceptance, or the life style...*and that's where depression comes into play.* Reviewing your list of depressive characteristics, odds are you named a lack of energy (in some form). With that in mind, consider the following. *Depression can drain neurotic individuals of energy, which neutralizes anger and therefore can avoid conflict, chaos, being seen as bad, as well as other undesirable outcomes.* However, similar to turning off a circuit breaker that cuts power to many appliances, depressive lethargy isn't selective or precise; therefore, it can reduce the energy to do various things.

Angry About Getting Angry

Why might neurotic persons ironically get angry with themselves for getting angry?

First, for those who need to be good, anger may be a result of not acting as they expect to behave. Second, anger can acknowledge to themselves and others that their initial anger was improper, which safeguards self-esteem, status, and acceptance. Third, anger can act as self-imposed punishment that controls future anger, and this attempt to improve themselves allows a sense of superiority. Fourth, self-directed criticism and guilt feelings may merely wipe the slate clean so they can get angry again. Fifth, self-imposed punishment allows them to control the discipline, as well as its duration, severity, and frequency. Sixth, as long as they're beating themselves up others are prohibited from issuing a rebuke they might otherwise give — and perhaps even become supportive in the face of harsh self-damnation.

Those with generalized anxiety may employ anger in a way that (to them) doesn't violate their need to be good or endanger their self-esteem, acceptance, status, or life style, and can elevate their sense of goodness and competency.

Control Finances

Neurotic parents or spouses in charge of the finances can benevolently give allowances, dole out money, or finance trips, vehicles, shopping sprees, and the like. Conversely, when they're anxious about something (e.g., grades, parenting skill, how money is spent), they can dry up an otherwise free flowing river of money and privileges. This can maintain an air of goodness through charity as well as power by denying it. *Neurotic persons may control others through generosity or by being in charge of money.*[484] Being in control of the finances, or things dependent on them, say housing and transportation, can keep people as close by and dependent as unweaned calves and corral them into particular behavior.

Create Excitement and Agitation

While it's a common belief the anxiety's intense energy is merely an unintended side effect that unsettles and derails individuals, remember that people are societal individuals. With that in mind, how might being frantic and agitated influence others?

Well, consider how neurotic individuals' anxiety can stir others to grant amnesty for unaddressed responsibilities (e.g., "I'll let you hand in the paperwork late because I know you've been so frazzled"), as well as solve problems or address threatening circumstances (e.g., worry about walkway slipperiness may prod others to shovel and salt, agitation about possible layoffs may pressure coworkers to work harder, concerns about break-ins can push others to check door locks and install a security system). Anxiety can be a method of exercising power, which has notable social implications.[485] Indisputably, dramatic symptoms demand attention.[486] However, repeatedly pulling the symptomatic fire alarm takes a physical and psychological toll on all involved. *Symptoms can generate excitement internally and externally, energizing people and environments as well as enraging others.*[487]

Escalating Worries

Symptoms can be quite subtle in the budding stages of generalized anxiety. However, why over time (often many years) might symptoms intensify? For instance, neurotic individuals may occasionally worry about passing an unimportant college exam, but later in life find themselves incessantly worrying about life-or-death medical issues, losing their home, or their children's safety. At first you might say that with increased responsibilities come bigger fears. Sure that's a valid answer, but there's something else to think about: the body's remarkable ability to adapt to stimuli. How might this impressive capacity be a distinct disadvantage for neurotic persons?

Given that they focus on particular thoughts, images, sounds, or circumstances that generate anxiety which fuels goal-attaining action or inaction, adapting to that stimuli decreases anxiety, which makes them progressively powerless to symptomatically reach their goals. So what might be their solution? They magnify and multiply their worries, making them more central, frequent, and dangerous.

Suicide, Parasuicide, and Suicidal Ideation

It's necessary to clarify and familiarize yourself with three distinct terms: suicide, parasuicide, and suicidal ideation. Suicide is the willful killing of oneself. Parasuicide is a deliberate suicidal threat, gesture, or non-fatal attempt that isn't intended to be fatal. Suicidal ideation is defined as suicidal thoughts and planning.

Recall that generalized anxiety is significantly correlated with suicidal ideation, but ultimately those diagnosed *only* with it have a low risk of attempting suicide.[488]

However, comorbidity with another mental disorder *significantly increases the risk of suicide attempts.*[489] *This critical subject requires the highest priority care, and must be treated seriously and thoroughly.* Unasked questions may perpetuate dangerous incomprehension. So, as grim, unpalatable, and delicate as the question is, could suicidal ideation, parasuicide, and suicide serve a purpose?

Perhaps it's best to start by considering those with inescapable and intolerable medical issues that anesthesia may barely soothe, (e.g., severe burns, neuropathic pain, cluster headaches, pancreatitis, shingles). You can imagine how sufferers may contemplate a suicidal escape when they reach their endurance limit. Similarly, some neurotically anxious persons may wish to flee their relentless and agonizing symptoms and believe that suicide will end the pain, be a means of evading future failure, ridicule, rejection, and abandonment. In fact, those who need to be good may rationalize what's otherwise inexcusable and socially detrimental, by viewing others as burdened and reframing suicide — or even the consideration of it — as socially benevolent (e.g., "My children would be better off without me in their lives").

Some with no intention of committing suicide may experience a sense of relief through suicidal ideation. (Not to be flippant or insensitive, but as an analogy consider the desperately impoverished who dream of winning the lottery and get an artificial thrill, a fleeting vacation, from their economic difficulty — even if they never buy a ticket.) Although suicide is clearly against oneself, what are the possible social implications and goals of suicide, parasuicide, and suicidal ideation?

• Could suicide's social purposes be seen in the details? For example, where a suicide is committed (e.g., at work, in the bedroom); who's likely to find the body (e.g., a tyrannical boss, a cheating spouse); how it's committed (e.g., in a spouse's cherished sports car); what's worn or not (e.g., job uniform, wedding ring); when it occurs (e.g., wedding anniversary, a parent's birthday); what's nearby (e.g., divorce papers). Might parasuicide or suicide be a means of power or revenge? For instance, such actions may lead others to carry lifelong guilt feelings, remorse, shame, and self-doubt for some perceived injustice (e.g., "If only I had been a better spouse [parent, boss, friend, sibling])."

• Might neurotic individuals who speak about, threaten, or attempt suicide dramatically draw others' attention or create tension that mobilizes or immobilizes others (and empower those who feel powerless)? Indeed, a reason for threatening suicide may be to impact others.[490] Although falling short of immediate professional intervention (e.g., authorities, healthcare providers), passive hints at suicide can get others riled up and take over obligations, retract demands, and generally put people in motion or arrest their requests and actions.

• Could suicidal ideation or parasuicide be a display of inadequacy that expresses an impulse to give up on seemingly irresolvable problems (e.g., "I just can't handle working for my boss anymore"), permits greater leeway or special privileges (e.g., "I have to take a break from this marriage before I walk in front of a train"), or rationalizes desires (e.g., "This project is driving me to the brink, I deserve to treat myself well after it's done")?

Double Insurance

Your insurance company awards you financial compensation to cover expenses or allow repair or replacement for the loss or damage of what you insured. However, what if your insurance company also charitably refunded your money if no problems occurred? It would be a win-win situation; you would be financially secure regardless of whether something adverse occurred.

Anxiety can safeguard acceptance, self-esteem, status, and life style, say by fueling action on the useful side of life or enabling retreat from a seemingly unconquerable challenge. However, why might it arise when it doesn't allow for retreat or fuel beneficial behavior? For instance, symptoms that spoil a first date, a job interview, or socializing, say by arriving late, being insecure, distracted, frenetic, or forgetful.

First, imagine that neurotic persons face and unfortunately fail a challenge. If they identify and blame anxiety for spoiling their chance at success they can protectively explain away poor outcomes. Moreover, others who reject them due to symptoms may be deemed unsympathetic, which allows self-esteem and status to remain unsullied. Second, when neurotic individuals move toward a challenge and symptoms undermine their efforts and knock them back a few steps, there's back-and-forth movement. This underscores their noble intent (e.g., "I gave it my best, but my anxiety overwhelmed me"). Third, when anxiety prohibits full participation, neurotic persons aren't fully vulnerable and cannot be genuinely assessed; therefore, any possible negative judgment has room for reinterpretation.

Yet, what benefit might appear when they attain a goal while anxious?

They are doubly triumphant as they achieved their goal *despite* their symptoms. So even if they have the same results as symptom-free others, their results are superior.

Neurotically anxious persons can employ symptoms to be heroes when they succeed, and if they fail they have a ready excuse that preserves and perhaps augments self-esteem and status for having the strength to approach challenges under the burden of villainous symptoms. *"Buying double insurance" symptomatically enables neurotic individuals to take a chance and be safe regardless of the outcome.*[491]

Attempt to Fool Fate

Consider how starting in infancy people develop a sense of safe behavior limits when their bodies provide a feedback mechanism for hazardous actions (e.g., upset stomach, muscle pain). They also learn vicariously; say by watching others engage in dangerous actions and get hurt. Also, concerned others inform them of good and bad consequences for their actions (e.g., studying, exercise, proper diet). In addition, people witness how those who breach social norms and laws suffer ostracism, bad reputations, and imprisonment. Now factor in the metaphysical concepts of rewarding and punishing afterlife such as heaven and hell and various forms of reincarnation. Knowing this, what general concept is learned?

A "just world" hypothesis or "balanced universe" belief wherein good behavior is rewarded and bad behavior is penalized. While you may readily grasp how such perceptions can be associated with the need to be good, how might they relate with the need to be in control?

Well, start by examining why actors may tell one another to "Break a leg" before going up on stage. Simply, the idea behind this apparent curse is that by wishing someone ill fortune they superstitiously avoid tempting fate, paradoxically wishing success rather than jinxing them as they fear would happen with a positive bidding such as "Good luck!"[492] In this way, they play off of the just world concept as a way to metaphysically control outcomes.

Now consider how people refrain from partaking in some pleasurable or indulgent activity to evade negative consequences (e.g., avoid cookies to prevent weight gain). Living within acceptable behavior guidelines can be an attempt to control for negative outcomes. Those who believe in a balanced universe may hold onto the notion that if they enjoy things or overindulge then fate (kismet, karma, chance, god[s], etc.) will inevitably balance the scales of the universe and cause something unfortunate to occur.

With this in mind, how might symptoms be a means to control for undesirable outcomes?

Some neurotic individuals believe they're often wrong and nothing goes their way. This puts them in a troubling, anxiety-producing conflict. They believe if they don't worry (or worry enough), then something undesirable will surely occur. On the other hand, if they take the time and energy to address a concern, nothing unfortunate will happen and they'll have wasted their time. So not only does this put them in an unwinnable situation, but also by their logic if they don't worry in the beginning, they'll certainly have to worry in the end. *From this perspective they may superstitiously worry to assure that nothing bad will happen.* For instance, some worry in a willful attempt to "ward off bad spirits," fate, bad karma, etc., as a means of un-jinxing themselves.[493]

Think about those who workout strenuously at the gym not for fitness, but rather to give themselves permission to later indulge in a calorie-dense dessert or notable alcohol consumption without guilt feelings. Similarly, *neurotic persons may experience symptoms prior to an event so they can enjoy some activity, or otherwise prohibited luxury, without worry or guilt feelings as if they have deposited in a karmic bank account only to freely withdraw from it later.* Neurotic individuals may feign symptoms to deceive "The Fates" and subsequently take pleasure in activities and extravagances free from misery.[494]

Pessimism

Reflect on how the military motto Semper Vigilantes ("Always vigilant") succinctly emphasizes the importance of being alert for dangers. Likewise, those with generalized anxiety may be constantly eagle-eyed for any threats. However, like a fighter jet on afterburner, remaining persistently alert and responsive rapidly depletes the energy required to sustain those safeguarding measures. Knowing this, what might be the symptomatic solution?

Neurotically anxious persons can be painfully pessimistic, for example, strongly believe "good times never last," and continuously "wait for the other shoe to drop," perpetually expecting an inevitable emergency. *Pessimistic conceptions incite and sustain anxiety, which fuels vigilance, preparation, and action.* Maintaining a belief that at any moment something could go out of control or that acceptance, closeness, peace, success, and prosperity are short-lived justifies and sustains guardedness and control. Unfortunately, *when a wary mindset is perceived as maintaining safety, there's a risk of it becoming all encompassing and overused.* For instance, anxious individuals see problems on the horizon that either have a microscopic chance of occurring or simply do not exist. Yet, they do not relinquish their goal of safety or their means to it. So, how might they override logic and low probability with a dismissive proclamation so they can preserve their way of thinking and acting?

They can say, "With *my* luck something bad will happen," "I have the *worst* luck in the world," "I'm sure everyone else will be fine, but *I'll* get caught," "Are you saying that I *shouldn't* protect myself or my children?" or similar phrases. By castrophizing, using blanket statements, and predicting worst-case outcomes, they protectively brace themselves. With this in mind, why might they be the "bad news first" type of people?

They're compelled to look for problems, real, possible, or imagined. Therefore, fearing the bad news chaser and being caught flat-footed or celebrating prematurely, they couldn't enjoy and appreciate the good news if they heard it first. Accordingly, they can justify, for example, going through others' phones, Internet history, text messages, diaries, credit card statements, etc., snooping for anything that could give a predictive advantage for an otherwise unforeseeable situation (e.g., a spouse's infidelity or overspending). (You can see how this can parallel hypochondria when people have repeated medical testing to discover some fatal disease before it consumes them.) But what if nothing bad happens?

Rather than renounce their beliefs, neurotic persons often cling tighter to them, believing that it's *because* of their pessimism that nothing bad occurred. In addition, pessimism can be strengthened due to negative reinforcement, as their worry is removed (perhaps only temporarily) and this subtraction of distress reinforces their pessimism (vigilance, control, etc.), which increases the likelihood of it reoccurring. Well then, are their beliefs shattered and pessimism extinguished when wonderful things occur?

No, especially if they believe in a balanced universe, wherein bad things soon follow the good or magnificent. Knowing this, can you see why some neurotic persons grow progressively tenser as situations improve or become calmer? While seeming illogical and paradoxical, it makes sense when you realize they're waiting for the next adverse thing to arise. *Neurotic pessimism makes it incredibly difficult to enjoy the good times, live in the moment, or find peace.*

Also, when those with generalized anxiety believe that people will take advantage of them or do something incorrectly, they believe others are bad while giving themselves authorization to be driven and take control. For instance, they may do their own home repairs and renovations out of fear that contractors will damage their home, steal, or go through their personal belongings.

When people pessimistically place burden for unemployment, remaining unmarried, or other unenviable conditions on others or circumstances (e.g., bad luck, down economy, deceitful siblings, selfish parents) they faultlessly avoid life's demands and the possibility of failure, as well as the action needed to successfully face their fears and develop a sense of competency. *Pessimism allows people to evade situations and conditions that risk exposure of their perceived inadequacies that imperil self-esteem and status.*[495]

Suffering

Ponder how people endure short-term financial pain, such as forgoing vacations, dining out, or luxury vehicles, so they can save for retirement or afford their children's schooling. Or, consider those who exercise strenuously to enjoy a healthier and longer life. Clearly, suffering can be a byproduct of healthy goal achievement. Some neurotic persons may be stressed simply due to their hard work associated with their drive and extraordinary acts of goodness. In addition, psychological and physical suffering can be the natural outcome of inefficient or ineffective life style convictions, reveal the limits of the neurotic solution, and appear to negate the possibility of self-imposed symptoms. Fair enough, but can suffering serve a purpose?

Given the unconscious aspect of neurotic symptoms, people aren't mindfully generating their misery. As previously mentioned, if those with generalized anxiety are able to achieve while suffering, they may be viewed as genuinely competent or superior.[496] Last, suffering can allow an excuse for, and justify potential, failure.[497]

Given the importance of understanding an individual in the social environment, reflect on how it's quite common and healthy for people to go out of their way for those who have lost a loved one, perhaps by preparing meals or babysitting. Similarly, people may provide relief and assistance to anxious persons. For example, excuse them from responsibilities or adjust expectations of what they can do.

Those with generalized anxiety may express their distress in a way that draws attention to their competency or superiority, (e.g., "It's really frustrating that I can't make it to your party, but I'm so stressed with all of the work they've given me after they fired everyone else in my department. I really need to relax, and your party sounds great, but my bosses gave me the responsibility of ten people"). This illustration shows how people's suffering can enable a sense of superiority, a fictional plus, compared to those who aren't pained. If this allows avoidance from a task that risks vulnerability, hurt or failure, there's also an evasion of a felt minus. *People may interpret their pain as a form of superiority, which may be nothing more than eluding a challenge they believe they would fail and appear even worse.*[498]

Sulk and Suffer in Silence

Why might those with generalized anxiety say or do something similar to the following?

• "Nothing's wrong. Everything's fine. You can go on vacation without me if you want. Have a good time. You don't have to worry," said with a sigh.

• Attend a party, but not talk with others or enjoy the food, and remain relatively inanimate, without being explicitly negative.

When neurotically anxious individuals express positive statements with inappropriate affect such as a sigh, a frown, or with no emotion, their words communicate one thing, but their sulking, tone of voice, or body language can subtly express hostility, disinterest, disappointment, or hurt, that may prompt particular action from others. This allows adherence to the need to be good (perhaps by willfully suffering through action deemed especially awful), control by avoiding confrontation or discord, and can elicit support and behavior change from others (e.g., leave a party early). *When neurotic individuals perceive that life and/or others have mistreated them, they may protest, suffer in silence, and sulk, which point an accusing finger.*[499] Indirect assertions of mistreatment may get others to alter their behavior and it may elevate neurotic individuals who regard themselves better than those they accuse.

Martyrdom

Why might neurotic individuals say statements similar to the following?

"I should be more social, but I have to tend to my spouse because I feel that something bad is going to happen when I least expect it. Besides, I couldn't enjoy myself knowing my better half needs me."

"I'm so lonely and really want to settle down and get married, but it just wouldn't be right. I'm just not that selfish to inflict my anxiety on another person. I'll get used to being alone."

"I was so anxious on Monday, but I didn't want to call at the last minute and take someone else's appointment or make you stay late."

"I was so worried about the grandkids that I rushed to buy their cough medicine, and ended up smashing my car into a lamppost. But as long as they're okay, then it was worth it."

First, recognize how people attempt to quell anxiety through action, or allow anxiety to forbid behavior. Why are some behaviors permitted and others impeded? It all depends on the goal and personality. Again you can see that anxiety doesn't automatically and mechanistically lead to a singular result, but is a vehicle that is given direction to a destination.

Second, neurotic persons may portray their symptoms as acceptable losses for a noble cause. Note the distinction between a martyr and a victim in that the "'martyr' dies for a cause or for principle," "whereas the 'victim' merely 'dies'…".[500] In this way, their sacrifice makes the world a better place. By being martyrs, they attempt to elevate their self-esteem, status, and acceptance with symptoms serving as evidence of how they have the morality to worry and take costly action when others are seemingly indifferent. Those with generalized anxiety may generate symptoms to demonstrate their superiority over their antagonists and persecutors.[501] For example, people may suffer with an intolerable spouse for the good of the children, and express to others how much better they are than their spouse.

Third, agonizing sacrifice for others may be an attempt to attain some sort of legendary immortality and reverence; for instance, "I hope you remember what I did for you after I'm no longer here," or "No one worries about your health and happiness more than I do."

Fourth, people can make sacrifices to control others. For example, "I've been looking for a year for a new home for you and I've found one on the next street. It was worth the effort so you can be close to us and your grandparents." Or, consider anxious parents who repeatedly voice how much they've sacrificed to pay for their children's education to get them to perform well academically.

Why may distressed neurotic persons decisively decline any suggestions to take a break, or others' offers to assume some demanding obligation?

By citing their principles, conscience, or some socially-acceptable construct, those with generalized anxiety can refuse relaxation, recreation, or anything that alleviates their symptoms. Consequently, they can view themselves as responsible, caring, and with exceptional strength and praiseworthy integrity as they persevere in their uphill climb while burdened with a weighty and cumbersome backpack of symptoms.

Take Advantage of the Transient

Why might those who fear vulnerability and rejection confess their flaws and express irritations about their children or spouse to strangers in a store or while on vacation, yet be distant with those they see regularly and have a strong association such as family, friends, and coworkers?

Transient and carefree interactions with strangers allow neurotic persons to be seen as friendly, approachable, good people, while avoiding the obligations and risks inherently tethered to long-term communication where those words can come back to haunt them. Likewise, fleeting, expendable expressions of imperfections, failures, frustration, and anger are relieving soulful confessions to others unlikely to be seen again. These liberating, anonymous admissions are without consequence, like an unsigned message in a bottle cast into the ocean.

Divide Vulnerability

Think about how corporations in a competitive marketplace have the goal to generate profit. They want to avoid other companies poaching vital employees and intellectual property. In addition, there's significant interest in minimizing the likelihood of employee public speculation about future products that could tip-off competitors. Consequently, businesses may segregate the design and production of essential components among various teams housed in guarded, windowless offices on various campuses. This ensures that no team or employee can determine the entire project. As long as most employees remain isolated from others, respective ideas remain secret. Such mystery and smokescreens protect corporations from financial loss by minimizing widely available information. With that in mind, why might those with generalized anxiety tell a friend about certain faults and contemptible actions and reveal to a coworker other flaws and failures?

Neurotic individuals may disclose distinct thoughts, feelings, and actions to numerous, yet non-communicating others, say by maintaining multiple E-mail addresses that enable discreet correspondence, telling far away people online under a nebulous username, divulging certain actions and thoughts (but not everything) in confidential therapy or the confessional, or inform coworkers of negative thoughts about family members and tell family about inferiorities at work. *Neurotic persons can feel accepted by expressing information in segmented ways, which maintains a sense of safety as no one person knows their entire biography nor is able to deduce it.* By compartmentalizing their lives, emotions, and thoughts they limit vulnerability to protect their self-esteem, acceptance, status, and life style.

Matryoshka Doll

A Matryoshka (a.k.a. Russian) doll contains several progressively smaller ones nested inside a large one. With this image in mind, what might neurotic persons attempt to accomplish with the following?

• Give the impression that they're attached to a significant project, when they aren't.

• Refrain from, or significantly delay, revealing such things as their (or their family's) troublesome medical, legal, substance abuse, job, or academic history.

People may display an impressive public image, while protecting their perceived smaller, inner selves. They may maintain an admirable veneer and withhold information, slowly revealing themselves layer after layer, progressing only when they're ready. Anxiety may fuel vigilance, unnecessary guardedness, or quick escape. If they're rejected or ridiculed at any of the early stages they avoid devastating harm, as they never revealed the core of their genuine selves.

Date Those Committed to Another

Why might neurotic persons have affairs with married individuals, especially those with no interest in divorcing or being fully invested in a relationship, when that behavior imperils self-esteem and status, is doomed to fail, and prohibits participation in a healthy relationship?

• They can flee the relationship at any time by defining it as unworkable.

• Dating those committed to someone else guarantees limited vulnerability.

• They don't have to be on their best behavior or vulnerable for extended periods.

By seeking a relationship with married persons, neurotic individuals can get attention and physical intimacy — even a bit of anxious excitement — without genuine and full vulnerability or long-term obligation. However, it's like leasing a relationship. There's no long-term commitment, and they can break the agreement at will with little or no penalty. But how might neurotic persons date those committed to another without violating their need to be good? They may attribute their actions to the virtuousness of their hearts' whims and unable to control cupid's arrow or as altruistically attending to those with selfish, inattentive spouses. Also, consider how they can end the relationship with a moral display and anxiously proclaim they're acting in the best interest of the unaware spouse. But how might neurotically anxious persons protect their self-esteem and status if the married persons end the relationship? They may portray the married individuals as duplicitous victimizers and themselves as the hopeful, patient, trusting, and innocent victims.

Relatedly, why might neurotic individuals seek those monogamously superglued to someone else, hoping the person will end the relationship? Devoted longing without an expiration date can portray good intentions of wanting to date, while simultaneously precluding it. This can enable virtually limitless avoidance of vulnerability and failure. This tactic can also be employed when seeking an unobtainable job, home, vehicle, etc.

Characterize Themselves as "Lazy"

People with generalized anxiety may call themselves "lazy." Yet, consider how laziness is decidedly irreconcilable with driven individuals who often have plenty of pep and many accomplishments. Moreover, given human goal orientation people can energize themselves toward their desires (e.g., people find the energy to get off the couch when they get sufficiently hungry, do the laundry when they're out of clean clothes). Consequently, there's *no objective reason* to define themselves as lazy. Yet, as a person's perception defines a distinctive reality, it can trump facts — especially when the perception is in accord with one or more goals.

So why might people make such a disparaging and incorrect self-definition of laziness?

First, consider how driven individuals can have a high, perhaps unrealistically so, self-ideal (their belief of what they *should* be doing as well as the accomplishments they *should* have...according to them). By comparison their self-image (how they see themselves and their achievements) is disconcertingly low, which has a painful side effect: the misperception of laziness.

Second, like insufficient or confusing desk assembly instructions, conflicting or inadequate life style convictions can prohibit goal achievement. Unable to achieve their desires, neurotic persons may mistakenly appear to themselves and others as lazy. In reality, they may be frustrated, discouraged, and fear failure to the point where they're drained of exhilaration and interest to pursue their desires.

Third (and this is where it starts to get interesting), *driven individuals must generate emotions that fuel dedicated effort.* With that in mind, if they maintain impressive, yet perhaps unrealistic, objectives the resultant chasm between self-image and self-ideal can create an anxiety-soaked perception of falling behind, idleness, or some other undesirable characteristic that produces anxiety, which energizes productive behavior. The same outcome may occur by merely contemplating settling for or condoning common accomplishments.

Fourth, why might those well aware they're ambitious insist they're lazy (or continually fear becoming that way)? Well, consider those who say they're poor not because they are, but to prompt them to reduce their spending before it becomes problematic. Similarly, driven, accomplished persons may say they're lazy to sustain effort as well as vigilance for any threats (e.g., financial, social, occupational) before any problems occur. Although such negative self-reference appears to imperil self-esteem, status, and acceptance, what's their safety net? Its inaccuracy ensures it never shatters their basic self-perception. (Often, patients will confess that they know they're "not really lazy," but they "feel lazy.")

Fifth, neurotic persons' anxious self-rebuke can draw reassuring others who offer factual support and reassurance of their diligence, encourage efforts, as well as praise their goals.

Sixth, given the importance of social acceptance, how might neurotic persons secure a sense of ability, protect status, and maintain their life style by calling themselves lazy?

By stating their immobility is due to laziness rather than ability, they give the impression they *could* succeed if only they applied themselves (e.g., "I'd complete the Sunday crossword puzzle [run a marathon, write a book, etc.], if I weren't so lazy"). This is an attempt to present a positive image of competency without having to demonstrate it.

Seventh, when those with generalized anxiety say they're lazy, they can avoid specific actions and challenges they'd rather not face and pursue desired ones. For example, others take on responsibilities because they presume the work won't get done or completed properly. Perhaps the task isn't neurotic individuals' goal (e.g., "I'm too lazy to paint the fence" may mean they just don't want to do it, even though they need to and have plenty of energy to do something else). Or, by attributing laziness to their immobility toward a stated goal, (e.g., "I'm too lazy to apply for that job [date, go to that party, etc.]") they can achieve an objective that supersedes the proposed ambition. It can keep them safe from attempting that which they might fail; yet it demonstrates a lack of courage.[502] After all, *people must bravely face their fears to overcome them*. For many, "lazy" is a less threatening label than "afraid" or "incompetent." Some describe themselves as lazy and evade employment, for instance, not due to genuine laziness, but rather to avoid being enslaved to a schedule or be under someone else's control.

Excel In One Area, Neglect Another

The maxim "Nothing ventured, nothing gained" encourages people to be adventurous and realize some reward and that not trying maintains the status quo. However, when some neurotic persons encounter opportunities to improve their lives, but fear failing and ending up in a worse situation, anxiety can protectively restrict participation and enable avoidance. In this way, "Nothing ventured, nothing lost."[503] Yet, others' anxiety-fueled efforts, say at work, garner praise, awards, and various perks, and exhibit competency that legitimizes and fortifies their self-esteem, status, and life style. Although some say anxiety is the price paid for their success, what vital and revealing information is missing?

To assess people it's necessary to examine the environments they select or create for themselves.[504] It's equally important to see where anxiety propels and prohibits people and analyze what they avoid and is incompatible with their admirable achievements.

Neurotic persons can protectively cordon off areas of functioning they believe they'll fail, and put their effort and attention in other pursuits, selecting and creating environments in which they can succeed.[505] They may excel in one life task while falling short in the others.[506] For instance, they may be exceptional workers while failing at the social and intimacy tasks.[507] Consider driven employees who work impressively long hours and simultaneously avoid parenting responsibilities (e.g., changing diapers, maintaining a watchful eye, or going over homework in a regularly loud and chaotic home), intimacy, being an involved and communicative spouse, as well as periods of inactivity when their minds race and they feel unproductive. Their spouses and children may be akin to unopened fine wine: showy, yet unattended possessions. Simply, their hard work may allow them to cast a noble appearance while they evade areas that risk failure, rejection, ridicule, and abandonment. This protective tactic may also enable the belief that given their drive and success, they could do well in the remaining life tasks...if only they had the time and energy. Their praiseworthy action may effectively distract others from what's avoided. Neurotic anxiety may allow an escape into work or play, for example, but avoiding the critical issue means that those evasions are short-lived.[508] Case in point, a spouse of a driven individual may repeatedly plead for a more engaged partner.

Run Late and Out of Time

Why might symptoms arise for neurotic persons in the following circumstances?

1. Unfailingly punctual patients experience symptom escalation before a scheduled therapy session that doesn't prevent attendance, but delays arrival to some point after the scheduled time.

2. Those who energetically thrust themselves into a task, say landscaping, however, after buying various trees, bushes, and tons of decorative stone, symptoms soon surface and silence their efforts and (hint) remain until winter.

3. Patients who arrive early to every session, are exquisitely polite and congenial, yet who talk in a free-flowing, and virtually uninterruptable, stream of words from the moment the session starts to its conclusion.

In the first illustration, why did their symptoms make them arrive late to an appointment when such action imperils acceptance and apparently violates the need to be good, perfect, right?

Imagine their therapist assigned therapeutic homework those patients deemed too difficult or revealing. However, to avoid conflict, disappointing the therapist, or risk being seen as bad, they refrained from being assertive when the homework was assigned, which put them in a bind. Their solution was to maintain the belief that they'd get to their homework before the next session, but didn't start or complete it, which intensified the problem. As the appointment time approached, they didn't wish to cancel the session on short notice and leave the therapist with an hour free (perhaps fearing that would look bad) just to avoid admitting they didn't do their homework. So how do they attempt to resolve their dilemma?

By unconsciously running late they demonstrate good intentions by attending the session, yet control the temporal window of vulnerability and accountability, as there's less time to process why the homework wasn't completed. Patients can multiply this effect by starting the belated session with a new problem or crisis that supersedes reviewing the homework.

In the second example, when neurotic persons enthusiastically start a project they display admirable intentions, but if they fear failing and wish to avoid criticism (self-imposed or by others), symptoms can arise that put the project on pause until the point when it cannot be done due to some other criteria (e.g., weather). *Neurotic symptoms can be maintained until a more legitimate excuse arises.*[509] The excuse "It isn't done yet" may be preferable to confessing, "I don't know what I'm doing. I'm afraid I'll fail and that you'll judge me negatively." This is why a project may take years to complete or remain unresolved until a professional is called in to finish the work. *Symptoms can enable an illusion of movement and good intentions that can safeguard acceptance and self-esteem.*

In the third illustration, you may be tempted to say that anxiety forces patients' non-stop pressured speech until the session is over. While this can occur, also consider how as long as they speak ceaselessly they prevent being asked questions. This controls the conversation, limiting the time of vulnerability or accountability, while venting their thoughts and demonstrating to themselves and others their commitment to treatment.

Start and Stop Treatment

Those with generalized anxiety may start therapy eagerly, schedule weekly sessions for months in advance, and solemnly vow to finally address their aggravating symptoms they've had for years. Yet, why after a few sessions might they swiftly and resolutely cancel all remaining appointments with the rationale that their symptoms are unassailable and impenetrable?

Those who believe that their symptoms are genetic or biological in origin may have difficultly accommodating a different concept, and surrender their therapeutic pursuits. Others' impatience might lead them to be supremely reluctant to allow the time necessary to address their symptoms. But additional clarity may come from factoring in goal orientation, symptom purposefulness, and what movement is symptomatically enabled or prevented.

First, the prospect of peace from overwhelming and long-standing anxiety symptoms can prompt treatment.

Second, dedicated interest in addressing symptoms displays good intentions to the therapist, as well as family members or places of employment that issue ultimatums that either neurotic persons start treatment or divorce proceedings, or job-reassignment paperwork, begins. Also, some psychiatrists insist their patients attend therapy to solve their cognitive functioning while the medications lessen symptoms. Starting therapy can pacify (read: control) others who prod them to resolve their symptoms.

Third, while neurotic persons wish to rid themselves of suffering, as long as symptoms can achieve aims, they might be unconsciously maintained. Accordingly, people may attend a few sessions to reduce surface tension without diving deeper into their functioning. They can do the same for medication, only taking it at times of high stress or crisis and then terminate usage, perhaps by claiming that it was unproductive or they fear unrealized negative side effects. By investigating the movement made you can see how anxiety can be employed to generate action in any direction. Note how people may delay things for a long while, say cleaning up and painting the house, or going to the gym and losing weight, but then done in a flurry to achieve an important goal, such as a month before putting a house up for sale, or months prior to asking for a divorce and returning to dating. Likewise, people may avoid treatment for years — even with irritating symptoms — and then approach it full force when it's their goal to reduce symptoms.

Miraculous Cure

Why shortly after starting therapy might those with a long and pervasive symptom history declare they're symptom-free (or nearly so) and terminate treatment?

While you might guess they started medication or experienced a sudden resolution of a long-term stressor, what if neither occurred? Well, there's another possibility. Suppose their therapist accurately articulated the problematic mindset and corrective course of therapy. Although eliminating painful symptoms is the therapeutic goal, reflect on how treatment can be demanding and uncomfortable as it requires that people be vulnerable, urges individuals to be accountable for their actions, examines their histories and flaws, and prompts people to abandon their unhealthy coping mechanisms and adopt new cognitions and actions — which to them are foreign, frightening, and untested. *Neurotic persons may say their symptoms have vanished to avoid the challenging process of therapy and maintain their purposeful, though agonizing, symptoms.* Perhaps praising the therapist for being so insightful and helpful and "much better than previous therapists" satisfies the need to be good and can be an attempt to ensure a smooth, unquestioned, and non-confrontational exit.

Trivia question: What is the modal number of therapy sessions (regardless of diagnosis)?

Here's a clue: Although gyms are often crowded shortly after ambitious New Year's resolutions are made, attendance dwindles rapidly soon after.[510] Those who wish to improve their weight, fitness, or appearance, join the gym with the best intentions, but may soon give up their exercise regimen because they don't want to give up their eating habits, admit how out of shape they are, exert the effort necessary to improve their physical health, etc. Similarly, despite how distressing psychological symptoms can be, odds are that people only attend *one* session — irrespective of the treatment model used.[511] In other words, patients are most likely to only go to the initial therapy session and then terminate treatment rather than 10, 20, 50, 100, etc. to address their symptoms. This reveals their resistance to changing their thinking and life style as well as can obliquely suggest the strategic importance of maintaining symptoms. When people wish their symptoms would disappear, but don't want to alter their life style, for instance, the latter goal can supersede the former.

Infrequent and Rescheduled Sessions

Although some symptomatic persons who require regular and frequent therapy end treatment after one session, why might others of equal need attend therapy only a few times a year?

While infrequent sessions are likely of little value — like going to the gym and working out only once a month — people can give a virtuous image of trying, while minimizing vulnerability and the difficulty of change. Relatedly, they may reschedule a therapy appointment for one that's maybe a few days or weeks ahead. In this way, they show good intentions, as they aren't outright canceling their appointment, and avoid confronting certain challenges and changing their life style. Some people feel shamefully inferior when they contemplate needing regular appointments; therefore, may reduce session frequency to protect their self-esteem and status.

Return to the Familiar

When neurotic persons have tension related to their present situation (e.g., painfully single, in a miserable marriage, unemployed) and want to improve it, they may experience a symptomatic pendulum. Elevated anxiety prompts them to address their symptoms and circumstances. This decision lowers their symptoms. However, what might happen when they pursue new goals or ways of thinking that risk ridicule, rejection, abandonment, and failure? Symptoms rise to the point of immobilizing them. Unfortunately, this lack of movement can maintain the original tension-filled situation. Yet, how might symptoms enable predictability, control, and alleviating action? (Hint: Think about how sequels to popular movies, video games, and books capitalize on familiar names, faces, settings, styles, and personalities, yet are seldom as good as the original.)

People may anxiously return to an old lover, rationalize reconnecting with long-lost friends, or reapply to an old job. By going back to what's familiar, predictable, and perhaps more controllable than the alternatives, they can flee their current stressful situation and avoid the pitfalls associated with new people and unknown conditions. Regrettably, their pursuit of convenience and safety is ultimately a temporary and unsatisfactory solution, as they previously escaped those disagreeable situations.

Water Power

While some neurotic individuals avoid crying for fear of losing control of their emotions, being vulnerable, distressing others, or appearing weak, why may others cry readily and profusely, perhaps with later remorse, fearing they've created an awkward situation, appeared shameful, or burdened others?

You may be tempted to say that crying is merely the aftermath of distress that enables an emotional catharsis. Yet, this isn't always true — particularly if issues remain unresolved *or if others disregard or disapprove of the crying.*[512] This provides a captivating clue. Recall that there are distinct types of tears (basal, reflex, and emotional) that differ by how they're initiated, with emotional tears being psychologically based and linked to communication.[513] Again you see symptoms' interactional characteristic. Crying has a social component, and perhaps most important is how crying influences others *and how others react to those tears.*[514]

Now imagine anxious individuals interacting with those who are confrontational, ruthlessly critical or demand action neurotic persons wish to avoid. How might they take control of the situation in a way that avoids escalating conflict, or looking mean or defiant?

Either a gentle stream or flood of tears may get others to relent, thereby effectively control them.[515] This is why crying is referred to as "water power."[516] This tactic can be used with others who have a legitimate point, but one that neurotic persons wish to avoid (e.g., others who prompt those with generalized anxiety to find employment, mind their own business, socialize). Sometimes, raining of tears allows a reign of power. This is particularly probable when neurotic individuals have sensitive spouses, friends, or family who wish to avoid conflict or inflicting emotional distress.

A Battle of Wills

Those who need to be in control can face others who are tenacious to their preferences and either deny neurotic persons what they want, or insist they do things they don't want to do. So what might be a symptomatic solution to such an impasse?

Neurotic individuals may provoke anxiety, fear, panic, irritability, anger, crying, and repeatedly voice their concerns, and amplify symptom severity, frequency, and duration in a battle of wills until others surrender. *Symptoms can be employed to strengthen neurotic persons' correctness and logic, used to guide and sometimes coerce, or overrule dissenting others into compliance.*[517]

An interesting situation occurs when neurotic individuals create a battle of wills within themselves. For example, imagine driven individuals who are extremely motivated to overcome an intense worry, say drive on the thruway, date, or go on cross-country flights. They may experience an intrapersonal tug-of-war that publicizes their exasperating dilemma. While this can lead to standing still or hesitation, symptoms may also eventually tip the scales. Whatever the victorious action or inaction from the symptomatic skirmish, it unveils their goal.

Pamper Themselves

Reflect on those times in which you felt stressed and took remedial action by treating yourself well in some small way. Maybe you bought a gourmet meal, clothing, or a gadget, perhaps you took a break, got a massage, or called a humorous and reassuring friend. Such endeavors are rather healthy as you were able to assess and sufficiently address your distress.

Now picture neurotic persons who want some indulgence (e.g., a vacation, new car, or housekeeper), but can't justify the financial or time expenditure to themselves or others. There's an objective and an obstacle to it. Consequently, they may dwell on some agitating event, be it in the recent or remote past, or something they fear will happen. They brew a progressively poisonous potion of worries they either sip in silence and seclusion or spill socially. Though pained, why might they be reluctant to accept assistive feedback, futilely follow others' advice, or readily dismiss their solace, as if determined to worry endlessly?

Observe what's occurring. They generate increasing anxiety that deteriorates their quality of life, as well as others' (say, a frugal spouse, demanding boss, or controlling parents who will, or have, denied those desired indulgences). Abrasive symptoms may eventually become unendurable. Therefore, extinguishing them takes precedence over preceding prohibitions, with exasperated others accepting what anxious individuals deem medicinal. Yet, how might those with generalized anxiety justify what's otherwise off limits?

First, they concede that their symptoms have degraded not only the quality of their lives but others' lives as well, and take full responsibility for their role in discord and problems.

Second, others may be particularly open to suggestions when medication and therapy have been ineffective or boycotted. Accordingly, neurotic individuals make statements such as, "I need a vacation to clear my mind and get back to the old me."

Third, concerned others who allow asserted solutions may be receptive to statements that characterize them as kind, flexible, and altruistic. Neurotic persons may prematurely appreciate others' benevolence to coax a commitment, and they may label those who challenge their suggested remedies as petty, self-centered, uncaring obstructionists who despicably want to perpetuate agonizing symptoms.

Fourth, supplying remedies enables neurotic individuals to commendably define themselves as driven self-starters invested in resolving their symptoms. Moreover, they may portray their proposed antidote as "the right thing to do," and good for all involved.

When pampering is viewed as appropriate, charitable, crucial, and remedial, permission may be granted for some indulgence that reduces or eliminates symptoms...*temporarily.*

Interestingly, why might symptom reduction be fleeting?

First, when some extravagance alleviates anxiety it becomes a proven remedy, therefore it can be justifiably re-administered. Second, consider how individuals may experience some pain reduction from taking the recommended dosage of aspirin or ibuprofen, and then increase the dose to experience greater relief. Or, think about how people start off drinking alcohol or coffee one at a time, but later must increase the amount to attain the previous effects. Similarly, if the pampering is insufficient to fully extinguish symptoms or becomes decreasingly effective, neurotic persons can suggest, pursue, and rationalize larger or more lavish indulgences. Third, recall that removing an aversive stimulus (e.g., disruptive symptoms) is the crux of negative reinforcement. Accordingly, when some indulgence reduces symptomatic distress for neurotic persons as well as supportive others, the strategy is stealthily sustained.

Accuse Others to Distance Them

Why might people with generalized anxiety be needlessly suspicious of innocent others, issuing false, inaccurate, or prolonged accusations?

Although unappetizingly imperiling self-esteem and status as well as inviting conflict, the answer lies in examining what it enables. When neurotic persons want to control their vulnerability, for instance, they may seek to distance others — including the virtuous and guiltless. Unfortunately, distance prevents nourishing and beneficial closeness. So, how might they justify such otherwise indefensible and illogical action?

Simply, accusations can push others away. Yet, there's that pesky problem of the truth — the claims are unfounded. Ah, but validity can be virtually irrelevant as long as neurotic persons view their allegations as accurate. (Indeed, everybody —

neurotic or not — can devoutly believe untrue things.) When emotional and physical distance is viewed as prohibiting harm, that safeguarding mechanism is reinforced and perpetuates anxiety. In other words, if people aren't hurt while away from others, distancing may be sustained. (Think of this as akin to those who fear swimming and state that as long as they're not near water they won't drown, but they needlessly avoid a healthy activity.) Moreover, watching distanced others faithfully rebound can reassure neurotic individuals of the relationship's strength, which also can reinforce this tactic.

So why, for example, might people with generalized anxiety remain married to those they regularly and harshly accuse?

Though they could get a divorce and liberate themselves from the professed stress and strain, consider what they might gain by remaining married. They can push their spouse away...but just far enough to be a nearby target, endlessly under the microscope, deemed inferior and held responsible for errors. This can displace neurotic persons from examination and judgment. Accused others may recurrently attempt to prove their dedication and good character, which benefits neurotic individuals. In addition, those with generalized anxiety can defend denying sex and other signs of affection (but allow them when desired) and limit cooperation (for weeks, months, years, or decades), among countless other things. Or, consider how they can maintain a socially desirable image of being married and keeping their marriage intact, or stay in their home and retain their current friends and neighbors. Also, they may escape facing financial hardship, moving to a less desirable location, or returning to dating that threatens failure, rejection, ridicule, and abandonment. *Neurotic persons may use symptoms to keep others within reach, but at arm's length.*

Double Standard

Although neurotic persons can have an extensive, strict, and precise rulebook of how they believe people should act, what do those sharp rules combined with human fallibility mean?

Simply, they may unavoidably and hypocritically breach their own guidelines. Yet perhaps more fascinating, *they may not see it.* For instance, those with generalized anxiety may chastise those who yell at others and plead for peace and rationality; yet scream at family members and be utterly unaware of how they violated the rules they readily impose on people around them.

Double standards give license for behavior denied to others, can protect self-esteem, provide assurance neurotic individuals are right (and others are wrong), as well as allow them to guiltlessly and righteously defend themselves. People with generalized anxiety can exhibit double standards in countless ways, such as when they try to control others, yet bristle and rebel when others try to control them; or, they can interrogate people, but evade even the most innocent, gentle personal questions, and deem them rude and intrusive.

Superiority Through Declarations of Inferiority

Why might neurotic individuals make statements similar to the following?

"I was never good at telling lies, I get really worried and my face turns red."

"I couldn't even look at someone other than my spouse. I know it's harmless and everyone does it, but I would feel so much guilt."

"I'm terrible at sitting still. I have to work otherwise I get extremely anxious. I wish I could be at peace just relaxing like you do."

Consider how these statements indirectly contend they're honest, trustworthy, moral, and industrious. *To avoid portraying themselves as smug showoffs, neurotic persons may boast of their abilities or laudable characteristics indirectly by labeling them as shameful inferiorities.*

Keep Busy to Evade Cognitive Discomfort

Driven persons may hate being idle, and persistently keep themselves in motion. While such energy can be employed productively on the useful side of life, what else might be going on?

Consider what likely happens when they aren't busy. Their minds may flood with countless distressing fears such as upcoming obligations, previous mistakes, flaws, failures, rejection, ridicule, or abandonment. However, being busy distracts them from their anxiety-producing concerns. They put their energy into gear rather than unproductively over-rev their engines in neutral.

Postpone Sleep

Neurotically anxious persons often have trouble falling asleep, experience unsatisfactory rest, and wake in the middle of the night, their minds racing with worries, and awash in sweat-saturated sheets. They lie awake frustrated and dwell on how they should be sleeping. Sometimes they do math — calculating how much rest they'd salvage if they fell asleep at that moment (e.g., "If I fell asleep right now, I could get three hours of sleep before I have to go to work.") There are those who perceive their sleeplessness not as an indicator of a psychological concern, but rather as a biological problem to be medicated. Intriguingly, why might some completely deny sleeping difficulties and pridefully state they "fall asleep quickly and deeply until morning and can easily live on 3 or 4 hours of sleep per night"?

First, declaring they can get by with only a handful of hours of sleep displays an enviable ability that elevates them above most mortals. By defining their sleeplessness as a strength — rather than an indicator of how their problematic thinking and perceptions require change — they protect their self-esteem, status, and life style.

Second, comprehending neurotic tactics regularly requires examining what's avoided. Knowing that, what does insufficient sleep prohibit?

Though you may guess that sleep would be a sanctuary from daily worries and flooded with buoyant dreams, the stressors that occur during waking hours can seep into sleep. Perhaps unsurprisingly, anxious dreams suggest mounting anxiety about problems in real life.[518] This poses an interesting problem. How can neurotic individuals safeguard their life style when stress-soaked slumber signals a need to change it?

They may dismiss anxious dreams as random, unrelated, and unfathomable, like a longtime smoker who ignores or rationalizes a sloppy, wet cough to keep nicotine within reach. While anxious dreams can wake people and disconcertingly shortchange their rest, how might this be a solution of sorts?

Examine what occurs in an anxious dream. People are the projectionists of a disturbing horror movie or fearful thriller. They sit on the edge of their seats, with their eyes glued to the screen. When their anxiety hits an intense climax, they wake. While insomnia has its downsides, reduced time asleep slashes the frequency, duration, and recollection of unsettling dreams. In other words, waking can act like a liberating intermission from an otherwise inescapable home movie.

In addition, as driven individuals are motivated to get things done, hibernating may be unbearable. They may experience guilt feelings for sleeping — especially if they sleep longer their usual hours of rest. Also, as anxiety can fuel action during waking hours, a surplus can keep people defenselessly awake as if they had a pot of coffee before bedtime. Ah, but if that's the case, then how are they able to fall asleep rapidly and soundly throughout the night?

They stay awake until they're completely exhausted. Generally, people need more than a few hours of sleep per night. So what might be a revealing clue that hints at a sleep deficit? These usually redline-revving individuals often crave copious amounts of caffeine upon waking. Why would anxious persons (especially those who deem their anxiety biologically or genetically innate) need caffeine to get them going?

Again, observe how neurotic tactics can be imperfect solutions to life's challenges. Though postponing sleep can allow people to avoid anxious thoughts and dreams, this is eventually counterproductive, as anxiety and sleeplessness can antagonize each other in an accelerative spiral. Ultimately, long-term sleep deprivation can elevate anticipatory anxiety.[519]

Dismiss or Undermine Suggestions

When people are in agonizing pain or life-threatening situations they're usually receptive to suggested solutions — even those previously far outside of their comfort zone. For example, they may try online dating if lonely, parachute out of a crashing airplane, try bizarre foods when starving, or undergo experimental surgery for a life-threatening condition. With that in mind, consider how sympathetic people may eagerly provide recommendations, set up appointments with healthcare professionals, and untiringly research solutions for anxiety-pained persons, who give responses similar to the following:

"Caffeine is unrelated to anxiety (says the person who drinks a pot of coffee daily). You can't ask me to give up coffee! I need it to function. Besides, I read that it's good for you!"

"I'm not going on medication. Psychiatrists want you to get hooked for life and pay them forever!"

"I want to go to therapy, but I'm too frazzled to pay attention and get anything out of it."

"I wouldn't want to waste a doctor's time. It's selfish of me to steal someone's appointment who's suicidal and needs treatment more than I do. I just couldn't allow that to happen."

"I don't believe in therapy. How can doctors possibly identify with what I've been through?"

Thankfully, clues unveil symptom purposes. First, what movement do these responses allow? None. Even when neurotic individuals are distraught and plead for symptom resolution, they may ignore, negate, forget, reject, sabotage, abandon, minimize, or halfheartedly attempt viable solutions. (Sometimes, patients resist a straightforward solution to their stated problem; for instance, "I'll *try* to do it" rather than "I will do it", "You make it sound easy," or "That's easier said than done"). Second, note that others may work harder on symptom alleviation than those afflicted. While this may be due to distracting and draining symptoms that prohibit action, could it also reveal that others want symptoms resolved more than neurotic persons do? If symptoms are protective, they may be maintained — despite their distressing character. But if that's true, why do people ask for helpful suggestions?

First, symptoms are genuinely painful and people usually strive to reduce pain. Second, neurotic individuals can be unaware of symptom purposefulness. They view symptoms as caused rather than an unconscious mechanism that safeguards self-esteem, acceptance, status, and their life style. Third, even if they never follow through on advice or therapy, asking for guidance displays good intentions and can validate symptom severity.

Symptom Strength and Recurrence

What do colds, fever, sweating, tiredness, urination, vomiting, tearing, ejaculation, sneezing, menstruation, coughing, rapid breathing, as well as the gag, blinking, and pupillary light reflexes reveal about the human body?

To ensure individual or species survival, symptoms and bodily actions may continue until their respective goals are achieved. For example, sufficient oxygen and nutrients have reached the muscles and brain, or harmful substances are evacuated from eye, stomach, throat, or gastrointestinal tract. Knowing this, it's easier to comprehend neurotic symptom duration. Just like people only run as far as the finish line, neurotic persons retain their symptoms only as long as required.[520]

Imagine those whose anxiety ruined previous relationships and who air their loneliness and unrelenting desire to be in a relationship and finally find "a perfect match" on the Internet. Unluckily, each person lives in different city and neither can relocate due to various constraints. Although symptoms have sabotaged past relationships, why might they be low or absent in this case?

When valid justification for distance is unavailable, neurotic individuals may generate symptoms as severe as necessary to allow goal achievement. In this example, as distance preexists, anxiety isn't needed to detach from others. When legitimate reasons appear that enable avoidance, symptoms may end.[521] However, if a nearby dating opportunity arises, symptoms may as well. *Neurotic symptoms exist for as long as they're able to be functional and fade when they're no longer needed or effective.*[522]

So how might this symptomatic phenomenon occur on the useful side of life?

Neurotic persons may experience anxiety to the magnitude necessary to achieve one or more challenging objectives, which can explain why they catastrophize even small concerns as a means to prioritize and address them.

Symptom Multiplicity

Consider how military commanders defending a highly valued target may establish multiple lines of snipers, land mines, barbwire, berms, flamethrowers, tanks, and unmanned aerial vehicles to multiply its safety. Comparably, *neurotic individuals may concurrently maintain several symptoms to achieve their goal.* For example, "I can't date because my symptoms will push others away. I don't have a job because I'm too anxious, so I don't have any money to take anyone out. I'm a stress-eater and I don't want to be rejected because of my weight."

Perhaps you're familiar with the arcade game *Whac-A-Mole* where one large plastic mole momentarily pop up in one of five holes that the player attempts to quickly bonk on the head with a padded mallet before the mole drops back down. Similarly, *neurotic persons may experience symptoms serially.* For instance, "I cannot look for a job because my car is unreliable and I'm afraid it'll breakdown and I'll get fired shortly after I'm hired." However, after someone identifies a nearby bus route, another concern arises, "I'm worried that my coworkers will ridicule me for taking the bus when they have cars. Besides, what if the bus runs late? I'll get fired on the spot!" This is known as symptom substitution, as one symptom replaces another in an unconscious process.[523] (Think of this as *Symptom Whac-A-Mole*, as one symptom or problem is knocked down, another one pops up.) Those with generalized anxiety can worry about anything, regardless of legitimacy or appropriateness, on the useful or useless side of life. Just consider driven people who worry about one healthy item after another on their To Do list (e.g., go shopping, exercise, make dinner) and achieve each in turn. Changing challenges can maintain anxiety-fuelled effort, as can adding things to their agenda.

MacGuffin

How might those with generalized anxiety socialize with minimal risk of conversation they deem too intimidating, intrusive, or revealing?

Consider how filmmaker Alfred Hitchcock routinely employed a MacGuffin in his movies. A MacGuffin is a detail or plot point that fundamentally exists to motivate characters and enable particular events to transpire; for instance, in secret agent movies elusive top-secret papers or gadgets can act as a plot device that supplies a rationale for interaction and advances the story.[524]

Interestingly, people can use a MacGuffin in real life. For example, you can imagine how after an individual catches a glimpse of an alluring store clerk, a conversation is started about some product or service not to purchase it, but rather as an easy and relatively non-threatening means to spur a discussion that may result in a date, with the ability to quickly escape without emotional risk if the conversation goes in an undesirable direction. With this in mind, could neurotic individuals use symptoms as a MacGuffin to gain notice and gratify their desire for unthreatening social interaction?

Indeed. People can use their suffering to garner attention.[525] Concerned others may encourage and empathize, discuss what occurred in therapy, symptom severity, duration, and frequency, as well as medication treatments, side effects, and effectiveness. Symptoms can be a safe topic that summons an attentive and accepting audience, which may be as small as one or as large a group as extended family, or anyone within earshot or e-mail. Those with generalized anxiety may enthusiastically narrate their story, taking on a role they deem accurate and necessary (e.g., hero, victim, martyr, expert). They can have a focused and intense perspective that may be more captivating than what others may be capable of creating.[526] Some cast interesting and compelling accounts of triumph, injustice, tragedy, or trauma to illuminate and substantiate their competency and goodness, how others or life have victimized them, or a catastrophic and perilous circumstance. They may convey the frightening, devastating, and incapacitating character of their symptoms. Prominent players such as a cheating spouse, critical parent, deceitful coworker, disobedient child, invincible competitor, controlling and vindictive ex-lover, or envious sibling can complete the ensemble and underscore a situation's unfairness, alarm, and immediacy. Such enthralling tales with convincing story lines draw intrigued and concerned advocates who readily assist and provide financial, social, physical, and emotional support.[527] Those who echo the narrative can bolster and testify to symptom severity and may, for instance, augment the probability of getting a sanctioned leave from situations deemed unendurable, counter therapeutic, or unsuitable, such as work or social functions. Also, supporters often applaud those who perform while draped under anxiety.

Neurotic persons may be especially sensitive to others who upstage them by achieving some admirable goal (e.g., buying a luxury vehicle, getting a promotion). In such circumstances, they may employ symptoms to make themselves the center of attention, level the playing field, and receive accolades.[528] For instance, anxiety may lure others away from a higher achieving sibling or spoil another's success. Anxiety related to notable achievements may also attract attention (e.g., frazzled during expensive home remodeling).

Given the need for attention, the fear of vulnerability and the related search for privacy, what might be the safest environment to use symptoms as a MacGuffin?

The therapist's office. Healthcare providers offer continuous attention, regularly encourage, recognize achievements, not dwell on failures, and are bound by confidentiality. So what can happen when therapists inevitably prompt patients to face their fear or change their life style convictions? Some patients terminate treatment and initiate therapy with another provider.

Concerned and Inquisitorial Pursuits

In accord with the need to be good, neurotic persons may ask questions such as, "Where are you from?", "Did you two drive together?", and "What school did you attend?" While those inquiries can initiate and maintain cheerful conversation, recall the need for control, predictability, as well as symptoms' safeguarding function, and the possible purposes of those types of questions surface. For instance, consider how as long as neurotically anxious individuals are asking questions they direct the conversation and can preclude others' inquiries, which avoids revealing information. In addition, sympathetic questions about others' flaws and fears can gather detailed data that can boost neurotic persons' self-esteem in comparison (e.g., "I'm devastated that your daughter dropped out of school after her unplanned pregnancy. My daughter will really miss her at commencement").

Sometimes people demonstrate the "I'll show you mine, if you show me yours" type of thinking, and are more willing to disclose their inadequacies and mistakes if others disclose theirs first. Patients fearful they'll disclose too much information may ask their therapists personal questions unrelated to treatment, say about their relationships, where they live, or what type of car they drive. This can be to gauge their healthcare providers (e.g., personality, wealth, life style), as well as make them somewhat vulnerable and invested before patients proceed with treatment. This can also occur after neurotic individuals believe they've inadvertently made themselves too vulnerable, either within or outside of therapy.

As personal questions risks appearing unacceptably meddling, how might those with generalized anxiety ask questions while protecting acceptance?

Sometimes they start off with a compliment. For instance, the statement, "Oh my gosh, you're such an attractive young lady, I bet men ask you out all the time," may be an indirect attempt to determine the therapist's sexual orientation, marital status, and life style. Often, neurotic individuals may safeguard their appearance by appending declarations of care such as, "I'm asking only because I'm worried and want you to be safe." Yet, what might allow you to discern protective curiosity from genuine compassion?

Topic focus. When questions only center on areas such as the salacious, financial, or potentially embarrassing, but none are asked of more overwhelming, yet boring topics or those of little social value, (e.g., an ailing family pet), then purpose may be revealed.

People with generalized anxiety may want to know about many things, including those they don't have a right to know, and may generate anxiety to permit otherwise impermissible actions. For instance, prying parents or suspicious spouses may generate anxiety to legitimize rifling through others' computers, phone, or other belongings. People can stir concern to prioritize and fuel investigation to allow predictably and control on either on the useful or useless side of life.

Neurotic persons can strongly believe that various threats loom constantly. They may foster alliances as well as maintain strong, redundant, and secure modes of communication that can be cross-referenced to ensure accuracy and augment predictability (e.g., multiple friends say the same thing about a particular individual), and provide guidance (e.g., how to approach the boss). Also, information can be treated as a form of currency; bartered with others to augment knowledge or doled out as reward, for instance, to reinforce others who voluntarily offer information. Furthermore, neurotic individuals may threaten to release gleaned information to stop others in their tracks or railroad them into action.

Although seemingly illogical and time-consuming, why might those with generalized anxiety ask questions to which they know the answers?

First, they keep conversations within their area of expertise, which allows a sense of competency and can avoid ignorance-exposing questions. Second, they can test others' knowledge — their flaws and strengths — as if the teacher's answer key were in hand. Third, they can assess others' trustworthiness. (This isn't terribly dissimilar from parents who quiz their teenagers about their whereabouts and activities after coincidentally and secretly seeing them out, tracking their children's phone location, or hearing about it from a third party.) This enables speculation about others' personalities (e.g., "What type of person would lie about such a thing?", "In what circumstances is this person likely to deceive me?"). However, verified trustworthiness may merely bring fleeting peace as apprehension is required to continually fuel vigilance, questioning, and verification of others' knowledge and intentions.

Anxious Company

While some anxious persons populate their world with calm and reassuring people who balance their worldview and soothe symptoms, why might others interact with those who are extremely anxious?

First, they can feel superior to those who suffer more intense symptoms. Also, this can attract attention, reassurance, and service, as well as get others to withdraw demands and criticism (e.g., "I know you're upset that my symptoms stop me from working regularly, but at least I'm not as bad as Chris or Jordan. They haven't worked in years!").

Second, other anxious individuals reinforce their worldview — their reality (e.g., life is unpredictable, diligence is necessary), which can unfortunately perpetuate symptoms.

Third, those with generalized anxiety may aggregate information that allows a broader neurotic response: gather new ways to be anxious, fortify symptom arrangement, develop novel strategies and tactics that enable a detailed and expansive set of symptoms rather than a new way of perceiving the world and acting in it.[529]

Fourth, being around anxious people may intensify symptoms, which initially appears counterproductive. For instance, "Going to therapy and seeing other nervous people in the waiting room makes me feel worse than before I walked in the door," can rationalize and authorize treatment withdrawal. Likewise, the presence of highly-driven anxious individuals can prod neurotic persons — especially highly competitive ones — to raise their standards and perform better, which reinforces their life style and allows significance on the useful side of life, say by being an exceptional parent, athlete, or employee.

Be People Readers and People Pleasers

When reviewing life style convictions it's necessary to examine their unstated — yet equally instrumental — obverse counterparts. For example, the need to be in control has the related logical converse corollaries: desiring predictability and the avoidance of chaos and/or conflict. Additionally, the need to be good reflects a desire to avoid being bad or disliked. Granted, there are exceptions to the rule. For instance, those with generalized anxiety may not care about chaos and conflict if they're irrelevant to the goal or can enable control. Similarly, they might not be concerned about being disliked when they champion a greater good; for instance, they may loudly protest and rebel against people or companies deemed exploitive. Nevertheless, neurotically anxious individuals often strive to avoid chaos, confrontation, looking bad, and being disliked. But what's a common catch?

Well, think about how, for example, anger may allow control, but it can violate people's need to be good and escalate the likelihood of unpredictability, chaos, and conflict, as well as sully their image. With this in mind, consider how some neurotic persons define themselves as people readers and people pleasers who are quick and keen judges of character, tolerant, compliant, flexible, accommodating, and gladly sacrifice for others' happiness. While they may believe these characteristics are in their nature, how might they allow goal attainment within the parameters of the Anxiety Code?

People pleasers want peace, tranquility, and to be liked (or at least avoid being disliked).[530] However, they must fulfill a number of requirements. First, they must determine what people prefer and what they detest. Anxiety can enable and sustain astute observation, vigilance of others' actions and words, extensive contemplation and speculation of what they mean, and fuel prediction of what may please or might offend. This provides awareness of acceptable and gratifying words and actions, as well as the social land mines to cautiously sidestep. Relatedly, they can have a near-clairvoyant ability to sense the tension in a room. However, recognize that reading people and interpreting intention is merely an assessment.

Second, people pleasers must apply their knowledge behaviorally; this explains their aforementioned characteristics and actions. Anxiety can fuel various attempts at pleasing as well as the recording of what works to achieve their goals and what doesn't. People pleasers develop social skills to gain acceptance.[531] They shape their presentation to what surrounding others appreciate, with others' evaluations serving as the measure of the people pleasers' value.[532] Pleasing can be in any form, but it's those gratified who define and direct neurotic individuals' actions. Relatedly, that which is considered pleasurable varies from audience to audience. People pleasers continually self-assess to assure acceptable presentation, filter information, and quickly correct any missteps. By gratifying others, people pleasers believe they achieve significance.[533]

People pleasers can be impressively diplomatic.[534] By charming, indulging, or satisfying, they can quell and avoid disharmony and disorder and achieve various goals (e.g., keep a marriage or family intact, remain employed when under direction of a tyrannical boss). In addition, some recurrently please when nothing chaotic or conflictual is occurring at that moment or recently because frequent pleasing in the absence of conflict and chaos can preempt them. In light of the preceding you arrive at an interesting conclusion: *People pleasers control the social environment.* Well, if that's the truth, then why don't they perceive themselves as controllers?

Because they deem that term as negative (e.g., selfish, mean, demanding, exploitive), it risks being seen as "bad." So what's the symptomatic solution? *They become unconscious of why they're people readers and people pleasers.* Consequently, they can view themselves positively; say as perceptive, flexible, selfless, generous, and accommodating, which erases any prohibitions to people pleasing as a means to control others.

People reading and people pleasing skills may be developed in childhood. For instance, a child in an unpredictably stormy household may abhor the conflict and chaos, and seek peace and predictability. Hence, the child may develop the ability to swiftly read moods and actions, as well as forecast turbulent situations that hover like a hurricane on the horizon. Often, people readers/people pleasers are the adult children of alcoholics, who learned to assess their social atmosphere and please others.[535]

Knowing what you do about people readers and people pleasers, why might they avoid or minimize texting, e-mailing, or even using the phone, and prefer face-to-face communication?

To minimize the risk of misreading others and being caught off guard, they want as much data as possible. However, those forms of communication are limited (e.g., they're unable to interpret facial expressions, body language, vocal intonations). Relatedly, anxiety may arise when they lack any sort of communication, as they're uncertain of others' thoughts, judgments, or actions (e.g., "It really bothers me that I don't know what they're thinking").

While people reading and people pleasing are means to a goal, like other neurotic tactics they're imperfect solutions for life's challenges, and have a constellation of associated, even paradoxical, risks.

People pleasers believe they *must* please others.[536] Their striving to please can be so paramount that they can be too responsible (e.g., take on others' concerns), and significantly sacrifice their time, money, effort, and consideration.[537] They may experience guilt feelings when unable to please, be conformist to their disadvantage, ceaselessly seek approval, be oversensitive to actual or perceived criticism, be supremely reluctant to accept or trust compliments, mercilessly crucify themselves as too self-indulgent or have guilt feelings for their otherwise common desires or needs, and be unwilling to solicit assistance.[538] Knowing this, why might people pleasers who prefer a certain course of action, or need to defend themselves from others' unfair actions, equate assertiveness with being aggressive?

Although assertiveness is a way for individuals to advocate their interests in a non-conflictual way, people pleasers may fear conflict to such an extent that they err on the side of caution and define assertiveness as a form of aggression that would lead to conflict, thereby avoid both. However, this maintains difficult situations as well as associated symptoms.

Their drive to please, and the fear of displeasing or failing to please, may lead to difficulty articulating what they want, perhaps fearing their preferences will irritate, disappoint, and distance others. For example, the circular dialog "What do you want for dinner?" "Anything you want is fine with me," illustrates a common frustrating stalemate. People pleasers may continually ask questions, assess what others want, if they're pleased, or what might please them more — pursuits that can paradoxically erode pleasing and eventually annoy others. For instance, people pleasers can make attentive, but distracting lovers whose questions in the midst of passion ruin the mood. Behaviors such as being humorous, paying the bills and keeping the house in order, solving others' problems or doing their work, remaining unobtrusive in a critical household, submitting to another's sexual desires, or standing down from pursuing a topic or course of action may unhealthily control chaos and confrontation and attain situational peace and predictability — as transient as they may be. People pleasers can become character chameleons who swiftly adjust to situations and people. Sometimes, they're perpetual actors in a dedicated role (e.g., comedian, confidant, colluder, comrade, supporter, soother, or servant). They may feel vague and undefined and have trouble distinguishing their likes and dislikes, their goals and what would make them happy — not knowing their true selves when they stop fulfilling a role or are alone.[539]

Though people pleasers want to be right, when and why do they readily admit they're wrong?

First, accountability is commendable; therefore, courageously owning up to the error can provide benefits that eclipse the risk to self-esteem and status. Second, it can avoid conflict. Third, by identifying when they're wrong, they can correct their misunderstanding and get to be good, perfect, right the next time and please others more efficiently and effectively.

What may occur when people pleasers' kind efforts go unrecognized or aren't reciprocated?

First, they may question the quality and longevity of their marriages, relationships, friendships, employment, etc., fearing they aren't pleasing enough or correctly. Anxiety may mount when they realize their means to a goal is inoperable and they're uncertain of what to do.

Second, if they perceive that matters are careening out of control, they can anticipate an unavoidable problem (e.g., asked for a divorce, fired), and experience symptom elevation. This can fuel safeguarding behavior, such as look for a lawyer, lover, or job, prior to receiving the expected news.

Third, symptoms can drastically decrease their ability to please. While this erodes their means of control and being good, can you see how it allows a break from fatiguing effort as well as be a means of passively and indirectly punishing others by depriving them of pleasing?

Fourth, people pleasers may expect others to recognize and reciprocate their kindness; after all, from their perspective it would be the good and right thing to do. However, when they inevitably encounter those who don't do things "the *right* way" or when life doesn't go the way "it *should*" they become irritated.[540] When their beliefs go unmet they may lash out in anger (perhaps due to unrealistic expectations and/or to gain compliance or create distance) then repent, perhaps through pleasing, to drain guilt feelings, remain good, and mend social connections.

Misdirection and Sideshows

Why might those with generalized anxiety exhibit the following behavior?

1. While in therapy for escalating symptoms related to an upcoming event, they stubbornly rummage through and analyze decades-old memories, endlessly explore their past, and discuss and theorize innumerable factors, certain they'll discover a symptom cause that will illuminate their mindset and symptoms and uncover a cure.

2. Persistently worry about a minor flaw that's distantly associated with — or completely unrelated to — the main issue. Self-criticize and redirect discussion to that flaw whenever conversation strays from it, insisting that it's important and revealing. For instance, anxiously dwell on being "nearly 10 pounds overweight" when their parenting is negatively impacting their children.

3. Although in great distress, ruminate about issues they have little or no influence over, such as nuclear war, upcoming movies, starving children in a distant country, or global warming.

4. Animatedly start a home project describing plans, materials, and rationale, but halfway through it become uninterested, and then passionately start another project which also remains unfinished.

Logically, anxious persons should dedicate their resources to symptom resolution. Yet when they don't, you must connect the dots to make a distinct and telling picture.

Here's a clue: Why do magicians use provocatively dressed assistants and dancers? It's to distract the audience from attending to what may reveal the illusions.[541] Likewise, the circus can have an impressive main act that occurs simultaneously as the routine sideshows. However, when you focus on the sideshows you can miss the main act. This hints at how those with generalized anxiety may protect their self-esteem, acceptance, status, and life style when the life tasks threaten failure, ridicule, rejection, and abandonment. "Sideshows" can preoccupy and distract from their main responsibilities.[542] *Deception and misdirection guide neurotic individuals' as well as others' attention from an important matter, or what risks exposure, to the harmless.*[543]

The first illustration shows how dwelling on the past avoids addressing the main issue and may divert attention. Such patients may be running in place, apparently active but not making any movement down the therapeutic path. Retrospection, living in the past, and scouring their histories for clues and causes, siphons attention from present thoughts and functioning, with little time and effort remaining to address current challenges. While continued therapy attendance gives the impression of effort, continually derailing the conversation maintains safeguarding symptoms.

In the second example, by broadcasting minor shortcomings neurotic individuals can claim they courageously express their flaws. However, their self-condemnation about some trivial fault or error, as well as emphasizing irrelevant topics, hijacks attention from attending to a notable failing (e.g., poor parenting) that requires effort and change. Also, their self-rebuke may attract support and encouragement while simultaneously curbing others' criticism, as they're unlikely to heap on additional blame. Focusing on and owning a minor problem enables neurotic persons to metaphorically plead guilty to a misdemeanor rather than a felony, which can be much less punishing to self-esteem, acceptance, status, and their life style.

In the third case, their handwringing attracts attention and maintains anxiety, but focusing on issues outside their influence and irrelevant gets others off the scent from that which can be improved and the lack of behavior change.

In the last illustration, moving back and forth between projects, but never finishing one gives the impression of industriousness and good intentions, while avoiding judgment that might occur if the projects were completed.

Interestingly, there are neurotic individuals who falsely claim certain ideas and behaviors to get their therapists off-track and create a delay or distance that protects against too much vulnerability or change. (Relatedly, some attest to untrue thoughts and actions to gauge their therapist's ability to identify inconsistencies as well as assess fact from fiction. If the therapist doesn't detect the contradictions and conflicts, then patients may lose confidence in the provider and end treatment, feel "superior to the expert," or somewhat safe as they can control, distract, and misdirect the course of treatment.)

Vague and Indecisive

What might you determine from the following?

• Extremely hungry individuals who quickly sit at a restaurant table and immediately order a meal.

• Those in dire need of a job who energetically apply to several and take the first one offered, and state that they'll find to a better one, or rise up the company, as time and effort permit.

• People who swiftly buy a house rather than be without a place to live.

• Those in a burning building who rapidly choose one exit from several possible choices.

People can decide quickly when it benefits them — even for life-altering, anxiety-saturated situations, when desired outcomes aren't possible or guaranteed, if the options are many or complex, and long-term effects are uncertain. Knowing this, why might neurotic persons say the following?

"I want to be happy, but I'm too anxious to focus on what would make me happy."

"I don't have any goals. I can't think of what I want. I can't concentrate on those things."

"I'm in a fog. Everything is gray, vague."

"I've been thinking about this for two years and I'm still torn between continuing my current job and going back to school and starting a different career."

While anxiety appears to make people indecisive, unable to articulate their desires, or have disconcertingly nebulous plans that prohibit goal achievement, how can this be for those who often have clear and comprehensive rules and think in binary terms like good or bad, right or wrong, and that people regularly make decisions relatively quickly, even when anxious?

When those with generalized anxiety attempt to assess and compare each factor associated with a choice, especially on an ever-changing landscape (e.g., home prices or car models that vary yearly), they create indecision through a logistical logjam that ultimately postpones or stops movement. So why might anxiety arise?

When those who like to be in control and right don't know the correct answer (or one doesn't exist) they may suffer paralyzing doubt that prohibits them from making the wrong decision.[544] As long as they're vague and uncertain, they can arrest their movement and avoid facing the issue temporarily or permanently, as a way to protect themselves.[545] They can endlessly contemplate every aspect possible to the point of uncertainty. This "analysis paralysis" exists to elude failure, ridicule, rejection, and abandonment. For example, by not deciding whether to get a divorce or pursue improving their marriage they can maintain a predictable and non-threatening co-existence. Or, consider how anxious indecision about which university to apply, may immobilize people for so long that they overshoot the application deadline, which evades the opportunity to fail, or prevents picking the wrong university or course of study.

What's another clue that reveals symptom purposefulness?

It's when habitually driven, decisive, binary thinkers, who regularly seek solutions to problems and determinedly resolve them, are *indifferent to their uncertainty or ambiguity.* As disinterest about indecision sustains their immobility, it's necessary to examine how frozen footsteps can enable goal achievement. Yet, if immobility is part of the goal-attaining equation, then why would people voice their distress when attempting to make up their minds?

They just want to be unshackled from their aggravating symptoms. (Remember that they're unaware of why they maintain symptoms and their function.) But there's more to it.

Airing symptom intensity and the breadth of worrisome topics can publicize neurotic persons' internal torment and validate their anguish. Such communication allows advantages.

When people painstakingly deliberate they can earn respect and elevation.[546] Agonizing over details — especially when others don't — demonstrates neurotic individuals' dedication and exhaustive integrity. "The best offense is a good pretense."[547] Just envision those torn between two socially acceptable and encouraged actions, say between dating and raising their children, being loyal to their current employer or searching for a higher paying job, and how they can spend weeks, months, or years painstakingly and meticulously going over the pros and cons.

When anxious individuals grapple with seductive endeavors and emerge victorious, they can substantiate (false) virtue.[548] A drawn-out internal tug-of-war can happen with virtually anything. For example, they may weigh having an affair with an alluring individual, only to conclude undying commitment to their marriage, or they may wrestle with themselves over a tempting dessert before declining it. They may believe that the more strenuous the struggle, the more valiant the endeavor. Such actions polish and showcase their shining mettle.

Now, consider how stressful indecision may pull others in for advice (e.g., "I know you're uncertain, but medical intervention hasn't worked and it's cruel and needless to prolong suffering. It's time to pull the plug" or "Stop worrying and order the ice cream sundae"). When others make decisions they liberate neurotic persons from the liability of making the wrong choice, and perhaps the guilt feelings associated with being "bad" as well.

Have Others Break Bad News

Certain situations such as a minor car accident, stealthily accrued debt, a costly mistake on a work project, a gradual erosion of attraction, or an affair may lead to conflict, chaos, criticism, or some other undesirable result. Although some prefer to conceal the information, disclosure may be inescapable. So how might people with generalized anxiety communicate controversial news in a way that minimizes risk?

Envision an overwhelmed employee in a tense and intolerable work environment who has to report an expensive miscalculation to a boss described as erratic, explosive, and unforgiving. The employee experiences overwhelming anxiety and starts going to therapy, testifying how the work caused the anxiety and urges the therapist to request a mental health leave of absence. In this way, anxiety enables an evasion of conflict and criticism…but only temporarily.

Consider a long-suffering and symptomatic spouse whose initial love for the other has evaporated and wants to leave the marriage, but fears verbal conflict and disapproval. Anxiety can prompt marital therapy, not to revive the marriage, but rather as a means to shift the burden to the therapist for bringing up the incendiary subject of divorce. In addition, divorce can become more serious and acceptable when a licensed professional discusses it.

Some people generate a small debt then hide the bills for a considerable period, wanting to maintain their spending and avoid accountability, chaos, and conflict. However, why might they incubate an otherwise small, but friction-prone, problem until it grows into an immense issue?

As unreasonable, imperfect, and counterproductive as this appears, it's *because* it increases conflict. Think about how it's the collection agency that informs the unsuspecting spouse who has to put anger on hold while fixing the problem. *Symptoms can assist in getting others to disclose bad news or broach a conflictual subject, to save face, minimize conflict, and achieve particular outcomes.*

Blame Biology

After identifying similar symptoms among family members, unable to remember an extended time in their lives when they were at peace, or have relatives tell them that they were anxious "since birth," neurotic individuals may strongly believe that biology, genetics, or some other domestic demon conjures their anxiety. Although this appears to be a reasonable, logical, and fact-based conclusion that others substantiate, why might people arrive at and maintain this understanding when they attended only a few therapy sessions or base their judgment solely on perception rather than medical tests?

While it appears that their attempts at comprehension were negligible and their verdict premature, neurotic persons may nevertheless resolutely clutch onto and emphatically express their belief that their anxiety is inherent and interminable. This makes sense once you realize that from that perspective they release themselves from having much, if any, responsibility for their symptoms (perhaps other than taking medication, if they choose). That obligation is primarily delegated to medical doctors and psychiatrists who are regarded as responsible for "fixing" the problem and "curing" the symptoms. And if symptoms remain, then *others* are viewed an inept and inadequate. In addition, by blaming biology those with generalized anxiety portray themselves as the innocent victims of their own bodies, which may draw more sympathy and latitude. Given the belief that symptoms are genetic in origin, parents and grandparents may strive to ameliorate symptoms by providing attention, encouragement, indulgences, and assistance. Furthermore, defining symptoms as innate and uncontrollable allows them to arise freely and without an expiration date or guilt feelings. When driven persons label biology as the incorrigible culprit that generates symptoms, they can sustain a life style that perpetuates anxiety-fueled successes.

Assessing for the presence of the Anxiety Code can assist differentiating genetic or biochemical origins from personality-based ones. If symptomatic individuals don't hold the relevant personality convictions, that may indicate an organic cause.

Influence Physiology

If you dwell on an embarrassing mistake you've made in front of respected others, fearfully examine whether a blemish is a melanoma, or face a challenging, yet inescapable project, you may cringe, feel sick to your stomach, or experience other physical consequences as thoughts can influence bodily functioning — at least to the degree which bodily organs can be persuaded. With increased intensity of focus, there's a magnification of related emotions that can initiate and escalate physiological changes.

Now consider how anxious individuals can exhibit somatization (physical symptoms without a physical cause).[549] They may experience muscle tension and soreness, sweating, twitching, trembling or shaking, dry mouth, nausea, upset stomach, diarrhea, exaggerated startle response, dizziness, lightheadedness, hot and cold flushes, numbness and tingling sensations, breathing difficulties, chest tightness, chest pain, and accelerated heart rate.[550] Although anxiety can cause these physical symptoms, how else might some of them be explained?

Well, think about how neurotic persons might not dismiss a simple gaffe or imperfect, yet common bodily function (e.g., dropping an object, misspeaking) as a natural characteristic of their humanness, but rather they fear they've imperiled acceptance. While some apologize or an attempt to hide their mistake, why might others experience an *increase* in physical or physiological symptoms?

Although symptom intensification may be from anxiously reflecting on how their error negatively impacted their acceptance or sense of competency, also contemplate how this can be a protective mechanism. With that in mind, why might those who mispronounce a word immediately cough and clear their throats even though there's nothing physiological or physically wrong? To deflect liability for the error from a cognitive matter (e.g., ignorance of correct pronunciation) and place responsibility onto a more acceptable, transitory issue, perhaps one that attracts sympathy (e.g., a cold, congestion, sore throat, dehydration). *Neurotic persons may experience symptom escalation to validate their claim, and blame their physiology to protect their image.*[551] In addition, people may influence their physiology to achieve goals on the useful side of life. For example, dwelling on a concern may lead to an elevated heart rate, which prompts driven individuals to anxiously get their paperwork done on time, "I've got to finish this project before I have a heart attack!"

Organ Inferiority

Knowing that physical symptoms can be associated with anxiety and that neurotic individuals may self-protectively experience physical problems, why might they unconsciously append or exacerbate congenital physical illnesses (a.k.a. organ inferiority)?

• Anxiety-related physical symptoms (e.g., migraines, sore back, chest pain) may be more obvious, tangible, relatable, and comprehensible than psychological symptoms, therefore exempt from scrutiny.

• When others are acquainted with existing physical conditions, sympathy, empathy, adjusted expectations, and assistance may exist. Consequently, perhaps only minimal change in others' action or understanding is needed for anxiety symptoms.

• Others might be more likely to accept and validate anxiety when it's related to existing physical concerns (e.g., "I'm afraid coworkers will ridicule me if I need help lifting something [have to take a break because of my migraines, etc.]").

• Given that people can be well-versed and intimately knowledgeable about their physical affliction's genesis, mechanics, presentation, and treatment (e.g., medication, side effects, progression), they can expertly trounce concerned others' suggestions and complaints.

• Those familiar with triggers may be able to swiftly (albeit unconsciously) develop physical symptoms by dwelling on certain issues or engaging in particular behaviors, perhaps controlling symptom severity, duration, and frequency as deemed necessary.

• Physical symptoms may allow for similar or indistinguishable outcomes as psychological symptoms (e.g., withdrawal, attention, distance).

• Employing organ inferiority and anxiety simultaneously may multiply the chance of goal attainment (e.g., many reasons to be driven ["Who knows how long I'll be able to work given my physical state. I need to work hard now"], or not find employment, socialize).

• There are more symptomatic avenues to achieve objectives. For example, they may accentuate psychological symptoms with those who are more attuned and sympathetic to them or elicit physical symptoms with others who deem them more legitimate and identifiable.

• When a personal, social, economic change, for instance, nullifies the reason for anxiety (e.g., better job, income, relationship), chronic physical issues may allow indefinite goal-attaining symptoms.

Though not congenital physical illnesses, injuries may be similarly employed (e.g., "An aggravated war wound" [or worry about it] may allow an exit from participation as well as provides an acceptable image: a patriotic hero).

Blame Others

Neurotic persons often seek to protect themselves by avoiding accountability for failure, mistakes, and the like, and may blame parents, teachers, or the environment.[552] For instance, "My parents never taught me patience (how to relax, save money, etc.)," dismisses responsibility for impatient acts, attempts to make others answerable for symptoms, and casually overlooks the opportunities to learn it from various sources or teach themselves. However, also note that although criticisms may be a way to elevate neurotic individuals and lower others, those accusations should be explored as they may contain some truth.[553]

People with generalized anxiety may blame society (e.g., laws, economy), others (e.g., criminals, duplicitous friends, biased bosses, politicians), fads (e.g., video games), and so on, to justify their anxiety, control, guardedness, worry, drive, frugality, etc. Yet, there's a clue to the accuracy of such accusations. For instance, when a person has a string of bad relationships might it speak more of the person than those dated? When an individual provides a list of others (or situations) deemed responsible for undesirable outcomes or symptoms, it's necessary to examine the common factor: the symptomatic person's role.

Now, imagine a neurotic person's spouse has decided to get a divorce and starts therapy to address various concerns — including how to request a divorce in the least symptom-provoking manner. Knowing this, why might the neurotic individual obstinately blame the therapist for the divorce even though the spouse made that decision prior to starting therapy?

It evades responsibility for any role in the failure of the marriage as well as the painful admission that the spouse is no longer in love.

Believe They're Ill-fated Victims

Why might those with generalized anxiety say something similar to the following?

"I don't know why the universe is against me! There's always a crisis and I can never relax!"

"The government is set up to keep people on the dole. I'd have a job if the laws weren't so prejudicial towards those who want to earn a decent living. I can't win no matter what I do."

"I think life is telling me I shouldn't date. Everyone I meet is selfish."

"If I don't work extra hard and be super nice to everyone, something bad will happen."

First, as long as the responsibility for failure and flaws, as well as symptoms, are squarely placed on serendipity, a gender, humanity, society, god(s), or some other unassailable entity, neurotic individuals skirt accountability for failure and justify how they cannot resolve the problem, which liberates them from action that risks failure, rejection, ridicule, or abandonment.

Second, what may be gained by identifying some large and faceless power, such as the Fates or formidable government agencies, as ruthlessly targeting neurotic persons?

As these forces are nebulous and uncontrollable, there's little or no avenue of recourse. Consequently, this mindset perpetuates symptoms. Additionally, people can take on greater significance when they portray themselves as the subject of these powerful constructs. After all, god(s), government, or some other immense and impressive entity has singled them out.

Third, neurotically anxious persons can imply they have a natural aptitude, an inborn capacity, but some cosmic cruelty or nefarious force villainously restricts them from growing to their full height. This may allow them to claim abilities without demonstrating them.

Fourth, by believing they're ill-fated victims, they can authorize their drive (perfectionism, goodness, control, etc.) on the useful side of life. For example, they believe they have to work industriously to overcome otherwise insurmountable hurdles, or they may perceive a biological link to family members' health problems which may not be genetic (e.g., obesity), but this belief allows them to rationalize obeying a strict diet and prompts dedicated exercise.

Lost Opportunity at Greatness

Some neurotic persons believe they've missed pivotal opportunities to be successful, generally or in one specific arena. When they say, "Only if someone gave me…" or "If only my parents…" they imply how life would be much better than it is right now, but they have missed the opportunity to attain success and prominence.[554] For example,

"I used to be phenomenal at math and could have been an accountant, but my school didn't offer that program. Now I'm stuck in a mediocre job and I'll never be an accountant!"

"My spouse has been nothing but mean and selfish. I want to get a divorce but I can't! I'm too old to get remarried and I don't want to die alone. The best years of my life are behind me."

"If only I had gone to Harvard I could have been running this company. Now I have to work my way up the corporation by working harder than everyone else."

So why might people with generalized anxiety hold the above perspectives?

First, it provides a historical account that explains current undesirable circumstances. Second, they can place responsibility for direction and action onto others, which severs their connection to a wrong choice, and can blame those whose advice they solicited. Third, as the deadline has passed, they're protectively prohibited from trying again (and possibly failing) and have an excuse as to why they cannot be successful in the future. Fourth, claiming a lost opportunity can fortify and galvanize their life style and make it mandatory to act in a certain way (e.g., driven, perfectionistic).

Revenge

Only symptomatic persons can fully experience their symptoms. Simply, no one else — including the most empathetic — can register 100% of what neurotic individuals endure. However, despite their notable suffering, why might those with generalized anxiety state their symptoms most negatively impact others, rather than themselves?

You might guess that it's part of neurotically anxious individuals' compassion that would allow them to be good people who are particularly sensitive to how their symptoms adversely affect others. However, the following examples hint at another answer:

"My symptoms have been so intense that my spouse had to cancel two vacations and lost the deposit on the hotel and the airfare. I'm sure that wasn't easy to handle. I feel terrible about that."

"I get so anxious on a plane that my boss has to send one of my coworkers on all out of town meetings. That's awfully unfair."

"I've been living at my parents' house when I should have been working all of these years. I know they're burning through their retirement savings. I feel so much guilt for that."

Such thoughtful responses and acknowledging others' distress demonstrates virtue and may avoid conflict. Yet, how might you perceive those sweet and sensitive statements if you found out the following?

• The spouse needlessly, yet strictly controlled financial expenditures.

• The coworker burdened with additional travel regularly annoys the symptomatic person.

• The retired parents have been critical and favored the anxious individual's siblings.

Like an optical illusion seen from a different perspective, one uncanny perception vanishes as a more authentic one takes its place. *Comprehension may be achieved quicker when healthcare practitioners examine at what or whom are the symptoms targeted.*[555] The answer to the question, "Who *else* is suffering because of these symptoms?" can be enlightening. Identifying one or more symptom targets, be it an individual, the opposite sex, an employer, or society, substantiates the psychology of use perspective and validates symptoms' social component and how they're used for a future objective rather than existing as an outcome of a previous experience.[556]

Symptoms can be unconsciously wielded as a way to retaliate for actual or misperceived injustices. For instance, there are patients who get upset when practitioners do not say or do what the patients want, or if they're unhappy with valid testing results. Rather than ponder clinical observations and suggestions or test data, some may contemplate retaliating against their healthcare providers, say by anonymously posting vitriolic comments online or making false reports to insurance companies or licensing boards. People who employ symptoms to take revenge are markedly discouraged, believing there are no other means to attain their goals.[557]

But there's one thing to resolve: If people revengefully employ symptoms, are their empathic feelings (among others) false?

No, as they may be unaware of how they use their symptoms to achieve goals. Accordingly, they express authentic sympathy, sadness, worry, guilt feelings, etc. for how their symptoms ruin others' plans, burden them with extra work, are a financial liability, require that others monitor them, take on chores, change plans, and so forth.

Reduce Drive and Goodness

The Anxiety Code can allow innumerable agreeable, commendable, and practical qualities that enable significance and benefit others. For example, those with generalized anxiety can be humorous, capable, responsible, attentive, trustworthy, moral, altruistic, compassionate, and industrious. Although their anxiety can fuel action when others relax or shy away from such efforts, why might it magnify to the point of incapacitating neurotic individuals from displaying those aforementioned characteristics?

Well, imagine others who profit from neurotic persons' efforts, but take those behaviors for granted, fail to acknowledge their work or results, dismiss their value, do not reciprocate acts of kindness and diligence, or in some other way do things that are unacceptable, critical, or exploitive. Indeed, while not being recognized, appreciated, or having their actions paralleled in some form (e.g., fair division of labor at home), can produce anxiety, say by leading neurotic individuals to doubt their worth or way of thinking, greater comprehension comes from searching for symptom purpose.

Those with generalized anxiety may be intimately familiar with how they believe things should be and how people should act. However, when others do not act as anticipated, neurotic persons may experience frustration, disappointment, and anger. Consider the Stoplight conflict. On the one hand, neurotic individuals could control the situation by using anger to gain compliance, yet some actively avoid an aggressive posture, as that would violate the need to be good and spark chaos and confrontation. On the other hand, they could adhere to the need to be good conviction and silence their rebuke, but that gives others control and perpetuates an undesirable condition. So how might symptoms achieve one or more goals in such situations?

First, anxiety can limit or prohibit people pleasing efforts, exertion, and compassion, among other commendable acts. As people notice when things don't get completed, or done well, anxiety-impeded actions draw attention to neurotic persons' importance and value. This compensates for when those beneficial actions and personality characteristics went unnoticed and unappreciated. Anxiety-based withdrawal can indirectly communicate things such as disapproval, disappointment, annoyance, and hurt.

Second, others may develop guilt feelings and make amends. For example, "I'm sorry I never realized how much you did. I'll never take you for granted again. How can I make it up to you?"

Third, if neurotically anxious individuals determine that their efforts won't be acknowledged, valued, or reciprocated, why would they continue to exert themselves? Symptoms can stop self-sacrificing, arduous endeavors when there isn't a benefit.

Fourth, by framing anxiety as the reason for withdrawal, neurotic persons can escape exploitive, conflictual, or rude people without violating their need to be good or in control. This avoids direct confrontation or disobedience and may control how people perceive them.

Fifth, given the unconscious aspect of neurotic symptoms, those with generalized anxiety can simultaneously stop their beneficial acts and plead for a return to their previous functioning. This protectively maintains an image of good intentions and integrity (not laziness, vindictiveness, or pettiness, for example) and cast symptoms as the undesirable obstacle, the unpredictable and uncontrollable saboteur of their noble desires.

Sixth, symptom-fueled retreat may punish others who must compensate for this withdrawal and face additional responsibilities (e.g., shop, watch the kids more often, do the laundry, go to events alone).

Exploit Reciprocity

Why might neurotic persons broadcast how distressed they are, yet instead of resting they voluntarily do some kind action for others, perhaps one that's needless or one someone else could have easily done (e.g., go to the store, mow a neighbor's lawn, or do a coworker's filing)? While the action is in accord with being good and driven, and perhaps they're merely voicing their fatigue or calling attention to their self-sacrifice, there's something else to consider.

Envision someone living at the poverty line (e.g., an unemployed or underemployed individual, a psychology graduate student) gave you a gift that took a long time to afford. Besides being appreciative, flattered, and honored, you would understandably be impressed with the gift's *relative* value — the financial toll given the person's near destitution. Therefore, might you reciprocate with a present that's not equal in price, but one that costs more and is proportionate to your (higher) income? Probably so.

Now, consider how being the first to display effort may gain others' compliance by reciprocity. For instance, envision two people having lunch at a Mexican restaurant and one says to the other, "I promise I won't dip my chip into the salsa after I eat part of the chip. I wouldn't want you to consume all the bacteria in my mouth. That would be inconsiderate of me." This prompts the same behavior from the other person without stating it. Now picture those who do a kind deed while overwhelmed with symptoms…and later indirectly, yet repeatedly, express their need for a babysitter over the weekend. *Symptomatic persons may do something for others with the unconscious anticipation they'll pay back the effort, perhaps with interest.*

Rightness, Orderliness, and Self-restraint

When some neurotic individuals are asked what they want to control, they blurt, "Everything!", often with a swift subsequent smile that confesses their realization of how their desire is unreasonably massive. While they want control of everything (or most things), they're certain they cannot, yet find it nearly impossible to relinquish their craving. So what might be their solution?

They selectively find competency, predictability, and stability in being right, orderliness, and what they can control.[558] Unable to control life or others, they may concentrate on controlling themselves as a substitute. They elect to be an expert on some narrow matter or specialized field (e.g., economics, housekeeping), controlling some fraction of their existence (e.g., budgeting, clean house), or by being punctual or systematic.[559] By making themselves experts or controlling a particular area of functioning, others may let them take charge. Note that neurotically anxious individuals may employ their knowledge and efforts on either the useful or useless side of life.

Focusing on a limited domain allows them to self-assuredly state that they have an eye for detail, but they have a telling blind spot. By attending to specific items they can make their world relatively insular and avoid what they perceive as frighteningly chaotic, complex, uncontrollable, and unpredictable.

By attending to controllable areas and functions, they're able to predict the result of some action, be effective, and avoid what's otherwise unbearable to contemplate, or might imperil status, self-esteem, and life style. Symptoms before or when situations become uncontrollable may liberate them from self-imposed, yet imprisoning obligations. For instance, symptoms may allow spending money, relaxing, or something else that was previously prohibited.

Some people refuse to express their thoughts and feelings, dance, drink alcohol, take drugs, or act in any way they fear might lead to a loss of control or invite shameful behavior that uncontrollably lives on, say when people recall it at will or post it online. They can take pride in their emotional, cognitive, or physical fortitude, ability to overcome obstacles, persistence through hardship and mistreatment, or ability to withstand situations that others avoid or concede defeat. They may never complain, and use this to demonstrate their mettle or significance. They can derive strength from their endurance and resilience, believing that a loss of control equals unacceptable weakness or failure. For example, "I'll *never* let them know they got under my skin. I wouldn't give them the satisfaction."

Callousness

It's common for patients cry in therapy. Indeed, it can be tremendously healthy to do so.[560] Yet, why would neurotically anxious individuals say something similar to (well, to be honest, it's usually this sentence verbatim), "I *promised* myself that I wouldn't cry"?

People prohibit themselves from crying to avoid a flood of tears (e.g., "I'm afraid that if I start crying, I'll never stop"). Interestingly, those who control their emotions may demonstrate an unshed tear when they reflexively wipe underneath their eye, as if they shed an actual tear. This reluctance to cry takes on greater meaning once you factor in the importance of social functioning.

Those who prevent themselves from crying when it's acceptable and encouraged (e.g., at their wedding, the birth of their child, a funeral) can risk appearing indifferent, cold-hearted, and emotionally bankrupt. So, how might they protectively reframe their actions?

They may say, "I need to be strong for others." Men are often reluctant to cry if they were taught that a "Real man" doesn't show emotion (other than anger). This is the "game face" or "business face" mentality that's often — and erroneously — deemed a sign of strength. Women also maintain this mindset, though seemingly less often. Some fear that if they cried others will think ill of them, so by not crying they vainly attempt to control how people may judge them (e.g., "I don't want others to think that I'm weak"). In this way, being callous is an attempt to control for negative judgment as well as the terrifying sense of powerlessness. However, people may merely postpone expressing their emotions until they're in isolated environments, such as while driving by themselves at night, in their bedrooms, or bathrooms (say weeping in the shower to conceal their emotions). Also, callousness can be a way to avoid being hurt. For example, when people aren't fully invested in a relationship, there isn't much to lose if it fails. Sadly, by curbing their emotions, people erode their connections with others and limit the amount of enjoyment they can derive from life.

Remain Quiet

Patients can be particularly quiet in session and perhaps declare they "can't remember anything" or regularly respond with a suspiciously terse "I don't know" to nearly every question. Some are selectively silent, say expressing thoughts about an event and not their feelings or vice versa. Often, people may discuss one situation but be curiously quiet on a somewhat similar other. Although some believe anxiety causes their silence, what might remaining quiet enable?

Although it can waste their time and money as well as perpetuate painful symptoms, it allows them to avoid expressing fears, flaws, and mistakes or change their ways of thinking and acting. Undiscussed matters cannot be critiqued. Fair enough, but what else may be going on?

Well, imagine loving, but exasperated spouses who strongly urge therapy for their symptomatic partners who don't want to go, but eventually do so reluctantly. By remaining quiet in treatment they appear to their spouses as invested in change and get credit for going to therapy, which gives the impression of being good and can avoid conflict. Passively rebelling by remaining quiet can control the amount of information given in a way that minimizes risk to being good, especially if silence is attributed to anxiety or poor memory. If loved ones are paying for treatment, the passive aggressive element increases. Yet, how do they explain their lack of therapeutic success?

Due to the unconscious process involved, as well as various risks, they cannot confess to thwarting the process. Rather, they may say, "I go to therapy every week, so it must be that the therapist is ineffective," "Therapy isn't working," "My anxiety must be genetic," or "My symptoms are too severe." As others can attest to the attendance record, yet not in session to see the still silence, they give such statements credence. However, this is like going to the gym, not working out, and then blaming the personal trainer for the lack of progress.

Circumlocution

What might happen when neurotic persons are asked questions that imperil self-esteem, acceptance, status, or their life style, yet evading the topic entirely risks the same result?

As outright avoidance may suggest responsibility for something unacceptable and worsen the situation (perhaps more than a truthful response), they may anxiously talk around the subject, never quite answering the question, but not fully backing down from it. Others may gracefully retract their questioning or be distracted, lowering the possibility for an undesirable outcome. (Indeed, when patients know an honest answer might shatter their defenses or prompt action they wish to avoid, they may talk around the topic rather than address it.)

Use Intellect to Evade Risk

How might neurotic persons handle situations when they don't know the right answer, and perceive displayed ignorance just as undesirable as being wrong?

They can use their intellect to guide it; for instance, by providing an answer to a seemingly related question or corralling the discussion into a field they know well.[561] In doing so, they can achieve two objectives. First, they deftly sidestep an area that would expose ignorance. Second, they showcase their intelligence. Also, consider how a black-and-white question can be morphed into a gray philosophical dialogue. For example, the question, "Who is the President of Germany?" might be parried with a philosophical query, "Wouldn't you say that the Chancellor of Germany or even the bourgeois is ultimately in charge of the country?" Answering a question with a question may effectively misdirect others. But what's another way in which people may use intellect to evade risk?

Any loss of control can be frightening to those who want an unhealthy amount of it. Now recall how one popular fear of those who like to be in control is the loss of psychological control, including the loss of control of their emotions. Therefore, neurotic persons may view life in mechanistic terms. Rather than express their feelings, they reflexively state facts and thoughts as a way to prevent a loss of emotional control, utterly unaware of doing so. (When I ask patients to describe their feelings about an event, sometimes they give a factual report. For instance, "The weather was sunny and warm. There were a lot of people there and many things to do." Tellingly, they genuinely believe that was an appropriate response to the question.)

When patients are encouraged to reduce the intensity and number of ways they exercise control by replacing many rules with a simpler and more flexible one, say "Do things randomly (e.g., try a restaurant that's unfamiliar to them, try a new meal)," they may respond, "Aren't I just controlling my control," or "Isn't doing things randomly just another rule?" This intellectual examination and rationale can reflect their reluctance to modify their convictions.

Vanity

Given humanity's vital need for interdependence as well as the unequalled joy of interaction, people seek acceptance — a virtually irresistible invigorating, reassuring, gratifying, and peaceful validation of worth and relatedness to others. However, what's the prerequisite?

Genuine acceptance and appreciation requires attention, interaction, and vulnerability (as they allow others complete assessment), as well as a demonstration of acceptable behavior, emotion, and thought (the acceptance criteria). Also, think about how — given the universality of human imperfection — a transparent and truthful presentation demands disclosing flaws and failures. Accordingly, people must summon the courage to progressively reveal themselves with the hope of others' allowance of certain quirks, mistakes, and differences. This process can be unnerving for anyone, and extraordinarily so for neurotic individuals. Knowing that, how might they strive to attain a sense of acceptance without exposing flaws and failures?

A clue is found in common teenage behavior. This isn't to say that teenagers are neurotic, but by using a prominent and familiar developmental stage you have a starting point for grasping another neurotic characteristic. Teenagers can be intensely aware of their appearance, spending countless hours in front of the mirror, or frequently and passionately communicating what actions, clothes, music, movies, apps, books, and people are acceptable, desirable, or enviable as well as what's unacceptable and should be avoided. They amass a strong and comprehensive understanding of what's valued, becoming finely familiar and fluent with permissible or praiseworthy presentation to the point of being able to sketch a detailed treasure map of acceptance. And keep in mind how as teenagers haven't achieved proficiency in a number of areas they may — similar to neurotic persons — have low self-esteem, which presents certain difficulties.

When teenagers don't accept themselves they can irresistibly seek others' acceptance, prize others' beliefs and perceptions, and fervently attempt to live up to others' values and preferences rather than their own. Accordingly, they may perpetually assess what the group or subgroup (e.g., peers, sorority, fraternity, teammates) cherish as well as compelled to assimilate, accommodate, and comply with others' rules, expectations, values, and actions. Knowing this, what are the related distinct and prominent challenges?

First, given the instability of fads and fashions, definitions can be exasperatingly fluid. Consequently, teenagers need to be continually sensitive to changes in routinely transforming trends.

Second, they have to persistently monitor and evaluate their compliance with what's acceptable and need a mechanism that signals when they've made any divergent and socially treacherous steps.

Third, they have to assess others' words and actions that convey acceptance or rejection.

Fourth, they would need to swiftly take corrective action such as increase compliance, recover from a misstep, or retreat from a threatening situation.

Fifth, teenagers might denigrate those considered unacceptable (the out-group). This allows them to self-elevate, fortify their bond to the in-group by reaffirming common goals and life style convictions, as well as emphasize the boundary between groups, which bolsters in-group acceptance by increasing between-group differences.

So what does the preceding describe?

Vanity, a well-honed understanding of what's socially acceptable as well as keen vigilance of one's appearance (perhaps to the extent of excessive and unjustified pride). Such teenage circumstances, mindset, behavior, and innate difficulties approximately illustrate a defining neurotic characteristic. At first, you might say that vanity is unbecoming and would counterproductively imperil acceptance, yet why might neurotic persons be vain and how might anxiety be usefully related?

While they're often reluctant to be vulnerable and display their flaws or errors, they don't give up their goal of social approval and maintaining or building self-esteem. They may not accept themselves, so they value and seek others' acceptance. With an increased threat to neurotic persons' vanity there's an amplified attempt to avoid that danger.[562] Accordingly, they may be relentlessly driven to determine what's acceptable and comply with socially-defined rules and goals. To prevent dangerous deviation, they may intensely and anxiously scrutinize their compliance as well as mercilessly reprimand themselves for mistakes. However, what are the associated challenges?

• The instability of what's acceptable requires constant monitoring.

• They must continually assess their compliance with what's socially allowable and adapt.

• Neurotic individuals have to attend to and gauge others' actions and reactions.

• They require feedback when they diverge from what's acceptable.

• Neurotic persons may need to retreat from situations or people who imperil acceptance, status, and self-esteem, and swiftly recover if they expose something that jeopardizes worth.

Once you recognize how the above requires an ocean of effort, you can see anxiety's relevance. It provides the energy to identify and adapt to what's desirable, sustain extensive assessments of self and others, empower obedience to what's acceptable by being part of a feedback mechanism when neurotic individuals stray from it, as well as energize avoidance, retreat, and recovery from that which imperils self-esteem, status, and their styles of living.

Vanity can include disparaging comments, which serves two functions. Neurotically vain persons may elevate themselves by sharply criticizing others, often with skill honed by years of practice.[563] (Indeed, some patients can deftly and tactically wield a sharp tongue that cuts others down with military precision.) This may also bond them to the in-group and distance the unacceptable out-group.[564] Yet, no matter how hard neurotic individuals attempt to balance the scales, they may perpetually feel inferior.[565]

Note that as what's acceptable may vary, any peace achieved through vain compliance is short-lived. Relatedly, anxiety-fueled vigilance for change concurrently erodes or prohibits a sense of peace. After all, how could anyone be serene when there's an undercurrent of anxiety and the continual risk of an unpredictable shift in knowledge that turns the tides of what's acceptable?

Paradoxically, neurotic vanity endangers what it attempts to protect. Although it may be a means to acceptance, it ultimately creates a dilemma: authentic acceptance is impossible without sufficient vulnerability. Also, when neurotic persons vainly retreat from particular areas of functioning (e.g., working, socializing, dating) where they expect others to participate, they demonstrate how they want exemption from common rules.[566] This double standard risks rejection and ridicule. Sometimes, those with generalized anxiety may use vanity not to be liked, but merely to avoid being disliked.

Unconscious Employment

People may experience frustration and unnerving tension when they're unable to determine why their symptoms occur, when they could erupt, how long they'll last, or their severity. With that in mind, how might the unconscious aspects of neurotic anxiety play a prominent role in perpetuating that unsettling state?

Imagine that to avoid negative judgment, an anxious parent wants to keep the house clean before guests arrive. However, there's something that prohibits this: children playing in the living room who are making a mess and resistant to stopping their play and cleaning up. The parent gets increasingly nervous as the clock inches toward the time of the guests' arrival. And, after asking nicely repeatedly without compliance, eventually gets angry and uses harsh words, loud volume, and not-so-subtle threats to have the children clean up. This should immediately strike you as an apparent violation of the need to be good. However, the parent states that symptom intensity, tone of voice, and threats did not register until afterward, and sincerely apologized the next morning. Knowing this, you must ask the following:

• Why might the parent be unaware of symptom development until after anger emerged?

• How can such behavior exist when it appears to violate a life style conviction?

• Why might genuine repentance occur after symptom flare up?

Sometimes those with generalized anxiety will say they "just snapped" and their symptoms were instant and irrepressible, and they were essentially unaware (therefore powerless) of their mood that stealthily and quickly overcame them. However, often anger wells up over time — as it did in the example. Knowing this, how might identifying goals assist in explaining symptoms?

Recognize that the kids' mess risked eliciting visitors' negative judgment, something the parent strongly wished to avoid. Dwelling on that negative outcome coupled with the children's misbehavior gradually generated and legitimized anger, which initiated and fuelled direct orders and yelling to prompt compliance. But how did the parent avoid violating the need to be good?

By being unaware of symptom buildup and action. Blissful obliviousness about the otherwise unacceptable behavior never flouts the need to be good conviction and simultaneously grants the parent freedom to act without the slightest qualms.[567] If the parent were aware of using anger to bully the children into compliance to protect status, then the anger may not have been generated or it would have been quickly extinguished. (However, bearing in mind goal orientation and symptom substitution, the parent may have used another tactic, say distraction, compliments, or bribes to achieve the same result.) By having the objective as well as symptom escalation remain unconscious, the subsequent guilt feelings are genuine. Yet if that's the case, then why does a moral sense of impropriety remain asleep throughout the night and not wake until the following morning?

Well, if it happened prior to the anger flare up, or in the midst of anger, it would imperil the goal of achieving compliance. Therefore, awareness does not arise until *after* the children change their behavior, and the postscript apology fortifies a sense of goodness (e.g., responsibility, remorse, reassuring the children). When life style convictions (e.g., the need to be good) prohibit goal-achieving emotion and action (e.g., anger, yelling), people may not relinquish their objective or means, but do what's otherwise forbidden without violating their convictions *from their perspective*. (Think of dieting individuals who eat mindlessly, or don't pay attention to the nutrition label or recommended serving size of the seductive foods they consume. Such inattention allows them to guiltlessly violate their self-imposed restrictions and fulfill their desires — to metaphorically have their colorful and calorie-dense cake and eat it too.)

Neurotic persons often camouflage or veil their actions; therefore, they're unable to perceive how their anxiety rises.[568] They need not be aware of their objectives or the psychodynamic mechanisms they use, they arrive at their goals all the same.[569] To protect their self-esteem and avoid accountability for socially unacceptable behavior, they employ symptoms unconsciously, and are unaware of their purpose.[570] They achieve their goals, while granting themselves personal clemency and, in some cases, attempting to achieve social amnesty. What's so captivating isn't that they're unaware of their symptoms' purpose, but rather how they *need to be* or face personal and social sanctions.[571]

It's also important to recognize how neurotic symptoms can also be unconsciously employed to attain altruistic goals. For example, people may unconsciously work up the anxiety that fuels their success at work, or exhausted parents can become increasingly and disproportionately alarmed about their children's long-term health and financial well being, which energizes them to make a well-balanced and nourishing dinner, remind the kids to brush their teeth, and have vitality to go over their homework. However, the unconscious aspects and deployment are, at best, only partial solutions. They imperfectly address a situation and can perpetuate symptoms (e.g., people remain frustrated and unnerved by being unable to resolve why their symptoms occur, when they could arise, why they exist, their duration or intensity).

Shyness

People with generalized anxiety may say that they want to make friends and socialize, but indelibly label themselves as shy and conceptualize their shyness as a nonnegotiable genetic hand-me-down or an eternally insurmountable biological obstacle to their stated desires. They make statements such as, "My parents are shy and I've always been shy. It will forever stop me from doing what I want." Yet, how could shyness be a veiled means of goal achievement?

At least initially in life, people want to be social. Alas, those who endure painful experiences may later avoid or completely renounce any opportunities or interest in socializing. But what about those with undeveloped social skills or formidable inferiority feelings who are determined to socialize, but agonizingly fear failure, ridicule, rejection, and abandonment?

Shyness can enable evasion while maintaining a more acceptable veneer of wanting to be social. This controls emotional hurt (allowing protection through distance) as well as others' opinions (by demonstrating socially-acceptable desires). Shyness can protectively limit socializing (e.g., stopping action, moving away) depending on the goal and assessed danger level. *Shyness is a form of control.*[572]

Sadly, if people forfeit pursuing socializing long enough they live reclusively. Interestingly, although some regularly bemoan their shyness and wished it vanished, it can be maintained because of its benefits. But there's one advantage you perhaps haven't considered: Could shyness facilitate socializing?

Consider how thoughtful others can see how their shy friends are distraught and frustrated then compassionately act on their behalf, say as a social liaison and set up a date. Or, neurotic individuals may use something as minimal as eye contact or a subtle smile to coax others to come to them without wagering anything more than a glance. Shyness can prompt others to increase their vulnerability while keeping neurotically anxious persons comparatively safe.

Resistant to Control

Why might those with generalized anxiety exhibit the following?

• Be so anxious they erode their ability to attend to another person.

• Despite given explicit directions, repeatedly do a task incorrectly.

• Regularly run behind schedule (e.g., show up late, not pay bills on time).

• Be so distracted they forget to do something (e.g., not pick up someone from the airport).

While your first thought might be that anxiety symptoms create such outcomes, it may be more advantageous for you to investigate the need to be in control. Sure, it urges domination, but what's the relevant obverse corollary?

Those who need to be in control are supremely reluctant to be controlled. Yet, there are inescapable times when others (e.g., supervisor, various officials) pull the strings — or social conventions prompt particular behavior (e.g., arrive on time to a wedding). So how could neurotic persons exert control in those situations?

Reflect on how in puppeteering lifting the string that's attached to a marionette's right arm will raise it. An individual who rebels against control may behave like a puppet that raises the left arm when the string to the right arm is pulled, and becomes a "reverse puppet."[573] In other words, those who need to be in control can have indirect incarnations of control when they rebel.

First, they sidestep others' control. Second, they get to control themselves (e.g., create situations and anxiety that lead them to be late). Third, they can control others behaviorally (e.g., make others wait,[574] have them take over some chore), financially (e.g., have others expend money on redoing a job), socially (e.g., a couple's tardy arrival at the spouse's important office event), and emotionally (e.g., provoke frustration and anger).

Interestingly, though rebellion appears to jeopardize acceptance and status, how might it be employed to elevate both?

Well, consider how defiance can allow achievements on the useful side of life; say protesting oppression, defying a discouraging and critical parent, or campaigning against unhealthy practices. This can elevate status and augment acceptance. But there's another social factor in this equation. How can rebellious individuals maintain control when social prohibitions, ridicule, and rejection threaten self-esteem, acceptance, status, and life style, as well as symptom use?

They may blame their symptoms (e.g., "My anxiety made me get up and say something," "My symptoms are too overwhelming for me to go on that trip with you"). This reduces or prohibits their accountability for defiance and passive-aggressive acts. In addition, when people depict their symptoms as uncontrollable and undesirable, others may view neurotic individuals as having good intentions, but at the mercy of their minds and bodies. Consequently, other people may be more apt to tolerate symptoms, which can enable their continued unconscious deployment.

Another common tactic to minimize disapproval while maintaining symptoms is apologizing for unchanging behavior...but this can only be used a limited number of times. For instance, those who run behind schedule and make people late may habitually and reflexively say, "I'm sorry." As you can imagine, when this occurs repeatedly, the apology is shown to be insincere. It exists to control others' perceptions.

Interestingly, when might being a reverse puppet be self-defeating, multiply symptoms, and erode power?

If people obediently believe they *must do the opposite* of another's direction, what happens when others' instructions coincide with neurotic persons' interests? For instance, if the spouse of an extremely tired neurotic individual suggests that it's time to go to bed, does the person remain awake just to rebel?

Relatedly, why might neurotic persons avoid the following?

1. Flying.

2. Driving on the thruway or on a long bridge.

3. An MRI exam.

4. An escalator.

5. An important or mandatory work meeting.

They may refrain from flying because they're not in control of the plane. Also, consider how as soon as the airplane door shuts, their movement is unnervingly limited, and they're unable to leave when they want (some fear panicking uncontrollably in front of others, which they believe invites negative judgment). Relatedly, those with generalized anxiety may not go on the thruway or a long bridge, as they cannot exit either at will. Some avoid the thruway because they don't want to be forced to make a decision quickly when merging into traffic as the onramp is ending. Also, people may avoid a claustrophobic MRI machine, being forced to time their step onto an escalator, or meetings they cannot leave without conflict, embarrassment, or jeopardizing their employment. (Sometimes, moments prior to the end of a therapy session, patients may display a spike in symptoms, ask a long-winded question, or make a dramatic statement, to be in charge of session length, rather than let it dictate their actions.) *Those who need to be in control can fear and rebel against situations, inanimate objects, or rules that limit or control them.* Interestingly, why might neurotically anxious individuals not like receiving gifts? They dislike being indebted in any way to others (e.g., they are obliquely urged to return the favor), and they may feel controlled as they're socially prompted to act happy and grateful.

"Yes, but..."

What's occurring in the following illustrations?

Patient: "I really need a job. I hate being unemployed."

Therapist: "They're hiring at the supermarket down the road."

Patient: "Yes, but I'm far too anxious to be able to work full time. I'll never be able to focus and I'll cost them money. They'll eventually fire me."

Patient: "I'm desperate to start dating again, but I won't find anyone at a bar."

Therapist: "Have you thought about online dating?"

Patient: "Yes, but I don't trust people who market themselves online."

Therapist: "How about volunteering where you can meet others?"

Patient: "Yes I could do that, but they're all strangers and I wouldn't feel comfortable."

These are examples of the neurotic "Yes, but...", a construction that realizes two goals. First, the "Yes" displays awareness of acceptable action as well as good intentions — which couldn't occur if the recommendations were immediately dismissed. Second, the "but..." *justifies rejecting the action just acknowledged as the correct thing to do.*[575] It's a rationalization that enables the safeguarding excuse to persist. (As an insightful patient confessed, "Everything after the 'but' is bull$#!+.")

Compassionate others may provide multiple suggestions, but become frustrated when neurotic persons furnish objections to each. *The "Yes, but..." skillfully sidesteps solutions people say they want, yet are reluctant or disinterested to do.*[576] People may thwart others' attempts to resolve the problem and eliminate symptoms because that would erase their perception of significance and prod them to meet the life tasks directly.[577] When others work harder than neurotic individuals on solving problems, it reveals symptom purposefulness and unconscious symptom maintenance.

So how might "Yes, but..." be used on the useful side of life?

Those with generalized anxiety may defend beneficial, yet unnecessary action. For instance, "Yes, I could skip exercising today (not decorate the house with countless Christmas lights, get my kids burgers and fries for lunch), but that wouldn't be healthy for me (nice to the neighbors, good for the kids)."

Sensitivity

Neurotic persons may be sensitive to innumerable matters such as socializing, relinquishing control, facing fears, getting a job, being vulnerable, admitting mistakes, talking about feelings, sex, or past lovers. Though some interpret sensitivity as a sign of unacceptable frailness, defensiveness, touchiness, suspiciousness, etc., what might be some benefits that explain its presence?

Increase Vigilance and Protective Action

Sensitivity is an element of inferiority feelings that can create intensified emotion.[578] So, why is this important?

Well, consider how being sensitive allows a heightened state of alertness and readiness for action. Now add in how emotions fuel behavior and you realize how high emotionality enables swift and determined action. For instance, increased sensitivity may allow quicker assessment when others enter a threatening realm of discussion and can facilitate faster responses when delicate matters are mentioned.

Sensitivity can be proactive as well as reactive. For example, people with generalized anxiety can be vigilant of what might irritate or disappoint others and take action prior to the opportunity for conflict or ridicule to arise. *Sensitivity and impulsiveness prompt people to find and perpetuate conditions in which their prestige is not imperiled.*[579]

Although stressful and symptom generating, think about how neurotic sensitivity can have beneficial outcomes, such as being an attentive new parent who constantly monitors and dramatically protects a newborn at the slightest hint of the child's distress. When the child is found to be well or if a problem is discovered and resolved, the resultant relieved tension reinforces sensitivity. Those with generalized anxiety can be sensitive to others' feelings, the mood of the room, etc., which allows rapid awareness and helpful reponse — but often with a symptomatic cost. For instance, vigilant parents may lose many hours of sleep as the attentively listen to the baby monitor for even the slightest hints of their child's distress.

Retreat

Just like you might protectively back away from foods or allergens to which you're sensitive, neurotic persons can be sensitive to matters and situations they deem dangerous and distance themselves. Alas, regular retreat can erode self-esteem, status, and acceptance. Also, if they progressively withdraw from life's challenges and label more situations overwhelming and threatening, they perpetuate and increase anxiety.

Control Others

Consider how compassionate people attempt to accommodate and care for those sensitive to things such as their child's death or a recent divorce. Knowing this, why might those with generalized anxiety experience symptom flare up when concerned others prompt them to take action that's beneficial, but not desired?

For example,

"It hurts me so much when you leave job openings on the table for me to read."

"I'm still heartbroken from when you didn't do much for my birthday last year."

"You're so cruel! If you knew the stress I endure you wouldn't even suggest what you did!"

Expressing sensitivity or "playing the hurt feelings card" halts others' suggestions, questions, and prodding, as they mercifully desist from pressing subjects that neurotic individuals want to avoid. Those with generalized anxiety may depict those who don't stop as callous bullies and themselves as innocent victims. Sensitivity can be proactive — like crying before the hurt, or a symptomatic shot across the bow, which gets others to back down. Unfortunately, continued avoidance prohibits or reduces the probability of accepting corrective feedback and further sinks self-esteem and capsizes social connections. Sensitivity can also prompt others to take action for neurotic persons (e.g., returning items to the store on behalf of those sensitive to conflict or easily embarrassed) or coax others to compensate for their accused insensitivity.

Indifference and Depression

Why might neurotic persons be utterly indifferent to immediate, legitimate, and inescapable matters that would otherwise spark tension, such as a cheating spouse who contracts a sexually transmitted infection or a favored child who gets arrested for drug possession?

If action would endanger one or more goals, then it may be suppressed or overridden. For example, those who wish to remain married and avoid moving out of their house and return to dating, might overlook their spouses' sexual indiscretions, and those who don't want to acknowledge their parenting flaws or their children's misbehavior may be unconcerned. *Given that emotions can fuel behavior and prioritize matters, indifference and depressive symptoms can arise and drain the emotional reservoir and de-emphasize those things neurotic individuals wish to ignore or not act upon.*

Relatedly, some discouraged, overwhelmed, or timid individuals state that this life is merely a temporary one — the opening act to the tremendous afterlife show that endlessly follows. This has a revealing corollary.

By minimizing the importance of present functioning and achievements, they become indifferent to them. Some imply that they can just coast through this life to reap the benefits of the next. This legitimizes their immobility and allows them to dismiss opportunities to face life's endeavors that pose the possibility of failure, rejection, ridicule, and abandonment.

Indirect Boasting

Given that those with the need to be driven can be high achievers, and those that need to be good may wish to avoid appearing as self-aggrandizing, how might anxiety and depressive symptoms allow them to obliquely brag about their accomplishments and superiority?

They may mournfully state they're without challenges within a specific arena because they conquered it (perhaps hinting they could do even more if given the opportunity). For example, "I used to really enjoy exercising, but after winning a few triathlons it just isn't interesting now. I'm anxious to try something new, but it's sad and unsettling that nothing else can take its place or is as challenging."

Move Toward Others

Perhaps unsurprisingly, driven patients are motivated to efficiently and effectively resolve their symptoms. Knowing that, why might they set an unrealistically ambitious treatment deadline?

While their self-imposed deadline unveils how long they want to take to achieve their goal, that's merely part of the equation. Sure they want to alleviate their painful symptoms as soon as possible, and can set hopeful dates, but if you look a bit further you'll see that there may be more to it.

You may say that the deadline is impractical simply because they're unfamiliar with how long it would take to acquire healthier ways of living, and the deadline is relatively unpredictable given the many unforeseeable variables involved. This too is part of the calculation, but not the most important factor.

Fortunately, a revealing hint about unrealistic treatment time limits lies in thinking about what might happen if the opposite were to occur. If these individuals gave themselves 20 or 30 years to complete treatment, they'd feel as though there's no hurry. This is decidedly not in accord with driven individuals' goal or way of living.

With the above in mind, examine how driven patients may become needlessly concerned about the number of sessions they've attended. This can occur after only a handful of them. In addition, they worry that they're doing an inadequate job and selfishly burdening their therapist. This too, is unnecessary and seemingly illogical…unless they allow something. When you add up the number of clues that exist, you come to a telling summation.

Unrealistic deadlines create a rapidly approaching target date that leads to sufficient tension that is used to move toward therapy as well as prod progress through it. This is in accord with driven individuals personalities. Ironically, they employ anxiety to reduce it. Interestingly, there's another related issue.

Why after successfully conquering a number of concerns might patients experience towering symptoms for trivial matters?

Well, think about how if they're profiting from therapy and want to continue, yet concurrently driven to conclude it, how can they overcome their self-imposed session limit? They can unconsciously generate significant symptoms that justify moving toward therapy and setting an appointment or extending treatment when their drive prompts them to stop prematurely. *Anxiety can prompt movement toward others on the useful or useless side of life.* For example, "I was worried about the grandkids so I thought I'd stop by and check on them," can authorize movement toward the grandchildren regardless if the visit is welcomed or beneficial.

Now consider neurotic persons who fear rejection and wish to avoid emotional or physical intimacy, yet feel equally compelled to be in a relationship, perhaps to comply with social expectations or goading (e.g., intrusive and demanding relatives who prompt marriage and children), for the enjoyment, or to satisfy biological needs. If they begin a relationship they protect their social image and quell others' pressure as well as reap many personal benefits, yet they make themselves vulnerable and risk emotional safety as well as peace of mind. However, if they safeguard their cognitive and emotional well-being by avoiding relationships, they imperil self-esteem, status, and acceptance, as well as preclude wonderful experiences. With this in mind, why shortly after starting a relationship might they do the following?

- Anxiously call and text ceaselessly.

- Demand their partner is constantly nearby or reachable.

- Insist on moving in with their significant other shortly after meeting.

• Divulge their most graphic thoughts, feelings, desires as well as embarrassing and problematic mistakes and faults (e.g., arrests, intoxicated indiscretions, suicidal ideation).

Such extraordinarily candid, controlling, claustrophobically close and clingy behavior appears to be counterproductive as it elevates the prospect of rejection and emotional hurt...yet this possibility whispers the answer.

Just consider how courageously pursuing a relationship may garner praise, or avoid criticism and disparagement, as well as allow various personal benefits (e.g., sexual intimacy). However, there's a downside. For those who wish to limit their exposure and the chance of emotional injury as well as others' influence, relationships can be increasingly unnerving. Therefore, to reduce their tension neurotic persons may wish to distance others. But how can they do so in a way that doesn't jeopardize acceptance or self-esteem?

By giving too much information (especially that which is unfavorable), displaying intense symptoms, and hurriedly pushing their relationship forward, their significant others may feel smothered, pressured, controlled, and uncomfortable, and end the relationship. This uncloaks another use of anxiety.

Those with generalized anxiety may employ symptoms to move toward others to ultimately distance them, which limits vulnerability and the possibility of emotional harm as well as maintains control. Also, while they displayed the good intentions and bravery to pursue a relationship, it was their significant others who retreated and are perceived or portrayed as guarded, self-centered, or exploitive. In addition, upon seeing symptoms, sympathetic people may invite stressed persons to come to them for reassurance and consolation.

Embellished Symptoms and False Flaws

Why might neurotic persons exhibit exaggerated symptoms or report untrue mistakes and fabricated weaknesses?

Well, imagine you had to cross a rope bridge above a perilous cliff and you're doubtful of the bridge's strength. Before crossing, you repeatedly jump full force on the bridge to assess its durability far beyond what's required to walk across. If you determine it isn't strong enough, you can avoid trusting it with your life. Similarly, excessive symptoms and fictional flaws can, for instance, test the strength of others' tolerance and loyalty. If they remain resiliently committed, neurotic persons may be somewhat assured they won't be abandoned when they're at their genuine worst (which is relatively better). However, they may perpetually fear others' devotion has waned and compelled to repeatedly test their fidelity, which can eventually alienate them. If others end their associations, neurotically anxious individuals can preserve self-esteem by believing such outrageous symptoms or confessed actions would push *any* person away. Also, they can swiftly dismiss or dissociate from those symptoms and undesirable characteristics given their inauthenticity.

Admirable Burdens

Those with generalized anxiety may identify numerous or crucial weaknesses and faults in others' logic or articulate systemic flaws (e.g., corporate thinking, political organizations) that led to unnecessary and massive problems (e.g., recalls, social discord). They then furnish a resolution that would — from their perspective — efficiently remedy the predicament. They state that the presenting problem initiates their tension, and their powerlessness to invoke change amplifies their symptoms.

While on the surface this seems to be simple frustration and anxiety related to an injustice or error about which neurotic persons are impotent, what could their symptoms allow?

First, why might they select issues outside of their control and unlikely to change (at least in the short-term)? This can generate and maintain symptoms. Second, note that their proposed solutions are untestable, therefore unfalsifiable. Consequently, they can assert they're correct (and others are wrong) in a way that evades failure. Third, easily providing a solution when others (usually experts) fail, enables indirect boasting of superior intelligence and judgment. They may distressingly plead for ignorance, "If only I didn't see where they could fix the problem I'd be as happy as the clueless masses." Relatedly, what might they communicate when they worry about the safety of their bountiful stock market cache, whether their luxury car will be safe in a parking lot, or feel anxiously obligated to take care of others' inconsiderate and disgraceful polluting? They can highlight their strong work ethic, moral caliber, financial standing, intelligence, selflessness, etc. *Anxiety symptoms can be employed to indirectly trumpet sense, strength, and superiority.*

Fortitude

Although perspiration is often seen as unattractive, embarrassing, and may draw ridicule, when might people not hide it, but display it as a badge of honor?

Picture gym goers who after a strenuous workout parade their sweat-saturated clothes — the telltale remnants of their impressive workout — that silently signal their devout dedication and Herculean effort. Evidently, something people hide in one situation, they can purposefully display in another.

Now consider how assuming common adult responsibilities (e.g., working, parenting, being married) testify to admirable drive and morals, but also can be occasionally overwhelming. Yet, as society often expects such actions, they may be relegated to mere pedestrian achievements. Knowing that, what might be the purpose of the following statements?

"My anxiety is crushing me. Yesterday, I frantically drove the kids to football practice, came home and hurriedly mowed the lawn before I went back and picked them up, rushed back home where I quickly made dinner and then cleaned up, and went over their homework before putting them to bed."

"I was so worried about the upcoming performance review at work that it was nearly impossible to concentrate on getting the project done on time and I didn't sleep for a month. Surprisingly, my supervisor raved about it to the CEO."

By persevering with anxiety, neurotic persons exhibit superior vigor, goodness, integrity, and work ethic than others.[580] Their suffering testifies to their fortitude and praiseworthy morals, as they're not resting on their achievements as lesser others might.[581] Relatedly, they may conclude that their symptoms build character, forging them into stronger individuals.[582] They may amplify their prideful elevation by facing challenges despite others' pleas to relax and abandon or delegate responsibilities. *Anxiety symptoms can be worn as a badge of determination, exertion, morals, courage, etc.*

Also, anxiety can be used to discount others' achievements. For example, "Yeah, I know how difficult it is for you to raise children, but if you had to do it with my symptoms — like I had to do for decades — then you'd realize just how much more challenging it can get!"

However, does this construct of fortitude apply when people don't express their symptoms?

They may believe that suffering in silence is ennobling and they can perceive themselves as *doubly* strong as they have the courage and resilience to persevere and be the model employee, devoted spouse, good friend, etc. while conscientiously not bragging, being confrontational, or "burdening others" with their distress. Also, they may reframe their isolation and distancing from people as being resilient, independent, and not reliant upon others, when it's merely a way to avoid vulnerability and change.

Underdogs

Why might people with generalized anxiety define themselves as underdogs?

First, by portraying life or people as unfair, citing things such as bad luck, a sluggish economy, meager job market, advantages of the affluent, prejudicial policies, a biased supervisor, siblings who had more parental attention and encouragement, and so on, they list reasons why through some advantage others had — or life denied them — they couldn't or didn't succeed. This protectively liberates them from accountability for failure.

Second, by believing the cards are stacked against them, and therefore in an unwinnable position, they can forgo future challenges.

Third, they can maintain and profess the belief that if they weren't unfairly disadvantaged, they'd be as successful as others. This not only protects self-esteem and status, but also allows them to claim unearned success.

Fourth, the underdog label connotes pure spirit and noble motivation in the face of uphill struggles and unfair competition. Consequently, even with genuine comparative inferiority (e.g., lower income, lesser work position), they can gain a sense of superiority (moral, ethical, etc.)

Fifth, how can driven individuals exploit the underdog perception? When they perceive that others have an unjust advantage, or that life or circumstance fated difficulties upon them, for instance, they can strengthen their grit to work harder than others, or motivate themselves to outpace life's hurdles, to balance the scales of fairness.

Sixth, when neurotic individuals attain the same achievements that others do, they can advantageously apply the underdog label. By perceiving an unfair disadvantage, they can bias the calibration and definition of winning. For example, as long as they believe they had to work harder, their successes can trump others' achievements of equal caliber.

Seventh, by deeming life and others as unjust and wrong, they can insist that other people or circumstances must change, which sustains the neurotic life style.

Eighth, by characterizing others, entities, or life as unfair victimizers, neurotic persons can also perceive themselves as innocent victims, all of which permit particular behavior. For example, they may believe that they have to "level the playing field," "right a wrong," "fight the good fight," or "stick up for the little guy." This can spur action on the useful side of life or allow unhealthy or otherwise impermissible behavior.

For example,

"The company is unfair, so I don't have any problem taking a long lunch (calling in sick [even when not], taking office supplies, etc.)."

"My parents have always treated my siblings better than me, so they should watch my kids while I'm at work (pay my student loan, buy me a new car, etc.)."

"My spouse is so mean and controlling, so what if I cheat? It'll even things out."

"I've got to work twice as hard and make sure everything is perfect because I'm sure my boss gave my coworkers every advantage possible over me."

Extending this a bit, contemplate how those with generalized anxiety may identify others as downtrodden and act with a sense of duty and righteousness. For instance, being especially generous to a downtrodden child (perhaps by using a miserly spouse's credit card), being excessively protective, or showing special attention and effort.

Impossibly High Standards

Why might neurotically anxious persons make plans so unrealistically ambitious that failure is unavoidable?

First, telling others of admirably impressive plans demonstrates goodness and drive, and may gain social acceptance and favor.

Second, extraordinary aspirations can make others' goals comparatively inferior.

Third, when people with generalized anxiety take on astounding challenges, friends, family, employers, etc. may allow leeway on other obligations and tolerate various symptoms such as irritability and anger, or dole out tasks and requests to others (e.g., parents or bosses ask others to help out).

Fourth, attempts at grand feats may get others to refrain from criticism when failure eventually occurs — it's safer to fail at the impossible than the ordinary.

Fifth, an overwhelming To Do list can enable most tasks to remain partially completed for an extended period, perhaps forever. As an incomplete project cannot be evaluated, neurotic persons may evade judgment, and they can always say they're working on, or thinking about, it.

Sixth, when neurotic persons either fail to complete, or they perform unsatisfactorily on, some task they may criticize their performance rather than their self-imposed stratospherically high goals.[583] This can garner praise and encouragement in the face of failure, especially when anxiety makes goal attainment more challenging. In addition, misdirecting others from unobtainable objectives to performance enables anxious persons to keep pursuing unattainable goals, which sustains the safeguarding tactic.

Seventh, failure maintains low self-esteem that perpetuates painful, yet purposeful, anxiety.

Eighth, consider how failing may allow neurotic persons to face fewer, or less taxing, challenges as others are less likely to give them responsibilities. This avoids future failure and associated tension.

Ninth, if they fail on remarkable challenges, they may claim that they could succeed at more common tasks without proof. For example, "I may have failed at raising six children, but I'm sure I could have been an excellent parent if I only had one kid," or "I couldn't write a world-class novel. I should have just poured myself into writing an exceptional poem for *The New Yorker*."

Self-castigation

People with generalized anxiety may relentlessly criticize what they do, haven't done, their emotions, appearance, past interactions, failures, and limitations, among countless other factors. So why might such irrepressible painful rumination and accusation exist?

Maintain the Life Style

When neurotic persons try new ways of thinking or acting and make a mistake or fail, they can get upset and express various forms of negative self-reference (e.g., call themselves disparaging names). Although it appears their self-rebuke is unwarranted and counterproductive, self-imposed sanction for straying from their life style convictions may motivate them to "keep on the right path." In other words, to not make the same error again, they rigidly obey their original convictions, and not try to change them.

Fair enough, but why might they do this when nothing goes wrong or even in times of success?

Well, think of those who criticize themselves after spending a small amount of money not because they cannot afford it, but as a means to reign in their spending *before* it gets out of control. Similarly, neurotic self-criticism may arise when people fear they have wandered too far from their philosophical home and want to return before something goes wrong.

The need to be good, perfect, right, driven, and in control requires energy employed in unique and interesting ways. Knowing this, why may neurotic persons be harshly and persistently self-critical and unswayed by others' solace?

To assess whether what they're doing is good, perfect, or right, and to avoid being caught flatfooted by someone else's criticism, those with generalized anxiety may self-monitor and scrutinize themselves with microscopic precision and a high standard of acceptability. In this way, they can identify, correct, or hide their flaws and mistakes before anyone spots them, or swiftly defend them if noticed. But this process may consume their resources. Rather than give up on this manner of living, they seek to sustain or multiply their anxiety-fueled efforts. Yet, how might they do that?

They may worry that others are equally or more exacting, perceptive, and judgmental. Indeed, neurotic persons may act almost as if the paparazzi were perpetually following them watching for faults and flaws. Also, neurotic individuals may fear they're "crazy" or losing their minds as a way to be aware of, and rein in, any behavior they believe is unacceptable.

Prevent Movement

Why might neurotic persons quickly dismiss others' encouragement and valid testimony of their notable and legitimate accomplishments by defining those successes as easily achieved?

First, those with low self-esteem can have significant difficulty acknowledging their abilities and achievements. As they don't perceive it, they cannot testify to it. Second, if they do see their capacities and accomplishments, they may want to avoid appearing pretentious. Third, by perceiving their previous successes as easily achieved, they increase the chasm between their perceived ability and the next challenge. For example, patients who've attained several therapeutic goals, but are apprehensive about moving forward, may fail to acknowledge their successes or discount them, "The last few things were easy, but I can't do what's next." By making future endeavors appear intimidating, people can slow their movement or immobilize themselves. This can minimize the risk of failure, ridicule, rejection, or abandonment.

Accentuate Extraordinary Performance and Standards

Why might neurotic individuals anxiously and unmercifully criticize themselves after a genuinely remarkable achievement, perhaps decrying how they disappointed themselves as well as others?

You might say that blatant self-congratulation is unbecoming and can be irreconcilable with the need to be good. This, while true, doesn't explain the self-rebuke. You must look for the purpose. *By criticizing their extraordinary achievement they obliquely and surreptitiously attract attention to it in a manner that avoids, or minimizes, being seen as arrogant.*[584] In addition, public frustration about monumental achievements implies impressively high standards, as well as being able to do better without evidence. Also, think about how brutal self-criticism may pull others to reassure and praise first-class accomplishments.

Show Piety and Compassion

What might the following anxious, self-critical statements allow?

"I feel like such an idiot! I was so distracted this morning that I forgot to put change in the donation canister by the register. How could I forget? I've been donating every day for six years! The cashier now probably thinks I've lost my job or that I'm cheap and selfish!"

"Last weekend, I was so nervous about my brother's breakup with his girlfriend, that I drove 1,400 miles in two days to visit and bring him gallons of homemade soup and presents so that he didn't get lonely or depressed. My spouse told me not to go and that we couldn't afford it right now. I'm sure there's going to be hell to pay at the end of the month, and it may not have been the smartest thing to do, but I had no choice."

First, what's the legitimate risk to self-esteem and acceptance? It's minuscule. Such misdemeanors are easily pardonable, especially when those actions are counterbalanced by good intentions and ultimately exceptional acts in the face of harsh internal and external punishment.

Second, dwelling on and scrutinizing minor events can misdirect attention from bigger flaws or problems (e.g., being intrusive, emotionally distant, overprotective, controlling).

Third, although the criticism could remain a silent thought, public self-flagellation gathers and informs an audience of concerned and compassionate others who may attempt to reduce suffering by pointing out neurotic individuals' commendable qualities and actions. Engaging in self-criticism for a purported flaw or shortcoming allows them to draw attention to their goodness.[585] Self-criticism masks symptom purposefulness, and indirectly bolsters self-esteem and status. Therefore, it may be a preferred alternative. *Self-rebuke can be veiled grandstanding.*

Fourth, harsh faultfinding to minor offenses publicizes their sensitivity level. This warns others to speak softly and refrain from being critical, which controls them.

So how might you know that the symptoms are purposeful and maintained?

When others readily forgive neurotic individuals, yet they deny themselves such mercy, disregard compliments, are unresponsive to reason, and determined to feel remorse or regret. (In therapy, some patients admit that although forgiven and accepted by their god[s], they reject and disapprove of themselves — then smirk when they realize they have higher standards than their respective god[s].)

Denigrate Others

Neurotic self-criticism takes on greater meaning when it's assessed against a social background. For instance, imagine a slightly overweight individual, who engages in self-rebuke about failing "at losing the last 5 pounds" while on a diet. Now, think about how this statement takes on different meaning when it's said in front of an overtly overweight coworker.

Similarly, envision those who make acidic self-critical statements about not saving enough money to fully pay for their children's university education when it's said in front of siblings whose children dropped out of high school. *Anxious self-castigation may elevate neurotic persons and indirectly assault others.*

If chastised, they may defend their actions with socially acceptable rationale. For example, "My doctor told me that I need to lose weight to be healthy," or "I don't care what I have to give up to ensure my children have the best." Neurotic individuals' self-criticism can contain camouflaged accusations against others (e.g., poor parenting, inadequate genes, rejection) and minimize their value.[586] For instance, "I never learned (can also be read as, 'was never taught') how to be a good parent (do laundry, be handy, etc.)."

"First Worst"

Why might people with generalized anxiety repeatedly proclaim they have the worst luck, are the worst at something, or are the world's biggest failures?

"Worst" can come in many forms, and can be subjective (e.g., the worst for a particular individual) as well as comparative (say, having symptoms longer than others). Consider how the "worst anxiety" may appear on the useful side of life, as when people's symptoms prioritize a challenge, and motivate them to be successful at a healthy or socially beneficial endeavor.

Or, it may appear on the useless side of life.

Experiencing the most extreme symptoms can gain attention or power (say, sympathy and allowances) when previous levels of anxiety are no longer effective to attain a goal. For instance, when some people don't want to wait, they may incessantly dwell on their concerns and unconsciously generate the "worst anxiety ever" to allow certain actions.

Being the worst at something can allow people to override all forms of encouragement to face challenges, believing they'll certainly fail.

Having the "worst anxiety" can magnify neurotic individuals' accomplishments (e.g., "I've never been so stressed in my life as I have after getting this promotion.")

Having symptoms longer or more tenacious than others experience, and impervious to healthcare professionals' efforts, may allow some distinction. Furthermore, bravely and consistently facing the most persistent or pervasive symptoms demonstrates intestinal fortitude, which elevates them above non-anxious individuals as well as other symptomatic persons.

Being "first worst" is a way people can portray themselves as superior and illustrates "downward ambition."[587] In addition, having the "worst luck" may explain away failure, or authorize immobility (e.g., "I can't win") or movement (e.g., "I have to leave early, otherwise with my luck I'd get stuck in traffic").

The Trampoline Effect

People may jump up when they need to reach something high up on a shelf. Yet, what's occurs prior? They crouch down a bit before launching upwards. Those who want to jump very high may use a trampoline to create supernatural flight, taking advantage of elastic mats and springs that store the energy that rockets them skyward. But how is energy imparted into the trampoline? Those mats and springs also allow people to get down even lower than would otherwise be possible before launching into the air. With this in mind, consider how those with generalized anxiety may use the "Trampoline effect" by harshly admonishing themselves and then in an attempt to balance the scales, lavish themselves with florid bouquets of unrealistic admiration.[588] By pushing themselves downward with self-criticism they're able to achieve greater heights. Although such changes in mood and action may at first appear illogical and unpredictable (and some may erroneously employ the term "bipolar"), neurotic persons may symptomatically push themselves down to ultimately self-elevate, with more pronounced worry and self-criticism associated with a corresponding height on their rebound.

Blame Themselves

Imagine neurotic individuals who host a party, but few people attend. While this could be quite a blow to their self-esteem, how might blaming themselves protect their self-esteem and status?

Although this appear to add insult to injury, consider how the following self-critical statements handily explain low attendance:

"Ugh! I'm so dumb. I must have told everyone the wrong day. Now that I think about it, I didn't do a good job of giving people directions. Only I could do something so poorly!"

Though it appears self-injurious, blaming themselves is ultimately a safeguarding tactic. After all, it's easier to accept their mistakes than the alternative — most people weren't interested in attending.

Dismiss Legitimate Offenses

Picture someone with generalized anxiety saying the following:

"I'm absolutely the worst parent ever! I yell nearly constantly, criticize nearly every move my kids make, and never encourage them. I'm always telling them what to do, whom to talk to, I search through their phones and computers, and I really should mind my own business. I wouldn't blame them if they don't talk to me when they're older. I'm the most wicked and least suitable parent in the world! I should be shot and hung out as a bad example."

But later those excessively negative statements are soon appended with this:

"How silly of me, of course I shouldn't be shot. I'm sure I'm not the *worst* parent ever. It's not like I beat my kids, *or worse*, like some parents. I've seen how other parents let their children stay out all night and talk to the most undesirable people in the world. That's terrible for them. It's only because I love my children so much that I want them to have what I didn't, that I take the time to go the extra mile for them, to protect them. You don't see that too often."

Neurotically anxious individuals may make searing statements of self-censure that contain massively exaggerated fictions, but also harbor stowaways of truth. While confessions of flaws and wrongdoing vent tension, what's gained when factual statements are interwoven with hyperbole?

Excessive self-castigation enables neurotic persons to discredit and discard all preceding — including legitimate — criticism; thereby safeguard self-esteem (as well as acceptance, status, and their life style).[589]

Next, what might the following communicate?

"I feel so bad about being such a terrible sibling while we were growing up. I teased you, stole your things, I said you broke the living room window when I did it, and mocked you in front of others. Those things keep me awake at night. Sadly, that's so long ago and there's no way I could ever make that up to you."

First, confessing to distant crimes, while defining them as beyond the statute of limitations, grants neurotic individuals amnesty, which liberates them from making amends. Second, acknowledging misconduct is in accord with being good; therefore, it can protect self-esteem, status, and acceptance. Third, they can preempt others' criticism and protect against condemnation and retaliation. After all, who's going to criticize those in the midst of a flurry of self-directed attacks? In fact, the administration may be so intense that others may not even be able to get a word in, or might beg them to stop. Fourth, neurotically anxious people may be able to dismiss their self-criticism with statements such as, "I was being too emotional," "I wasn't thinking rationally," or "I'm too critical of myself." *Self-critical admissions of willful mistreatment and neglect can safeguard self-esteem, acceptance, status, and the life style.*

Evade Accountability and Future Responsibilities

What might be gained when those with generalized anxiety reprimand themselves, say for being an unsuitable parent, employee, lover, or friend? For instance, "Didn't I tell you I was a terrible person? You had to know this wouldn't work!"

Self-criticism can enable neurotic individuals to avoid accountability.[590] By broadcasting such negative statements they inform everyone within earshot that any responsibilities placed on their shoulders will end up being a disaster, which may lead others to avoid assigning them formidable jobs as well as mundane, yet crucial, tasks. *For the reason that it appears that self-criticism surrenders self-esteem, it can powerfully protect it by not seeming as though one is defensive or evading responsibility.*[591]

Motivation

Why might driven, high-achieving people with generalized anxiety criticize themselves or dismiss their accomplishments?

Start by looking at what's known as the Impostor syndrome (a.k.a. Impostor phenomenon, Fraud syndrome) whereby accomplished persons mistakenly believe their achievements were based on factors other than their competence, such as timing, luck, others' generosity, working significantly harder than others, perhaps misrepresenting themselves and deceiving others on their ability.[592] Though appearing illogical and false could there be a purpose to it?

First, note that the Impostor syndrome can prevent movement and maintain vanity. After all, if people think their successes are not due to their abilities or effort, they can refrain from taking action or perpetually monitor themselves (as well as others) to make certain they're acting acceptably. Second, imagine driven individuals running a cross-country race believing they're doing extraordinarily well, but somewhere in the middle were told they were near last place. Might they exert themselves more, rather than be complacent and keep the current pace?

When high achieving individuals believe they're impostors, they may generate anxiety as well as self-directed anger, fear, jealously, or some other emotion that spurs greater action to achieve socially useful goals. For example, "I'll surely fail if I don't do it perfectly," or "I'm not as smart as others, so I must try harder." They might say, "I've always felt different from others," which can coincide with the misperception that everyone else is competent.

Guilt Feelings

As neurotic self-criticism may regularly include guilt feelings, it's necessary to explore their presence and possible purposes.

Thwart Temptation

Examine how some actions, say eating healthy and exercise, have physical feedback mechanisms with positive and negative consequences, e.g., fitness, endurance, and feeling well physically, as well as obesity, heart attacks, and diabetes, yet may be deficient to prod healthy practices. Even external prompts for obedience may be insufficient, e.g., not everyone pays their taxes even though they can be fined or imprisoned. So, even though such external and internal feedback mechanisms may prompt compliance, they don't guarantee it. Note that given life's infinite temptations, such as leaving work early, alluring affairs, or unscrupulous business dealings, this poses a challenge for those who need to be good. So, what can multiply the probability of compliance?

Conscience. It's something which monitors and guides behavior and thoughts to ensure that people comply with common sense and be good.[593] *However, conscience merely provides insight of what's good.* So, what other internal mechanism may increase the probability of moral action?

Well, consider how guilt feelings can stop people from violating social conventions, for instance, taking the last seat on the bus that would leave a prominently pregnant woman standing. Guilt feelings can extinguish temptation of "unsocial impulses."[594] *Guilt feelings can mirror a community's morality, cherished ethics, and principles, boost the probability of acceptance, and attract sympathy, forgiveness, and leniency.*[595] While not mandatory for good action, they're part of a behavior management system as they alert people to their conduct and urge them to do the socially right thing.

Similar to social interest, guilt feelings aren't inborn. Rather, they can be socially promoted and instilled, personally chosen, or a combination, but are ultimately a unique composition. They can arise to prompt compliance with what's deemed good, perfect, right, and bolster self-esteem, strengthen acceptance, as well as maintain a life style. Guilt feelings can thwart temptation and prompt behavior deemed good as defined by social rules or an individual's life style convictions (e.g., "I would feel bad if I broke my diet"). *Guilt feelings can prompt people to abide by rules, regardless of if they're societally advocated or personal.*[596] But before you deem them as wonderful, recognize their distressing character makes them problematic symptoms.

Elevation and Hidden Boasting

Being praised usually requires that people do more than what's expected. For that reason, those with generalized anxiety may surpass society's values by crafting unnecessary personal rules they deem superior, with accordant behavior that goes above and beyond the norm. With that in mind, why might they say something similar to the following?

"I'm such a bad parent. I watched the first four hours of my daughter's tennis competition, but I wanted to get back home to watch the football game live, but I felt so bad for almost abandoning her that I stayed for the remaining three hours. I'd feel miserable if I didn't."

When neurotic persons use guilt feelings to squelch unacceptable conduct they can concurrently celebrate their virtue and compassion.[597] Guilt feelings enable them to live by their convictions, garner attention and admiration, as well as prove significance. Knowing that, how might they demonstrate outstanding morals, attention to detail, compassion, and sensitivity?

Their inward-directed cannon of criticism fires at the tiniest violation of their ethics or society's guidelines, or at the most trivial concerns. Thunderous self-condemnation may be the flare that draws attention to their goodness, first-rate work, admirable expectations, respectable ethics, etc. Although pained, some may engage in roundabout self-flattery (e.g., "I feel so bad that I keep winning at this game"). *Neurotic individuals can slyly brag of their character and work by expressing guilt feelings and finding fault with extraordinary effort.*[598]

What might you infer about the guilt-riddled expression, "I feel terrible about those poor, suffering children (in some distant place). Some times I can't sleep. Yet, most people don't pay any attention to them"?

Guilt feelings allow people to paint an image of being morally superior martyrs who elevate themselves from others by their suffering when others don't.[599]

While guilt feelings are frequently associated with improving behavior, change can terrify those with generalized anxiety. Now, consider how guilt feelings for things such as world hunger, child labor, or nuclear proliferation allow people to broadcast praiseworthy characteristics such as compassion, while liberating them from taking action as those issues are beyond their control. *Neurotic persons may harbor a sense of accountability for those things of which they're innocent or powerless, but evade responsibility for which they're accountable.*[600] Guilt feelings can allow an elevating point of view with an exonerating blind spot.

Misdirection, Guilt Feeling vs. Regret and Remorse

Why might those with generalized anxiety state that their symptoms have either prohibited acceptable action or caused some inappropriate conduct, express guilt feelings and promise not to act that way again, yet do so repeatedly?

When people experience a behavior gone wrong (e.g., overextending their physical abilities) they endure a significant and swift consequence (e.g., chipped teeth, broken bones), experience regret and vow to never engage in that behavior again — and don't. Regret is a thought or expression of an *action taken* that, in hindsight, was wrong and shouldn't have happened, nor is likely to occur in the future. Simply, those who regret their actions will take responsibility for their behavior and change, improve.[601] On the other hand, remorse is a thought or articulation of *failure to take action*, and if a similar opportunity arises, people will act differently having learned from their remorse. *People will change their behavior to attain their goals.*

So, how might neurotic individuals do what they want (perhaps frequently) when it goes against what society values, with little or no negative personal or social repercussions?

Here's a clue: the original definition of apology meant to *defend* one's actions.[602]

People can engage in otherwise impermissible behavior and, *after reaching their goal*, profess a prompt postscript of guilt feelings: acknowledgement, apologies, and promises of change to assure others and/or themselves. This illustrates how they can act without conscience only to later declare disobedience *of the conscience they didn't demonstrate.*[603] In this way, they get to do what they want, and then broadcast they know the right thing to do. This is an attempt to protect self-esteem, acceptance, status, and life style.

Yet, what might reveal their true goal as well as whether their guilt feelings are camouflage?

As movement can expose goals and values it's important to minimize words and scrutinize behavior. It's the action *after* those statements that unveils if they were expressions of guilt feelings or sincere regret or remorse.

Guilt feelings can misdirect others' attention from neurotic individuals' undesirable actions to their admirable intentions, even when they engage in the same conduct repetitively; for instance, "I'm really sorry for forgetting to take out the garbage," yet it happens every week. *Guilt feelings can wipe the slate clean for misdeeds so that people can engage in the behavior repeatedly once they have atoned.*[604] Guilt feelings can reveal the importance neurotic persons put on retreating from responsibilities rather than improving their behavior.[605] When individuals experience regret (or remorse) they concentrate on their acts, and when they experience guilt feelings they focus on themselves.[606]

Immobility

There are times when apparent discord among goals, actions, and emotions symptomatically prohibits people from achieving their stated desires. For example, "I would love to start dating, but my children rely on me and would be helpless without me. I would feel like a terrible parent and worry constantly" or "I would leave this relationship in a heartbeat because I've been cheated on too many times, but I'd feel so much guilt abandoning someone I've dated for years." However, as the unity of the personality asserts there's consistency among goals, thoughts, emotions, and actions, how might you explain those expressed guilt feelings as well as seemingly conflictual thoughts, actions, and emotions?

While it looks as though the person has the kids' best interest at heart and the goal to take care of them supersedes dating, what if the children were in their mid-20s, employed, and had their own families? Or, might guilt feelings about leaving a duplicitous lover hint that the person doesn't want to be alone, start dating unfamiliar individuals, or go without readily-available sex? Anxiety-based guilt feelings can create behavioral gridlock that gives the impression of compassion and good intentions, while protecting people from engaging in action they'd rather avoid. *Guilt feelings can be used to initiate or maintain immobility.*[607] This can also be employed on the useful side of life, say when experiencing guilt feelings that stop people from cheating on a test or making a snide comment.

Permit Otherwise Unallowable Action

Why might those with generalized anxiety express guilt feelings *before and while* they're engaging in otherwise unacceptable action?

Consider how, for example, saying "I feel ashamed doing this..." can allow them to take some pleasure from the activity, but as long as they experience some guilt feelings, then they aren't that bad as at least they have a conscience about it. This enables them to see their behavior as merely bending their rules without breaking them. *Guilt feelings can allow people to enjoy what they prefer, but limit their enjoyment and avoid paying the full penalty for their wrongdoing.*[608]

Hidden Aggression

How might you interpret the apology, "I feel dreadful about the affair. I was lonely for too long and our sex life lost its spark long ago"?

Living by the need to be good conviction doesn't mean that aggression is always avoided or repressed. For instance, the apology above can be an oblique rebuke of a distant and flavorless lover that suggests the affair wouldn't have occurred if the person had been more available and attentive. Guilt feelings may be a sheath of goodness that cloaks a cutting remark. *Guilt feelings may veil aggression and competition camouflaged by a presentation of passivity and compliance.*[609]

Control

While trying to make others have guilt feelings can be a means of prodding compliance (the infamous "guilt trip"), how might self-directed guilt feelings control others?

Well, envision those who express the following,

"I was such a bad parent, I never taught you how to eat properly and exercise, and now you're 30 years old and still single. It's completely my fault that you don't want to date."

"Although it was refreshing and exhilarating to get compliments for once, I shouldn't have spent our savings on trying to make myself look better. It was wrong and I feel ashamed."

The first example illustrates how self-directed guilt feelings can prompt the adult child to exercise, lose weight, and date. The second shows how guilt feelings may coax more attention and compliments. *Self-directed guilt feelings can be used to control others.* Relatedly, why might those with generalized anxiety experience guilt feelings and believe some difficult situation (e.g., a messy basement) is their fault when it isn't?

By assuming responsibility for a problem, they can grant themselves permission to take control and push their solution to fix it (e.g., throw out what they don't want and restore order). They can do what they want while under the guise of being good and doing the right thing.

Nonexistent Good Intentions

Imagine an anxious person cheerfully accepts a party invitation; however, doesn't feel competent at small talk and meeting new people, and fears revealing inadequacies either in form (e.g., being awkward) or in content (e.g., being in an unsuitable career, being unfamiliar about the topics discussed, expressing a fact or perspective that risks disapproval). On the morning of the party, symptoms arise and preclude attendance. However, a week later the neurotic individual unexpectedly encounters the host who extended the invitation. Although anxiety apparently averted a crisis, it merely postponed one as breaking a promise and isolating is frowned upon. So, how can symptoms safeguard self-esteem, acceptance, stats, and life style?

Consider how for this to occur the person must:

• Avoid criticism.

• Apologize for the absence.

• Refrain from hurting the host's feelings.

• Provide rationale that legitimizes the absence.

• Express the admirable characteristics of social awareness and good intentions.

The individual solemnly says, "I feel miserable about missing your party. My anxiety just floored me and I didn't leave my house all day. I'm so sorry about not being there."

Accepting the invitation enabled the person to be good, as well as controlled confrontation and questions that may have occurred if the reply were "No." While anxiety allowed an avoidance of a threatening situation, the contrition demonstrated upon meeting the host is revealing. First, failure to express guilt feelings about behavior that violates socially acceptable rules (e.g., breaking a promise, giving the impression the person isn't valued) suggests a lack of self-awareness, respect, empathy, and accountability. Accordingly, demonstrating guilt feelings and apologizing proves them, and may garner praise and reassurance. Second, anxiety is identified and blamed as the obstacle that justifies the absence. Third, painful guilt feelings and repentance decrease disapproval as well as exhibit social awareness and good intentions. Yet, how do you know those good intentions are false?

People strive toward their goals, often minimizing threats or those things that obstruct goal achievement. Symptoms do not make goals unobtainable, but rather reveal a superseding objective (e.g., safety over socializing). If the neurotic person really wanted to attend the party, there would be little or no symptomatic obstacle (e.g., if a $20 million check for that person were at the party, anxiety wouldn't prohibit party attendance, but may energize action toward it — and then perhaps a quick retreat).

Guilt feelings may be a display of nonexistent good intentions.[610] They may compensate for social offenses, minimize personal and social sanction for transgressions, and help escape social cooperation and obligations while pursuing personal objectives. Expressing guilt feelings can demonstrate knowledge and adherence to social conventions and reflect commendable ethical convictions, and allow people to save face.[611] Such communication enables an avoidance of rejection and criticism, as well as protects self-esteem.[612]

Moving Away

Imagine one spouse who demonstrates dutiful fidelity, while the other feels smothered, uncomfortable with the attention, vulnerability, and commitment a healthy marriage requires. With that in mind, what might be the purpose of guilt feelings in the following?

"My anxiety burdens you. I'm never interested in sex. I'm moody and continually critical. I feel awful that I'm holding you back from enjoying your life. It'll pain me, but you deserve someone who can treat you better."

Although this suggests an act of selfless kindness, as the person appears to sacrifice happiness and a marriage so that the other can be happy, recall that movement can reveal goals. Simply, the expression of guilt feelings allows action away from the attentive and patient spouse — who might be seen as overwhelmingly intrusive. Neurotic individuals may proclaim guilt feelings for the burden they place on others and for getting a disproportionate amount of attention.[613] This can occur for a couple of reasons. First, for those who garner attention, their expression of guilt feelings may be a veneer that protects acceptance. Second, when neurotic persons feel too attended to, they can use guilt feelings to distance themselves. Guilt feelings can be a redundant symptom because they, like other symptoms, can preclude participation and enable retreat.[614]

Moving Towards

Why might a recently divorced person who started another relationship state the following?

"I worry so much about how I left my spouse. It was disgraceful the way I behaved. My lawyers were too aggressive and I got full custody of our kids. I feel as though I've got to check in a bit more often. I have to make things right!"

Sure this is a display of goodness through the expression of guilt feelings, but there's more to it. What if you knew that the individual misses the ex-spouse as they connected in ways unparalleled in other relationships — including the person's current one?

Guilt feelings allow movement toward the ex-spouse and enable a relationship that might be otherwise impermissible. *Guilt feelings can be a means by which to move toward others under the presentation of social interest.*[615]

This chapter has presented numerous personality-based neurotic strategies and tactics that can be employed to unconsciously achieve goals on the useful and useless side of life. However, given the virtually-limitless horizon of human creativity, the preceding may merely be a hearty sampling.

In addition, although having strategies and tactics neatly dissected and labeled enables easier instruction, life is seldom so clear and straightforward. Indeed, neurotic anxiety can be a puzzling mystery with subtle clues that arise over time and require a keen eye to detect and decipher. If only you had illustrations that better approximated real life conditions that you could analyze…

Chapter 17: Illustrations

Fully comprehending neurotic anxiety requires more than just accommodating information from a dictionary-like format, with topics and tactics neatly separated and defined. In reality, the lines between tactics are blurred, and signs can be so elusive and faint that they're difficult to discern. Therefore, thorough learning requires how to detect clinical evidence, distinguish tactics, decrypt purposes, and decipher goals from a format that closer approximates how people present. To that end, the following examples portray fictional therapy sessions. For the sake of manageable brevity, a necessary concession is the distillation into vignettes that which regularly requires many meetings to surface and observe. Nevertheless, each is a mini-mystery of sorts, with numerous clues for you to discover some common and revealing manifestations of generalized anxiety. These illustrations are presented only for illumination, not for developing a diagnosing skill. (In other words, even if you're really tempted, please refrain from using what you learn in this chapter to casually analyze friends and family members — or anybody else.)

Controlling Spouse

In his first therapy appointment, a middle-aged man states, "Doctor, I'm really concerned about my wife."

"How so?" asks the psychologist while taking a seat and gently encouraging the patient to do the same.

"Well," the patient says as he abruptly crashes down on the couch, "she's a hoarder." He starts vigorously massaging his temples, "She has so many things randomly strewn about the house."

"You looked stressed."

"I am. Her compulsion has created a dangerous household."

"Dangerous?" the therapist parrots.

"Absolutely. I'm constantly worried that the kids will fall over her mess and break a bone or poke out an eye. And, I think if it gets any worse it will be a fire hazard."

"How long has this being going on?"

"*Years*," the man emphatically replies. "She keeps bringing things into the house."

"Interesting. What types of things?"

"You name it," the patient says while roughly wringing his hands.

"Such as…?"

"Oh, various things. They're all junk. I really don't want to dwell on it. That would only make me feel worse," the man says as he sinks into the couch.

"Things will be okay," the doctor reassures. "Is there anything else going on that concerns you?"

"Oh sure. Not only does she waste money on needless things, but also she won't buy off-brand clothes and generic food like I tell her, nor does she use the coupons that I go out of my way to cut out for her. I think she's concerned with how others view her. She doesn't want to look bad in comparison to the neighbors or her sister. But Doc, we only make so much money and there's no need to waste it like that. She buys what she wants without taking my needs into consideration, nor does she consider the future, say our retirement or the kids' college tuition. I'm afraid we'll end up in the poor house. She doesn't get the importance of being a team player in the marriage. This frustrates me and hurts my feelings. Sometimes, I think she's doing it on purpose."

"I'm sorry you're pained."

"Oh, it gets worse," the patient appends.

"How so?"

"I'm worried that her hoarding behavior is teaching our kids that it's okay to be a packrat. I don't want you to get the impression that I'm a neat freak. I'm not. I just don't want my kids to learn that it's okay to take on these types of behaviors," the man punctuates with outstretched arms. "I'm not panicking over this, but I have constant worry."

"Are the kids demonstrating any hoarding behavior?"

"No, not yet…but I think it's only a matter of time. My anxiety has become so intense that I can't sleep. My mind races about all the bad things that are happening and how things are going out of control in the marriage. I can't sleep unless I have some background noise. Usually, I leave the TV on."

"I see," the psychologist acknowledges. "How did your wife adjust to the sound and light from the TV?"

"Well, it wouldn't be nice to keep my wife awake all night; so I started sleeping on the living room couch," the man says as he vigorously rubs his eyes. "But unfortunately, this isn't a great solution. First, the kids see that I have to sleep on the couch. What does this teach them? My kids see that my wife and I aren't together. I'm fearful that this will make them curious and upset them to the point where it impacts their schoolwork or future relationships. They probably think their parents don't love one another. That's got to be awful for my kids."

"What do your kids say?"

"Nothing. But they're kids — almost teenagers. They don't always know what's best for them and I fear that they're used to it by now. Maybe they don't want to rock the boat or they're protecting my feelings. They don't know another way of living at this point — I'm guessing of course. However, sleeping on the couch is killing my back every morning and it makes me really irritable about the smallest things that wouldn't bother me otherwise. I end up losing my temper. Anger overcomes me and I'll yell. I feel terrible about it."

"Sounds aggravating. What do you get angry about?"

"Gee, it could be anything. But mostly, it's the mess in the house, that she doesn't properly address her mental illness, how she's a bad influence on the kids, or how my wife neglects my feelings. I always apologize to her afterward. She knows my back aches in the morning."

"Do you experience anger at other places, such as work?"

"Thankfully, no. I guess that by the time I take a hot shower and get into work my back feels better and my body isn't rebelling."

"I'm glad you're not suffering all day," the psychologist says.

"Thanks, but there's something else that bothers me."

"What?"

"My symptoms have been so overwhelming that I've been unable to perform sexually, and my poor wife has gone without sex for nearly a year," the man says as he hunches forward.

"So you sleep in a different room and haven't been intimate for almost a year. That must be difficult for both of you."

"It is. I'm embarrassed and feel massive amounts of guilt about it."

"I understand you're stressed, but you don't have to beat yourself up about it. We'll figure this out."

"Thanks…I wish my wife were as compassionate. She's blinded to how bad her symptoms are and how not only they're ruining our marriage and my kids, but also how they come back on her."

"Can you give me an example?"

"Well, for instance, the house is such an embarrassment that we don't have company over because I'm worried how others will judge us. This drives my wife crazy because she's a very social, but I refuse to horrify our friends. But, she can be so stubborn, and disrespectful, and selfish."

"How so?"

"Recently we were at her best friend's house for her friend's birthday party," the man says before adding, "I never did like her — always thought she was a bad influence."

"I understand," the doctor acknowledges.

The man continues, "Anyway, I could tell that my symptoms were on the rise and I wanted to leave. After I told my wife this, she turns around and tells me that we just got there and we should stay for at least an hour otherwise it would be rude. Well, I told her that it was rude to *me* that she wasn't honoring my wishes and was siding against me."

"What happened?"

"Well, this only made my symptoms worse. I couldn't stop dwelling on how she always puts other people first. That's very disrespectful. Also, I wear my emotions on my sleeve. I mean my symptoms had to be obvious to everyone at the party — and that they must be judging me. I kept on thinking about her self-centeredness. All I wanted was to leave and she wasn't having any of it. Every time I signaled her to come over to me, she kept on chatting with her friends. I was getting increasingly anxious and angry. She was ignoring her husband," the man says with exasperation.

"What did you do?"

"I walked straight over to her and I expressed my frustration. I'm sure my voice was escalating, but I didn't car who heard me. I was trembling so much that I accidentally spilled red wine all over her friend's new white carpet. I was so embarrassed. When I told my wife that my symptoms were going through the roof and that we had to leave immediately, she had no choice but to make some lame excuse and we left the party."

"That sounds intense. How did your wife respond to your symptoms?"

"She was extremely vulgar in the car. She started telling me that *I'm* selfish and that an hour at the party wouldn't have killed me. At that point I interrupted her. I told her that I can't control my symptoms and that they come out of nowhere. Also, I told her that what she was saying was hurting my feelings — but she didn't stop. I started to tremble more and cry, and she eventually calmed down."

"How was your anxiety after leaving the party?"

"Thank God by the time we got home it had mostly disappeared. But I told you the story to show you how my wife disregards my concerns about her symptoms."

"How often do you discuss your worries with your wife?"

"Oh, I wouldn't say we *discuss* it. I express my thoughts and feelings all the time, but she won't even consider my concerns and tunes me out entirely. My wife completely dismisses my pleas to stop her compulsion and clean up her mess. Sometimes she gets up from where she's sitting and goes into another room," the man says as he launches up from the couch and starts pacing. "She's not being fair. She doesn't even acknowledge how her actions are disrespectful and her symptoms that are making me a nervous wreck. It's like she doesn't care how her actions traumatize me or the kids!"

"It must be frustrating," says the psychologist.

"It's terribly frustrating for me — like you say — but I stick with it."

"Stick with it?"

"Yeah, I know that her memory isn't as good as mine, so I have to compensate for that."

"How?"

"I realize that I have to remind her just about every day that she doesn't need to keep spending money and cluttering up the house, and that she has to be more thoughtful. Those things she buys aren't necessary and I don't like them," the man says with pressured speech while continuing to pace. "I have to let her know how bad her symptoms are. But no matter how many times I tell her that I'm concerned about her health, that all I want is her to feel better, she doesn't care. On top of that, I've told her countless times that my anxiety is relentless and unnerving, and that it's making life very difficult! But her compulsion controls her. I've been very patient, but I can't take it anymore," the man expresses his exasperation with increasing volume, "and it's gotten bad recently," that man says as he returns to the couch.

"How bad?"

The man pauses, "I hate to say it, but I'm really starting to resent her, and I don't want to do that. Sometimes I get so irritated that I've got to take things into my own hands."

"Really? How so?"

"Well, for instance, I keep sneaking some of her clutter to my car and throw it out at my office."

"And she doesn't notice?"

"There's so much clutter that I doubt she does. In fact, she has made me so anxious and hurt and angry, that I blurted out that maybe we should think about divorce."

"Do you want to divorce her?"

"No, no," the man says rapidly as he shakes his head. "I'd *never* divorce her. She's the only person I ever loved and wanted to marry. I couldn't leave her — and I couldn't to do that to the children."

"So why bring up separating?"

"Who knows?" the man says with a smile and a shrug. "Maybe if I hint at divorce she'll get that I mean business about how she causes my symptoms and has driven me to bring up the subject, then she might change."

"Is it fair to make threats like that?"

"You don't get it. Look, my wife has a serious medical problem that needs treatment. Her symptoms disrupt the house and threaten our marriage as well as our family. I've told her repeatedly how unhealthy her behavior is, and she doesn't change. Even though we don't sleep in the same bed and haven't had sex in nearly a year, she doesn't change. I tell her that her compulsions are endangering our children, and she doesn't change. She needs help, but no matter how many times I ask her, she refuses to start therapy or medication. She's completely unfazed by how her compulsions debilitate me and how her disrespect hurts my feelings, which makes me question her love for the children and me. Her behavior concerns me so deeply that *I* have to seek treatment."

"What's your goal for therapy?"

"I want my symptoms to go away forever."

"Okay," the doctor acknowledges.

"But for me to get rid of my symptoms my wife has to change."

"Ah," the doctor utters. "I see your point of view, but as she's not here, we can only work on your symptoms."

"Yes, but my symptoms won't go away until she changes! What do you want me to do? Do you want me to forget about her suffering or dismiss how her symptoms control her and ruin our family? I just can't do that!"

"I understand what you're saying, but might you be painting yourself into a corner?"

"How so?"

"Are you saying that if she's unwilling to change, then your symptoms stay?"

"Well, what if you explain to my wife how her compulsions cause my symptoms. You could get her to see how dangerous her symptoms are, and how she needs to change her ways. She can benefit from an outside perspective that can show her the error of her ways. I'm at the end of my rope. My symptoms are killing me, and she's has been causing my anxiety for years. She's got to treat me nicer and she's got to start throwing out all that garbage that's collected in the house over the years and has become a fire hazard and stop wasting all my money," the man pleads. "Here, let me show you some pictures of how bad it is!" The patient produces his phone and swipes through several pictures of his home.

The psychologist looks at the pictures and sees some clutter, several knickknacks, and a couple of children's items. While not immaculate, it appears relatively ordinary in neatness.

The patient asks, "Do you see the problem?"

"I might now."

Controlling Spouse, Revisited

The many forms of symptomatic evidence in this example are simple to spot (Why not start with an easy one?) Given the last piece of information, you might be tempted to say that the patient is delusional — rather than suffering with generalized anxiety. However, note that there's some truth to his claims. For instance, his home is a bit messy and not as neat as he prefers, his wife does move into another room when he brings up his concerns, and his insomnia is related to anxiety. But the main reason why his anxiety arises remains shrouded. Thankfully, there are many clues that unveil his symptoms' purposes.

Out of all of the things people can focus on, what they attend to generates particular emotions, and those emotions spark or impede certain behavior, which may achieve a goal. Accordingly, what this man observes and disregards can be as revealing as an x-ray. With that in mind, what does he zero in on? What emotions does this perspective generate? What related behavior occurs? And, in what direction do his actions point?

For a man who states that he loves and would never divorce his wife, you may assume that she has a number of attractive and wonderful characteristics. Yet, throughout the vignette does the patient ever acknowledge his wife's good efforts and attributes? No, he solely focuses on what she does wrong. This lack of balance in perspective reveals a confirmation bias — a tendency to see things that confirm his conceptions. Knowing that the patient only attends to what his wife does incorrectly (from his point of view), you can suspect that he wants her to change. But how does he prompt her?

Well, consider that his perspective allows the use of words that are alarmist and disproportionate to the circumstance. For example, the man defines his wife as a "hoarder," and that his wife's clutter creates a "dangerous household" — a fire hazard that jeopardizes the entire family, that she has and will "waste money on needless things," that the kids won't simply trip or knock something over — but rather they'll "break a bone or poke out an eye," he says that the state of his home will "horrify" friends, that his wife's actions "traumatize" him. These extreme words mirror his perspective and reveal his type and level of emotions about the subject. Indeed, he's focusing on those matters to generate and perpetuate particular emotions and at a certain level. If you were to stop your investigation at this point, you'd be missing the larger picture, as the man appears to be suffering pointlessly. So, what might his anxiety allow?

Reflect on his goal: he wants his wife to change. Additionally, you know that she hasn't responded to his direct suggestions and mandates (e.g., curb her spending, use coupons, keep the house clean). So rather than surrender his desire, he employs symptoms to achieve it. With that in mind, by perceiving his wife as causing his anxiety, what might he accomplish?

As long as he deems her as responsible for his symptoms, *she's* the one that must change. This liberates him from examination or altering his perspective, goals, and life style convictions. Moreover, his belief grants him license and rationale to frequently attempt to prod his wife to act the way he wants, say by repeating statements or subtle threats. Additionally, he fortifies his argument by defining his wife as petty, vain, and competitive, as — from his perspective — she buys things to prevent her sister or the neighbors from outshining her. The man describes his wife's behavior as a threat on multiple fronts: their finances, the children's education, role modeling unhealthy behavior that jeopardizes the kids' future, the children might be physically injured, etc. He claims that his wife's actions negatively impact the kids presently and in the future. Yet, the children may be completely unfazed and unaffected, as evidenced by their lack of complaints or any mention of it. This fact isn't in accord with the man's perspective, so what does he do? He rationalizes his children's lack of protest (e.g., they're trying to spare his feelings) and states that problems will arise in the future. Odds are, the children don't complain because they don't see a mess.

Moreover, as long as he defines his wife as helpless against an innate compulsion, and that she cannot see the alleged damage she's doing, the patient can further fortify his drive to push her to change. Also, the worrisome implication that visitors to their home would be horrified can be another attempt to provide more reasons why his wife should alter her behavior. Furthermore, by believing his wife has memory problems or doesn't listen to him, he can convince himself that it's acceptable and necessary to frequently remind her about what he wants her to do. (Odds are that she knows *exactly* what he wants as he hasn't kept his preferences a secret, she just tunes out his repetitive statements because she has different goals.) The patient fails to see that his wife is the co-captain of the family team and has just as many rights in the home as the patient does. His pleas for her to change come in the form of "I" statements (e.g., "I want…" or "All I want…"). The patient doesn't acknowledge what his wife wants, or her rightful privileges within the home.

The man employs a number of tactics to protect his self-esteem, acceptance, status, and life style. For instance, he implies that he's smarter and more compassionate than his wife, and states that he's worried about the children and implies his wife isn't concerned about their well-being. He believes that he's able to see what's wrong and what needs to change, and she does not have such insight. This can be an unconscious attempt to elevate him above her and strengthen his argument.

The patient defines his wife as stubborn, distancing, and uncooperative, yet he's unaware of his cognitively rigidity. He cannot see his role in marital discord, he uses righteous indignation and gets angry to tell her what the "right" thing is to do. Yet, even though the patient has such rationale and points, his wife doesn't change. (Interestingly, did you notice how his back pain and the related anger dissipate as soon as he leaves the house?) So what other symptoms and tactics arise when she doesn't comply with his desires?

Consider the unity of the personality. His anxiety-based insomnia prods him to sleep in the living room. This creates physical distance and punishes her in ways that evade responsibility (e.g., blaming his symptoms for not sleeping in the same bed and denying sex). In this way, his symptoms may be used to take revenge. This hints at another face-saving tactic. While he blames her for causing his anxiety which has led to a nearly year-long sex drought as he sleeps on the couch, he reframes his related back pain in martyr-like terms — he sleeps on the couch to prevent disturbing his wife's slumber, thereby stating that he suffers for his wife's sake. After all, if he needs background noise to sleep, he could stay in bed and wear earbuds or headphones.

Where else was the unity of the personality evidenced?

Well, reflect on when his wife didn't want to leave the party. There was a battle of wills between the man's symptoms and his wife's interest in respectfully attending and enjoying her best friend's party. This enabled the man to control his wife. Though an unconscious process, he appeared to focus on symptom-producing thoughts that made his presence increasingly difficult (e.g., increased volume and content of speech that annoyed and aggravated his wife, staining the carpet). It was an arms race of sorts. She wanted to stay at the party, and he did not. His symptoms began to prompt her to leave. Her response? She ignored him. Then, his symptoms exploded until she appeased him by surrendering her goal to be at the party. Also, reflect on their car ride home. What symptoms arose when the wife expressed her annoyance and anger at her husband? His sensitivity, trembling, and tears ("water power") coerced her to stop her criticism. The unity of the personality is demonstrated in many ways: increased speech volume, body language, the use of tears, only focusing on those things that produce select and powerful emotions (e.g., reframing her desire to stay at the party as disrespect), and muscle weakness. In fact, the battle of wills escalated to the point where the man used the (empty) threat of divorce to control his wife. You can see how impatience and dramatic symptoms can create excitement and agitation to gain attention and compliance. Although the man expresses his regular dissatisfaction with his wife, he says he loves her and has no intentions of a divorce. Moreover, he cites his children's well-being as a noble rationale to keep his marriage intact. By stating that a divorce would harm the children he can portray himself as a martyr who suffers for others' benefit, and this is in compliance with the need to be good. Yet, all he may be doing is giving himself license to remain immobile in the marriage and continued permission to prod his wife.

The patient is driven to have things his way, and he may view a "Real" man as one who controls his wife, is smarter and more compassionate, etc. and he unconsciously uses his symptoms to gain compliance and portray himself as superior. Furthermore, he believes that he's an innocent victim and his wife the victimizer. The man also demonstrated his cognitive rigidity and defense mechanisms when the doctor highlighted the patient's use of a threat. At that point, the patient attempted to minimize the therapist's ability by implying a lack of cognitive capacity and insight to "get it." Indeed, given the patient's perspective and goal, he may not be able to discern a different point of view. Rather than ponder the therapist's observation — and its implications for change — the patient attempted to misdirect the psychologist by returning focus to his wife and making unsubstantiated claims.

The patient displayed present-ism in his impatience to leave the party. He states that he's powerless against his symptoms and unaware of why they exist other than as the result of his wife's lack of cooperation. Ultimately, the man uses neurotic anxiety symptoms to dominate his wife and elevate himself, in an attempt to protect his self-esteem, status, acceptance, and life style. Here you see that the presenting issue isn't the real issue. This is quite common in therapy and one of the reasons why a logical answer may be ineffective when a *psycho*-logical answer is needed. Make no mistake, the patient is truly suffering. However, note that his stipulation that his wife causes his symptoms, which will only evaporate once she changes. The patient goes so far as to attempt to recruit his doctor to validate and legitimize the patient's claim that his wife must alter her behavior. However, recall that the person with the symptoms is the person who must change.

Driven Parent

In her initial therapy session, a middle-aged woman enters a psychologist's office. Her eyes dart among various items, examining the displayed degrees and décor as if she were a detective investigating various clues. She hesitantly descends onto the couch and asks about the doctor's educational background, theoretical orientation, number of anxious people treated, success rate, how long the psychologist has been at the present location as well as years in practice. They discuss the rules of confidentiality, and the woman declines the option to sign a release of information so the psychologist can keep in touch with the patient's primary care physician for continuity of care. The woman states, "I don't think it's necessary that my medical doctor knows I'm in therapy."

"I understand," the psychologist replies. "It's no problem."

"I Googled you before I set the appointment," the woman says holding her phone up before setting it on the couch next to her.

"People do that," says the doctor.

"This is my first time in therapy and I wanted to make sure you're good," the woman confesses. "I'm a bit apprehensive."

"No worries," the psychologist smiles. "New experiences can be a bit daunting. I appreciate your courage in following through. I'm glad to answer any questions along the way."

"Thank you. Do you have a back door here?"

"Yes."

"Can I enter and exit through it if I'm to continue therapy?"

"Sure."

"Do you start your sessions promptly on time?"

"Yes, unless there's an emergency," the doctor clarifies.

"I had to wait in my car for nearly 15 minutes before I came up here."

"How come?"

"I got here early, but I didn't want to sit in your waiting room and run into somebody I know."

"I see. What concerns you?"

"I don't want to be judged and I certainly don't want to hang out with other people who have to see you for who-knows-what. I'm probably not like your other patients."

"I understand," the psychologist reassures. "How can I be of best use to you?"

"I'm anxious."

"How long have you been anxious?"

"Well, I was a bit anxious when I was younger, and it has been on and off for years, then it went away until the last few years."

"Is there anything that you can identify as related to your anxiety?"

The woman inhales deeply then blurts out, "My daughter is driving me crazy!"

"How so?" her psychologist asks.

The patient furrows her brow, "She doesn't do anything all day."

"How old is your child?"

"She's 16."

"Only child?"

"Yes."

"Please continue," the doctor encourages.

"You see, I grew up on a farm. We'd have to work in the barn, feed the cows, clean the house, and I had to get up at daybreak and start working. That work ethic really benefitted me. Eventually I became the CEO of a company here in town. However, my daughter is on the computer all day chatting with her friends while doing her homework, and at night they text each other. She's constantly on her phone. I can't stand it."

"It sounds like your daughter has quite a different life style than yours."

"You said it!"

"What would you prefer her to do?" the doctor queries.

"She can start by contributing more to the family."

"How so?"

"I'm not talking about chores so much, but rather about being part of the family. For example, at dinnertime we should be eating as a family, but when she couldn't put her phone down, I forbade her from using it at the table. Her father and I just want her to be involved with the family, but she isn't. Is that asking too much?"

"It doesn't seem so. So, why might she detached from you and your husband?"

"Well, I've been thinking about this," the woman pauses. "It's not that we don't provide for her, or that we don't love her, or that we don't want the best for her. Then I thought it's because she's a teenager and that's common teenager behavior."

"Often," the psychologist adds, "but I suspect you believe it's something else."

"Yes you're right, I do. Not every teenager acts that way and there's no reason why my daughter would need to be so distant. I was curious what the problem was. So, I read online about various diagnoses and I'm certain my kid has some kind of attention deficit disorder or social phobia."

"Hmmm, interesting," the psychologist utters. "How did you arrive at that conclusion?"

"You wouldn't believe how many times I've got to tell her to do something," the woman shakes her head rapidly in disbelief.

"Like what?"

"Oh, that she's got to sit up straight, that she has to use full sentences, not drag her feet when she walks, that she can't slam the chair into the kitchen table, that she has to bring her dirty dishes into the sink when she's done eating, what to wear, who to associated with, that she's got to let me know when she needs to get a project done for school instead of waiting until the last minute — yet she never listens. I think about this all the time and sometimes I've got to yell to get her to do the right thing. Even then she drags her feet. That's why I think she has ADHD or some kind of attention deficit. Perhaps, I should have her tested. What do you think?"

"Well, I don't know..." the doctor replies, "tell me more."

"I think she has social phobia too because she spends so much of her time in her bedroom on the computer or her phone — away from her mother who loves her more than anything in the world. She almost never talks with me. Often, when I enter a room, she leaves. I want to know what's going on with her and why she's always so quiet. I tell her all the time that I didn't become CEO by being shy and distant. I impress upon her how she has to present well, not in tattered jeans like she always wears. I'm getting very concerned about her. She's not going anyplace in life looking like that."

"Sounds frustrating and exhausting."

"It is. There are times when I text her and she doesn't respond."

"How do you feel about that?"

"She's glued to that phone. She always has it within reach. She has it on her every second. There's no way she didn't see my text."

"I see," the psychologist says. "How are your daughter's grades?"

"Thankfully, she doing very well in school," the woman confesses.

"That's good."

"Yes, but that doesn't mean anything. There is more to life than just doing well at presentations, papers, and tests. She needs to engage people. She needs to become part of the family."

"Often, people's movement reveals their goals—"

"So?" the woman interrupts.

"I see that your daughter's movement is away from you. Can you identify any reason why she would create distance?"

"No," the woman replies reflexively.

"How would you characterize the way you speak with her?" the psychologist queries.

The patient sighs then states with pressured speech, "This has nothing to do with me. Don't make me out to be the bad guy! Can't you see that I'm the one who's trying when she's not? Maybe I shouldn't have made this appointment. It doesn't matter how I talk to her. I love her and what I tell her is useful. How else is she going to learn? I want her to have even more accomplishments than what I have. But, if she isn't able to pay attention, those lessons will be lost forever. I've got to repeatedly get on her to do her homework and I go over it line by line. I've got other things I'd like to do, but I need to make sure my daughter is doing well in life. If I didn't constantly remind her about her homework or chores or how to speak or how to present well she wouldn't get such good grades. She needs constant prodding or she'll fall behind. And if I didn't talk to her about her schooling, with whom to associate, and how to act, I'd never interact with her because she's so secretive and quiet. The only time I have an advantage is when we're in the car and she can't go anywhere, but she's usually silent there too."

"Is she always quiet and withdrawn from people?"

"Well, like I said earlier, she does talk and text a lot with her friends. Lord knows what they're talking about. Probably just wasting time. The point is that she's only this age once, and time is running out. All I want is to be the best parent I can be and for her to do well in life. However, her disrespect and distancing makes my job ten times more difficult and…look at me, I'm working up a sweat just thinking about it," the woman says as she takes a tissue out of her purse and wipes her brow and palms. "There are some nights I wake up worried sick about my daughter's future."

"I'm sorry that you're suffering. Everything will be okay," the psychologist comforts.

The woman lets out a slow exhale and she sinks into the couch. "Maybe. But there are some days I just can't envision that happening."

"How does your daughter act with your husband?" asks the psychologist.

"Oh, him? He's a pushover. He'll listen to her drone on about her day, what boy she's interested in, what music she likes, dumb TV shows, laughing and carrying on like idiots." The woman's speech increases in volume and rate, "He needs to be a father who guides her, but he's more of a pal. She'll have plenty of time for boys after college, and those brainless TV shows she watches are detrimental. At this point, I'm thinking about cancelling the service so she doesn't have as many shows to watch. I should also cancel her phone, but I need to know where she is at any time and to give her a way to reach me if necessary. But, to answer your question, she talks to her father regularly but..." the woman pauses, "about useless things. What's worse is that my daughter often asks him for advice rather than me. I'm the successful one. I make more money than he does and she's asking him for advice!"

"How does your husband respond to your daughter's interests?"

"He just kind of humors her, I think. He laughs at her silliness and hangs on every word she says. He looks really interested in it and he appears to be fascinated, but I think he's just being nice. He overpraises her."

"Overpraises?"

"He is her cheerleader, attending to every little thing she does. I think he spoils her."

"Hmmm. Interesting," the doctor utters while pondering the woman's statement.

"Exactly! You think so too, huh? Anyway, I don't think any adult could really relate to a child. Maybe my husband never grew up. He's too easy going — and that drives me crazy too. I, on the other hand, don't tolerate my daughter's giddiness or hollow pursuits."

"So what do you tolerate?"

"You probably noticed that I can be impatient. I tend to interrupt boring people if they drone on too long without getting to the point. I don't tolerate much and my patience is getting very thin lately with my daughter—." At that moment the woman's phone rings. While quickly drawing the phone to her ear she looks at the doctor and raises her index finger then subtly mouths, "One second." After briefly responding to the call she resumes, "Anyway, where was I? Oh yeah, I refuse to bankroll any interest that is a waste of time. That's especially true when my daughter doesn't do what she should. Why should I finance what she wants, when she doesn't do what I want? I role model hard work and how important that is. I'm always in motion doing something and that's what has made me who I am and what has allowed her to have her phone, clothes, and computer."

"I see," the psychologist responds. "It sounds like you work very hard. What's your typical day like?"

"I get up around 4:30 am, have some coffee before I go to the gym. I come home and get ready for work and I'm there before 7 most days. I work until 6 pm and I come home to dinner on the table at 6:30. I check on my kid's homework as well as my work e-mail and return necessary phone calls. I probably get to sleep at about 11 or midnight and I sleep right on through until I get up at 4:30 the next day to go back to the gym."

"What type of workout do you do at the gym?"

"Cardio, running mostly — I was always a runner — though I often go to a spinning class or on the elliptical machine. I can't skip a day, because when I do I get really edgy and keyed up."

"And are you anxious when you workout?"

The woman pauses, "No. I'm not. Actually, it's the only time I feel at peace."

"And, how much coffee do you drink in a day?"

"Let me see…maybe two before the gym, another in the car on the way to work, and then 4 or so throughout the day. Maybe one after dinner. But I don't go by the guide on the machine, that doesn't make a proper cup."

"That's a lot of coffee. Are you getting enough rest?"

"I've never suffered from insomnia. I fall asleep as soon as my head hits the pillow."

"Do you wake up in the middle of the night?"

"Rarely," she responds pridefully. "I never needed any sleep aid medication — nor do I need any for my anxiety — if you were thinking about putting me on drugs."

"So you wouldn't be interest in medications? They can be quite good at reducing symptoms."

"Psychiatry is like stomach stapling," she retorts. "I'm not interested."

"What do you mean?"

"Look," the patient says forcefully, "I believe people can lose weight if they try, but some don't have the will or tenacity. So they opt for the simple and easy route. They avoid being accountable for their behavior and want someone else or something to control their weight. The funny thing is, if they want to eat like crazy, stomach stapling isn't going to stop them in the long run."

"Anti-anxiety medications can be helpful," the doctor states, "but it's up to you, of course."

"I'm not taking medication. I need to be in control of my faculties and I don't want to get the side effects I've read about. I'm not going to take anything that changes my mood or energy level."

"But you drink coffee."

"So does everyone else with a job," the woman volleys back.

"Did you know that coffee can aggravate anxiety?"

"I can't go without it. I sleep so deeply that if I don't have it in the morning I'm super-groggy. I need something to wake me up and get me going to the gym. Also, I've got to be attentive at work all day. The fact is that it isn't the coffee that's causing my anxiety; it's my daughter. The problem is only getting worse as she gets older and faces real life. I'm worried sick about her. What do I need to do to cure my symptoms?"

Driven Parent, Revisited

People's actions provide clues about their goals and how they think. Before you get to the first words about why the woman is in therapy, you have evidence of her interest in predictability and her desire to know about things and others. Note that this isn't paranoia, just cautious curiosity. Yet, why might she act this way? Though it seems unnecessary — especially with a licensed professional — there should be some explanation. Perhaps, she wants to control for an undesirable outcome for therapy? This is a reasonable and prudent goal. Maybe she wants to limit who knows information about her? This can explain her disinterest in signing a release of information that would allow communication between her healthcare providers. Certainly, she doesn't want to accidently run into someone she knows. But why? She wants to avoid (read: control for) negative judgment. Over the course of years, such anxious scrutiny and forethought may have been reinforced and fortified when nothing undesirable followed. However, it appears to have needlessly crept beyond healthy boundaries.

The woman reports being anxious on and off for decades, with symptoms increasing during the last few years. Long-term and intermittent symptoms can suggest her anxiety may be due to how she handles life's challenges rather than because of genes that turn on and off repeatedly over the course of decades, for example. Presently, the patient identifies her daughter as the cause of her symptoms; however, what else may be going on?

As people are goal oriented, it's helpful to start your investigation by assessing the woman's goal — to parent her daughter so she's successful. This is a virtuous and socially-beneficial objective. But which perceptions, rules, and goals does she attempt to instill in her child?

Well, reflect on this woman's upbringing. She learned early on that children fulfill parentally-imposed responsibilities and that hard work and tenacity are productive. In fact, her strategies for life appear quite successful and relatively healthy, as she has checked all the boxes for socially-defined success: married, employed, financially stable, athletic, and is a parent who loves her child. Accordingly, she attempts to instill her proven strategies in her daughter, and expects her to put in diligent effort in her schoolwork, present properly, make good social connections, interact with her and her husband, and not waste time on frivolous things. These expectations appear good and reasonable. However, when the daughter doesn't live up to them, the patient is frustrated, anxious, and upset. At this level of examination the woman's symptoms appear to be a natural consequence associated with parenting challenges. Yet, how else might you explain her daughter's behavior as well as the patient's symptoms?

Consider how the woman is driven, seeks control and predictability, and is tenacious in pursuing her goals. To that end, she often attends to her daughter's behavior and regularly offers guidance. Ah, but *how* does she do this with her daughter? Well, consider how this woman is a problem solver who looks for errors and attempts to fix them. She even searches for possible problems on the horizon that haven't materialized to avoid them. By focusing on what's wrong — or what could go wrong — she generates tension and anxiety that she employs to fuel beneficial behavior. Apparently, she also uses this strategy in parenting.

The woman's embellished and inaccurate worry about her child empowers vigilance of her behavior. In addition, it grants the patient permission to frequently correct her daughter and give unsolicited advice. For instance, examine the ratio of positive and encouraging interactions to the negative and discouraging ones the patient has with her child. The ratio is disproportionately critical, with much prodding. There's very little — if any — reported encouragement and warm exchange with her daughter on her level or about her passions. The mother doesn't ask about her child's friends or interests and doesn't offer much acceptance. She just continually pushes her daughter to be better. However, this has an unintended outcome. It risks giving her daughter the impression that she's inferior, that her pastimes are not valid or important, and — despite the woman's declarations — unloved by her mother. This is palpably different from her warm, encouraging, attentive, and flexible father. So what may happen after years of this type of mother-daughter interaction? Perhaps, the daughter initially put up a fight, but given her mother's desire for control and her power over finances, transportation, household rules, etc., the child learned a direct attack — an insurrection of sorts — was unwinnable. So, how might the daughter maintain autonomy and defy her mother's control and negativity?

The daughter demonstrates another coping mechanism: passive rebellion. She physically avoids her mother and tunes out her mother with indifference. (Interestingly, such deficit of attention has been labeled "mother deafness."[616] Please note that despite the name, it's not an exclusively maternal condition. Fathers can be icily ignored as well.). So even though the patient has good intentions, and her strategies for life have been successful, it's likely her presentation sabotaged her strivings. Yet, if people strive toward their goals, and the woman's desire is to improve her daughter's chances for success in life, and the patient is a problem solver who readily identifies errors, why doesn't she see her role in unwanted behavior and change her parenting style?

Being seen as an ineffective parent imperils self-esteem, acceptance, status, and requires a review and revision of the patient's life style. Yet, neurotic symptoms safeguard those things. The woman devoutly believes in her life style convictions and is supremely reluctant to renounce them. Consequently, she may seek to fortify them as well as her parenting style. By making her role in the problem and related need to change unconscious, she severs all connections she has to those possibilities and responsibilities. However, she still has to explain her daughter's behavior in a protective way. Rather than blame herself, in accord with her life style, the woman identifies problems with her daughter's behavior and scours the Internet for what those actions (deemed symptoms) mean. She unofficially diagnoses her child with an attention deficit disorder and social phobia. By blaming the daughter in this way, the patient liberates herself from changing her belief system and improving her behavior. She supports her position by identifying only that behavior that fits those diagnoses. The woman uses her concern to turn up the volume and frequency of criticism, and declares her noble intent to allow continued negativity. The patient uses phrases such as "All I want…" to justify her goals and related actions, but she doesn't take into account what her daughter wants.

Kids may do things differently from how their parents did when they were younger. But, you may suspect that the child's fractured and rapidly divided attention among people and things (e.g., TV, phone, family, friends) indicate some kind of attention deficit disorder. Perhaps (after all, she isn't in the room to be assessed), but take into account how the daughter may merely be multitasking on a scale the parent is unfamiliar. (Indeed, just consider how the pacing of movies, TV shows, and commercials has generally increased in tempo throughout the decades.) When you look at the data, it's unlikely that she's lazy, or has an attention deficit disorder or social phobia, as the mother asserts. Her grades are well above average. This suggests that she's industrious rather than lazy, and is quite capable of focusing her attention — on her teachers as well as her books — for extended periods. Next, although the patient reports that her daughter is disengaged from the family, that's simply untrue. The daughter frequently attends to her father. People often don't register when their perceptions and beliefs are negated or disproven. For example, did you catch how the patient protectively reframes and discounts her husband's ability to successfully bond with their daughter as an undesirable weakness? She labels him a "pal" and a "pushover," and that proper, mature adults cannot connect with children the way her husband does. Did you notice how the patient projects onto the therapist the belief that her husband's behavior is questionable? The doctor merely stated a relatively vague "Hmmm. Interesting," which could mean many things — including something related to the patient, rather than her husband.

In addition, the daughter's regular communication with her friends provides evidence counter to the contention that she's socially phobic. Ah, but how do you explain the girl's retreat to her bedroom or copious amounts of texting rather than face-to-face communication? Does such distancing suggest social phobia? Well, consider how the daughter may be social in ways her mother is unfamiliar, but it doesn't mean that the child has a social phobia. The patient may unconsciously prefer to see her child as lazy, or having an attention deficit disorder or socially phobia, because that's easier to believe than the woman is failing at parenting and has alienated her beloved daughter.

From her point of view, the patient is experiencing symptoms because her daughter's life style doesn't mirror hers. She believes her daughter is imperiling her future. This is unnerving for the mother. But rather than view her symptoms as a feedback mechanism to improve her thought patterns and actions, the patient doubles-down on her original bet. She focuses on what's going wrong and uses various forms of resultant anxiety to ratchet up her drive and control of her daughter's behavior. The patient depicts her actions as altruistic, self-sacrificing, and necessary, which gives her authority to keep pushing her teenager. Additionally, she contemplates cutting her daughter's conduit of communication with others (phone and computers) to corral her daughter's behavior. Controlling finances (with accompanying anxiety and anger) is another means to goad her child into particular behavior. In fact, this woman bolsters her anger through many means, such as having unrealistic expectations. For instance, teenagers are normally interested in surveying what's acceptable and they commonly communicate what is, and is not, cool. Yet, the woman projects her goals onto her daughter and defines this as unnecessary and counterproductive.

There are a number of ways in which the patient unconsciously provokes anxiety (as well as the physiological correlates) to achieve her goals. Anxiety revs her up like her morning coffee, often allowing her to achieve amazing, productive, and defining feats on the useful side of life — something that she may not be willing to relinquish. Yet, that which makes her great is that which works the greatest against her. The woman uses her anxiety to push herself, and has employed this strategy to push her daughter. Yet, her drive, determination, and use of anxiety to achieve lofty and socially-beneficial goals, has indeed pushed her child — but away from her. Though the woman's anxiety has been employed fruitfully in the past, presently it's splintering her family. Yet, people can be very tenacious to their beliefs and not recognize when they act in a hypocritical manner. For example, did you notice the woman's double standard? Though she finds her child's use of her phone disrespectful at the dinner table, the woman didn't hesitate to receive a call while in session — completely unaware of the hypocrisy. Things may become conscious or unconscious in accord with goal achievement. Also, consider how the unity of the personality is demonstrated in her physical movements: eyes that dart around the room, her furrowed brow, rate of speech, perspiration, and reported sleeplessness. Moreover, note how the woman unabashedly acknowledged being impatient. She wears it as a badge of honor rather than a fault to be worked on, but why? As unnerving as it is, it can be used to control others or situations, say by making them get to their point quicker or to cut them off so that she doesn't have to listen to what they say. In fact, tremendous drive, impatience, anxiety, and sleeplessness often cluster together.

Did you notice how the woman responded to the psychologist's question about her feelings about the daughter's lack of reply to her text? The woman did not express a feeling, but rather a string of thoughts and facts. This may reveal preference for concrete and predictable matters as well as difficulty in handling emotions, which can be vague and unpredictable. Also, did you pick up on her use of a "Yes, but..."? She employed it when the psychologist noted the daughter's good grades. As her daughter's good grades could dismiss the woman's point of view and minimize her worry, she attempted to discredit it.

Now, reflect on the woman's description of her average day. It's double-parked with obligations. Why might that be? First, it's correlated with being driven. Second, being busy can preclude ruminating about what she has to do, dwelling on awkward or painful things in the past, racing thoughts that arise prior to falling asleep, and — given her drive — any cognitive discomfort from being idle. Third, by postponing sleep until she's utterly exhausted, she's able to evade distressing cognitive discomfort. This explains why she's able to fall asleep as soon as her head hits the pillow, as well as why someone with pronounced anxiety would seek (and defend the use of) copious amounts of coffee. The caffeine can overcome the exhaustion from an insufficient amount of sleep and generate the desired amount of systemic arousal that approximates her eventual anxiety level. Overall, though her anxiety has been employed to achieve various socially-beneficial goals, you know that it's an imperfect solution because it lessens the quality of her life, as well as those around her. But given its ability to allow intermittent success, its unconscious operation, nearly lifelong duration, and how the woman defines herself, it may be difficult for her to change.

Fearful Son

An overweight 26-year-old man dressed in sweatpants, untied sneakers, and a t-shirt attends his first therapy appointment.

"What brings you in?" asks the psychologist as he encourages the man to have a seat.

"My dad."

"What about him?"

"No, he drove me here," the patient responds.

"Actually, I was asking about what symptoms you're experiencing that led you to make the appointment."

"Well, my dad made the appointment for me," said the man while bouncing his foot frenetically. "He knows that I've been anxious since high school...maybe earlier. I live with him."

"Describe your anxiety," the psychologist urges.

"It's really frustrating."

"How so?"

The man continues, "There are so many things I want to do, but my anxiety paralyzes me."

"Can you give me some examples?"

"It stops me from doing all the things I want to do."

"Such as?"

"Well, currently I'm unemployed," the patient states. "And that's been very difficult."

"I can imagine. How has it been difficult?"

"I really want to work — even my dad sees my efforts — but my anxiety sidelines me."

"Sidelines?"

"Yes, in a couple of different ways."

"How?" the psychologist investigates.

"Well, last year I was so anxious that I missed two important job interviews that my father set up for me."

"That must have been upsetting."

"My poor father was very disappointed," the man quickly replies.

"What happened?"

"With the first interview I noticed a couple of hours before the appointment I was really anxious so I thought I'd relax by playing a video game to get my mind off of it. But I ended up losing track of time."

"And the second one?"

"I was so anxious beforehand that I just couldn't function. I thought that there was no way they'd hire me. Then I though, why go to the interview if I was only going to fail it?"

"I'm sorry to hear that. You said that was last year. Any job interviews this year?"

"No."

"What's stopped you?"

"I thought that maybe I should get an adult job, not some minimum wage job and be stuck working with high school kids."

"Okay," the psychologist acknowledges. "So what was your plan?"

"I thought I should go to college rather than immediately find a job."

"That sounds like a nice goal. Did you enroll?"

"I never made it that far," the man admits.

"I'm sorry to hear that. What happened?"

"It was my anxiety again. I just couldn't decide which career path to take. I thought rather than waste more of my father's money, I needed to be absolutely sure that I pick the right education path. But I was torn, so I never applied to any school."

"So you were being considerate of your father's finances. That's very thoughtful."

"Thank you," the man nods with a slight smile.

"What was the last job you had?"

"Actually, I never had one. But now I need to get one."

"Why do you need to?"

"Again, it's the money. I want to help out my dad. I'm sure I'm an expense. After all, he pays for all of my food, my car, my insurance...everything, really. I need to help him out. But that's not the only reason why I need to get a job."

"Why else?"

"He's been alone since my mother died. But, I'm sure he'd like to date."

"What stops him?"

"As long as I'm around the house, he has been busy with me. He checks in on me regularly and always sacrifices his time, money, and energy to try to distract me from my worries, reassure me, or lighten my burden. I feel terrible about how I'm still living off of him. It's a bit embarrassing. Besides, I don't think any woman would want to date him given that I'm still in the house. I really miss my mom — no one will be as good as she was."

"I'm sorry about your mom's passing."

"It's okay. I still have very fond memories of her."

"That's nice to hear," the psychologist says warmly.

"I remember this one time when I was about 6 my mother and I were in the kitchen and she was helping me go over some worksheets from school — colors or patterns, something like that. She was dividing her time between making dinner and me. I remember looking at those worksheets and thinking that I couldn't do them right and I started to get a bit tense. I started to fidget in my seat and might even have teared up. But my mom, she was sharp as a tack. Once she saw how stressed I was she came over and calmed me down. She saw that the worksheets were stressing me out. She picked up my pencil and did the worksheets for me. She saw my anxiety evaporate on the spot. I really felt loved and protected at that moment — probably more than I've ever felt since. I recollect it often."

"I'm sorry for your loss. I'm sure your mother loved you tremendously."

"Thank you, she did. But, thinking about it now I guess I've always had anxiety. It's probably genetic."

"Did you ever have any genetic testing done?"

"No, but I can *feel* it. I'll probably have it for the rest of my life," the man says as he falls back deep into the couch.

"Don't worry. This can be figured out," the doctor reassures. "A moment ago you said you were unable to pick a career path. Let's focus on the positive. Sometimes it's helpful to find your passions as they can make excellent and rewarding careers. When you were younger were there any jobs you dreamed of having?"

"Originally, I wanted to be a surgeon," the patient's mood lightens. "When I was a kid I'd watch all those doctor shows and I thought being a doctor would allow all the things I wanted: respect, financial stability, and a lot of flexibility to do what I wanted."

"That's great," the psychologist encourages.

"Yeah, but over time my anxiety intensified and I eventually shied away from it."

"That's too bad. I'm sure you would be a wonderful doctor."

"I don't know. I could never see myself responsible for anyone else's life. It's too much pressure all the time. And there's the work involved. Becoming a doctor requires tremendous intelligence and effort and constant assessment of how much you know and how good you are. There's no rest, you always have to keep on top of things. I just could never take on that level of pressure and judgment. All those tests. I just want a career that's reliable and non-threatening."

"I understand. What other passion might interest you?"

"Well, I like to read — I always have. When I was younger I also thought I'd be a college professor or something with tenure where I'm guaranteed a job and that I'd really have to goof up to lose the position."

"Job security is nice to have."

"I prefer to silently go into work and not draw a lot of attention. I just want to do my job and go home."

"So would you like to become a professor?"

"That would be nice, but..." the patient trails off.

"But...?"

"Well, I'm getting too old to try a new career path or go back to school."

"There's no need to worry," the psychologist reassures with a smile. "You can do it. I have a friend who returned to school when he was 50 to get his doctorate."

"Yes," the patient pauses, "I guess that's possible. But like I said earlier, my symptoms always stop me from doing what I want to do. No matter what I try, I can't win."

"I'm sure you have untapped skills and abilities. You're young and you can grow and learn new things."

"I don't know. I can't even pay attention to those free online classes."

"What happens?"

"I get anxious and my mind wanders."

"I understand," the doctor acknowledges. "How's your social life?"

"As I've gotten older I've lost touch with most of my friends from high school. It's mostly my dad that I associate with now. I still keep in contact with a few friends online though."

"Do you ever go out?"

"No money."

"Do they every visit?"

"I'd hate for them to see me cooped up in my house. It'd be too embarrassing."

"I understand your concerns, but it connecting with others can reduce anxiety."

"Maybe for most people, but I don't think that's the case with me. I only keep in contact with one friend, but it's a long drive to his house."

"How often do you see him?"

"I drive out there every week."

"And what do you do?"

"Well, to be honest, I only talk to him because he gets me pot."

"How long have you been using marijuana?"

"Years. It's the only thing that calms me," the man says while his foot bounces rhythmically.

"I see," the doctor says. "How often do you use it?"

"Just about everyday."

"I see," the psychologist says.

The patient quickly changes the topic, "I'd like to start a family one day."

"That sounds like a nice goal. Tell me about your dating history."

"Well, in high school there was this girl I thought was cute. I talked to her a couple of times, but when it came time to ask her out — even for a coffee — I just couldn't get the words out."

"How about other women?"

"When I was in my early 20s I dated two women for a couple of months each."

"How did that go?"

"It was okay...no sex or anything," the patient appends.

"Well, everybody would like a close and healthy relationship — and a lot of people get married—"

"But for every two marriages there's one divorce," the man interjects.

"Sure relationships can be challenging and intimidating at times — even end. While not all last, relationships are like most other things in life, they require effort and practice to be successful. You're not supposed to know everything about relationships, or life, in your 20s. Be patient and there's no need to beat yourself up about it."

"Yeah I guess, but every one of my previous relationships failed," the patient persists.

"That puts you in good company."

"I don't get it," the man says quizzically. "What's your point?"

"Have you have thought about how every relationship prior to marriage failed for each happily married person?"

"So?"

"Even though these individuals had a 100% failure rate in their relationships, it didn't stop them from getting married."

"That may be, but I don't know," the man pauses. "I mean I'd like to get married and start a family. But I often think about how I'm not getting any younger."

"Well, that's true for all of us," the psychologist smiles. "You're still a young man."

"No, I think I'm getting too old to have children. Even if I met someone this week, I'd want to date for at least three years before I propose. The engagement would take at least a year. We'd have a 'Honeymoon year' together of just being a couple before we started to try to get pregnant which may take a year or two depending on how old she is, and by that time I'd be about 33 years old. And, who wants to chase after a five-year-old when they're pushing 40?"

"People do," the psychologist assures. "Perhaps you would be a more patient father at that age."

"I don't have the energy now and I'm too frazzled to have the attention span necessary to be a good parent. I think my opportunity to be a parent is lost forever."

"You never know."

The patient slightly shifts his focus and with an increasing rate of speech says, "Well, I can't start dating if I don't have any money. I won't have any money until I get a job. And, I can't get a job until I get over my anxiety. And that's why my dad made this appointment for me. He's concerned," the man looks at his watch.

"It was very nice of him to assist you in setting up the appointment."

"Yes. He's really thoughtful and knows how easily I can get anxious. He often takes care of things for me."

"Is there any downside to that?" the psychologist asks.

The patient pauses, "I think it shows his care as a father."

"Indeed it does, but are there any drawbacks that he helps out so much?"

"Oh I see what you're saying. Yeah, like I said, he doesn't have as much money or free time because he's so helpful."

"Anything else?"

The patient pauses again, "No. I don't think so."

"Okay. So let me see if I get this right. You want to work and you want to date and get married and have a family, but your anxiety as always stopped you in your tracks."

"Yes, that's right."

"What are your strengths? I'm sure you have many."

"Many? I don't think I have any," the patient ricochets.

"Perhaps they need to be found. While I understand that your anxiety stops you from achieving your stated goals, is there anything it allows?"

"No. Nothing."

"Okay," the doctor responds. "So, what do you do during the day?"

"I usually just stay around the house. I really can't enjoy anything. I spend some time on the computer. Perhaps I look up jobs, but I usually watch TV or movies on the couch and go on the Internet. And, I read a lot."

"What do you read?"

"I just got done with The Lord of the Rings trilogy," the patient says energetically.

"Did you enjoy it?"

"Very much. I think I finished all three in less than two weeks."

"That's impressive."

"Thank you. But one problem is that I graze a lot when I read, and when I'm on the computer or watching TV."

"Graze?"

"Yeah, I'm constantly eating. You can see that I'm about 40 pounds overweight because of it," the patient grabs his stomach and shakes it. "Food seems to ease my anxiety. But being overweight tends to make me anxious. I can't win."

"There are many ways to improve your eating habits."

"Yeah, maybe, but I have to get rid of my anxiety first," the patient glances at the clock on the doctor's desk.

"Well, it's useful to identify why symptoms arise. Sometimes there are genetic and biological factors that can come into play as well as psychological ones. Medications can be tremendously helpful in reducing or even eliminating symptoms. Have you ever tried them?"

"Oh yes. I was on them for awhile and they worked really well."

"Was? You're not taking medication presently?"

"No."

"What stopped you?"

"They didn't work anymore."

"I'm sorry to hear that. How did your prescriber handle that?"

"Well, I just stopped taking them. I never told my doctor."

"I see. Well, there are different dosages and many different medications that may reduce symptoms—"

"Yeah," the patient interrupts, "but I think that my body will overpower whatever I put into my system. You just can't beat Mother Nature. I think I'm doomed to be anxious. I can't figure it out."

"That sounds frustrating. Are you able to identify a pattern in your symptoms?"

"Hmmm. No. No, I can't," the patient shakes his head.

"How about your dad? He sees you at home, has he noticed any patterns?"

"No. While my dad has been helpful in a lot of ways, he never mentioned seeing anything."

"Well, perhaps an identifying pattern or two will surface as we discuss it over time," the doctor responds. "Off the top of your head, what's your biggest fear?"

"Failure," the man promptly responds.

"That's common. Don't worry," the doctor says soothingly.

"I don't know," the patient continues his thought. "Getting back to my dad, there are some times when I can't help but get mad at him and think he's at fault in some way."

"How so?"

"While he has never been domineering or forced me to do things I find stressful, he never encouraged me."

"That's too bad, but now that you're a bit older you can motivate and encourage yourself."

"It's kind of late for that. The time has passed, those formative years are so important. I feel like I'll always be anxious," the patient takes a deep inhale. "Besides I think I also blame him because I think my symptoms are genetic. That's also why I think why the antianxiety drugs worked once and why talk therapy isn't right for me," the man says as he looks at his watch and gets up from the couch. "I want to get over my symptoms, but I really think that therapy isn't going to be any help. No offense."

"I understand. Perhaps you would like to follow up with medical and genetic testing?"

"Perhaps. I know my dad wants me to speak with you, but I don't think I should be here. I see that it's the top of the hour and I should be leaving. Thank you for your time," that man says as he shakes the doctor's hand and promptly walks out of the office.

Fearful Son, Revisited

There's a revealing misunderstanding in the beginning of the session. The man mistakes the doctor's question in such a way that reveals how the patient is reliant on his father. Just consider how it's the patient's father who made the appointment and drove his son to the initial session — even though the patient is an adult, has a license, and drives regularly. However, this tellingly suggests something else.

Given that symptoms can fuel behavior as well as immobility toward a goal, the patient's anxiety may have equally prodded him to make the appointment and drive himself there. But it didn't. Perhaps the father is more invested than the patient in symptom alleviation, as he appears to be working harder than his son towards it.

Note how the patient's anxiety prohibited him from attending two job interviews. Moreover, his well-intended remedy — playing video games to reduce tension — ended up being a distraction that led him to overshoot the scheduled interview time. Did you notice the patient's response when the doctor states that it must have been upsetting when the patient missed the two job interviews? The man doesn't say that he was very disappointed, but rather that *his father* was. Perhaps the patient didn't want to go to those interviews or the therapy session. This foreshadows his fear of failure as well as his exit from treatment.

Throughout the session the patient broadcasts admirable intent...then gives reasons why he cannot engage in the behavior that he recognizes as the right thing to do. The man expresses his interest in furthering his education so that he can get a better job, yet does he do it? No, as his symptoms (being torn with anxious indecision) prohibited action. In addition, he fortifies his standstill and highlights his tension by expressing his noble concern of not needlessly spending his father's money on tuition. Yet, the patient never acknowledges that he could have taken out a student loan, for example. This simultaneously allows a sense of being good and paralyzes forward movement. The man has never had a job. It seems unlikely that he couldn't have found employment for even a few hours per week at anytime during his youth and young adulthood. Unfortunately, as long as his symptoms arrest his actions toward employment, he erodes self-esteem and increases his distance from healthy behavior. The man demonstrates awareness of how he is costing his father money, the benefits of getting a job, the need to socialize and date, and even how his symptoms make it difficult for his father to date. The man's symptoms cripple his, and his father's, movement. (Could it be that part of the reason why the patient has symptoms is to control his father's love life and not — in the patient's mind — replace the patient's beloved mother with another woman? Might it be that if his father dated, he would have less time, energy, and money for the patient?)

Given the unconscious character of neurotic symptoms, the man genuinely suffers and experiences guilt feelings for not working, socializing, dating, or furthering his education, as well as for being a financial stressor on his father and impinging his life style. Yet, they may be merely the byproduct — the collateral damage — of his symptomatic solution. So what clue does the patient give about his way of living and his symptomatic goals in his early recollection of his mother?

He demonstrates how his anxiety drew his mother's attention, support, as well as led her to alleviate his stress by fulfilling his obligations. He equates her actions to a display of affection, which has been unmatched since. His father has taken on that role; subjugated by symptoms. His father's attention may be the only connection the patient has to affection and acceptance. Something he may not be willing to jeopardize.

Early in the session the patient states, without proof and with nothing more than a gut feeling, that his anxiety is genetic. He may have this impression because he has experienced anxiety for years, or that others tell him he has always been anxious. And, indeed, there can be genetic factors related to generalized anxiety. However, consider how this perception may magnify and maintain his anxiety if he believes that he's doomed to have a chronic condition. This seems counterproductive, yet could there be a reason why he clings to this unsubstantiated claim? Could it be that he believes it because it allows it to perpetuate a coping mechanism that safeguards his self-esteem and life style? Relatedly, did you notice that throughout the session the doctor's reassurances are not acknowledged nor do they relieve the patient from even the smallest amount of stress? Why might he not be comforted with the possibility that he isn't shackled to his symptoms for the rest of his life?

When the psychologist investigates the patient's career options, the patient discounts each one (sometimes employing the "Yes, but..." tactic, for instance). The same dynamic occurs with socializing, dating, and having children. Again, you can see how the patient broadcasts socially-acceptable desires, but constructs a series of insurmountable symptomatic obstacles that stop his forward movement. The patient repeatedly demonstrates rationalization and psychological resistance to various options in accord with his stated goals. This is revealing. For every solution the psychologist offers, the patient states an opposing point — almost reflexively at times. Yet, the man is unaware of how he protectively employs his symptoms. Consider how he is able to see how he impacts his father's life, but he is unable to see how his father enables a retreat from facing the life tasks directly.

The patient reveals the many ways he self-medicates his anxiety: food, reading, watching TV, and using marijuana. In fact, you have evidence that the patient can put himself in motion regularly, as he reported driving a long way every week to get his marijuana.

At first you may say that it's low self-esteem that is bringing on the patient's symptoms. Though low self-esteem is certainly related to his symptoms, recall that low self-esteem — a sense of inferiority — can prompt people to take action that ultimately can prove competency and build confidence. The key to solving this mystery is looking at what movement is symptomatically allowed as well as prohibited. While you know that anxiety has immobilized the man in many areas of functioning, what doors does it unlock?

Examine what he does with his time. He spends his day watching TV, eating, and using the Internet, which enable him to avoid certain challenges while his father finances and enables his life style. This patient isn't lazy — indeed neurotically anxious individuals can have tremendous drive — rather he has a goal that supersedes working, socializing, and dating. He may be determined to avoid his biggest fear: failure. As long as long as he doesn't try, he cannot fail.

In addition, the patient demonstrates a strength. He's a voracious reader. How do you know that this is an area of superiority that's important to him? It's the only time he acknowledges the doctor's positive words. His dedication to his reading proves that he can attend to, and follow through on, a rather difficult task when it's in accord with his goal. (Just think about how some people may be quite anxious if they were to attempt to read The Lord of the Rings trilogy in less than two weeks.) Nevertheless, the patient may view himself as incapable as this strengthens his perspective that he will fail in life, which justifies retreating from life's challenges.

While the patient complains about his weight, when the psychologist attempts to reassure him that weight can be addressed, the patient creates what initially appears to be an unnecessary stipulation — he has to reduce his anxiety first. Why might he do this? It's because that rule allows him to maintain another element of his life style, eating what and when he wants. The appended statement that he "can't win" suggests that he shouldn't even try to change his diet and life style.

Next, though the patient believes his symptoms are inborn, what's his perception on maintaining a medication regimen?

Although his medication experiences have effectively reduced his symptoms — something he pleads for — he quits taking what was prescribed without interest in fine-tuning his medication. Additionally, he didn't tell his prescriber that he stopped taking his medication. This is interesting. If medications allowed the patient to achieve his stated goal, but with an adjustment, it would appear logical that he would pursue a better suited brand and/or dosage of medication. Could it be that he abandoned his medication because that allowed for purposeful symptoms to persist? When the psychologist offered support and encouragement to revisit medication, the patient interrupted with a firm dismissal.

The patient partially blames his father, stating that he didn't provide enough encouragement when the patient was younger. However, when the psychologist points out that the patient is an adult who can encourage himself, the man states that the deadline for encouragement has passed. This solidifies the patient's immobility.

You can see how symptoms stop the patient from facing a number of challenges, and that he's able to have a non-threatening (though painfully symptomatic) existence. In addition, his father appears to enable his adult's son's avoidance of vital areas of functioning. It's likely that while the patient's father wants his son to address his symptoms, it may also be that the patient knows that his father will support and not abandon him. Life painfully, yet needlessly, intimidates the patient. The patient's symptoms are an imperfect solution to achieve his goal, the avoidance of failing socially, romantically, occupationally, or in raising a family. Many clues reveal the man's resistance to treatment: his lack of effort in attending therapy or addressing his symptoms medically, cognitive rigidity, regularly looking at the time, reflexively dismissing contrasting information, rationalizing immobility, etc. Yet, he communicates admirable aspirations, which may protect his self-esteem, acceptance, and status, as can expressed guilt feelings that give the impression that he wants to do many things — if it weren't for his symptoms that block his movement.

The patient blames his father for symptom development and the lack of success in life. This is merely another way to sidestep accountability and change, as perhaps is the unsubstantiated belief that his symptoms are biological or genetic in origin. However, when the psychologist prompts the patient to follow up with medical and genetic testing, the patient doesn't express an interest in doing so. Perhaps he fears results not in accord with his presumption?

The patient ends the session with the statement that he believes he shouldn't be there. While this appears odd, recall the modal number of therapy sessions is one. Most people only attend the initial session and not continue treatment. This may speak of an unconscious desire to maintain purposeful symptoms. This man has many strengths, yet does not see them. Treatment that identifies his abilities and encourages growth may erase his fears in approaching and conquering life's challenges.

People Pleaser

A 30-year-old well-dressed woman sits with perfect posture in a psychologist's waiting room. The woman smiles brightly and rises from her chair upon seeing the approaching doctor. "I want to thank you for seeing me on such short notice," she says.

"It's no problem. It's my pleasure to help out whatever way I can," says the psychologist as they enter the therapy room. "Please have a seat," the doctor says while closing the office door.

Upon the door latching, the woman immediately bursts into tears. "I needed to speak with you. I just can't take it anymore." The patient pauses, "I'm sorry to cry."

"Nothing to worry about," the doctor says while gently extending a suggestive hand in the direction a box of tissues next to the patient. "Crying can be a necessary and healthy thing. What's going on?"

"I worry all the time," the patient says as she grabs a couple of tissues and dabs around her eyes.

"What do you worry about?"

"Everything!" the woman says with a mix of humor and dread.

"How long have you been anxious?"

"Years and years. I don't know exactly when it started."

"So, you worry about everything all the time?"

"Yes. I hate it."

"Have you ever experienced a panic attack?"

"I know what they are, but I never had one."

"Okay," the psychologist says. "Well, that's good. Tell me about your worry."

"It doesn't make any sense."

"Can you give me an example?"

"Sure," the woman says. "I worry about work."

"What do you do for a living?"

"I'm a math teacher."

"Do you enjoy your work?"

"Very much," she says with authority. "And, I love my students and I love teaching them."

"Terrific."

The woman continues, "But, the funny thing is that even though I know I'm very good at my job — not that I'm bragging — I can't help thinking that someone will find a flaw in my teaching, or I'm going to make a mistake that will get me fired."

"Sounds stressful."

"It keeps me up at night." The patient wrings her hands, "...I have this fear that I'm an impostor and it's just a matter of time before someone finds out."

"That must keep the anxiety going."

"Yes, and I can't stand it."

"Yet, you know you're very good at your job," the doctor testifies.

"That's what makes it illogical. It's maddening."

"We'll figure it out," the doctor reassures.

"I hope so," the woman utters.

"How important is it that you do a good job?"

"Extremely important. I love my job. It's the only thing I've ever wanted to do, and I can't imagine doing anything else."

"Hmmm..." the psychologist ponders. "Is there anything about your job which is unclear?"

"No. All the rules and requirements are clear — what I need to do, what I should do, what I can't do."

"Okay."

"I have no problem following rules. As a matter of fact," the woman continues, "I *like* clear rules to follow."

"So you fear that people will see you as incompetent and that you in some way have faked your abilities — even though you know that to be false?"

"Yes..." the woman acknowledges then adds, "I know, it's crazy."

"Not really. These things have their own logic. There's no need to be down on yourself."

"If you say so…" the woman surrenders. "You're the doctor."

"So, you're worried about what other people think about you at school."

"I'm always worried about what other people think of me *everywhere*. I can't relax."

"I'm sorry you're so stressed."

"There's no need to apologize."

"I'm just trying to be comforting," the doctor explains.

"I'm sorry to be rude. I didn't mean anything bad."

"It's fine. I didn't take it that way," the psychologist reassures. "Can you please describe your social life?"

"I have plenty or friends and people generally like me," the woman pauses before adding, "I'm not saying that I'm great or anything."

"So, are you saying that you fear they don't like you?"

"No, I fear that they *won't*," the woman clarifies.

"Please explain."

"I worry that even though people presently like me, I'll do something that will cause them to hate me or be disappointed in me."

"Have you?"

"No."

"Are you in conflict with anyone?"

"No. I hate conflict. I'm very flexible. The problem is that I'm constantly thinking."

"About…?"

"My mind races with countless possibilities and outcomes, as if I have to predict what people will say and do and what they think of me — or will think of me if I act the wrong way. I'm a people reader. It's torture. I'm never at peace and I'm uncomfortable in my own skin. I tend to worry about everything, even things I know aren't true or are unlikely to happen, but I can't stop the worry. No matter what I do, I'm always waiting for something bad to happen."

"Has anything bad happened?"

"No."

"Tell me what else you worry about."

"I worry about everything," the woman shifts in her seat, "and my worries have increased in intensity over the years. I worry about getting cancer or my children's health and education, our financial future, what the neighbors think, what strangers think, and it never ends."

"How are those things?"

"Well, that's what's crazy about it. My family is in good health. We have enough money. The house is paid off. We get along well with our neighbors. There's absolutely nothing to worry about, yet I can't stop worrying."

"What does the worry lead you to do?"

"Different things. I can't figure it out. Sometimes it stops me in my tracks. Other times I feel compelled to do something. As a prime example, I'll be up to 2 o'clock in the morning working on a presentation until it's perfect."

"You sound dedicated."

"Maybe, but I know deep down that nobody cares about the presentation or most things I worry about."

"I see."

"Sometimes," the woman continues, "my anxiety will lead me to go to the gym. I'm constantly working out. I'll worry about what we eat. I refrain from spending money needlessly. I go the extra mile for my kids and husband. I don't want anyone to think I'm lazy or a bad mother."

"Yet, nothing bad has happened? Like a negative review at work?"

"No. Never. But the odd thing is, with a presentation, for example, when it's all done and everything went fine, I think how stupid it was of me to worry so much. But, I'll do it again with the next project. Sometimes, I'll proofread an e-mail five times before sending it as a way to avoid saying something wrong. It's bizarre."

"It's not uncommon," the doctor informs her.

"No?" the woman halfheartedly accepts. "Well, that's comforting in a way. I always thought I was the only one. I'll worry about something only to find out later on that I didn't need to worry about it. I do it all the time."

"A lot of people worry like you do. It'll be okay."

"Often, I dwell incessantly about something that I said or should have said or something I did or should not have done and I'll go over it endlessly until I drive myself crazy about it. There are some days when I'm so frustrated and upset that I'll even tell some stranger I see in line at the store how difficult things are. I feel bad for burdening that person, but sometimes I just have to get it off my chest."

"I understand. It's good to vent." The doctor continues, "Tell me what was it like growing up in your house?"

The woman furrows her brow for a split second, "My father was an alcoholic and he had a short fuse. Still does, to be honest."

"And your mom?"

"Well," the woman looks up at the ceiling, "...she was a real sniper."

"A sniper?"

"I'd think that everything was okay, and I was doing fine, but she's like a patient sniper in hiding. And as soon as she saw a shot that she could take, she'd hit me with some critical comment that would just knock me down when I least expected it."

"That must have been a very difficult home to grow up in."

The patient laughs, "It wasn't easy." The patient inhales then the muscles in her face relax, "...I hated it."

"How did you cope?"

"I learned that as long as I did well in school, didn't get into trouble, and presented well at church and out with my parents, things weren't bad unless one of my parents was in a really bad mood."

"What did you do then?"

"Well, I developed kind of a sixth sense. I could tell when my dad had too many and was irritable, or my mom was frustrated and wanted to take it out on someone."

"And this sixth sense," the psychologist asks, "allowed you to do what?"

"It's like I had a heightened state of awareness. Like I said, I'm a people reader. I could tell just by the footsteps or the sound of a door closing who was in the house and what mood they were in. Sometimes, I would bring my dad a beer or turn on the TV for him, or I'd help my mom with laundry or cleaning the bathrooms — she hated doing that. Sometimes I'd do that before they were in a bad mood."

"How did your parents respond?"

"Oh it worked out well. They usually calmed down. I'd do anything to avoid chaos or confrontation. I just can't stand it. To this day I can sense the tension in a room from a mile away. My parents were either fighting at full volume or irritated to the point of uncomfortable silence. I was continually aware of my parents' moods. Sometimes I'd escape."

"Escape?"

"To a neighbor's house or the school library," the woman offers. "Thankfully, I can still find peace in reading."

"I'm glad to hear that. What types of books do you read?"

"I guess I'm pretty simple in my tastes," the woman says. "I never could get into subtle literature. I like fantasy or science fiction with a clear moral to the story."

"I see. That kind of mirrors your job."

"How so? I teach math to elementary school students, not reading."

"Out of all of the subjects you could teach, why do you like math?"

"I get it. It comes naturally to me."

"Fair enough. And, you're very good at it. But, is there anything else?"

"Well, I like how you can always figure out the answer. It's very black-and-white. The answer is either right or wrong."

"Could it be that you like math and reading the types of books you do because they're both straightforward, with an unambiguous right answer?"

The patient smiles, "I never thought about it that way, but you're right."

"That might be related to your symptoms."

"How so?"

"Well, if you're a perfectionist who seeks black-and-white matters in a gray, imperfect world you might become a bit anxious."

"Explain."

The psychologist sat a bit more upright, "People aren't like math. They can be gray and difficult to figure out."

"Tell me about it. I'm always worried about what people think and I try to make sure they're happy. I feel like I'm there to make sure others are enjoying themselves but I never can."

"Never?"

"Well, that's not quite true. I do have a moment's peace when I see others relax. It's as though a giant weight has been lifted from my shoulder. But soon thereafter I find myself worried about the next problem I have to fix. All I want is peace and quiet and for everyone to be happy. You wouldn't believe how difficult that is."

"I believe you," the psychologist says with a kind smile. "How is your relationship with your kids?"

"My students? It's very good."

"That's excellent, but I was referring to your children."

The woman hesitates, "I think they see how much I worry about what other people think and they know that if they cry or get angry with me I cave in immediately. I just can't stand chaos or confrontation or people disliking me. They're smart. They know how to push my buttons, but I just can't stop from giving in to them. I love them, but I fear that instead of acknowledging me and being nice they just take advantage of my kindness. I feel like the more I bend, the more I give them, and the more they want."

"So they learned that as long as they are upset with you, then you'll give in to their wants?"

"Yes!" the woman laughs upon her realization.

"Ah, so you've trained them how to treat you," the doctor observes.

"I guess I have," she humbly concedes before insightfully adding, "...and I fear I have done the same with my husband."

"How so?"

"For example, while I wanted a child — two at the most — my husband came from a family of five children, three boys and two girls, and he wanted a large family. I just couldn't deny him that; it would have disappointed him so much. We have four children."

"You must have your hands full."

The patient smiles and nods, "I'm more than a bit overwhelmed. But it's not the kids that are the problem."

"What is?"

"More like who," the woman hints.

"Who?"

"I don't want to speak ill of my husband, but it seems like every time I ask for his help, he gets very upset quickly, so I just don't ask him anymore."

"With parenting?"

"Usually, but other things as well. I'm so frustrated."

"I understand. Tell me more," the doctor prompts.

"I keep expecting him to see all the work I'm doing and reciprocate. My parents are like that too. I do everything right, but I just can't seem to get where I need to be with him — or my parents. Sometimes I'm at a loss as to what to do."

"How long has your husband been that way?"

"As long as I've known him."

"So you're expecting him to act differently than the way he has always acted."

"Well, that's what I would do if I saw my spouse struggling or if I weren't contributing fairly."

"I'm sure," the doctor affirms.

"My husband on the other hand, he doesn't cooperate and he doesn't bend. I'm always the one who yields. There isn't any acknowledgement of what I do. Nothing."

"I'm sorry. That must be very difficult."

The woman continues, "I'm always the one solving problems and making sure others are happy — and I did the same thing with the family I grew up in. Even now, I think I do everything right by my parents and they don't visit the grandkids or return my phone calls. I've done everything right, but I still failed. It's aggravating."

"You are a strong person."

"Thank you. But, I have to persevere. I have no choice. After all, who is going to take care of the kids otherwise? They're dependent on me. That's why I can't afford to lose it in front of them."

"What do you mean when you say 'lose it'?"

"Actually," the patient concedes, "I don't want *anyone* to see me lose my cool — or cry, for that matter. I can hold it in really, really well."

"Like out in the waiting room?" the doctor recollects.

"Yes, exactly."

"So, when do you cry?"

"Usually," the patient says, "when I'm all alone — say driving in my car, or in my bedroom with the door locked, or when I'm in the shower. But there was this one time we were flying to Boston — my husband's family lives there — and as soon as they closed the plane door I had anxiety and I couldn't stop crying. I don't know why. I don't fly now because of it. Unfortunately, it has put quite a damper on my family's vacation plans."

"You could drive to Boston," the psychologist offers.

"I hate driving on the thruway."

"How come?"

"I don't know. I feel like I'm trapped somehow. I can't explain it."

"So you don't go to Boston?"

"Not any more," the woman states. "My poor husband," she adds.

"What about him?"

"He has to fly to Boston with the kids, without me. It must be difficult for him to handle four kids all by himself."

"I'm sure."

"And, his family gives out all of these gifts and makes elaborate plans," the patient exhales.

"How do you feel about that?"

"I don't like it."

"How come?"

"I love giving gifts and making people happy, but I hate accepting gifts from anyone. I'll do it to be nice, but I hate it."

"Because...?" the doctor prompts.

"I hate owing anybody anything. I hate being indebted in some way to people and then they have a one-up on you. I don't even care for his family's gifts. But it doesn't make a difference because I still have to act phony-nice and reciprocate."

"What has his family said about you not visiting?"

"Well, whatever they said, it couldn't be good."

"What makes you say that?"

"They're a critical bunch. I swear that if they saw God face-to-face they'd find an imperfection."

"Tough crowd."

"You have no idea," the woman says with exasperation and a hint of humor.

The doctor pauses before asking, "Do you like control?"

"No. I'm not a controlling person *at all*. I usually give in to what people want. I'm very flexible and don't make any demands on others," the woman says with certainty. "What makes you say that?"

People Pleaser, Revisited

Right from the start you can spot revealing clues. The woman is dressed well and sitting attentively. In addition, she is respectful and thankful when she meets the psychologist. These are admirable attributes and characteristics, but might they also hint why she's in treatment? In other words, does this woman know how to present well, engage in behavior customarily defined as "good," and is she vigilant of her surroundings? Yes, and what follows her brief introduction unveils exactly that.

The woman is able to control her tears while in the waiting room, yet her tears flow as immediately and freely as if from a faucet when the therapy room door shuts. This demonstrates how well she can control her emotions — but to what end? She also apologizes for her crying — something that doesn't need an apology. Yet recall the original meaning of the word "apology" meant to defend one's actions. Why might she feel the need to defend her crying? Do others not allow it? Does she deem it as a sign of inferiority? Does her desire for control include the need to overpower her tears? Of course, you know the answer.

The patient states that she worries all the time and about everything. This hints at how long she has had her symptoms. Odds are, a recent event wouldn't lead to such symptom prevalence. More likely, she may need to control several areas of life, or that she needs such widespread worry to maintain a certain anxiety level. Indeed, she reports having symptoms for years and she is uncertain of when her symptoms started. Perhaps, this is because she has employed symptoms since she was a girl. She denies having any panic attacks. So, her symptoms of anxiety are generalized and have existed for years. But what does she worry about?

The patient expressed symptoms related to her job as an elementary school math teacher. Thankfully, she loves her work, excels at it, and truly enjoys her students. Yet, she's burdened by the perpetual fear that she'll be found to be an impostor — that someone will spot a flaw and she'll lose her dream job. Why would this be when the woman knows that she's good at her job? Why would she have unjustifiable worry? Are her symptoms biochemical or genetic? That might explain why she cannot always predict them and that they appear illogical to her.

When the psychologist investigates whether the woman is anxious about her job because of some lack of clarity, the woman states that everything is clear — and she leaves a hint: "I *like* clear rules to follow." Simply, the woman likes clarity as well as knowing a right way to do something. Though these are healthy characteristics, they may open the door for further investigation. Why might she emphasize liking clear rules? Perhaps she loathes ambiguity? Maybe she wants to be right and to not get into trouble? So why would a woman who likes clarity and does excellent work at her dream job, fear that she'll be found out to be a fraud?

Well, she does say that she worries about what everyone thinks of her everywhere. So why might a woman who is very successful continue to worry about what other people think of her? She is particularly sensitive to others, and remember that sensitivity is a prominent neurotic characteristic. Whenever there is a question about symptoms, its important to examine what movement symptoms allow or prohibit and what that may achieve.

You know that she cherishes her job, so could it be that she's overly concerned with what others think about her at work so she can prioritize doing her job well? In addition, could her needless and over-the-top worry about being found out that she's an impostor be her way of generating anxiety which fuels consistent and top grade performance at work? Could such perfectionistic performance enable her to achieve the goal of keeping her beloved job by avoiding the possibility of losing it?

Did you notice the number of times the woman clarifies her statements (e.g., "not that I'm bragging," "I'm not saying that I'm great or anything")? Why might this woman say such things? A hint lies in what precedes those clarifications. Each time she acknowledges a strength. It's almost as if she's apologizing when she recognizes a legitimate competency. This is interesting. Could it be that she doesn't want to look arrogant as that risks lessening other people's opinions of her? In this way, her clarifications are an attempt to control what other people think about her to avoid negative judgment. The woman worries about rejection, ridicule, and abandonment that are unlikely. She fears that her many friends won't like her some day in the future. Her fear of disappointing them may fuel the flame of continued actions that maintain those friendships. She may needlessly filter her presentation to avoid rejection. The stick of anxiety, rather than the carrot of success, motivates her.

The patient does readily acknowledge her flexibility. At this point, you might get the feeling that she's inconsistent as she discounts certain abilities while testifying to others. What's important to focus on is *why* it's important to her to let her psychologist know that she's flexible and that she hates conflict. Those two things are related to each other and linked to a defining characteristic. Think about as long as the woman is flexible, she reduces the probability of conflict. She hates conflict; therefore she must be flexible to avoid it. So why does she hate conflict. Well, for at least two reasons. First, conflict is unpredictable. Generally, those who like control also like predictability. The exception to that rule is when they use unpredictability to control others, say by doing dramatic things that energize others to take notice or action. Second, conflict significantly increases the probability of being seen as "bad," which imperils acceptance. In brief, the patient may broadcast her notable flexibility to the therapist to illustrate how important it is to her to avoid conflict. It's safe to assume that the woman goes out of her way to be flexible for others, and often takes a loss of some kind (e.g., time, money, effort, attention).

The woman reports that her mind races with "countless possibilities and outcomes." You can imagine how anxiety can fuel such intense cognitive processing. The patient reveals her insight about why she's experiencing such symptoms; she's trying to predict what people will say and do and what they think of her. While this is very distressing, she's attempting to gain predictability and know how to present to others. Her mind races with supercomputing processing to determine the best practices to control how others perceive her and how to do things perfectly (at least as perfectly as things can be done).

Relatedly, the patient confesses to being a people reader. This is a practice that requires vigilance and processing. But *why* is she a people reader? Well, she may be able to figure out what people are thinking, their preferences as well as their dislikes. This information can allow predictability and be accumulated and used to guide the patient's behavior. But there's more to it than that. The woman confesses to the torture of the process. This underscores how neurotic symptoms are an imperfect solution, but which may be maintained because they have a partial payoff. The woman is genuinely suffering, and isn't at peace. While people may jump to the conclusion that neurotic individuals are faking their distress, that's untrue. Their pain is authentic and requires thorough investigation and compassionate care.

This woman experiences unnerving anxiety symptoms, including pervasive worry that touches every area in her life. She worries about everything — even things which are going very well. Though at first this appears illogical, clarity comes from examining what it can allow. She states that her worry is not only widespread, but also has amplified over the years. Why might this be? You may be tempted to say that her condition is getting worse as she faces increasing stressors associated with more varied and intense demands of living (e.g., parenting). This is correct, but also only part of the answer. Recall when people, for instance, start drinking coffee or alcohol for their effects, these individuals may get their intended outcomes from just one serving, but over time increase their consumption to achieve the same level of effect as their bodies adapt to the chemicals within those beverages. Now keep this in mind when examining increased anxiety symptoms. First, people may have increasing worry upon approaching concerns. For example, university students may have mild anxiety when a research paper is assigned, but their tension may increase in accord with the nearness of the deadline. Second, when neurotic individuals employ anxiety over the course of many years, they may habituate to their original stressors. Rather than relinquish their anxiety tactics, they may dwell on concerns that have increasing negative consequences. Patients may worry about relatively minor things that generate anxiety that's sufficient to stop or motivate them (depending on their goal), but in due time they will worry about divorce, bankruptcy, their and their children's health. Some may make themselves concern about life and death matters due to their error because they're the only things left to generate the effect needed. Indeed, people can worry — as the woman in the example demonstrates — about things they know aren't problematic. She may engage in worry that generates the energy to prioritize a task and do it perfectly. Even though she knows that it's overkill, she does it anyway. This highlights how driven individuals can over prepare to control for a desired outcome.

The woman can worry about things, such as finances and health, to prod her to reduce her spending and to get to the gym. These are healthy endeavors, but they are achieved with needless symptoms. Also, she reveals that some of the reason why she goes "the extra mile" for her children and husband is to control what others think about her. Her diligence and thoroughness is also evidence in her work when she will worry, do something well, realize that her worry was needless, but repeatedly engage in the same behavior again. Why might she do this? Because her successes reinforce her worry, meticulousness, and perfectionism.

When the psychologist informs the woman that her behavior is relatively common, this somewhat eases her distress. But why? Well, consider how this woman goes out of her well to present well to control what others think about her. Accordingly, she's likely to be supremely reluctant to tell anyone about her worries, fearing that others will view her as inferior. Consequently, she has kept these thoughts to herself. However, when her doctor lets her know that she isn't the only person with those symptoms, it allows the woman the relief of not being that different, of not having to filter, of having certain connections to others. When the woman does vent her thoughts and stress, she makes certain to do so in a way that doesn't jeopardize her social connections — she tells strangers. And as way to maintain goodness, she genuinely has guilt feelings for "burdening" others.

Remember that much of the personality and coping mechanisms are developed early in life. Knowing that, the psychologist asks the woman about her family of origin, and growing up in that household. The patient describes her parents as unpredictably volatile and hurtful. It was a situation she hated. This is valuable therapeutic information. At this point you get a glimpse of her struggles as a young girl. She needed to adapt to that situation. She sought predictability and control. When the doctor asks the woman about how she coped, the answer shouldn't come as a surprise. She worked hard, presented well, and attempted to read her parents' mood to provide predictability as well as be a guide for her behavior. In short, she cultivated coping skills that allowed her to negotiate the environment and get as close to her goals as possible. Note that she could have coped in many ways, but she (unconsciously) chose this constellation of coping mechanisms. She became a people reader and people pleaser. She was attentive to all forms of data that might allow predictability and control — as least as much as was possible in that environment. She also was able to escape physically and psychologically from that situation, either by going to a neighbor's home or the library where she was able to escape in reading. And this reveals another clue. What type of reading does she like and why? Recall that she likes clarity. Her reading as well as career preferences evidence that. Obversely, seeking clear understanding and answers may lead her to avoid gray, uncertain areas of life.

There's additional evidence that she's a people pleaser who seeks peace, yet who also dwells on anxiety-producing material, which simultaneously erodes her tranquility and fuels efforts to maintain control. This woman can briefly relax when others are at peace (pleased, non-confrontational, non-chaotic), but that peace is short-lived, as she soon focuses on the next problem. She continually waits for the other shoe to drop. Why? Because this generates the anxiety she uses to maintain vigilance and control.

It's important to recognize that neurotic solutions as incomplete and flawed. Yet, her anxiety may enable a partial payoff that may sustain symptom development — like superstitions that chance inadvertently reinforces. So other than the woman's suffering, how else are her symptomatic tactics counterproductive?

Well, think about her relationship with her children. Given her desire for controlling chaos, embarrassment, and negative judgment, she employs pleasing to appease and quite her kids. One prominent problem is that she has essentially trained her children that they can get what they want as long as they create chaos beforehand. This is the opposite of what the woman expected or desires. The patient is aware that she has done the same with her husband. Just consider how she says that she's done everything right and still her husband doesn't recognize her contributions and reciprocate. The patient has repeatedly placated her husband by giving in to his wants. This has largely avoided conflict; however, it has sent the indirect message that he can get what he wants if he threatens or demonstrates conflict or hurt feelings. She alludes to how she has done everything right with her parents as well, but they don't reward her efforts. In fact, those who follow the rules believing they're doing the right thing, yet fail, can become anxious as they don't know what to do to achieve their desires.

The woman has to do the majority of parenting given her husband's disinterest and reluctance. This frustrates the woman who naturally expects co-parenting, acknowledgment of her efforts as well as her husband's reciprocation of them. Given this woman's desire to avoid conflict she has chosen to persevere rather than be assertive with her husband. How does she fortify her stance? She states that she must continue doing the same behavior for the sake of the children. This allows her to be good, but also avoid what she wants to. She employs the excuse of not harming her children to give license to not "lose it" — to show emotions or symptoms in front of them. This illustrates how powerful goal orientation, the unity of the personality, and control are when people curb their naturally-occurring emotions to achieve their aims. The woman admits to delaying her emotions to a less-jeopardizing time and place: her car, her bedroom, and her shower. This is in addition to her venting to strangers. These actions control how others perceive her as well as limit chaos and conflict. Indeed, despite having painful symptoms, the woman is excellent at her job, takes care of her children is a wonderful friend, among other admirable characteristics.

The patient is capable of so much, yet how might you explain her fear of flying?

Those who like more control than what's healthy commonly fear flying. Perhaps this is due to a fear of crashing, or not being in control of the plane, or they fear they'll experience symptoms in front of others. They may state that they'd get onto a plane, as long as they were the ones flying it. Or, some say that they hate being trapped on a plane, knowing that they cannot leave once the airplane door shuts. These individuals hate being corralled into action, so something as simple as being on a locked plane, or on a thruway they cannot exit, can lead to symptom development.

Now examine what movement is related to this woman's anxiety.

Her symptoms allow her to avoid the plane or the thruway — but there's something else to note: her husband and his family. As long as the woman doesn't travel to Boston her husband must be in charge of their children. This can allow him some insight to what the patient endures while parenting without his help, which may goad him to changing his behavior. It can allow the woman a break from parenting children who are occasionally unruly, thereby allow some peace. In addition, her in-laws are a caustic, critical bunch. And, as long as she fears either flying or driving to Boston, she can avoid negative judgment and uncomfortable situations.

So what might you make out of the patient's desire to avoid receiving gifts? After all, gifts are nice to receive and can acknowledge the patient's goodness among other things. Ah, but take into account her desire for control. Those who really like being in control can go to great lengths to not allow others to control them *in any way*. This includes being indebted to them. Those who like to be in control may avoid situations in which others may call upon a debt — at any time — that mandates particular action. This can be extraordinarily unnerving. In fact, neurotically anxious persons can do some remarkable feats to avoid being indebted to others (e.g., move by themselves, paint their homes, accomplish chores when physically ill).

So if the woman likes control that much, why does she immediately dismiss her psychologist's inquiry as to whether she likes control?

Well, take into account the need to be good. People pleasers (among others) may define controlling people as those with an iron fist, who always — and sometime quite violently — force others against their will to do something (e.g., by yelling, threatening, creating chaos and conflict). People pleasers may not view themselves as controllers because they do not describe controlling in that way. But why don't they? It's because it would tarnish their self-perception as well as imperil acceptance and status if they were to view themselves as manipulating others in some way — and often for self-interested reasons (e.g., to control for negative judgment).

The above vignettes show how symptoms and tactics can be employed on the useful as well as the useless side of life. However, these are significantly condensed artificial stories, crafted merely to illustrate various points relevant to generalized anxiety. While painful and distressing symptoms can be maintained because of their ability to achieve various objectives, that's only part of the picture…

Chapter 18: Sustaining Symptoms

Those with generalized anxiety suffer, feel frenzied and seldom at peace, and often expect a crisis or something grievous to occur. They may be distressingly unaware of why symptoms arise and baffled why they persist. Their symptoms rob them of joy and may unnervingly erupt without warning, perpetuate mercilessly, erode self-esteem, imperil relationships, make work and socializing insufferable, and vary in severity, frequency, and duration. Although you know the Anxiety Code, as well as why and how symptoms can be purposeful, what maintains neurotic anxiety?

Cause and Effect Mindset

Occluded Perspective

Human beings are pattern-seeking creatures that tend to seek causes to explain circumstances (deemed as effects). This predisposition and perspective shape psychological symptom assessment, treatment, and prevention. Just recall that early therapists were medical doctors who applied the cause and effect paradigm, as well as their medical terminology, to psychological symptoms. While implementing a popular and proven medical theory and practice with familiar concepts and terminology made the transition easier, repurposing an off-the-rack mindset may be ill-suited. Furthermore, an existing and productive mindset and practice with greater relative popularity and duration risks making other perspectives appear less legitimate or effective. Moreover, it may displace awareness they exist, pointlessly discount them, or reduce people's desire to investigate them — like how a pop singer's immense promotion and resultant popularity eclipses lesser known, but talented performers. Last, as people can have difficulty perceiving how disruptive and painful symptoms could be self-generated and purposeful, they may not contemplate the possibility. *A cause and effect mindset may preclude seeing factors that may accurately explain and remedy symptoms.*

Searching for Symptoms

People with generalized anxiety can be intensely driven to comprehend and resolve their symptoms, insightful and industrious in therapy, regularly attend sessions, do their therapeutic homework diligently, and enthusiastically investigate various treatment interventions, as well as continually assess symptom presence and consider possible causes. As impressive and helpful as those actions are, which of the preceding might sustain symptoms?

When individuals frequently ask themselves if they're anxious, what previously caused their anxiety, as well as what might initiate symptoms, they dwell on anxiety-related factors — perhaps to the point of inadvertently waking, maintaining, and amplifying anxiety. In addition, such practices supplant healthier questions and activities such as "How can I relax?", "What other perspectives can I take?", and "How often is my worry unnecessary?"

When people research their symptoms they may studiously pore over medical reports, psychological texts, and online resources to understand symptom development and presentation as well as various modes of effective treatment. Yet, what are the possible problems?

As laypersons aren't trained in diagnosing and treatment, they might misinterpret some vague and common symptom as an indicator of a serious malady, which can escalate anxiety. For instance, many ordinary experiences as well as anxiety symptoms — say fatigue, headaches, and back pain — are also signs of cancer. Moreover, as anxiety can be related to many things, they may seek treatment that's irrelevant to the essence of their issues. For example, if people see a pattern among their direct relatives, they might assume their anxiety is genetic or biochemical, and only seek treatment in accord with that point of view. An unsubstantiated belief their symptoms are innate and immutable may convince them that their symptoms are eternal and only responsive to medical intervention. Accordingly, they may unsettlingly infer an imprisoning and inescapable lifelong sentence of symptoms and medication.

Neurotic persons who research their prescribed anxiolytic medication for possible side effects (which they might see as numerous and alarming) may either fear the possibility of experiencing them or believe they're experiencing side effects when they aren't. Consequently, they may not fill their prescriptions, be too anxious to take them, or get rid of them for fear of losing control while on them or becoming addicted. Unfortunately, this prohibits at least temporary symptom relief and might intensify symptoms.

A Cause Can Always Be Found

As anxiety can fluctuate during the course of a day, week, month, year, and lifetime, among various settings, and in front of or in the absence of others, people have innumerable factors to consider when contemplating causes. On top of that, human memory is often populated with inaccuracies, alterations, fabrications, and open to recollections deemed genuine even if merely suggested. Accordingly, everyone could pick an instance or experience and conclusively state it's *the* cause that explains anxiety. In fact, even people who never had generalized anxiety could select a tense or worrisome event or condition from their past as a source of symptoms they don't have. *As symptom origins can be readily and frequently selected, there can be an endless supply of identified initiators.* If people are determined to discover their symptoms' cause, they're likely to find one. However, even if their assumption is inaccurate, they may nevertheless use it as the foundation of (correspondingly misguided) treatment.

Medical Causes in a Social Context

When you examine things such as parental role modeling of generalized anxiety-related life style convictions, or being an enabling spouse or parent that shapes and reinforces others' anxiety growth and continuation, why might people conceive of their child's or spouse's symptoms as medically based?

As long as symptoms are understood to be innate to anxious individuals, significant others are liberated from altering anything about themselves or acknowledging their role in production.[617] Parents who don't wish to see how their parenting is associated with their children's behavior will underestimate or disregard their role in childrearing, and remain oblivious to their part in the genesis and perpetuation of their children's bad habits.[618] For example, those parents who frequently discipline their children without success may fail to contemplate how it's their parenting style that's problematic and not their children's problem.[619] Regrettably, blaming children weakens their self-confidence, which may perpetuate the behavior their parents want to cease.[620] People may protect their self-esteem, acceptance, status, and life style by asserting that medical issues cause their children's or significant others' anxiety symptoms.

What other social factors might lead neurotic persons to believe their symptoms are inborn?

First, believing symptoms have a genetic, biochemical, or physiological basis may permit them to criticize and indict parents and grandparents, who may attempt to compensate for their accused role in symptom presence, say by allowing more latitude, attention, or something else that can reinforce and perpetuate symptoms. This perspective may allow neurotic persons to elevate themselves by blaming and criticizing family members as well as attempt to make them accountable and control them (e.g., "If I didn't inherit your anxiety I'd be working right now, so stop pressuring me to find a job!"). This point of view may perpetuate symptoms.

Second, a perception of anxiety as innate may lead those with generalized anxiety to deem talk therapy as utterly useless, leading to statements such as, "I've been anxious for as long as I can remember, my parents are anxious people, and my symptoms are due to a chemical imbalance. It's in my genes. What good is talking about it going to do?" Neurotic persons may avoid treatment preferring to allude to a family history of nervous disposition.[621] Interestingly, even though people can readily see generationally-replicated behavior and thought patterns — such as language and holiday traditions — they may have notable difficulty perceiving symptom generation and perpetuation similarly.

Third, conceiving symptoms as due to an inborn factor rather than personality, provides an excuse from revealing flaws and faults, as well as allows people to avoid the challenging process of developing insight and initiating change.

Fourth, bandied about pejorative labels such as, "crazy," "unbalanced," "mental," "nutter," and "insane" can devastate self-esteem as well as imperil acceptance. For that reason, perceiving symptoms as a medical affliction — rather than psychologically-based — may be more personally and socially palatable. Accordingly, neurotically anxious individuals may seek medication rather than change their symptom-inducing perceptions, rules for living, goals, or other variables. Moreover, symptom reduction through anxiolytic use may fortify the medical perception of symptoms. Unfortunately, as long as anxiety remains purposeful, medication may have little or no efficacy or merely submerge symptoms that continually strive to surface.

A medical analogy can indirectly illuminate another cause and effect difficulty related to neurotic anxiety. Some women soon after childbirth may experience anger, depression, as well as anxiety, and — given the temporal proximity between childbirth and psychological symptoms — logically believe they have a medical diagnosis of Postpartum depression. Although this is a common and legitimate biologically-based condition, when might women mistakenly believe they have it?

Well, consider how new mothers are burdened with recuperation from childbirth, perhaps return to work, and resume various other obligations. Sadly, some have clueless, selfish, unsupportive husbands (boyfriends, partners) who do not sufficiently assume their expected parenting duties (feeding, changing diapers, laundry, food preparation, etc.), and leave a majority of parenting to their wives, *and* continue to expect pre-newborn levels of attention. These men do not grasp nor appreciate the scope and intensity of what their wives do (often a disproportionate amount of exhausting work). On top of that, new moms may feel trapped as they cannot, or don't want to, leave their marriages, afford nannies or time off work, or motivate their husbands to shoulder more responsibility. These women can become anxious, depressed, and angry; and due to the nearness in time between childbirth and psychological symptoms, popular perception, and authentic medical symptoms that often occur after childbirth, they may incorrectly self-diagnose.

Similarly, friends or family members may tell those with neurotic anxiety (or they convince themselves), that they have, for example, Attention-deficit hyperactivity disorder (ADHD). Yet, consider how anxiety can make it difficult to focus as well as encode and/or decode information. (This is an increased risk for those who consume copious amounts of caffeine.) Though Postpartum depression and ADHD are diagnostically different from generalized anxiety, they help illustrate how people may misperceive psychosocially-based symptoms as biological in origin. This misunderstanding can lead to neurotic symptom persistence.

Presenting Issue Isn't the Real Issue

Imagine those immensely worried about how their adult children got tattoos and what negative impact that might have on employment or dating. Perhaps, they're concerned that their adult children are dating those deemed undesirable, they fret over their children's lack of drive, or fear their children got into the wrong line of work. These parents repeatedly express their concern and offer unsolicited advice which exasperates and distances their children. Although the reasons for symptom development appear legitimate to the parents, their children are genuinely happy in their relationships as well as their careers with no objective troubles. So if the presenting issue or the chief complaint isn't the real issue, what is?

It's how the parents are controlling and have unhealthy boundaries, and their symptoms give them license to coax or control their children. *When the presenting issue isn't the real issue, it can mislead and blind people to the factors that account for anxiety, thereby maintain symptoms.*

Pessimism

Pessimism can allow retreat and the accusation of others and environmental factors in an attempt to safeguard image.[622] Knowing this, how might it perpetuate symptoms?

External and Vague Attributions

When neurotic persons attribute their anxiety to external and frequently vague or uncontrollable factors, such as a miserable economy, or fate, they misdirect people's attention. Also, they can portray themselves as innocent victims, and life as unfair. This minimizes their role in symptom growth as well as has a specific and revealing corollary: To them, *others* and *life* have to change. When those with generalized anxiety are unable to specifically identify an issue or what needs improvement, or attribute symptoms to those things that are external, cloudy, and uncontrollable (e.g., fate), they prevent themselves from addressing their symptoms.

Accusations

Given generalized anxiety's unconscious character, neurotic persons may insentiently maintain it. However, they still seek to explain it — and in a way that protects their self-esteem, acceptance, status, and life style. To that end, some make accusations (regardless of validity) that others and life are unreliable, immoral, negligent, harmful, or some other toxic characteristic. This symptomatic point of view can be perpetuated in two ways. First, it allows a self-perception of comparative moral superiority. Second, it can evoke, maintain, and augment anxiety that fuels protective vigilance, control, distance, suspicion, readiness for action, secrecy, industriousness, and so forth. Interestingly, whether suspicions are confirmed or unfulfilled, neurotic persons can justify their perception as corroborated suspicions prove they were right, and unmet ones suggest their anxious precautions and guardedness prevented someone else's wrongdoing — or will eventually occur.

Catastrophize

People can view a diagnosis with such imposing weightiness and authority they deem themselves grossly inferior (e.g., "I'm so messed up that I have *clinical* levels of anxiety! Nobody will hire me and I'll be alone forever!"). If they're told, or solemnly believe, that some innate constituent causes their anxiety, they may catastrophize their situation and believe they're immensely, inherently, and immutably flawed.

Also, if anti-anxiety medications are either only mildly effective or completely impotent, people may perceive themselves as hopeless (e.g., "Even medicine can't help!"). Those who are prescribed anxiolytics may think they'll get all — or just the worst — side effects. Catastrophizing about medication may lead them to feel untreatable or, at the very least, unable to soothe or silence their symptoms. This is especially difficult for driven individuals who believe every problem has a solution, and if they can't find one, they feel powerless, as their symptoms appear alarmingly incomprehensible and irresolvable.

Unfortunately, those who believe in a balanced universe, in which bad people get their comeuppance and justice eventually prevails, can perceive their symptoms as retribution for some evil, say being bad, unfair, having sinned, violated society's rules, or lazy. This can reinforce and inflame a perception of inferiority. Consequently, they may avoid treatment to elude official labels deemed derogatory, damning, socially dangerous, and demoralizing.

Relatedly, some believe in Murphy's Law (a.k.a. Sod's Law), "If anything can go wrong, it will." With the belief that anything can go wrong, at any time, and will do so (perhaps when it's least expected or when something is most needed to go right), how could they not experience anxiety? Given this mindset it makes complete sense to them to be continually concerned, remain watchful, exert control, be right, do something perfectly, or be some other way that maintains symptoms.

Life Style Convictions and Private Logic

People choose their behavior based on how they perceive and comprehend their surroundings.[623] With this in mind, how might life style convictions maintain symptoms?

Selective Attention and Perception

People's brains are limited in strength and capability, only able to attend to relatively few of the countless variables in their surroundings, with no alternative but to choose, consciously or unconsciously, what to observe. Neurotic persons selectively attend to and perceive the world in a way that affirms and amplifies their perceptions and private logic.[624]

For example,

• Perceive only when others do something wrong.

• Reject or readily downplay others' compliments.

• Recognize when others are successful and praised.

• Remember when intense industriousness worked out well.

• Acknowledge criticisms and failures, but not their successes or accolades.

• Recall only when their anxiety enabled success or their worry was warranted.

• Just encode those times when being good or perfect benefitted them or others.

• Attend to chaotic, confrontational, and unfortunate events in the immutable past, but not on current and future conditions that are positive and serene.

The Anxiety Code influences how people perceive and act. That, as well as inflexible convictions, can perpetuate symptoms.

The Progressive Spiral of Private Logic

Consider how life style convictions influence what's attended to and how it's interpreted, which can reinforce the Anxiety Code. Second, recall that the deleterious drifting away from common sense may be so subtle as to be virtually imperceptible. For that reason, neurotically anxious individuals may continue to believe what they're doing and thinking is acceptable and healthy. To them, they've never strayed out of the realm of common sense, therefore may be unaware they need helpful guidance. Last, think about how by not seeking or permitting feedback, those with generalized anxiety may significantly intensify the deviation in their thought, like an imprecise clock that progressively becomes more remote from the actual time. Moreover, they may be resistant to ask for advice if they believe it will reveal a weakness. The neurotic life style creates increasing distance from common sense, contorting and renouncing the demands of reality.[625] *Decreased corrective feedback risks an ever-tightening spiral of unhealthy thoughts and action that maintains or worsens symptoms.*

Early Learning

If someone were to approach you with an outstretched hand you may reflexively extend yours and shake hands. Similarly, you may turn a door handle with virtually no conscious thought involved. These early-learned skills became second nature, like riding a bike. It's noteworthy that early learning can remain for an extended period — especially if regularly engaged — and can lead to automatic action without any remembrance of initial accommodation. Life has many such simple rules that people quickly incorporate or learn by rote. *Learning the Anxiety Code convictions early in life may lead to their long-term and seemingly instinctive use, which may make it difficult to change them or the associated symptoms.*

Simple Rules and Back to Basics

What might golfers do when they notice deteriorating performance on the fairway?

Often, they revisit fundamental lessons (e.g., "Put your feet about a foot apart, head down, left arm straight, follow through, keep your eye on the ball..."). Likewise, in times of crises, unpredictability, or failure, people may revert to straightforward, easily-accessible, and long-held rules to achieve their goals. This is perhaps most evident during catastrophic events, when they don't have ample time to contemplate various courses of action. For example, during an earthquake you might go under a table or in a doorway, or if you catch on fire, stop, drop, and roll to smother the flames. Simply, following rules can free up time and resources.[626]

Given the sheer complexity of life, people may gravitate toward what's more cognitively achievable — it's just less stressful that way. For instance, religious rituals and rigid belief systems may ease anxiety by paring or reducing the complexity of life to something more manageable.[627] While religious or political belief systems construct reality and guide behavior to gain understanding, predictability, and goal achievement, they're disadvantageously without detailed and nuanced comprehension. Relatedly, why might some individuals become markedly defensive and antagonistic when they debate politics or religion? Simply, changing any dearly held perceptual framework risks a frightening distortion of people's reality as well as jeopardizes goal achievement and significance. This isn't an attack against religion or politics; rather, examining belief systems may shine a light on generalized anxiety.

Some neurotic persons do not perceive their failure as due to their unhealthy convictions, but from not living them with the devout intensity and fidelity necessary for success. Consequently, they readily redouble their allegiance to their basic convictions in an attempt to gain clarity, predictability, and goal attainment. *Uncertainty compels stronger obedience to private logic, guiding principles, perceptions, and beliefs.*[628] *However, such strong obedience to simple rules can increase cognitive rigidity, limit actions and coping skills, which can dramatically increase the distance between private logic and common sense.* For instance, imagine those adults who feel compelled or obligated to be good children to their critical and selfish parents. They may experience symptoms for many reasons (e.g., edgily wait for the next parental complaint or demand, dread the self-imposed obligation to associate with those caustic individuals, experience anxiety that fuels their vigilance or prompts them to make obligatory visits, filter their presentation to avoid criticism, and suppress their anger to be good). People may return to and fortify the Anxiety Code when they face uncertainty, are in crisis or scarily distant from their fundamental beliefs, to reach their goals, and get reassuring clarity. Alas, this sustains symptoms.

Allegiance When Challenged

People can rally together to overcome a threat, say a neighborhood criminal, a blizzard that leaves people stranded, or a hostile supervisor whose subordinates defend each other or sabotage the boss's successes. Oppression can unite people for a common goal.[629] Knowing this, what may occur when compassionate others encourage neurotically anxious individuals to accept healthier ways of living?

When reality contrasts with neurotic persons' life style convictions they may perceive that as threats from various angles and in different areas.[630] When challenged, their inferiority feelings drive them to cling tighter to their private logic, guiding lines, and neurotic fictions making those individuals become even more rigid in their thoughts and actions.[631] The more intense the inferiority feelings, more probable their thoughts become dogmatic, unrealistic, and insufficient.[632]

Be the "Good Patient"

How might the need to be good sustain symptoms?

Given that therapists make educated guesses and patients' feedback guides assessment, therapy is a process of mutual exploration with accuracies and inaccuracies. However, patients who need to be good may wholeheartedly trust their healthcare professionals, praise them, and never question them or tell them when they're incorrect, perhaps fearing conflict, abandonment, looking bad, or being wrong. (Occasionally patients beam, "You'd be really proud of me!" for something they did that's in accord with their therapeutic teachings of which they're proud, and perhaps to please the therapist — as if the clinician needed to be gratified.)

Regrettably, being the "good patient" by obediently complying and avoiding dissent can misspend session time, misdirect treatment, be counter therapeutic. To avoid prolonging unproductive therapy, discord, or appearing like a failure, patients may say their symptoms have evaporated when they haven't, then terminate treatment without having resolved their symptoms. Sometimes patients filter and hold back telltale thoughts or experiences for fear of being seen as bad — or becoming too vulnerable. This deprives their therapists of vital information, which may prolong symptoms.

The Uncomfortable Comfort Zone

Why despite difficult symptoms might people doggedly maintain their way of living?

Altering the Anxiety Code convictions can make life appear chaotic, confusing, incomprehensible, and overwhelming, as people would need to shift their rules and perception of reality that enabled some predictability and competency. Intermittent reinforcement of the Anxiety Code fortifies and nurses them even through long infertile droughts. Reluctant to try another way of thinking and acting, people embrace their convictions and stay in their "comfort zone." But, is it actually comfortable?

As it certainly isn't pleasant, it's more of a familiar zone that's — at most — less stressful to them than what they perceive is outside of it. Symptoms remain as long as individuals are unknowing of their misconceptions, see their rationale and behavior as superior, and perceive reality as too threatening to their image that they've tried hard to protect.[633] *People may maintain and bolster unhealthy convictions rather than face the ambiguity and ensuing distress that may come from changing them.*

Unconscious Aspects

Neurotic persons may be completely unaware they use their symptoms for a purpose, which can protect their self-esteem and avoid accountability for socially unacceptable behavior.[634] After all, how could they perceive themselves as good and permit otherwise impermissible action and inaction if they were fully aware of their symptoms' purposes or mindful of the underlying mechanisms?

Unfortunately, those unconscious characteristics conceal connections and obscure logic, which can maintain symptoms. Also, not knowing when symptoms will strike, their duration, or severity, may terrorize symptomatic persons, intensifying and sustaining symptoms. Thankfully, there are many ways in which to identify unconscious associations and goals, say by assessing people's movement. Another is to decipher their early recollections.[635]

Believe Insight Leads to Change

Given the unconscious aspects of neurotic anxiety, some believe illuminating insight would rapidly and decisively turn off symptoms as if connected to a light switch. However, recollect that insight doesn't guarantee behavior change. So what essential factor distinguishes those who achieve their treatment goals from those who do not?

Though some believe it's the quality of the therapist-patient relationship that accounts for treatment success, that's untrue. (Indeed, practitioners acknowledge that some reserved patients reluctant to establish a strong relationship in treatment have conquered their anxiety; whereas some of the most agreeable and friendly patients continue to struggle with their symptoms.) Thankfully, a clue resides in an old joke:

How many psychologists does it take to change a light bulb?

One...*but the light bulb must want to change.*

The best predictor of therapeutic success is the patient's goal, not insight or the quality of the relationship with the therapist. This is akin to how if people want to lose weight they'll change their eating and exercise patterns. Yet, if they want to retain their life style, they'll break every diet regardless of the amount of insight about caloric intake and expenditure, physiology, nutrition, etc. Indeed, people often demonstrate insight to resolve their problem, yet don't employ their wisdom, as this would jeopardize their symptomatic tactics. (For example, when I ask patients what advice they would give their children or friends if they were in the same situation, patients may readily provide the healthy answer. Tellingly, sometimes they decline to answer or claim uncertainty. Consequently, they don't have to follow through on their own advice, as that would require change.)

Insufficient Self-esteem

How might low self-esteem maintain symptoms?

The High Hurdle of Low Self-esteem

Those who achieve their aspirations may have periodic, or areas of, self-confidence (e.g., certain they're good parents, meticulous, excellent at their jobs); however, remaining tasks can appear more challenging or wholly insurmountable. Unfortunately, those with low self-esteem may demonstrate little or no movement toward those areas that can benefit from increased confidence. Low self-esteem can be confining. Discouraged neurotic persons who have tried to reduce their symptoms but failed, might believe that future attempts will be disastrous, therefore may not try. They often state that *if* they had self-confidence in specific areas of functioning *then* they would approach them. Yet, this logic is inaccurate, immobilizing, and ultimately self-defeating given that *self-confidence can only come after successful action that proves competency to oneself.*

Retreat Erodes Confidence

People have the remarkable ability to assess dangerous situations and take anxiety-spurred protective action. However, for this goal-directed mechanism of assessment and response to work efficiently and effectively people must be able to correctly determine two things:

1. The risk of a situation (e.g., weather severity, cliff height).

2. Their ability to safely and competently manage the threat.

When these factors are accurately assessed, with amplified risk there can be a corresponding magnification of anxiety, which increases the speed, intensity, and determination of the resultant effort employed to maintain safety. However, what might confound this extremely useful ability?

First, people may be unable to properly determine threat severity, say misperceiving a dangerous environment as harmless. This, of course, is applicable to any challenge (e.g., social, intellectual, physical). Second, individuals who view themselves as inferior may underestimate their abilities and overestimate risk. This can generate worry and immobilizing fear, or prompt needless action including retreat from conditions or challenges they're capable of successfully addressing. This progressively shrinks their arena of functioning, limiting opportunities to achieve goals, and further erodes self-esteem that otherwise would flourish with each success.

Reinforced Motivator

Recall that high-achieving neurotic persons may (unconsciously) alter their self-perception to lower their self-esteem. By broadening the chasm between their self-image and what's acceptable, they can prompt and sustain anxiety-fueled, goal-achieving efforts (e.g., a belief they're not as intelligent as others and therefore need to work harder, may enable them to become stellar employees). Task success reinforces and perpetuates this practice.

Perception of Others

How might those with low self-esteem view others in a way that maintains symptoms?

Neurotic individuals may modify their perceptions of others, perhaps believing they have immense powers of observation and can detect even the tiniest flaw or those that are inconsequential or nonexistent. This amplifies their fear of exposure and subsequent failure, ridicule, rejection, and abandonment, which can fuel vanity as well as other safeguarding mechanisms.

In addition, instead of neurotic persons regarding themselves, their work, or other things related to them as good or excellent, they might resist and discount positive feedback, and doubt others' assessments or faculties. For instance, after receiving a genuine compliment those with generalized anxiety may frustratedly ask, "Why can't anyone be honest?"

Intriguingly, when driven, perfectionistic individuals surround themselves with calm, accepting, and flexible people there can be increased anxiety, frustration, and anger. Rather than see themselves as cognitively rigid, perfectionists, or overachievers, they view others as lazy, having low standards, or other discordant characteristics.

Even though some neurotic persons continually fear or believe they're wrong, when might they stubbornly believe they're right and others are unarguably incorrect?

Revealingly, it can be when others insist and attempt to prove (correctly) that neurotic persons are capable or superior in some endeavor or overall. (Indeed, people with generalized anxiety often do not see the irony in their logic and action. Though they often doubt their abilities or correctness, they can be supremely secure in how right they are on this matter.) Given the desire for significance, it appears that defiance of truthful compliments may seem like the last thing neurotic individuals would do. However, clarity comes from recognizing that others' accurate assessment is inharmonious with neurotic persons' low self-esteem. In other words, those who regularly doubt themselves can become extremely confident they're right when they face perceptions different from their own that — in this case — jeopardize a conception that maintains symptoms.

Fear and Love Paradox

While those with generalized anxiety want to move toward treasured others, what are the intimidating difficulties?

First, if they perceive themselves as inadequate, they may conclude that nobody could genuinely love or accept them (after all, they do not accept themselves). Consequently, they believe that rejection, ridicule, abandonment, and failure are inevitable. Second, beloved others' extraordinary value can make even their lightest negative word, expression, or hesitation, devastating. This can be terribly unnerving, and people may not want to take on such a risk. Can you see how this leads to a paradox that generates and perpetuates anxiety?

People cannot simultaneously fear and love someone because love (rather than admiration from a distance) requires vulnerability and fear generates guardedness.

But there's something else to consider about the fear and love paradox.

Imagine neurotic individuals in a relationship who simultaneously fear vulnerability as well as being alone. If they feel too vulnerable, they may dwell on one or more factors that generate anger, suspicion, or any other emotion that creates distance. Yet, what may happen if the distance becomes too great?

As they become more independent, the fear of loneliness increases. This can create a rubber band effect, which pulls them back into their relationship. People's relationship status can ping-pong for years or decades.

Superiority Complex

Often, those who start therapy know their way of approaching life is problematic and strive to reduce symptoms by changing their thoughts, goals, and actions. However, many symptomatic individuals never contemplate therapy. Perhaps it's because they minimize their symptoms, defining them as how life is and always has been. Some believe they're right and most others are wrong and that the symptoms arise due to other factors (e.g., life circumstances, work, family members). Those with a superiority complex are prone to avoid or discount treatment — as well as psychology in general (e.g., "I don't believe in therapy"). For these individuals, the idea of being wrong and needing to change may be so painful that it doesn't enter consciousness. Consequently, they maintain a life style that perpetuates symptoms.

Neurotic Dilemma

Imagine those with generalized anxiety who must select a wedding gift for a dear friend. They go to the store and look for the perfect present, but soon develop anxiety. Perhaps you're tempted to say that their anxiety is due to the self-induced pressure to get the best gift or that anxiety prioritized getting to the shop and fueled extensive contemplation of various presents to ensure goal achievement. Perhaps...but there's something else you need to consider. Why would they experience frustrating indecision and overwhelming anxiety to the point of leaving the store, thereby fail in their quest?

To get the *perfect* present, they need to determine which gift is ideal. However, given the many incalculable and invisible factors involved, it's an impossible task. Consequently, they weigh and overanalyze their options and ultimately produce a flood of symptoms that wash them out of the store. Although anxiety prevented purchasing a present, what did it enable?

Consider how they face a dilemma; they must get the best gift, but cannot figure out what it is. A clue to symptom purposefulness appears once you assess what goal the movement achieves. Overwhelming anxiety facilitates retreat that disallows making the wrong choice. *Dilemmas associated with inflexible compliance with irreconcilable convictions, and perhaps needing to select one over another, can lead to and sustain anxiety.*

How do neurotic persons maintain their convictions when they live in a setting that maintains, espouses, and values different rules and perceptions?

They strive to serve two warring masters: private logic and common sense — living by their rules while demonstrating compliance with social norms and conventions. They strive "to do justice to both the real and imaginary requirements."[636] However, this requires vast amounts of energy to monitor themselves and others to ensure their presentation adheres to social standards. The compromise between neurotic individuals' life style convictions and their need to act within their society's boundaries is known as "Neurotic Camouflage."[637] *When neurotic persons attempt to follow their private logic as well as common sense they maintain their anxiety by means of a fatiguing and ultimately doomed tactic.* When overwhelmed with this double agent-like situation, anxiety can take them away from the conflict, to areas in which their private logic isn't challenged (e.g., avoid work or socializing and live with parents). *As long as neurotic dilemmas among convictions or between private logic and common sense exist, anxiety persists.*[638]

Reduce the Discernible

Indisputably, anti-anxiety medication can be a godsend, appreciably effective, and liberate people from intolerable symptoms. Indeed, in the initial therapy session some patients say, "I made the appointment because my anxiety was out of control, but I've started medication and feel much better. I don't know if I need to be here." While this appears to be a straightforward and practical solution, how might medicating symptoms sustain them?

Well, imagine a person who notices a disconcerting rash and applies a soothing balm. Yet, throughout the day increasing worry that the rash is a sign of serious medical illness prompts setting a physician's appointment. During the examination the doctor says, "Because the ointment eliminated the distinguishing attributes, I'm unable to determine the particular reason for the rash or what it was. If an outbreak reoccurs, please refrain from treating it and come in immediately." In this illustration, medicating the symptom prohibited comprehension and perhaps the necessary treatment as well. This has related importance to neurotic anxiety.

Medically overpowering anxiety symptoms erases distinguishing information and blots out revealing clues, such as possible triggers, which symptoms occur, symptom timing, duration, and severity, variation in presentation, who's nearby or absent when anxiety appears or subsides, and what actions are enabled and prevented. This prohibits data that can be used in assessment and treatment, therefore, may inadvertently prolong anxiety. In addition, as much as anxiolytics can be beneficial, they aren't a cure — they merely anesthetize symptoms. Consequently, they can give the impression that all is well. Yet, how could that be if the underlying issues (e.g., Anxiety Code convictions, marital conflict, work stress, loneliness, inferiority feelings) remain? Third, symptoms continually swim upstream against the medications that squelch them, nether backing down from the fight. Therefore, medication administration without addressing the underlying psychological factors may prolong medication use. Last, with the perspective that neurotic symptoms are an innate, organic mechanism that assists thriving and surviving, some individuals conclude that medically restraining them makes anxiolytics equivalent to a psychiatric chastity belt that forcefully restrains a naturally occurring function.

Self-Medicate

Some people may self-medicate with alcohol, marijuana, and aerobic exercise to reduce anxiety.[639] Although they might regularly, preemptively, or in the face of increased tension engage in such palliative practices, they may merely maintain intermittent symptoms as long as the stressor and/or problematic life style convictions remain.

So, why might anxious persons consume vast amounts of caffeine and/or use tobacco?

As they usually have an abundance of energy it would appear unnecessary and illogical yet, for instance, some drink one to two *pots* of coffee per day, and/or numerous energy drinks. While in certain amounts nicotine can subtract anxiety (and may explain why anxious individuals use tobacco), keep in mind that caffeine and nicotine can multiply anxiety, as can nicotine and alcohol withdrawal.[640] Consequently, those who self-medicate with nicotine and/or alcohol may perpetuate their use as people may experience symptom decrease that reinforces their use, and suffer symptom elevation when they stop self-medicating. Fair enough, but how might you explain caffeine use?

Neurotically anxious individuals may use nicotine and caffeine to achieve an "optimal level" of tension. After all, if symptoms are purposeful, people may unconsciously seek to stir and maintain them. Some state that they need their coffee to get them started in the morning. This may explain why when ceasing caffeine or tobacco use is discussed, some become argumentative and defensive, perhaps protesting, "I *need* my coffee to start my morning. You can't ask me to give up my coffee!" Moreover, they may not identify caffeine or nicotine as symptom perpetuators — perhaps defining them as relaxing, (e.g., taking a smoke or coffee break) — and the same goes for alcohol use (e.g., have a good time, enjoy a glass [or more] of wine). *Self-medicating can control when and how much arousal or anxiety arises, which provides additional evidence that people can unknowingly generate, regulate, and maintain symptoms.*

Terminate Medication Use

Those with generalized anxiety can have a strong resistance and apprehension to taking medication. They may fear side effects, that they'll lose control of their presentation, or become addicted and enslaved to their medication regimen. There even may be an oblique awareness that they'll forfeit their symptomatic means of goal achievement. Consequently, they may unconsciously sabotage symptom reduction or adjust medication use to control symptom ebb and flow with more specificity. People may state they've had anxiety on and off for years, using anxiolytics until they're over some rough patch, and terminate medication use once excessive symptoms have subsided, but they never address the undercurrent of psychological and social factors that perpetuate anxiety. Some state their medications couldn't win the wrestling match with symptoms, which could only be held down for just so long or only to a particular degree. Ultimately people may give up their meds out of frustration or dissatisfaction.

Tools Paradox

While some people may start therapy, notebook in hand, with the goal of acquiring the therapeutic "tools" to end anxiety, how might this practice maintain it?

First, consider how some cognitive and behavioral techniques, like medication, are akin to a fire extinguisher that can be employed when necessary. While it's a good and healthy thing to extinguish symptomatic fires, if they occur regularly then there's a bigger issue that must be addressed. After all, it's better to not have fires than to be obligated to put them out frequently. Second, solely focusing on psychological tool acquisition to reduce anxiety disregards symptom purposefulness and the importance of the life style. It's necessary to address the Anxiety Code to evoke change, which highlights an important treatment distinction. The difference between counseling and psychotherapy is that counseling strives to change the behavior *within* the life style, whereas *the goal of psychotherapy is to change the life style.*[641] If the life style isn't addressed, anxiety remains. In other words, if someone wants to lose weight, the counseling approach would discuss various tools such as understanding caloric intake versus expenditure, distractions, high protein and high fiber foods, exercise, and so on. However, if the person doesn't lose weight then therapy must address the life style factors that perpetuate overeating (e.g., to distance others and the possibility of dating and rejection).

Neurotic persons may value, devalue, and dismiss contradictory information, pleas, and suggestions, ignoring that which isn't in accord with their values or achieving their goal.[642] So even if they know the tools, they may refuse or neglect to use them, or soon forget them.

Impatience and Vulnerability Quandary

Impatient individuals want to rocket through treatment to end their symptoms as soon as possible. This speaks of impressive motivation and appears to be a strong indicator of treatment success. But what's the catch? Therapy requires time and vulnerability. Patients can be reluctant to let a relative stranger walk into their home of memories, misperceptions, flaws, mistakes, and illogical rules. Consequently, they may prematurely end treatment.

Treatment Deadlines

Imagine someone walking into a gym and asking a personal trainer how long it will take to be able to bench press 200 pounds. Due to variations among many factors, such as physical build, exercise frequency, workout duration, diet, genetics, exercise difficulty, other exercises engaged, and perhaps sleep patterns and amount, there cannot be a precise answer.

Similarly, anxious individuals may start therapy and ask, "How long will treatment take to get rid of my symptoms?" In accord with their ambition and intolerance for ambiguity, they seek a treatment deadline to have predictive clarity, motivate themselves toward their goal, assess their progress along the way, and avoid feeling as though they're endlessly tethered to therapy. But, due to many unknowable and influential variables, this is an unanswerable question.

Nevertheless, given their drive and discomfort with unpredictability, they may set an inexperienced and overambitious deadline. Unfortunately, this may sustain or increase symptoms when they do not achieve their therapeutic goals by their projected treatment termination date. Relatedly, some ask about their progress in comparison to other patients as a way to gauge success and prod action. Additionally, it can lead to symptom development that can prioritize efforts, or arise when they feel inferior to others.

Wait for Treatment

Some people persevere with anxiety for years or decades and come in for treatment only when they (and often others) can no longer bear the symptoms. However, impatient individuals can become frustrated with the "slow progress" (the realistic time needed to address such long-standing and rampant symptoms), and terminate therapy before changing what's necessary for symptom resolution.

Just Below the Boiling Point

Envision someone peering out of a high-rise office window witnessing suspicious activity on the streets below. That person dials the police and warily hovers a finger over the send button, primed to push it at the first identifiable sign of misconduct. Such precautionary actions in the presence of a possible threat enable the quickest possible response that prevents or minimizes harm or damage. With this in mind, why might neurotic persons dwell on unsettling past events, as well as present and future concerns?

As long as anxiety is purposeful then either to have it not occur, or arise too late, is useless. For neurotic anxiety to fulfill a purpose, people need a way to unconsciously generate it when necessary. With this in mind, consider how those with generalized anxiety may be preoccupied with worrisome matters. They may exist in a tense-filled life, which rapidly escalates their emotions.[643] This strained state lowers their resistance and makes them more susceptible to symptoms.[644] In fact, they can maintain tension just below the flashpoint of anxiety development. (Interestingly, people may fight with themselves and brew tension that precipitates symptoms.[645]) Emotional tension can precipitate physical symptoms; and without tension there cannot be neuroses.[646] However, this readiness comes at a painful price: prolonged anxiety.

Also, as some become uncomfortable or bored when things are calm, perhaps due to its unfamiliarity or the anticipation that something bad will happen, they keep tension at a middling amount — not too stressful and not too calm. People do this in a number of ways. For instance, they can be stressed by having insufficient funds, but if they have a minor windfall they only partially address their bills to stave off immediate problems, then go on an expensive vacation or needlessly buy a car, which sustains their tension.

Keep Busy

People with generalized anxiety may take on numerous obligations and refuse to take a break or slow down. This reveals their ambition, a desire to be good, a way to motivate themselves, a way to avoid opportunities for their minds to wander into unnerving areas, a desire to take control of situations, etc. However, as long as they keep overwhelmingly busy they maintain anxiety.

Keep a Symptom in Reserve

A car's spare tire, a fire extinguisher, and an extra house key at a neighbor's home illustrate how people may keep items they don't need immediately, or ever, to ensure goal achievement in case of an emergency. Now consider how people may try something new, perhaps an untested, but promising recipe, the latest exercise, a new TV show, but may go back to their old habits when their experiences aren't as profitable as expected. Knowing this, why might those who are progressing well in therapy withdraw from treatment despite remaining issues?

While factors such as time constraints or financial limitations may come to mind, it's also necessary to reflect on how even when they have acquired healthier actions and a new perspective, they may fear putting full faith in them. Neurotic individuals may keep one or more symptoms in reserve rather than relinquish them, and employ them when needed.[647]

Keep Symptoms As Long As Necessary

Imagine a driven employee who persistently worries about getting a project completed on time. Anxiety leads to insomnia and fuels efforts to complete the project. However, once the assignment is handed in and given a positive review, anxiety drops significantly...until the next project. *Symptoms persist as long as they're functional and recede when they're not needed or no longer effective.*[648] Neurotic individuals can maintain anxiety as long as it serves a purpose.

Chapter 19: Epilogue

Preexisting factors shaped the field of psychology's development. Most notably, the medical mindset guided concepts such as "mental illness," and viewing symptoms as the outcome of some genetic, biological, chemical, or physiological initiator. Although the cause and effect perspective is accurate and beneficial in comprehending and treating medical concerns, its application to the assessment and treatment of psychological symptoms has certain limitations, and needed improvement. Over time, various contributions broadened understanding. For instance, the biopsychosocial model beneficially incorporates biological, psychological, and social factors when assessing and treating anxiety. Accordingly, the universal application of the cause and effect approach to psychological symptom development may be swiftly discredited with the realization that people aren't merely billiard balls on a pool table reacting in a predictable and mechanical way to outside forces. They're creative, social, goal-oriented, and have individual choice. People investigate, interpret, act upon, respond to, and anticipate stimuli in innumerable ways. This perspective more eloquently and comprehensively explains anxiety and introduces the growth model concept, which asserts that symptoms can be a function of development as people strive toward their objectives in life.

Infants are born in an inferior position and gradually acquire an understanding of themselves, others, and the world. They must increasingly address the life tasks and use their ever-growing compendium of life style convictions — the rules of perception, thought, action, and emotion that comprise their powerfully persuasive personalities — to achieve various aims as they strive toward competency. Simply, each person's unique personality is a handwritten manuscript of a personal narrative that's used to get through life. As bodily systems work cooperatively, people can focus their attention on whatever will generate specific emotions that fuel goal-achieving behavior. This unity of the personality may also explain characteristic neuronal functioning and neurotransmitter levels (among other biochemical and physiological factors) that medications alter to reduce symptoms. Although biological constituents can play a role in symptom development, it's necessary to assess psychological and social factors. Tellingly, generalized anxiety is also referred to as neurotic anxiety, and neuroses can be equated to personality disorders. Therefore, investigating relevant life style convictions can demystify generalized anxiety and augment treatment. As it happens, neurotically anxious individuals have three distinct and revealing convictions that I've nicknamed the Anxiety Code: the need to be good, perfect, right, the need to be driven, and the need to be in control.

Unfortunately, strict adherence to the Anxiety Code prohibits necessary flexibility in thought, emotion, and action. People may experience anxiety when, for example, convictions clash or are unsuitable for a situation. Although life style convictions can be problematic and lead to anxiety, people may be stubbornly reluctant to adjust or relinquish them as that goes against well-entrenched learning, may jeopardize their conception of reality, as well as initially risk reducing goal achievement while they acquire new ways of perceiving and acting. Consequently, they may strive to attain their objectives while abiding by the Anxiety Code, which can be beneficially employed to achieve goals on the useful side of life. Anxiety can arise to meet the demands of living, as people must have the energy to be industrious, perfectionistic, athletic, etc. However, it can inflict a distressing toll, such as sleeplessness, rumination, tension, distraction, social discord, as well as physical symptoms. Nevertheless, goal achievement reinforces the Anxiety Code as well as anxiety-fueled behavior. This, coupled with the difficultly of changing problematic convictions, maintains symptoms. Indeed, people can persevere through many difficulties, and may not start therapy until their symptoms are well rooted and widespread.

As each person is part of the larger and influential community, the social aspects to an individual's psychological symptoms must be recognized. Undeniably, the most exhilarating and peaceful moments people experience are often linked to love, acceptance, harmony, and competence — and the most devastating times are regularly related to a social factor: ridicule, rejection, abandonment, and failure. While anxiety, as well as the Anxiety Code, can enable achievements on the useful side of life, for those whose convictions are too rigid, inadequate, or who judge themselves as inferior, are discouraged, or perceive life's challenges as intimidating, they may unconsciously employ anxiety symptoms on the useless side of life to protect their self-esteem, acceptance, status, and style of living. However, as symptomatic persons genuinely suffer and may be deemed innocent victims of their biology, circumstances, etc., the purposefulness perspective may appear categorically incorrect, controversial, and taboo, as it seems to callously blame suffering victims for their own — as well as others' — suffering. Yet, there's a biological precedent to consider.

First, people's bodies can employ rather painful and unattractive protective physical mechanisms, such as immune functioning and healing (e.g., bruising, vomiting, diarrhea, pus, phlegm). Second, physical symptoms can inadvertently harm others (e.g., coughing and sneezing may pass on a cold, sexually transmitted infections are easily communicable). Similar to physical symptoms, psychological symptoms can be employed to assist in survival and thriving, as well as have a social component — even a cost to others' well-being. Sadly, people can be cruel to each other under even the simplest circumstances (see, for example, Milgram's obedience to authority studies,[649] Zimbardo's prison study,[650] Sherif's Robber's Cave experiment[651]). Neurotic symptoms' unconscious characteristics may prohibit people from seeing how, when, and why their symptoms exist as well as how their symptoms negatively impact others. Accordingly, they may not be any more willfully malicious than those who unintentionally transmit a cold.

Taking the biological analogy a bit further, examine how people's naturally-allied, self-protective immune system can mount a lethal self-directed attack in the case of human autoimmune diseases. Likewise, the healthy intestinal bacteria and enzymes that are beneficially employed while people are alive are what putrefy their bodies after they die. (My apologies for such an unsettling example.) With that in mind, consider how neurotic symptoms can safeguard the self, but ultimately can be personally and socially catastrophic as the neurotic response is an imperfect solution to life's challenges. Thankfully, new convictions can be acquired to address anxiety symptoms. Therapy may also be employed like a yearly medical physical that assess and preempts problems, as well as encourages the maintenance of healthy perceptions and endeavors.

Rather than focusing on what's wrong with patients, psychological assessment and treatment can be positive, stimulating, and uplifting. Symptomatic persons can to be encouraged to build on their strengths, overcome their worries, courageously challenge their life style convictions, and select healthier goals. The most successful patients are committed to change, accept feedback readily, as well as recognize their fears and obstacles may be their protective creations. Additionally, they may use their symptoms as an internal compass that points out what they need to confront and conquer. While patients often believe that they're the only ones with generalized anxiety, they can be somewhat relieved when they find out their thoughts, fears, emotions, and actions are relatively common.

Interestingly, while people can quickly acknowledge they're insufficiently trained to do their own surgery, many unhesitatingly believe they can do their own therapy. After all, it's common for people to be psychologists-in-training, detectives since infancy who've been reading others and trying to figure out life. However, when you consider the need for extensive training to notice symptom development, comprehend complex psychological functioning, as well as implement interventions on symptoms that are unconsciously employed, people may not be suited to do their own therapy. For the same reasons, this book cannot be a self-help text.

The growth model asserts psychological symptoms can be purposeful. This enriches the cause and effect perspective and may improve comprehension, assessment, and treatment that not only reduces symptoms, but also may be socially beneficial (e.g., less stressed friends and family), financially advantageous to patients (e.g., fewer co-pays, less travel and time off from work) as well as insurance companies (fewer sessions needed, less medication prescribed).

Perhaps, the knowledge about generalized anxiety disorder can be somewhat applied to other anxiety diagnoses as a means to broaden comprehension and treatment. Certainly, knowing psychological principles and interpersonal dynamics can be beneficially employed in court cases (e.g., determining intent and truths) and can enable better screenplays and novels, say with an increased realism of characters and movement. (Amusingly, if you want a sneak peak of what being a psychologist is like, imagine watching 100 movies or reading 100 books, five minutes at a time, in random order, and remembering distinct storylines, character development, notable facts such as job title, work location, friends, foes, and family members, multiple subplots, psychodynamics among individuals, identifying behavior and thought patterns, etc. — but on an interactive level and while trying to predict what may happen next.)

Life is like a game with countless players. There are general rules as well as personal strategies, and cooperation is required. But, it's not about winning or losing in comparison to others; it's about enjoying various passions. Yet, as the Italian proverb cautions, "After the game, the king and the pawn go into the same box."[652] As the game clock ticks, each person writes a unique autobiography. Alas, every one has an ending, a final chapter. However, by facing fears, maintaining healthy and flexible convictions, establishing positive and authentic social connections, finding love, as well as bravely striving and struggling down unpredictable paths in pursuit of desires, each person can author an extraordinary and noble narrative.

References

[1] Adler, A. (1996b). What is neurosis? *Individual Psychology, 52*(4), 318-333. (Original work published 1935)

Mozdzierz, G. J. (1996). Adler's "What is neurosis?": Clinical and predictive revelations from the past. *Individual Psychology: The Journal of Adlerian Theory, Research and Practice, 52*(4), 342-350.

[2] Maniacci, M. P. (2002). The DSM and individual psychology: A general comparison. Journal of *Individual Psychology, 58*(4), 356-362.

[3] Lombardi, D. N., Florentino, M. C., & Lombardi, A. J. (1998). Perfectionism and Abnormal Behavior. *Journal of Individual Psychology, 54*(1), 61-71.

[4] Adler, A. (1927). *Understanding human nature.* (Walter Béran Wolfe, Trans.). Garden City, NY: Garden City Publishing Company, Inc.

[5] American Psychiatric Association. (2000). *Diagnostic and statistical manual of mental disorders: DSM-IV-TR.* Washington, DC: American Psychiatric Association.

World Health Organization. (1992). The ICD-10 classification of mental and behavioural disorders: Clinical descriptions and diagnostic guidelines. Geneva: World Health Organization.

[6] Rygh, J. L., & Sanderson, W. C. (2004). *Treating generalized anxiety disorder: Evidence-based strategies, tools, and techniques.* New York: Guilford Press.

[7] Rygh, J. L., & Sanderson, W. C. (2004). *Treating generalized anxiety disorder: Evidence-based strategies, tools, and techniques.* New York: Guilford Press.

[8] Mosak, H. H. & Phillips, K. (1980). *Demons, germs and values.* Chicago: Alfred Adler Institute.

[9] Mosak, H. H. & Phillips, K. (1980). *Demons, germs and values.* Chicago: Alfred Adler Institute.

[10] Jackson, M., & Sechrest, L. (1962). Early recollections in four neurotic diagnostic categories. *Journal of Individual Psychology, 18*(1), 52-56.

[11] Seligman, M. E. P. (1971) Phobias and preparedness. *Behavior Therapy, 2,* 307-320.

Leonard, D. C. (2002). *Learning theories: A to z.* Westport, CT: Greenwood Press.

[12] Noggle, C. A., & Dean, R. S. (2013). *The neuropsychology of psychopathology.* New York: Springer Pub. Co.

Roemer, L., Orsillo, S. M., & Barlow, D. H. (2002). Generalized anxiety disorder. In D. H. Barlow (Ed.). *Anxiety and its disorders: The nature and treatment of anxiety and panic* (2nd ed.) (pp. 477-515.). New York: Guilford Press.

[13] Mosak, H. H. & Di Pietro, R. (2005). *Early recollections: Interpretative method and application.* New York: Routledge.

[14] Moscovitch, M., Chein, J. M., Talmi, D., & Cohn, M. (2007). Learning and memory. In B. J. Baars & N. M. Gage (Eds.), *Cognition, brain, and consciousness: Introduction to cognitive neuroscience* (pp. 255-291). Amsterdam, The Netherlands: Elsevier.

[15] Loftus E. F., Coan J., & Pickrell, J. E. (1996). Manufacturing false memories using bits of reality. In L. M. Reder, (Ed.), *Implicit memory and metacognition* (pp. 195-220). Mahwah, NJ: Lawrence Erlbaum.

Loftus, E. F. (1997) Creating False Memories. *Scientific American, 277,* 70-75.

Lommen, M. J., Engelhard, I. M., & van den Hout, M. A. (January 01, 2013). Susceptibility to long-term misinformation effect outside of the laboratory. *European Journal of Psychotraumatology, 4.* Retrieved June 3, 2013 from European Journal of Psycho-traumatology website:
http://www.eurojnlofpsychotraumatol.net/index.php/ejpt/article/download/19864/pdf_1

[16] Bartlett, F. C. (1932). *Remembering: A study in experimental and social psychology.* New

York: Macmillan.

Mosak, H. H. & Di Pietro, R. (2005). *Early recollections: Interpretative method and application.* New York: Routledge.

[17] Mosak, H. H. & Di Pietro, R. (2005). *Early recollections: Interpretative method and application.* New York: Routledge.

[18] Bartlett, F. C. (1932). *Remembering: A study in experimental and social psychology.* New York: Macmillan.

Mosak, H. H. & Di Pietro, R. (2005). *Early recollections: Interpretative method and application.* New York: Routledge.

[19] Patihis, L., Frenda, S. J., LePort, A. K. R., Petersen, N., Nichols, R. M., et al. (December 24, 2013). False memories in highly superior autobiographical memory individuals. *Proceedings of the National Academy of Sciences, 110,* 52, 20947-20952.

[20] Mosak, H. H. & Di Pietro, R. (2005). *Early recollections: Interpretative method and application.* New York: Routledge.

[21] Mosak, H. H. & Di Pietro, R. (2005). *Early recollections: Interpretative method and application.* New York: Routledge.

[22] Schacter, D. L. (1996), *Searching for Memory.* New York: Basic Books.

Bartlett, F. C. (1932). *Remembering: A study in experimental and social psychology.* New York: Macmillan.

Mosak, H. H. & Di Pietro, R. (2005). *Early recollections: Interpretative method and application.* New York: Routledge.

Loftus E. F., Coan J., & Pickrell, J. E. (1996). Manufacturing false memories using bits of reality. In L. M. Reder, (Ed.), *Implicit memory and metacognition* (pp. 195-220). Mahwah, NJ: Lawrence Erlbaum.

Loftus, E. F. (1997) Creating False Memories. *Scientific American, 277,* 70-75.

[23] FDA.org (2011, December, 6) *Cigarette Health Warnings.* Retrieved December 11, 2011 from http://www.fda.gov/TobaccoProducts/Labeling/CigaretteWarningLabels/default.htm

[24] Gostin, L. O. (2014). *Global health law.* Cambridge: Harvard University Press.

Haber, D. (2013). *Health promotion and aging: Practical applications for health professionals.* New York : Springer Publishing Company.

[25] Corsini, R. J. (1999). *Dictionary of psychology.* Philadelphia, P. A.: Brunner/Mazel, Taylor & Francis.

[26] apophenia (n.d.). *The Skeptic's Dictionary.* Retrieved July 8, 2011, from The Skeptic's Dictionary website: http://www.skepdic.com/apophenia.html

Shermer, M. (December, 2008). Paternity: Finding meaningful patterns in meaningless noise. *Scientific American,* Retrieved July 8, 2011 from Scientific American website: http://www.scientificamerican.com/article.cfm?id=patternicity-finding-meaningful-patterns

Shermer, M. (2011). *The believing brain: From ghosts and gods to politics and conspiracies--how we construct beliefs and reinforce them as truths.* New York: Times Books.

[27] Vyse, S. A. (1997). *Believing in magic: The psychology of superstition.* New York: Oxford University Press.

[28] Carroll, R. T. (2003). *The skeptic's dictionary: A collection of strange beliefs, amusing deceptions, and dangerous delusions.* Hoboken, NJ: Wiley.

[29] Fullerton-Smith, J. (2007). *The truth about food.* London: Bloomsbury.

Kida, T. E. (2006). *Don't believe everything you think: The 6 basic mistakes we make in thinking.* Amherst, NY: Prometheus Books.

Brown, J. E. (1999). *Nutrition now.* Belmont, CA: West/Wadsworth.

[30] Mack, A., & Rock, I. (1998). *Inattentional blindness.* Cambridge, Mass: MIT Press.

[31] Crowe, R. R. (2012). The genetics of phobic disorders and generalized anxiety disorder in

Principles of Psychiatric Genetics In J. I. Nurnberger, Jr, and W. Berating (Eds.). *Principles of psychiatric genetics* (pp 112-120). Cambridge: Cambridge University Press.

Smoller, J. W. Genetics of mood and anxiety disorders (2008). In J. W. Smoller, B. R. Sheidley, & M. T. Tsuang, (Eds.). *Psychiatric genetics: Applications in clinical practice* (pp. 131-176). Washington, DC: American Psychiatric Pub.

McGrath, P. J. & Miller, J. M. (2010). Co-occurring anxiety and depression: concepts, significance, and treatment implications. In H. B. Simpson, Y. Neria, R. Lewis-Fernández, & Schneier (Eds.). *Anxiety disorders: Theory, research, and clinical perspectives* (pp 90-102). Cambridge, UK: Cambridge University Press.

[32] Lambert, M-P, & Herceg, Z. (2011). Mechanisms of Epigenetic Gene Silencing. In H. I. Roach, F. Bronner, & R. O. C. Oreffo (Eds.). *Epigenetic aspects of chronic diseases* (pp. 41-54). London: Springer.

Grange T. & Lourenço E. E. (2011) Mechanisms of Epigenetic Gene Activation in Disease: Dynamics of DNA Methylation and Demethylation. In H. I. Roach, F. Bronner, & R. O. C. Oreffo (Eds.). *Epigenetic aspects of chronic diseases* (pp. 55-73). London: Springer.

Ballestar, E. (2011). *Epigenetic contributions in autoimmune disease*. New York: Springer Science+Business Media.

[33] Lightfoot, J. D., Seay, S. J, & Goddard, A. W. (2009). Pathogenesis of generalized anxiety disorder. In D. Stein, E. Hollander, & B. Rothbaum (Eds.), *Textbook of Anxiety Disorders* (pp. 173-192). New York: American Psychiatric Publishing, Inc.

Weiner, I. B., Stricker, G., & Widiger, T. A. (2012). *Handbook of psychology: Clinical psychology*. Hoboken, NJ: Wiley.

Rygh, J. L., & Sanderson, W. C. (2004). *Treating generalized anxiety disorder: Evidence-based strategies, tools, and techniques*. New York: Guilford Press.

Cowen, P., Harrison, P., & Burns, T. (2012). *Shorter Oxford textbook of psychiatry*. Oxford: Oxford University Press.

Hudson, J. L. & Rapee, R. M. (2004) From anxious temperament to disorder. In R. G. Heimberg, C. L. Turk, & D. S. Mennin (Eds.). *Generalized anxiety disorder: Advances in research and practice* (pp. 51-74). New York: Guilford Press.

Barlow, D. H. (2004). *Anxiety and its disorders: The nature and treatment of anxiety and panic*. New York, NY: Guilford Press.

Crowe, R. R. (2012). The genetics of phobic disorders and generalized anxiety disorder in Principles of Psychiatric Genetics In J. I. Nurnberger, Jr, and W. Berating (Eds.). *Principles of psychiatric genetics* (pp 112-120). Cambridge: Cambridge University Press.

Smoller, J. W. Genetics of mood and anxiety disorders (2008). In J. W. Smoller, B. R. Sheidley, & M. T. Tsuang, (Eds.). *Psychiatric genetics: Applications in clinical practice* (pp. 131-176). Washington, DC: American Psychiatric Pub.

McGrath, P. J. & Miller, J. M. (2010). Co-occurring anxiety and depression: concepts, significance, and treatment implications. In H. B. Simpson, Y. Neria, R. Lewis-Fernández, & Schneier (Eds.). *Anxiety disorders: Theory, research, and clinical perspectives* (pp 90-102). Cambridge, UK: Cambridge University Press.

[34] Hasher, L., Goldstein, D., & Toppino, T. (1977). Frequency and the conference of referential validity. *Journal of Verbal Learning and Verbal Behavior, 16,* 107-112.

[35] Rygh, J. L., & Sanderson, W. C. (2004). *Treating generalized anxiety disorder: Evidence-based strategies, tools, and techniques*. New York: Guilford Press.

Sadock, B. J., Kaplan, H. I., & Sadock, V. A. (2007). *Kaplan & Sadock's synopsis of psychiatry: Behavioral sciences/clinical psychiatry*. Philadelphia: Wolter Kluwer/Lippincott Williams & Wilkins.

Collier, J. A. B., & Collier, J. A. B. (2009). *Oxford handbook of clinical specialties*. Oxford: Oxford University Press.

Ferri, F. F. (2012). *Ferri's clinical advisor 2012: 5 books in 1*. Philadelphia, PA: Elsevier Mosby.

Marks, I. M. (1987). *Fears, phobias, and rituals: Panic, anxiety, and their disorders*. New York: Oxford University Press.

Martens, E. J., de, J. P., Na, B., Cohen, B. E., Lett, H., & Whooley, M. A. (January 01, 2010). Scared to death? Generalized anxiety disorder and cardiovascular events in patients with stable coronary heart disease: The Heart and Soul Study. *Archives of General Psychiatry, 67*, 7, 750-8.

Portman, M. E. (2009). *Generalized anxiety disorder across the lifespan: An integrative approach*. New York: Springer.

36 Rygh, J. L., & Sanderson, W. C. (2004). *Treating generalized anxiety disorder: Evidence-based strategies, tools, and techniques*. New York: Guilford Press.

37 Rowa, K., Hood, H. K, & Antony, M. M., (2013). Generalized Anxiety Disorder. In W. E. Craighead, D. J. Miklowitz, & L. W. Craighead, (Eds.). *Psychopathology: History, diagnosis, and empirical foundations* (2nd. Ed.) (pp. 108-146). New York: John Wiley & Sons.

Rosen, J. B. & Schulkin, J. (1998). From normal fear to pathological anxiety. *Psychological Review, 105*, 325-350.

Bishop, S. J., Duncan, J., & Lawrence, A. D. (2004). State Anxiety Modulation of the Amygdala Response to Unattended Threat-Related Stimuli. *Journal of Neuroscience, 24*(46), 10364-10368.

Herwig, U., Abler, B., Walter, H., & Erk, S. (2007, January). Expecting unpleasant stimuli--An fMRI study. Psychiatry Research: *Neuroimaging, 154*(1), 1-12.

38 Martin, E. I. & Nemeroff, C. B. (2010). The biology of generalized anxiety disorder and major depressive disorder. In Goldberg, D. P., Kendler, K. S., Sirovatka, S. J., and Regier, D. A. (2010). *Diagnostic issues in depression and generalized anxiety disorder* (pp. 45-70). Arlington, VA: American Psychiatric Association.

39 Etkin, A., Prater, K. E., Schatzberg, A. F., Menon, V., & Greicius, M. D. (January 01, 2009). Disrupted amygdalar subregion functional connectivity and evidence of a compensatory network in generalized anxiety disorder. *Archives of General Psychiatry, 66*, 12, 1361-72.

40 Lightfoot, J. D., Seay, S. J, & Goddard, A. W. (2009). Pathogenesis of generalized anxiety disorder. In D. Stein, E. Hollander, & B. Rothbaum (Eds.), *Textbook of Anxiety Disorders* (pp. 173-192). New York: American Psychiatric Publishing, Inc.

Rowa, K., Hood, H. K, & Antony, M. M., (2013). Generalized Anxiety Disorder. In W. E. Craighead, D. J. Miklowitz, & L. W. Craighead, (Eds.). *Psychopathology: History, diagnosis, and empirical foundations* (2nd. Ed.) (pp. 108-146). New York: John Wiley & Sons.

41 Martin, J. L., Sainz-Pardo, M., Furukawa, T. A., Martín-Sánchez, E., Seoane, T., & Galán, C. (January 01, 2007). Benzodiazepines in generalized anxiety disorder: Heterogeneity of outcomes based on a systematic review and meta-analysis of clinical trials. *Journal of Psychopharmacology, 21*, 7, 774-82.

42 Lightfoot, J. D., Seay, S. J, & Goddard, A. W. (2009). Pathogenesis of generalized anxiety disorder. In D. Stein, E. Hollander, & B. Rothbaum (Eds.), *Textbook of Anxiety Disorders* (pp. 173-192). New York: American Psychiatric Publishing, Inc.

Rowa, K., Hood, H. K, & Antony, M. M., (2013). Generalized Anxiety Disorder. In W. E. Craighead, D. J. Miklowitz, & L. W. Craighead, (Eds.). *Psychopathology: History, diagnosis, and empirical foundations* (2nd. Ed.) (pp. 108-146). New York: John Wiley & Sons.

Cutler, N. R. (2010). *Critical pathways to success in CNS drug development*. Chichester, West

Sussex, UK: Wiley-Blackwell.

Mantella, R. C., Butters, M. A., Amico, J. A., Mazumdar, S., Rollman, B. L., et al. (January 01, 2008). Salivary cortisol is associated with diagnosis and severity of late-life generalized anxiety disorder. *Psychoneuroendocrinology, 33,* 6, 773-81.

Steudte, S., Stalder, T., Dettenborn, L., Klumbies, E., Foley, P., et al. (January 01, 2011). Decreased hair cortisol concentrations in generalised anxiety disorder. *Psychiatry Research, 186,* 2-3.

[43] Glenberg, A. M. & Andrzejewski, M. E. (2008). *Learning from data: An introduction to statistical reasoning* (3rd ed.). New York: Taylor & Francis.

[44] Wansink, D. (2012) Hidden persuaders: Environmental contributors to obesity. In S. R. Akabas, S. A. Lederman, & B. J. Moore, (Eds.). *Textbook of obesity: Biological, psychological, and cultural influences* (pp. 108-122). Chichester, West Sussex, UK: Wiley-Blackwell.

Simmons, W. K., Martin, A. & Barsalou, L. W. (2005, October). Pictures of Appetizing Foods Activate Gustatory Cortices for Taste and Reward. *Cerebral Cortex, 15*(10), 1602-1608.

Rolls, E. T. (2005, May). Taste, olfactory, and food texture processing in the brain, and the control of food intake. *Physiology & Behavior, 85*(1), 45-56.

Brunstrom, J. M., Yates, H. M. & Witcomb, G. L. (2004, March). Dietary restraint and heightened reactivity to food. *Physiology & Behavior, 81*(1), 85-90.

Naslund, E., & Hellstrom, P. M. (2007, September). Appetite signaling: From gut peptides and enteric nerves to brain. *Physiology & Behavior, 92*(1-2), 256-262.

Hinton, E. C., Parkinson, J. A., Holland, A. J., Arana, F. S., Roberts, A. C., & Owen, A. M. (2004, September). Neural contributions to the motivational control of appetite in humans. *European Journal of Neuroscience, 20*(5), 1411-1418.

Sewards, T. V., & Sewards, M. A. (2003, June). Representations of motivational drives in mesial cortex, medial thalamus, hypothalamus and midbrain. *Brain Research Bulletin, 61*(1), 25-49.

Picco, M. (2007, April 16). *Stomach noise: What makes my stomach growl?* Retrieved February 22, 2009, from http://www.mayoclinic.com/health/stomach-noise/NU00189

[45] Karama, S., Lecours, A. R., Leroux, J-M., Bourgouin, P., Beaudoin, G., Joubert, S., et al. (2002, May). Areas of brain activation in males and females during viewing of erotic film excerpts. *Human Brain Mapping, 16*(1), 1-13.

Halaris, A. (2003, March). Neurochemical aspects of the sexual response cycle. *CNS Spectrums, 8*(3), 211-216.

Sadock, B. J., & Sadock, V. A., (2007). *Kaplan & Sadock's synopsis of psychiatry: behavioral sciences/clinical psychiatry.* (10th ed.). Philadelphia, PA: Wolter Kluwer/Lippincott Williams & Wilkins.

[46] Rowa, K., Hood, H. K, & Antony, M. M., (2013). Generalized Anxiety Disorder. In W. E. Craighead, D. J. Miklowitz, & L. W. Craighead, (Eds.). *Psychopathology: History, diagnosis, and empirical foundations* (2nd. Ed.) (pp. 108-146). New York: John Wiley & Sons.

[47] Rowa, K., Hood, H. K, & Antony, M. M., (2013). Generalized Anxiety Disorder. In W. E. Craighead, D. J. Miklowitz, & L. W. Craighead, (Eds.). *Psychopathology: History, diagnosis, and empirical foundations* (2nd. Ed.) (pp. 108-146). New York: John Wiley & Sons.

[48] Martin, J. L., Sainz-Pardo, M., Furukawa, T. A., Martín-Sánchez, E., Seoane, T., & Galán, C. (January 01, 2007). Benzodiazepines in generalized anxiety disorder: Heterogeneity of outcomes based on a systematic review and meta-analysis of clinical trials. *Journal of Psychopharmacology, 21,* 7, 774-82.

Rygh, J. L., & Sanderson, W. C. (2004). *Treating generalized anxiety disorder: Evidence-based strategies, tools, and techniques*. New York: Guilford Press.

Sadock, B. J., & Sadock, V. A., (2007). *Kaplan & Sadock's synopsis of psychiatry: behavioral sciences/clinical psychiatry*. (10th ed.). Philadelphia, PA: Wolter Kluwer/Lippincott Williams & Wilkins.

Canadian Psychiatric Association. (January 01, 2006). Clinical practice guidelines. Management of anxiety disorders. *Canadian Journal of Psychiatry, 51*, 8 supplement 2, 9S-91S.)

[49] Craighead, W. E., Miklowitz, D. J., & Craighead, L. W. (2008). *Psychopathology: History, diagnosis, and empirical foundations*. Hoboken, NJ: John Wiley & Sons.

Lightfoot, J. D., Seay, S. J, & Goddard, A. W. (2009). Pathogenesis of generalized anxiety disorder. In D. Stein, E. Hollander, & B. Rothbaum (Eds.), *Textbook of Anxiety Disorders* (pp. 173-192). New York: American Psychiatric Publishing, Inc.

[50] Schneier, F. R. (2012). Tricyclic antidepressants and monoamine oxidase inhibitors. In S. G. Hofmann (Ed.). *Psychobiological Approaches for Anxiety Disorders: Treatment Combination Strategies* (pp. 41-60). Chicester: Wiley.

[51] Schneier, F. R. (2012). Tricyclic antidepressants and monoamine oxidase inhibitors. In S. G. Hofmann, (Ed.). *Psychobiological Approaches for Anxiety Disorders: Treatment Combination Strategies* (pp. 41-60). Chicester: Wiley.

Ranga Rama Krishna, K. (2013). Monoamine oxidase inhibitors. In A. F. Schatzberg, & C. B. Nemeroff, (Eds.). *Essentials of clinical psychopharmacology* (pp. 119-136). Washington, DC: American Psychiatric Pub.

[52] Lightfoot, J. D., Seay, S. J, & Goddard, A. W. (2009). Pathogenesis of generalized anxiety disorder. In D. Stein, E. Hollander, & B. Rothbaum (Eds.), *Textbook of Anxiety Disorders* (pp. 173-192). New York: American Psychiatric Publishing, Inc.

Davidson, J. R. T., & Dreher, H. (2004). *The anxiety book: Developing strength in the face of fear*. New York: Riverhead Books.

Rowa, K., Hood, H. K, & Antony, M. M., (2013). Generalized Anxiety Disorder. In W. E. Craighead, D. J. Miklowitz, & L. W. Craighead, (Eds.). *Psychopathology: History, diagnosis, and empirical foundations* (2nd. Ed.) (pp. 108-146). New York: John Wiley & Sons.

[53] Martin, E. I. & Nemeroff, C. B. (2010). The biology of generalized anxiety disorder and major depressive disorder. In Goldberg, D. P., Kendler, K. S., Sirovatka, S. J., and Regier, D. A. (2010). *Diagnostic issues in depression and generalized anxiety disorder* (pp. 45-70). Arlington, VA: American Psychiatric Association.

[54] Starcevic, V. (2009). *Anxiety disorders in adults: A clinical guide*. Oxford: Oxford University Press.

[55] Martin, E. I. & Nemeroff, C. B. (2010). The biology of generalized anxiety disorder and major depressive disorder. In Goldberg, D. P., Kendler, K. S., Sirovatka, S. J., and Regier, D. A. (2010). *Diagnostic issues in depression and generalized anxiety disorder* (pp. 45-70). Arlington, VA: American Psychiatric Association.

[56] Frosch, D. L., Krueger, P. M., Hornik, R. C., Cronholm, P. F., Barg, F. K. (2007). Creating Demand for Prescription Drugs: A Content Analysis of Television Direct-to-Consumer Advertising. *Annals of Family Medicine 5*: 6-13

Hollon, M. F. (1999). Direct-to-consumer marketing of prescription drugs: creating consumer demand. *Journal of the American Medical Association, 281*(4):382–384.

[57] Lee, V. C. (October 01, 2011). Direct-to-Consumer Pharmaceutical Advertising Therapeutic or Toxic?. *P and T, 36*, 10, 669-684.

[58] Lee, V. C. (October 01, 2011). Direct-to-Consumer Pharmaceutical Advertising Therapeutic or Toxic?. *P and T, 36*, 10, 669-684.

[59] Starcevic, V. (2009). *Anxiety disorders in adults: A clinical guide*. Oxford: Oxford University Press.

[60] Lightfoot, J. D., Seay, S. J, & Goddard, A. W. (2009). Pathogenesis of generalized anxiety disorder. In D. Stein, E. Hollander, & B. Rothbaum (Eds.), *Textbook of Anxiety Disorders* (pp. 173-192). New York: American Psychiatric Publishing, Inc.

[61] Baran, R., & Dawber, R. P. R. (2001). *Baran and Dawber's diseases of the nails and their management*. Malden, MA: Blackwell Science.

Linton, S. (2005). *Understanding pain for better clinical practice: A psychological perspective*. Edinburgh: Elsevier.

Cervero, F. (2012). *Understanding pain: Exploring the perception of pain*. Cambridge, Mass: MIT Press.

[62] Cervero, F. (2012). *Understanding pain: Exploring the perception of pain*. Cambridge, Mass: MIT Press.

[63] Linton, S. (2005). *Understanding pain for better clinical practice: A psychological perspective*. Edinburgh: Elsevier.

[64] Sadock, B. J., Kaplan, H. I., & Sadock, V. A. (2007). *Kaplan & Sadock's synopsis of psychiatry: Behavioral sciences/clinical psychiatry*. Philadelphia: Wolter Kluwer/Lippincott Williams & Wilkins.

Kandeel, F. R. (2007). *Male sexual dysfunction: Pathophysiology and treatment*. New York, NY: Informa Healthcare USA.

Weiten, W. (2010). *Psychology: Themes & variations*. Belmont, Calif: Wadsworth/Cengage Learning.

[65] Apter, M. J. (1992). *The dangerous edge: The psychology of excitement*. New York, NY: Free Press.

Schachter, S., & Singer, J. (1962). Cognitive, Social, and Physiological Determinants of Emotional State. *Psychological Review, 69*, pp. 379–399.

[66] Spiegel, R., & Fatemi, S. H. (2003). *Psychopharmacology: An introduction*. Chichester, West Sussex, England: John Wiley & Sons.

Wyszynski, A. A., & Wyszynski, B. (2005). *Manual of psychiatric care for the medically ill*. Washington, DC: American Psychiatric Pub.

Fisher, G. L., & Roget, N. A. (2009). *Encyclopedia of substance abuse prevention, treatment, & recovery*. Los Angeles: SAGE.

Everly, G. S., & Lating, J. M. (2002). *A Clinical guide to the treatment of human stress response*. New York: Kluwer Academic/Plenum.

Winokur, G., & Clayton, P. J. (1986). *The Medical basis of psychiatry*. Philadelphia: Saunders.

Wood, J. C. (2007). *Getting help: The complete & authoritative guide to self-assessment and treatment of mental health problems*. Oakland, CA: New Harbinger Publications.

Muse, M. D., Moore, B. A., Stall, S. M. (2013). Benefits and challenges of integrated treatment. In Stahl, S. M. & Moore, B. A. *Anxiety disorders: A guide for integrating psychopharmacology and psychotherapy* (pp. 3-24). New York: Routledge.

Clark, D. A., & Beck, A. T. (2012). *The anxiety and worry workbook: The cognitive behavioral solution*. New York: Guilford Press.

Holsboer, F., & Ströhle, A. (2005). *Anxiety and Anxiolytic Drugs*. Berlin: Springer.

Heckers, S. (January 01, 1997). *Neuropsychiatry*, edited by Barry S. Fogel, M.D, and Randolph B. Schiffer, M.D. Associate Editor: Stephen M. Rao, Ph.D. Psychosomatics, 38, 3, 295.

Simpson, H. B. (2010). *Anxiety disorders: Theory, research, and clinical perspectives*. Cambridge, UK: Cambridge University Press.

Maxmen, J. S., Kennedy, S. H., & McIntyre, R. S. (2008). *Psychotropic drugs: Fast facts*. New York: W. W. Norton & Co.

Janicak, P. G., Marder, S. R., & Pavuluri, M. N. (2011). *Principles and practice of psychopharmacotherapy*. Philadelphia: Wolters Kluwer Health/Lippincott Williams & Wilkins.

Antony, M. M., Ledley, D. R., & Heimberg, R. G. (2005). *Improving outcomes and preventing relapse in cognitive-behavioral therapy.* New York: Guilford Press.

[67] Portman, M. E. (2009). *Generalized anxiety disorder across the lifespan: An Integrative approach.* New York, NY: Springer.

Muse, M. D., Moore, B. A., Stall, S. M. (2013). Benefits and challenges of integrated treatment. In Stahl, S. M. & Moore, B. A. *Anxiety disorders: A guide for integrating psychopharmacology and psychotherapy* (pp. 3-24). New York: Routledge.

Pull, C. B. (2007). Combined pharmacotherapy and cognitive- behavioural therapy for anxiety disorders. *Current Opinion in Psychiatry, 20,* 30–35.

[68] Muse, M. D., Moore, B. A., Stall, S. M. (2013). Benefits and challenges of integrated treatment. In Stahl, S. M. & Moore, B. A. *Anxiety disorders: A guide for integrating psychopharmacology and psychotherapy* (pp. 3-24). New York: Routledge.

[69] Kahneman, D., Slovic, P., & Tversky, A. (1982). *Judgment under uncertainty: Heuristics and biases.* Cambridge: Cambridge University Press.

Fiske, S. T., & Taylor, S. E. (1991). *Social Cognition* (2nd ed.). New York: McGraw-Hill.

[70] Gilovich, T. (1993). *How we know what isn't so: The fallibility of human reason in everyday life.* New York: Free Press.

[71] Aronson, E. (1999). *The social animal.* New York: Worth.

Nickerson, R. S. (1998). Confirmation bias: A ubiquitous phenomenon in many guises. *Review of General Psychology, 2,* 175-220.

[72] Roeckelein, J. E. (1998). *Dictionary of theories, laws, and concepts in psychology.* Westport, Conn: Greenwood Press.

Corsini, R. J. (1999). *The dictionary of psychology.* Philadelphia, PA: Brunner/Mazel.

[73] Mosak, H. H. (1973). *Alfred Adler: his influence on psychology today.* Park Ridge, NJ.: Noyes Press.

Lombardi, D. N., Florentino, M. C., & Lombardi, A. J. (1998). Perfectionism and Abnormal Behavior. *Journal of Individual Psychology, 54*(1), 61-71.

[74] Freeman, A. (1993). *Foreword.* In L. Sperry & J. Carlson (Eds.). Psychopathology and psychotherapy from diagnosis to treatment (pp. iii - vi). Muncie, IN: Accelerated Development.

[75] Huppert, J.D. & Sanderson, W. C. (2010). Psychotherapy for generalized anxiety disorder. In Stein, D. & Hollander, E., (Eds.), *Textbook of Anxiety Disorders* (2nd ed.) (pp. 219-238). Washington, DC: American Psychiatric Press, Inc.

[76] Mosak, H. H. & Phillips, K. (1980). *Demons, germs and values.* Chicago: Alfred Adler Institute.

[77] Mosak, H. H. & Phillips, K. (1980). *Demons, germs and values.* Chicago: Alfred Adler Institute.

[78] Bitter, J. R. (1996). On neurosis: An introduction to Adler's concepts and approach. *Individual Psychology: The Journal of Adlerian Theory, Research and Practice, 52*(4), 310-317.

Sperry, L. (1996). Adler's conception of neurosis in the contemporary treatment of personality disorders. *Individual Psychology: The Journal of Adlerian Theory, Research and Practice, 52*(4), 372-377.

Mozdzierz, G. J. (1996). Adler's "What is neurosis?": Clinical and predictive revelations from the past. *Individual Psychology: The Journal of Adlerian Theory, Research and Practice, 52*(4), 342-350.

[79] England, G. W., & Misumi, J. (December 01, 1986). Work Centrality in Japan and the United States. *Journal of Cross-Cultural Psychology, 17,* 4, 399-416.

Corcoran, B., & Berger, W. (2008). *Nextville: Amazing places to live the rest of your life.* New York: Springboard Press.

Gini, A. (2000). *My job, my self: Work and the creation of the modern individual*. New York: Routledge.

Dykema-Engblade, A., Stawiski, S., Autism and Developmental Disabilities: Current Practices and Issues. (January 01, 2008). Employment and retirement concerns for persons with developmental disabilities. *Advances in Special Education, 18*, 253-272.

[80] Centers for Disease Control and Prevention (CDC). (2013, April 24). *FASTSTATS - Marriage and Divorce*. Retrieved August 17, 2013, from http://www.cdc.gov/nchs/fastats/divorce.htm

[81] Carducci, B. J. (2009). *The psychology of personality: Viewpoints, research, and applications*. Malden, MA: Wiley-Blackwell.

Plomin, R. (2008). *Behavioral genetics*. New York: Worth Publishers.

Joseph, J. (2006). *The missing gene: Psychiatry, heredity, and the fruitless search for genes*. New York: Algora Pub.

Hoffmann, J. P. (2011). *Delinquency theories: Appraisals and applications*. New York, NY: Routledge.

[82] Buss, D. M., & Hawley, P. H. (2011). *The evolution of personality and individual differences*. New York: Oxford University Press.

Bruder, C. E., Piotrowski, A., Gijsbers, A. A., Andersson, R., Erickson, et. al. (January 01, 2008). Phenotypically concordant and discordant monozygotic twins display different DNA copy-number-variation profiles. *American Journal of Human Genetics, 82*, 3, 763-71.

[83] Mosak, H. H. (1972). Life style assessment: a demonstration focused upon family constellation. *Journal of Individual Psychology, 28*, 232-247.

Shulman, B. H. & Mosak, H. H. (1988). *A manual of life style assessment*. Muncie, IN: Accelerated development.

Withrow, R, & Schwiebert, V. L. (2005). Twin loss: Implications for counselors working with surviving twins. *Journal of Counseling & Development, 83*, 21-28.

[84] Aronson, E. (1999). *The social animal*. New York: Worth Publishers.

Ford, C. S. & Beech, F. A. (1951). *Patterns of sexual behavior*. New York: Harper Row.

Smith, E. R., & Mackie, D. M. (1999). *Social psychology* (2nd ed.). Philadelphia: Psychology Press.

Abramson, P. R. & Pinkerton, S. D. (1995). *With Pleasure: Thoughts on the Nature of Human Sexuality*. New York: Oxford University Press.

[85] Deci, E. L. (1980). *The psychology of self-determination*. Lexington, Massachusetts: Lexington Books.

[86] Deci, E. L. & Ryan, R. M. (1985). *Intrinsic motivation and self-determination in human behavior*. New York: Plenum Press.

[87] Schacter, D. L. (2001). *The seven sins of memory: How the mind forgets and remembers*. Boston, MA: Houghton Mifflin.

Schacter, D. L., Chiao, J. Y., & Mitchell, J. P. (January 01, 2003). *The seven sins of memory: implications for self*. Annals of the New York Academy of Sciences, 1001, 226-39.

Ebbinghaus, H. (1885/1964). *Memory: A contribution to experimental psychology*, (trans. H. A. Ruger and C. E. Bussenius). New York: Dover Publications.

[88] Wheatley, T. & Wegner, D. (2001). Automaticity of Action, Psychology of. In N. J. Smelser & P. B. Baltes, (Eds.), *International encyclopedia of the social & behavioral sciences* (pp. 991-993). Oxford, UK: Elsevier Science Limited.

[89] Wheatley, T. & Wegner, D. (2001). Automaticity of Action, Psychology of. In N. J. Smelser & P. B. Baltes, (Eds.), *International encyclopedia of the social & behavioral sciences* (pp. 991-993). Oxford, UK: Elsevier Science Limited.

[90] Wheatley, T. & Wegner, D. (2001). Automaticity of Action, Psychology of. In N. J. Smelser &

P. B. Baltes, (Eds.), *International encyclopedia of the social & behavioral sciences* (pp. 991-993). Oxford, UK: Elsevier Science Limited.

[91] Wheatley, T. & Wegner, D. (2001). Automaticity of Action, Psychology of. In N. J. Smelser & P. B. Baltes, (Eds.), *International encyclopedia of the social & behavioral sciences* (pp. 991-993). Oxford, UK: Elsevier Science Limited.

[92] Coon, D., & Mitterer, J. O. (2009). *Introduction to psychology: Gateways to mind and behavior.* Belmont, CA: Wadsworth, Cengage Learning.

[93] Kahneman, D., & Tversky, A. (1979). Intuitive prediction: Biases and corrective procedures. *Management Science, 12,* 313-327.

Buehler, R., Griffin, D., & Ross, M. (2002). "Inside the planning fallacy: The causes and consequences of optimistic time predictions." In T. Gilovich, D. Griffin, & D. Kahneman (Eds.), *Heuristics and biases: The psychology of intuitive judgment* (pp. 250–270). Cambridge, UK: Cambridge University Press.

[94] Weiner, I. B., & Craighead, W. E. (2010). *The Corsini encyclopedia of psychology (4th Ed.).* Hoboken, NJ: Wiley.

Roeckelein, J. E. (1998). *Dictionary of theories, laws, and concepts in psychology.* Westport, Conn: Greenwood Press.

[95] Spence, C. & Santangelo, V. (2010) Auditory Attention. In C. J. Plack (Ed.). *The Oxford handbook of auditory science: Volume 3* (pp. 249-270). Oxford: Oxford University Press.

[96] Cherry C. (1953) Some experiments on the recognition of speech with one and two ears. *Journal of the Acoustical Society of America, 25*:975–979.

Craighead, W. E., & Nemeroff, C. B. (2001). *The Corsini encyclopedia of psychology and behavioral science: Volume 4.* New York: Wiley.

[97] Zwicky, A. (2005, Aug 7). *Just Between Dr. Language and I. Language Log.* Retrieved May 21, 2013 from http://itre.cis.upenn.edu/~myl/languagelog/archives/002386.html

Bellows, A. (2006, Mar 19). *The Baader-Meinhof Phenomenon. Damn Interesting.* Retrieved May 21, 2013 from http://www.damninteresting.com/the-baader-meinhof-phenomenon/

[98] Lader, M., Cardinali, D. P., & Pandi-Perumal, S. R. (2010). *Sleep and Sleep Disorders: A neuropsychopharmacological approach.* Boston: Springer.

[99] Krebs, R. E. (1998). *The history and use of our earth's chemical elements: A reference guide.* Westport, Conn: Greenwood Press.

[100] Kouider, S., Andrillon, T., Barbosa, L. S., Goupil, L., & Bekinschtein, T. A. (September 01, 2014). Inducing Task-Relevant Responses to Speech in the Sleeping Brain. *Current Biology.*

[101] Adler, A. (1973). *Superiority and social interest.* (3rd. Rev. ed.). H. L. Ansbacher, & R. R. Ansbacher, (Eds.), New York: Viking Press.

[102] Bridges, J. W. (1932). *Personality, many in one: An essay in Individual Psychology.* Boston: Stratford Company.

[103] Adler, A. (1929b). *The science of living.* New York: Greenberg, Publisher, Inc.

[104] White, R. W. (1959). Motivation Reconsidered: The concept of competence, *Psychological Review, 66* (5), pp. 297-333.

[105] Banerjee, J. C. (1994). *Encyclopaedic dictionary of psychological terms.* New Delhi: M.D. Publications.

[106] Banerjee, J. C. (1994). *Encyclopaedic dictionary of psychological terms.* New Delhi: M.D. Publications.

[107] Adler, A. (1929a). *The practice and theory of Individual Psychology.* (P. Radin, Trans.). New York: Harcourt, Brace & Company, Inc.

[108] Clancy, B., Finlay, B. L., Darlington, R. B. & Anand, K. J. S. (2007). Extrapolating brain development from experimental species to humans. *Neurotoxicology 28,* 931-937.

[109] Warren, H. C., & Carmichael, L. (1930). *Elements of human psychology*. Boston: Houghton Mifflin Company.

Ratan, V. (1993). *Handbook of human physiology*. New Delhi: Jaypee Bros. Medical Publishers.

[110] Sadock, B. J., & Sadock, V. A., (2007). *Kaplan & Sadock's synopsis of psychiatry: behavioral sciences/clinical psychiatry*. (10th ed.). Philadelphia, PA: Wolter Kluwer/Lippincott Williams & Wilkins.

[111] Adler, A. (1956). *The Individual Psychology of Alfred Adler: A systematic presentation in selections from his writings*. H. Ansbacher & R. Ansbacher (Eds.), New York: Basic Books.

[112] Adler, A. (1956). *The Individual Psychology of Alfred Adler: A systematic presentation in selections from his writings*. H. Ansbacher & R. Ansbacher (Eds.), New York: Basic Books.

[113] Adler, A. (1956). *The Individual Psychology of Alfred Adler: A systematic presentation in selections from his writings*. H. Ansbacher & R. Ansbacher (Eds.), New York: Basic Books.

[114] Dreikurs, R. & Mosak, H. H. (1967). The tasks of life II. The fourth life task. *Individual Psychologist, 4*(2), 51-56.

[115] Mosak, H. H. & Dreikurs, R. (1967). The life tasks III: The fifth life task. *Individual Psychologist, 5,* 16-22.

[116] Mosak, H. H. & Maniacci, M. P. (1999). *A primer of Adlerian psychology: The analytic-behavioral-cognitive psychology of Alfred Adler*. Philadelphia: Brunner/Mazel.

[117] Darwin, C. (1859). *On the Origin of Species by Means of Natural Selection, or the Preservation of Favoured Races in the Struggle for Life* (1st ed.), London: John Murray, Retrieved February 14, 2009, from http://darwin-online.org.uk/content/frameset?itemID=F373&viewtype=text&pageseq=1

Dawkins, R. (1989). *The selfish gene*. New York: Oxford University Press.

[118] Lundin, R. W. (1989). *Alfred Adler's basic concepts and implications*. Muncie, Indiana: Accelerated Development Inc.

Adler, A. (1973). *Superiority and social interest*. (3rd. Rev. ed.). H. L. Ansbacher, & R. R. Ansbacher, (Eds.), New York: Viking Press.

[119] Adler, A. (1956). *The Individual Psychology of Alfred Adler: A systematic presentation in selections from his writings*. H. Ansbacher & R. Ansbacher (Eds.), New York: Basic Books.

Smuts, J. C. (1973). *Holism and evolution*. Greenwood Press. Oxford, UK

[120] Adler, A. (1996a). The structure of neurosis. *Individual Psychology, 52*(2), 351-362. (Original work published 1935).

[121] Adler, A. (1956). *The Individual Psychology of Alfred Adler: A systematic presentation in selections from his writings*. H. Ansbacher & R. Ansbacher (Eds.), New York: Basic Books.

[122] Adler, A. (1939). Sur la "protestation virile". [On the "masculine protest"]. *Courage, 2*(1). 8-10. As cited in Mosak, H. H. & Maniacci, M. P. (1999). *A primer of Adlerian psychology: The analytic-behavioral-cognitive psychology of Alfred Adler* (p. 5). Philadelphia: Brunner/Mazel.

Mosak, H. H. & Schneider, S. (1989). Masculine protest, penis envy, women's liberation and sexual equality. *Journal of Individual Psychology, 33*(2), 193-202.

Mosak, H. H. & Maniacci, M. P. (1999). *A primer of Adlerian psychology: The analytic-behavioral-cognitive psychology of Alfred Adler*. Philadelphia: Brunner/Mazel.

[123] Dreikurs, R. (1973). *Psychodynamics, psychotherapy, and counseling* (Rev. ed.). Chicago: Adler School of Professional Psychology.

[124] Dreikurs, R. (1973). *Psychodynamics, psychotherapy, and counseling* (Rev. ed.). Chicago:

Adler School of Professional Psychology.

[125] Yerkes R. M. & Dodson J. D. (1908). The relation of strength of stimulus to rapidity of habit-formation. *Journal of Comparative Neurology and Psychology 18*, 459–482.

[126] Postman, N. (2006). *Amusing ourselves to death: Public discourse in the age of show business*. New York, NY: Penguin Books.

Smith, G. W. (2004). *The politics of deceit: Saving freedom and democracy from extinction*. Hoboken, NJ: John Wiley.

[127] Dreikurs, R. (1973). *Psychodynamics, psychotherapy, and counseling* (Rev. ed.). Chicago: Adler School of Professional Psychology.

[128] Adler, A. (1958). *What life should mean to you*. A. Porter (Ed.). New York: Capricorn Books. (Original work published 1931)

Orgler, H. (1963). *Alfred Adler: The man and his work*. New York: Capricorn Books. (Original work published 1939)

Beecher, W. (1959). Guilt feelings: Masters of our fate or our servants? In K. A. Adler & D. Deutsch (Eds.), *Essays in Individual Psychology: Contemporary application of Alfred Adler's theories* (pp. 59-70). New York: Grove Press, Inc.

Mairet, P. (1928). *A B C of Adler's psychology*. London: Kegan Paul, Trench, Trubner & Co., LTD.

[129] Adler, A. (1996a). The structure of neurosis. *Individual Psychology, 52*(2), 351-362. (Original work published 1935)

[130] Dreikurs, R. (1973). *Psychodynamics, psychotherapy, and counseling* (Rev. ed.). Chicago: Adler School of Professional Psychology.

[131] Dreikurs, R. (1973). *Psychodynamics, psychotherapy, and counseling* (Rev. ed.). Chicago: Adler School of Professional Psychology.

[132] Ollendick, Thomas H., & Schroeder, Carolyn S. (2013). *Encyclopedia of Clinical Child and Pediatric Psychology*. Springer Verlag.

[133] James, W. (1890). *Principles of psychology*. New York: Smith.

Aronson, E. (1999). *The social animal*. New York: Worth.

[134] Hoehn-Saric, R., & McLeod, D. R. (1993). *Biology of anxiety disorders*. Washington, DC: American Psychiatric Press.

Hutchison, E. D. (2013). *Essentials of human behavior: Integrating person, environment, and the life course*. Los Angeles: SAGE.

[135] Gilbert, D. T., Pinel, E. C., Wilson, T. D., Blumberg, S. J. & Wheatley, T. P. (1998). Immune neglect: A source of durability bias in affective forecasting. *Journal of Personality and Social Psychology, 75*, 617-638.

[136] Dreikurs, R. (1973). *Psychodynamics, psychotherapy, and counseling* (Rev. ed.). Chicago: Adler School of Professional Psychology.

Aronson, E. (1999). *The social animal*. New York: Worth.

[137] Tyerman, A., King, N., & British Psychological Society. (2008). *Psychological approaches to rehabilitation after traumatic brain injury*. Malden, MA: BPS Blackwell.

Granacher, R. P. (2008). *Traumatic brain injury: Methods for clinical and forensic neuropsychiatric assessment*. Boca Raton: CRC Press/Taylor & Francis Group.

Zasler, N. D., Katz, D. I., & Zafonte, R. D. (2007). *Brain injury medicine: Principles and practice*. New York: Demos.

Parker, R. S. (1996). The spectrum of emotional distress and personality changes after minor head injury incurred in a motor vehicle accident. *Brain Injury, 10*:287-302.

Jorge, R. E., Robinson, R. G., Moser, D., Tateno, A., Crespo-Facorro, B., & Arndt, S. (2004). Major depression following traumatic brain injury. *Archives of General Psychiatry, 61*, 42–50.

Aitken, L., Simpson, S., Burns, A. (1999). Personality change in dementia. *International*

Psychogeriatrics, 11, 263-271.

American Psychiatric Association. (2000). *Diagnostic and statistical manual of mental disorders: DSM-IV-TR.* Washington, DC: American Psychiatric Association.

Blanchard, R. J. (2008). *Handbook of anxiety and fear.* Amsterdam: Academic Press.

Marks, I. M. (1987). *Fears, phobias, and rituals: Panic, anxiety, and their disorders.* New York: Oxford University Press.

Starcevic, V. (2005). *Anxiety disorders in adults: A clinical guide.* New York: Oxford University Press.

Candland, D. K. (2003). *Emotion.* New York: Authors Choice Press.

Lerner, R. M. (1999). *Adolescence: Development, diversity and context.* New York: Garland.

[138] Bernstein, D. A., & Nash, P. W. (1999). *Essentials of psychology.* Boston: Houghton Mifflin.

Bartholow, B. D., & Heinz, A. (2006). Alcohol and aggression without consumption: Alcohol cues, aggressive thoughts, and hostile perception bias. *Psychological Science, 17,* 30-37.

[139] Schwartz, B. (2004). *The paradox of choice: Why more is less.* New York: HarperCollins.

[140] Haselton, M. G. & Ketelaar, T. (2006). Irrational emotions or emotional wisdom? The evolutionary psychology of emotions and behavior. In J. P. Forgas (Ed.), *Hearts and minds: Affective influences on social cognition and behavior* (pp. 21-40). New York: Psychology Press.

Bechara, A., & Damasio, A. (August 01, 2005). The somatic marker hypothesis: A neural theory of economic decision. *Games and Economic Behavior, 52,* 2, 336-372.

Cameron, C., D. & Payne, B., K. (2011). Escaping Affect: How Motivational Emotion Regulation Creates Insensitivity to Mass Suffering. *Journal of Personality and Social Psychology, 100*(1), 1-15.

Crawford, C. (2010). *Evolutionary Psychology, Public Policy and Personal Decisions.* (pp. 93-109.) United States of America: New Jersey. Lawrence Erlbaum Associates Inc.

[141] Dreikurs, R. (1973). *Psychodynamics, psychotherapy, and counseling* (Rev. ed.). Chicago: Adler School of Professional Psychology.

Zeelenberg, M., Nelissen, R. A., Breugelmans, S. M., & Pieters, R. (2008). On emotion specificity in decision making: Why feeling is for doing. *Judgment and Decision making, 3*(1), 18-27.

[142] Baumeister, R. F., Vohs, K. D., DeWall, C. N., & Zhang, L. (2007). How Emotion Shapes Behavior: Feedback, Anticipation, and Reflection, Rather Than Direct Causation. *Personality and Social Psychology Review 11,* 167-203.

[143] Dreikurs, R. (1973). *Psychodynamics, psychotherapy, and counseling* (Rev. ed.). Chicago: Adler School of Professional Psychology.

[144] Haselton, M. G. & Ketelaar, T. (2006). Irrational emotions or emotional wisdom? The evolutionary psychology of emotions and behavior. In J. P. Forgas (Ed.), *Hearts and minds: Affective influences on social cognition and behavior* (pp. 21-40). New York: Psychology Press.

[145] Klein, S. B & Thorne, B. M. (2006). *Biological psychology.* New York: Worth Publishers.

[146] Klein, S. B & Thorne, B. M. (2006). *Biological psychology.* New York: Worth Publishers.

[147] Sadock, B. J., & Sadock, V. A., (2007). *Kaplan & Sadock's synopsis of psychiatry: behavioral sciences/clinical psychiatry.* (10th ed.). Philadelphia, PA: Wolter Kluwer/Lippincott Williams & Wilkins.

[148] Seligman, M. E. P. (1971) Phobias and preparedness. *Behavior Therapy, 2,* 307-320.

Leonard, D. C. (2002). *Learning theories: A to Z.* Westport, CT: Greenwood Press.

[149] Feinstein, S. (2006). *The Praeger handbook of learning and the brain: Vol. 2.* (The Praeger handbook of learning and the brain.) Westport, Conn.: Praeger.

McGaugh, J. L. (2003). *Memory and emotion: The making of lasting memories.* New York: Columbia University Press.

Dierkes, M., Antal, A. B., Child, J., & Nonaka, I. (2003). *Handbook of organizational learning and knowledge.* Oxford, UK: Oxford University Press.

Reisberg, D., & Hertel, P. (2004). *Memory and emotion.* Oxford: Oxford University Press.

[150] Wilmore, J. H., Costill, D. L., & Kenney, W. L. (2008). *Physiology of sport and exercise.* Champaign, IL: Human Kinetics.

Haibach, P. S., Reid, G., & Collier, D. H. (2011). *Motor learning and development.* Champaign, IL: Human Kinetics.

[151] Aiello, M. (n. d.). *Memory and memory loss.* Retrieved March 12, 2009 from Duke University Medical Center, Department of Psychiatry and Behavioral Sciences Web site: http://psychiatry.mc.duke.edu/CMRIS/ED/Memory.htm

Ebbinghaus, H. (1885/1964). *Memory: A contribution to experimental psychology,* (trans. H. A. Ruger and C. E. Bussenius). New York: Dover Publications.

[152] Beattie, G. (2004). *Visible thought: The new psychology of body language.* New York: Routledge.

Fast, J. (1988). *Body language.* New York: Pocket Books.

Dimitrius, J. & Mazzarella, M. C. (1999). *Reading people: How to understand people and predict their behavior – anytime, anyplace.* New York: Ballantine Books.

[153] Titelman, G. Y. (1996). *Random House Dictionary of Popular Proverbs and Sayings.* New York: Random House. p. 94

[154] Adeleye, G., Acquah-Dadzie, K., Sienkewicz, T. J., & McDonough, J. T. (1999). *World dictionary of foreign expressions: A resource for readers and writers.* Wauconda, Ill: Bolchazy-Carducci Publishers.

[155] Ekman, P., & Rosenberg, E. L. (1997). *What the face reveals: Basic and applied studies of spontaneous expression using the facial action coding system (FACS).* New York: Oxford University Press.

[156] Ekman, P. (2009). *Telling lies: Clues to deceit in the marketplace, politics, and marriage.* New York, NY: W. W. Norton.

[157] Kleiner, M. (2002). *Handbook of Polygraph Testing.* San Diego, CA: Academic Press.

Gamer, M., Verschuere, B., Crombez, G., & Vossel, G. (2008, October). Combining physiological measures in the detection of concealed information. *Physiology & Behavior, 95*(3), 333-340.

Grubin, D., & Madsen, L. (2005, June). Lie detection and the polygraph: A historical review. *Journal of Forensic Psychiatry & Psychology, 16*(2), 357-369.

[158] Burgess, R. & Baldassarre, C. (2006). *Ultimate guide to poker tells: Devastate opponents by reading body language, table talk, chip moves, and much more.* Chicago: Triumph Books.

[159] Ekman, P. (2007). *Emotions revealed: Recognizing faces and feelings to improve communication and emotional life.* New York, NY: H. Holt.

Ekman, P. (2009). *Telling lies: Clues to deceit in the marketplace, politics, and marriage.* New York, NY: W. W. Norton.

[160] Nummenmaa, L., Glerean, E., Hari, R. and Hietanen, J. K. (2013, December 30) *Bodily maps of emotions.* Proceedings of the National Academy of Sciences. Retrieved January 5, 2014 from http://www.pnas.org/content/early/2013/12/26/1321664111.full.pdf+html

[161] Vingerhoets, A. J. J. M. (2013). *Why only humans weep: Unravelling the mysteries of tears.* Oxford: Oxford University Press.

[162] Mancia, G. et al. (January 01, 1983). Effects of blood-pressure measurement by the doctor on patient's blood pressure and heart rate. *Lancet, 2,* 8352, 695-698.

[163] Harman, M., Waldo, M. & Johnson, J. (1998). The sexually dysfunctional couple: Vaginismus and Relationship Enhancement Therapy. In J. Carlson & L. Sperry (Eds.)

The disordered couple (pp. 83-95). Bristol, PA: Brunner/Manzel, Inc.

Mitchell, D. R. (2009). *A concise encyclopedia of women's sexual and reproductive health*. New York: St. Martin' s Press.

Wincze, J. P., Bach, A. K., & Barlow, D. H. (2008). Sexual Dysfunction In D. H. Barlow (Ed.). : *Clinical handbook of psychological disorders, a step-by-step treatment manual* (4th ed.) (pp. 615-661). New York, NY: Guilford Press.

Sadock, B. J., Sadock, V. A., & Sadock, B. J. (2008). *Kaplan & Sadock's concise textbook of clinical psychiatry*. Philadelphia: Wolters Kluwer/Lippincott Williams & Wilkins.

Boyer, S. C., Goldfinger, C., Thibault-Gagnon, S., & Pukall, C. F. (2011). In R. Balon (Ed.). *Sexual dysfunction: Beyond the brain-body connection*. Basel: Karger.

Jannini, E. A., McMahon, C. G., & Waldinger, M.D. (2013). *Premature ejaculation: From etiology to diagnosis and treatment*. Milan: Springer.

Winn, P. (2001). *Dictionary of biological psychology*. London: Routledge.

Schiff, J.D. & Mulhall, J. P. (2005). Epidemiology of erectile dysfunction. In G. A. Broderick (Ed.). *Oral pharmacotherapy for male sexual dysfunction: A guide to clinical management*. Totowa, NJ: Humana Press.

Bennett, P. (2011). *Abnormal and clinical psychology: An introductory textbook*. Maidenhead, Berkshire, England: McGraw Hill.

Rakel, R. E., & Rakel, D. (2011). *Textbook of family medicine*. Philadelphia, PA: Elsevier Saunders.

Bartlik, B. D., Kolzet, J. A., Ahmad, N., Parveen, T., & Alvi, S. (2010). Female sexual health. In M. J. Legato (Ed.). *Principles of gender-specific medicine*. Amsterdam: Academic Press.

Deveci, S. and Mulhall, J. P. (2010). Male sexual dysfunction. In M. J. Legato (Ed.). *Principles of gender-specific medicine*. Amsterdam: Academic Press.

Craighead, W. E., & Nemeroff, C. B. (2004). *The concise Corsini encyclopedia of psychology and behavioral science*. Hoboken, NJ: John Wiley & Sons.

Neighbors, M., & Tannehill-Jones, R. (2010). *Human Diseases*. New York: Delmar.

Smith, D. J., Barton, D., & Joubert, L. (2007). Psychological and social influences on male sexual function. In F. R. Kandeel (Ed.). *Male sexual dysfunction: Pathophysiology and treatment*. New York, NY: Informa Healthcare USA.

[164] Prinz, W. Aschersleben, G. & Koch, I. (2008). Cognition and action. In E. Morsella, J. A. Bargh, & P. M. Gollwitzer (Eds.), *Oxford handbook of human action* (pp. 35-71). Oxford University Press.

[165] Heap, M. (2002). Ideomotor effect (the "Ouija Board" effect). In M. Shermer (Ed.), and P. Linse (Contributing Ed.), *The skeptic encyclopedia of pseudoscience: Vol. 1* (pp. 127-129). Santa Barbara: ABC-CLIO.

Kelly, L. (2004). *The skeptic's guide to the paranormal*. New York: Thunder's Mouth Press.

[166] Stephens, R., Atkins, J., & Kingston, A. (January 01, 2009). Swearing as a response to pain. *Neuroreport, 20,* 12, 1056-1060.

Stephens, R., & Umland, C. (December 01, 2011). Swearing as a Response to Pain—Effect of Daily Swearing Frequency. *The Journal of Pain, 12,* 12, 1274-1281.

[167] Stephens, R., & Umland, C. (December 01, 2011). Swearing as a Response to Pain—Effect of Daily Swearing Frequency. *The Journal of Pain, 12,* 12, 1274-1281.

[168] Rakel, D. (2012). *Integrative medicine*. Philadelphia, PA: Elsevier Saunders.

Schacter, D. L., Gilbert, D. T., & Wegner, D. M. (2009). *Psychology*. New York: Worth Publishers.

Goldstein, I. (2006). *Women's sexual function and dysfunction: Study, diagnosis, and treatment*. London: Taylor & Francis.

Both, S., & Laan, E. (2003). Directed masturbation: A problem of female orgasmic disorder. In W. O'Donohue, J. E. Fisher, & S. C. Hayes (Eds.), *Cognitive behavior therapy: Applying emperically supported techniques in your practice* (pp. 144-151). New York: John Wiley & Sons.

Wiegel, M., Scepkowski, L. A., & Barlow, D. H. (2007). Cognitive-affective processes in sexual arousal and sexual dysfunction. In E. Janssen (Ed.), *Psychophysiology of sex* (pp. 143-166). Bloomington: Indiana University Press.

[169] Komisaruk, B. R., Beyer, C., & Whipple, B. (2006). *The science of orgasm.* Baltimore: Johns Hopkins University Press.

[170] Catel, P. (2011). *Surviving stunts and other amazing feats.* Chicago, Ill: Raintree.

Cappello, M. (2011). *Swallow: Foreign bodies, their ingestion, inspiration, and the curious doctor who extracted them.* New York: New Press.

[171] Reis, D. L. & Gray, J. R. (2008). Affect and action control. In E. Morsella, J. A. Bargh, & P. M. Gollwitzer (Eds.), *Oxford handbook of human action* (pp. 277-297). Oxford University Press.

[172] Cacioppo, J. T., Tassinary, L. G., & Berntson, G. G. (2000). *Handbook of psychophysiology.* Cambridge, UK: Cambridge University Press.

[173] Amy Cuddy: Your body language shapes who you are. (n.d.). Retrieved July 21, 2014, from http://www.ted.com/talks/amy_cuddy_your_body_language_shapes_who_you_are

[174] Zhong, C. B., & Liljenquist, K. (January 01, 2006). Washing away your sins: threatened morality and physical cleansing. *Science (New York, NY), 313,* 5792, 1451-2.

Lee, S. W. S., & Schwarz, N. (May 07, 2010). Washing away postdecisional dissonance. *Science, 328,* 5979.

[175] Corsini, R. J. (1999). *Dictionary of psychology.* Philadelphia, P. A.: Brunner/Mazel, Taylor & Francis.

Sadock, B. J., & Sadock, V. A., (2007). *Kaplan & Sadock's synopsis of psychiatry: behavioral sciences/clinical psychiatry.* (10th ed.). Philadelphia, PA: Wolter Kluwer/Lippincott Williams & Wilkins.

[176] Weger, U. W., & Loughnan, S. (December 13, 2012). Mobilizing unused resources: Using the placebo concept to enhance cognitive performance. *The Quarterly Journal of Experimental Psychology,* 1-6.

[177] Moore, R. J. (2012). *Handbook of pain and palliative care: Biobehavioral approaches for the life course.* New York: Springer.

[178] Weiner, I. B., Freedheim, D. K., Schinka, J. A., & Velicer, W. F. (2003). *Handbook of psychology.* New York: Wiley.

[179] Hicks, R. A., & Conti, P. (1991, June). Nocturnal bruxism and self reports of stress-related symptoms. *Perceptual and Motor Skills, 72*(3, Pt 2), 1182.

Schneider, C., Schaefer, R., Ommerborn, M. A., Giraki, M., Goertz, A., Raab, W. H.-M; et al. (2007). Maladaptive coping strategies in patients with bruxism compared to non-bruxing controls. *International Journal of Behavioral Medicine, 14*(4), 257-261.

Sapolsky, R. M. (1998). *Why zebras don't get ulcers: An updated guide to stress, stress-related diseases, and coping.* New York: W. H. Freeman and Company.

American Psychiatric Association. (2000). *Diagnostic and statistical manual of mental disorders: DSM-IV-TR.* Washington, DC: American Psychiatric Association.

Carleton. R. N. & Asmundson G. J. G. (2012) Dispositional fear, anxiety sensitivity, and hypervigilance. In M. I. Hasenbring, A. C. Rusu, & D. C. Turk (Eds.). *From acute to chronic back pain: Risk factors, mechanisms, and clinical implications* (pp 231-250). Oxford: Oxford University Press.

Sullivan, M. J. K. and Martel, M. O. (2012). Processes underlying the relation between catastrophizing and chronic pain: Implications for Intervention. In M. I. Hasenbring, A. C. Rusu, & D. C. Turk (Eds.). *From acute to chronic back pain: Risk factors, mechanisms, and clinical implications* (pp. 251-268). Oxford: Oxford University Press.

[180] Adler, A. (1929b). *The science of living.* New York: Greenberg, Publisher, Inc.

[181] Dreikurs, R. (1953). *Fundamentals of Adlerian psychology.* Chicago: Alfred Adler Institute. (Original work published 1935)

[182] Chesley, G. L., Gillett, D. A. and Wagner, W. G. (2008), Verbal and Nonverbal Metaphor With Children in Counseling. *Journal of Counseling & Development, 86*: 399–411.

[183] Sapolsky, R. M. (1998). *Why zebras don't get ulcers: An updated guide to stress, stress-related diseases, and coping.* New York: W. H. Freeman and Company.

Arslan, O. (2001). *Neuroanatomical basis of clinical neurology.* New York: Parthenon Pub. Group.

Rygh, J. L., & Sanderson, W. C. (2004). *Treating generalized anxiety disorder: Evidence-based strategies, tools, and techniques.* New York: Guilford Press.

[184] Bashour, T. T. (2011). *The broken heart: Protect your heart from daily stress and emotional upheavals.* Pittsburgh, Pa: RoseDog Books.

[185] Adler, A. (1956). *The Individual Psychology of Alfred Adler: A systematic presentation in selections from his writings.* H. Ansbacher & R. Ansbacher (Eds.), New York: Basic Books.

[186] Adler, A. (1930). *The neurotic constitution: Outlines of a comparative individualistic psychology and psychotherapy.* (B. Glueck & J. E. Lind, Trans.). New York: Dodd, Mead and Company.

[187] Adler, A. (1973). *Superiority and social interest.* (3rd. Rev. ed.). H. L. Ansbacher, & R. R. Ansbacher, (Eds.), New York: Viking Press.

[188] Adler, A. (1973). *Superiority and social interest.* (3rd. Rev. ed.). H. L. Ansbacher, & R. R. Ansbacher, (Eds.), New York: Viking Press.

[189] Adler, A. (1973). *Superiority and social interest.* (3rd. Rev. ed.). H. L. Ansbacher, & R. R. Ansbacher, (Eds.), New York: Viking Press.

[190] Adler, A. (1996a). The structure of neurosis. *Individual Psychology, 52*(2), 351-362. (Original work published 1935)

[191] Goldfeld, S., Wise, P., & Zuckerman, B. (2002). The Impact of Maternal Health on Child Health Status and Health Service Utilisation. *Journal of Paediatrics and Child Health, 38*(5):A8.

Debes, F., Budtz-Jorgensen, E., Weihe, P., White, R. F., & Grandjean, P. (2006). Impact of prenatal methylmercury exposure on neurobehavioral function at age 14 years. *Neurotoxicology and Teratology, 28*(5), Sep-Oct 2006, 536-547.

Burns, L., Mattick, R. P., & Wallace, C. (2008, June). Smoking patterns and outcomes in a population of pregnant women with other substance use disorders. *Nicotine & Tobacco Research, 10*(6), 969-974.

Shea, A. K., & Steiner, M. (2008). Cigarette smoking during pregnancy. *Nicotine & Tobacco Research, 10*(2), Feb 2008, 267-278.

Salihu, H. M., Sharma, P. P., Getahun, D., Hedayatzadeh, M., Peters, S., Kirby, R. S., et al. (2008, January). Prenatal tobacco use and risk of stillbirth: A case-control and bidirectional case-crossover study. *Nicotine & Tobacco Research, 10*(1), 159-166.

Cornelius, M. D., Goldschmidt, L., DeGenna, N., & Day, N. L. (2007, July). Smoking during teenage pregnancies: Effects on behavioral problems in offspring. *Nicotine & Tobacco Research, 9*(7), 739-750.

Yumoto, C., Jacobson, S. W., & Jacobson, J. L. (2008, November-December). Fetal substance exposure and cumulative environmental risk in an African American cohort. *Child Development, 79*(6), 1761-1776.

Vaurio, L., Riley, E. P., & Mattson, S. N. (2008, January). Differences in executive functioning in children with heavy prenatal alcohol exposure or attention-deficit/hyperactivity disorder. *Journal of the International Neuropsychological Society, 14*(1), 119-129.

Autti-Ramo, I., Autti, T., Korkman, M., Kettunen, S., Salonen, O., & Valanne, L. (2002, February). MRI findings in children with school problems who had been exposed prenatally to alcohol. *Developmental Medicine & Child Neurology, 44*(2), 98-106.

Autti-Ramo, I. (2000, June). Twelve-year follow-up of children exposed to alcohol in utero. *Developmental Medicine & Child Neurology, 42*(6), 406-411.

Aronson, M., Hagberg, B., & Gillberg, C. (1997, September). Attention deficits and autistic spectrum problems in children exposed to alcohol during gestation: A follow-up study. *Developmental Medicine & Child Neurology, 39*(9), 583-587.

Oberlander, T. F., Warburton, W., Misri, S., Aghajanian, J., & Hertzman, C. (2006, August). Neonatal Outcomes After Prenatal Exposure to Selective Serotonin Reuptake Inhibitor Antidepressants and Maternal Depression Using Population-Based Linked Health Data. *Archives of General Psychiatry, 63*(8), 898-906.

Gray, K. A., Day, N. L., Leech, S., & Richardson, G. A. (2005, May-June). Prenatal marijuana exposure: Effect on child depressive symptoms at ten years of age. *Neurotoxicology and Teratology, 27*(3), 439-448.

Willford, J. A., Richardson, G. A., Leech, S. L., & Day, N. L. (2004, March). Verbal and Visuospatial Learning and Memory Function in Children With Moderate Prenatal Alcohol Exposure. *Alcoholism: Clinical and Experimental Research, 28*(3), 497-507.

Dunn, C. L., Pirie, P., & Hellerstedt, W. L. (2004, March-April). Self Exposure to Secondhand Smoke Among Prenatal Smokers, Abstainers, and Nonsmokers. *American Journal of Health Promotion, 18*(4), 296-299.

Dominguez-Salas, P., Moore, S. E., Baker, M. S., Bergen, A. W., Cox, S. E., et. al. (2014, April 29). Maternal nutrition at conception modulates DNA methylation of human metastable epialleles. *Nature Communications, 5:3746* doi: 10.1038/ncomms4746

[192] Surowiecki, J. (2004). *The wisdom of crowds.* New York: Anchor Books.

[193] Adler, A. (1927). *Understanding human nature.* (Walter Béran Wolfe, Trans.). Garden City, NY: Garden City Publishing Company, Inc.

[194] Adler, A. (1956). *The Individual Psychology of Alfred Adler: A systematic presentation in selections from his writings.* H. Ansbacher & R. Ansbacher (Eds.), New York: Basic Books.

[195] Hardin, G. (1968). The tragedy of the commons. *Science, 13* December, vol. 162. no. 3859, pp. 1243-1248.

[196] Sherif, M., Harvey, O. J., White, B. J., Hood, W. R., & Sherif, C. W. (1961). *Intergroup conflict and cooperation: The Robbers Cave experiment (Vol. 10).* Norman, OK: University Book Exchange.

[197] Adler, A. (1996a). The structure of neurosis. *Individual Psychology, 52*(2), 351-362. (Original work published 1935)

[198] Adler, A. (1927). *Understanding human nature.* (Walter Béran Wolfe, Trans.). Garden City, NY: Garden City Publishing Company, Inc.

[199] Adler, A. (1956). *The Individual Psychology of Alfred Adler: A systematic presentation in selections from his writings.* H. Ansbacher & R. Ansbacher (Eds.), New York: Basic Books.

[200] Adler, A. (1958). *What life should mean to you.* A. Porter (Ed.). New York: Capricorn Books. (Original work published 1931)

[201] Adler, A. (1958). *What life should mean to you.* A. Porter (Ed.). New York: Capricorn Books. (Original work published 1931)

[202] Sloan, W. D., & Mackay, J. B. (2007). *Media bias: Finding it, fixing it.* Jefferson, NC: McFarland & Co.

Moody-Ramirez, M. (2013). *Obamas and mass media: Race, gender, religion, and politics.* New York.: Palgrave MacMillian.

[203] Bandura, A., Ross, D., & Ross, S. A. (1961). Transmission of aggressions through imitation of aggressive models. *Journal of Abnormal and Social Psychology, 63*, 575-582.

[204] Milgram, S. (1974). *Obedience to Authority: An Experimental View*. New York: Harper and Row.

[205] Gibson, E. J. & Walk, R. D. (1960). The "visual cliff.". *Scientific American 202*, April, 64-71.

[206] Dreikurs, R. & Soltz, V. (1990). *Children: The challenge*. New York: Plume.

[207] Cooley, C. H. (1902). *Human Nature and the Social Order*. New York: Scribner's. pp. 179-185.

[208] Janis, I. (1972). *Victims of Groupthink: A Psychological Study of Foreign-Policy Decisions and Fiascoes*. Boston: Houghton Mifflin.

[209] Asch, S. E., (1951). Effects of Group Pressure Upon the Modification and Distortion of Judgements. In H. Guetzkow (Ed.), *Groups, leadership and men* (pp. 177–190). Pittsburgh, PA: Carnegie Press.

[210] Durkheim, E. (1951). *Suicide: A study in sociology*. (J. A. Spaulding & G. Simpson, Trans.). Glencoe, IL: Free Press. (Original work published 1897)

Robertson Blackmore, E., Munce, S., Weller, I., Zagorski, B., Stansfeld, S. A., Stewart, D. E., et al. (2008). Psychosocial and clinical correlates of suicidal acts: Results from a national population survey. *British Journal of Psychiatry, 192*(4), Apr 2008, 279-284.

[211] Durkheim, E. (1951). *Suicide: A study in sociology*. (J. A. Spaulding & G. Simpson, Trans.). Glencoe, IL: Free Press. (Original work published 1897)

Luoma, J. B., & Pearson, J. L. (2002). Suicide and marital status in the United States, 1991–1996: is widowhood a risk factor? *American Journal of Public Health, 92*, 1518–1522. *Findings support suicide higher among widowed.

Kposowa, A. J. (2000). Marital status and suicide in the National Longitudinal Mortality Study. *Journal Epidemiology and Community Health, 54*, 254–261. *Findings support that divorce has significant correlation with suicide, but only among males.

Popoli, G., Sobelman, S., & Kanarek, N. F. (1989). Suicide in the state of Maryland. *Public Health Reports, 104*, 298–301. *Findings show widowed or divorced persons have higher rates of suicide than those single or married.

Smith, J. C., Mercy, J. A., & Conn, J. M. (1988). Marital status and the risk of suicide. *American Journal of Public Health, 78*, 78–80. *Findings show that married individuals have lowest suicide rates, with young widowed males having high suicide rates.

[212] Coleman, L. (2004). *The copycat effect: How the media and popular culture trigger the mayhem in tomorrow's headlines*. New York: Paraview Pocket Books.

Aronson, E. (1999). *The social animal*. New York: Worth Publishers.

Insel, B. J., & Gould, M. S. (2008, June). Impact of modeling on adolescent suicidal behavior. *Psychiatric Clinics of North America, 31*(2), 293-316.

[213] Randell, B. P., Wang, W-L., Herting, J. R., & Eggert, L. L. (2006, June). Family Factors Predicting Categories of Suicide Risk. *Journal of Child and Family Studies, 15*(3), 255-270.

[214] Sapolsky, R. M. (1998). *Why zebras don't get ulcers: An updated guide to stress, stress-related diseases, and coping*. New York: W. H. Freeman and Company.

House, J., Landis, K., & Umberson, D. (1988). Social relationships and health. *Science 241*, 540.

Berkman, L. F. & Breslow L. (1983). *Health and Ways of Living: Findings from the Alameda County study*. New York: Oxford University Press.

[215] Sapolsky, R. M. (1998). *Why zebras don't get ulcers: An updated guide to stress, stress-related diseases, and coping*. New York: W. H. Freeman and Company.

[216] Sapolsky, R. M. (1998). *Why zebras don't get ulcers: An updated guide to stress, stress-related diseases, and coping*. New York: W. H. Freeman and Company.

Kiecolt-Glaser, J. K., Garner, W., Speicher, C., Penn, G. M., Holliday, J., & Glaser, R. (January

01, 1984). Psychosocial modifiers of immunocompetence in medical students. *Psychosomatic Medicine, 46,* (1) 7-14.

[217] Sapolsky, R. M. (1998). *Why zebras don't get ulcers: An updated guide to stress, stress-related diseases, and coping.* New York: W. H. Freeman and Company.

Herbert, T., & Cohen, S. (1993). Stress and immunity in humans: A meta-analytic review. *Psychosomatic Medicine 55,* 364.

[218] Holmes, T. H., & Rahe, R. H. (January 01, 1967). The Social Readjustment Rating Scale. *Journal of Psychosomatic Research, 11,* (2), 213-218.

[219] Taylor S. E. (2011). Affiliation and Stress. In S. Folkman (Ed.). *The Oxford Handbook of Stress, Health and Coping.* (1st ed.) (pp. 86-100). New York: Oxford University Press Inc.

Uvnas-Moberg, K. & Petersson, M. (2005). Oxytocin, a mediator of anti-stress, well-being, social interaction, growth and healing. *Z Psychosom Med Psychother. 51*(1):57-80. (Retrieved May 9, 2013 from http://www.richardhill.com.au/oxytocin.pdf)

Fuchs, N. K. (2006). *The health detective's 456 most powerful healing secrets.* Laguna Beach, CA: Basic Health Publications.

Dayton, T. (2007). *Emotional sobriety: From relationship trauma to resilience and balance.* Deerfield Beach, FL: Health Communications.

[220] Hughes, M. & Waite, L. (2009, September). Marital Biography and Health at Mid-life. *Journal of Health and Social Behavior, 50,* 344-358. Online edition. Retrieved August 30, 2009, from http://www.asanet.org/galleries/default-file/Sep09JHSBFeature.pdf

[221] Olds, S. W., Marks, L., & Eiger, M. S. (2010). *The complete book of breastfeeding.* New York: Workman Pub.

[222] Meltzoff, A. N., & Moore, M. K. (November 01, 1989). Imitation in Newborn Infants: Exploring the Range of Gestures Imitated and the Underlying Mechanisms. *Developmental Psychology, 25,* 6, 954-62.

Reissland, N. (July 01, 1988). Neonatal Imitation in the First Hour of Life: Observations in Rural Nepal. *Developmental Psychology, 24,* 4, 464-69.

Field, T. (1990). *Infancy.* Cambridge, Mass: Harvard University Press.

[223] Effects of sexual activity on beard growth in man. (January 01, 1970). *Nature, 226,* 5248, 869-70.

Bribiescas, R. G. (2006). *Men: Evolutionary and life history.* Cambridge, Mass: Harvard University Press.

[224] Crozier, W. R., & Jong, P. J. (2012). *The psychological significance of the blush.* Cambridge, England: Cambridge University Press.

[225] Butler, J. G. (2002). *Television: Critical methods and applications.* Mahwah, NJ: Lawrence Erlbaum Associates.

[226] Sapolsky, R. M. (1998). *Why zebras don't get ulcers: An updated guide to stress, stress-related diseases, and coping.* New York: W. H. Freeman and Company.

House, J., Landis, K., & Umberson, D. (1988). Social relationships and health. *Science* 241, 540.

Holt-Lunstad J., Smith T. B., Layton J. B. (2010) Social Relationships and Mortality Risk: A Meta-analytic Review. *PLoS Med* 7(7): e1000316. doi:10.1371/journal.pmed.1000316

[227] Ridley, M. (1999). *Genome: The autobiography of a species in 23 chapters.* New York: HarperCollins.

[228] Ridley, M. (1999). *Genome: The autobiography of a species in 23 chapters.* New York: HarperCollins.

[229] Triandis, H. C. (1995). *Individualism & collectivism.* Boulder: Westview Press.

Markus, H. R., & Kitayama, S. (1991). Culture and the self: Implications for cognition, emotion, and motivation. *Psychological review, 98*(2), 224-253.

Markus, H., & Kitayama, S. (1994). The cultural construction of self and emotion: Implications for social behavior. In S. Kitayama, & H. Markus (Eds.), *Emotion and culture* (pp. 89-130). Washington, DC: American Psychological Association.

Cohen, D., & Gunz, A. (January 01, 2002). As Seen by the Other . . . : Perspectives on the Self in the Memories and Emotional Perceptions of Easterners and Westerners. *Psychological Science, 13*, 1, 55-59.

[230] Sapolsky, R. M. (1998). *Why zebras don't get ulcers: An updated guide to stress, stress-related diseases, and coping.* New York: W. H. Freeman and Company.

Lepore, S., Allen, K., & Evans, G. (1993). Social support lowers cardiovascular reactivity to an acute stressor. *Psychosomatic Medicine 55*, 518-524

Edens, J., Larkin, K., & Abel, J. (1992). The effect of social support and physical touch on cardiovascular reactions to mental stress. *Journal of Psychosomatic Research 36*, 371-381

Gerin, W., Pieper, C., Levy, R., & Pickering, T. (1992). Social support in social interaction: A moderator of cardiovascular reactivity. *Psychosomatic Medicine 54*, 324-336

Kamarck, T., Manuck, S., & Jennings, J. (1990). Social support reduces cardiovascular reactivity to psychological challenge: A laboratory model. *Psychosomatic Medicine 52*, 42-58

[231] Uchino, B. N., Smith, T. W., & Berg, C. A. (January 01, 2014). Spousal Relationship Quality and Cardiovascular Risk: Dyadic Perceptions of Relationship Ambivalence Are Associated With Coronary-Artery Calcification. *Psychological Science Cambridge, 25*, 4, 1037-1042. Retrieved February 7, 2014, from http://www.ncbi.nlm.nih.gov/pubmed/24501110

[232] Cialdini, R. B. (1993). *Influence: The psychology of persuasion* (rev. ed.). New York: Morrow.

Aronson, E. (1999). *The social animal* (8th ed.). New York: Freeman.

Sapolsky, R. M. (1998). *Why zebras don't get ulcers: An updated guide to stress, stress-related diseases, and coping.* New York: W. H. Freeman and Company.

[233] Wyatt, T. D. (2014). *Pheromones and animal behavior: Chemical signals and signature mixes.* Cambridge: Cambridge University Press.

Coon, D., & Mitterer, J. O. (2010). *Introduction to psychology: Gateways to mind and behavior.* Australia: Wadsworth, Cengage Learning.

[234] McClintock, M. K. (January 22, 1971). Menstrual Synchrony and Suppression. *Nature, 229*, 5282, 244-245.

[235] Doucet, S., Soussignan, R., Sagot, P., & Schaal, B. (January 01, 2009). The secretion of areolar (Montgomery's) glands from lactating women elicits selective, unconditional responses in neonates. *Plos One, 4*, 10.)

[236] Cutler, W. B., Friedmann, E., & Mccoy, N. L. (February 01, 1998). Pheromonal Influences on Sociosexual Behavior in Men. *Archives of Sexual Behavior, 27*, 1, 1-13.

McCoy, N., & Pitino, L. (March 01, 2002). Pheromonal influences on sociosexual behavior in young women. *Physiology & Behavior, 75*, 3, 367-375.

[237] Kirk-Smith, Michael; Booth, D. A.; Carroll, D.; Davies, P. (1978). Human social attitudes affected by androstenol. Research Communications in Psychology, *Psychiatry & Behavior, Vol 3*(4), 1978, 379-384.

Wedekind, C., Seebeck, T., Bettens, F., & Paepke, A. J. (January 01, 1995). MHC-dependent mate preferences in humans. *Proceedings. Biological Sciences / the Royal Society, 260*, 1359, 245-9.

Cutler, W. B. (January 01, 1999). Human Sex-Attractant Pheromones: Discovery, Research, Development, and Application in Sex Therapy. *Psychiatric Annals, 29*, 1, 54-59.

[238] Hays, W. S. T. (2003). Human pheromones: Have they been demonstrated? *Behavioral Ecology and Sociobiology, 54*(2), 89-97.

[239] Grosser, B. I., Monti-Bloch, L., Jennings-White, C., & Berliner, D. L. (January 01, 2000).

Behavioral and electrophysiological effects of androstadienone, a human pheromone. *Psychoneuroendocrinology, 25,* 3, 289-99.

[240] Haselton, M. G. & Ketelaar, T. (2006). Irrational emotions or emotional wisdom? The evolutionary psychology of emotions and behavior. In J. P. Forgas (Ed.), *Hearts and minds: Affective influences on social cognition and behavior* (pp. 21-40). New York: Psychology Press.

[241] Laslocky, M. (2013). *The little book of heartbreak: Love gone wrong through the ages.* New York: Plume.

Eisenberger, N. I., & Lieberman, M. D. (January 01, 2004). Why rejection hurts: a common neural alarm system for physical and social pain. *Trends in Cognitive Sciences, 8,* 7, 294-300.

[242] Hsu, D. T., Sanford, B. J., Meyers, K. K., Love, T. M., Hazlett, K. E., et al. (January 01, 2013). Response of the μ-opioid system to social rejection and acceptance. *Molecular Psychiatry, 18,* 11, 1211-7.

[243] Laslocky, M. (2013). *The little book of heartbreak: Love gone wrong through the ages.* New York: Plume.

[244] Laslocky, M. (2013). *The little book of heartbreak: Love gone wrong through the ages.* New York: Plume.

[245] Hsu, D. T., Sanford, B. J., Meyers, K. K., Love, T. M., Hazlett, K. E., et al. (January 01, 2013). Response of the μ-opioid system to social rejection and acceptance. *Molecular Psychiatry, 18,* 11, 1211-7.

[246] Sapolsky, R. M. (1998). *Why zebras don't get ulcers: An updated guide to stress, stress-related diseases, and coping.* New York: W. H. Freeman and Company.

[247] Freud, S. (1930/1989). *Civilization and its discontents.* New York: W. W. Norton and Company. p. 33

[248] Adler, A. (1956). *The Individual Psychology of Alfred Adler: A systematic presentation in selections from his writings.* H. Ansbacher & R. Ansbacher (Eds.), New York: Basic Books.

Mosak, H. H. & Maniacci, M. P. (1999). *A primer of Adlerian psychology: The analytic-behavioral-cognitive psychology of Alfred Adler.* Philadelphia: Brunner/Mazel.

[249] Adler, A. (1956). *The Individual Psychology of Alfred Adler: A systematic presentation in selections from his writings.* H. Ansbacher & R. Ansbacher (Eds.), New York: Basic Books.

[250] Adler, A. (1958). *What life should mean to you.* A. Porter (Ed.). New York: Capricorn Books. (Original work published 1931)

[251] Mitra, S., & Acharya, T. (2003). *Data mining: Multimedia, soft computing, and bioinformatics.* Hoboken, NJ: John Wiley.

Han, J., & Kamber, M. (2006). *Data mining: Concepts and techniques.* Amsterdam: Elsevier.

[252] Amazon. com, Inc. (n.d.). *Amazon.com: Help > Amazon.com Site Features > Your Content > Recommendations* Retrieved February 22, 2009, from http://www.amazon.com/gp/help/customer/display.html?nodeId=13316081#how

Apple, Inc. (2008, September 9). *Apple special event, September 2008.* Retrieved February 22, 2009, from http://www.apple.com/quicktime/qtv/letsrock/

Linden, G., Smith, B. & York, J. (2003, Jan/Feb). Amazon.com recommendations: Item-to-item collaborative filtering. *IEEE Internet computing, 7*(1), 76-80.

[253] Watson, J., & Crick, F. (1953). Molecular structure of nucleic acids; a structure for deoxyribose nucleic acid. *Nature 171* (4356), 737–738. Retrieved February 22, 2009, from http://profiles.nlm.nih.gov/SC/B/B/Y/W/_/scbbyw.pdf

[254] Mosak, H. H. (1977). The interrelatedness of the neuroses through central themes. In H. H. Mosak (Ed.), *On purpose* (pp. 138-143). Chicago: Adler School of Professional

Psychology. (Originally published in the Journal of Individual Psychology, 1968, 24, 67-70.)

Mosak, H. H. (1971). Lifestyle. In A. G. Nikelly (Ed.), *Techniques for behavior change* (pp. 77-81). Springfield, IL: Charles C. Thomas Publisher.

Mosak, H. H. (1979). Mosak's typology: An update. *Journal of Individual Psychology, 35*(1), 192-195.

[255] Mosak, H. H. (1977). The interrelatedness of the neuroses through central themes. In H. H. Mosak (Ed.), *On purpose* (pp. 138-143). Chicago: Adler School of Professional Psychology. (Originally published in the Journal of Individual Psychology, 1968, 24, 67-70.)

Mosak, H. H. (1971). Lifestyle. In A. G. Nikelly (Ed.), *Techniques for behavior change* (pp. 77-81). Springfield, IL: Charles C. Thomas Publisher.

Mosak, H. H. (1979). Mosak's typology: An update. *Journal of Individual Psychology, 35*(1), 192-195.

[256] Weiner, I. B., & Craighead, W. E. (2010). *The Corsini encyclopedia of psychology*. Hoboken, NJ: Wiley.

[257] Mosak, H. H. (1977). The interrelatedness of the neuroses through central themes. In H. H. Mosak (Ed.), *On purpose* (pp. 138-143). Chicago: Adler School of Professional Psychology. (Originally published in the Journal of Individual Psychology, 1968, 24, 67-70.)

Mosak, H. H. (1971). Lifestyle. In A. G. Nikelly (Ed.), *Techniques for behavior change* (pp. 77-81). Springfield, IL: Charles C. Thomas Publisher.

Mosak, H. H. (1979). Mosak's typology: An update. *Journal of Individual Psychology, 35*(1), 192-195.

[258] Adler, Alexandra. (1938). *Guiding human misfits: A practical application of Individual Psychology*. New York: Macmillan.

[259] Mosak, H. H. (1977). The interrelatedness of the neuroses through central themes. In H. H. Mosak (Ed.), *On purpose* (pp. 138-143). Chicago: Adler School of Professional Psychology. (Originally published in the Journal of Individual Psychology, 1968, 24, 67-70.)

Mosak, H. H. (1971). Lifestyle. In A. G. Nikelly (Ed.), *Techniques for behavior change* (pp. 77-81). Springfield, IL: Charles C. Thomas Publisher.

Mosak, H. H. (1979). Mosak's typology: An update. *Journal of Individual Psychology, 35*(1), 192-195.

[260] Wynbrandt, J., & Ludman, M. D. (2008). *The encyclopedia of genetic disorders and birth defects*. New York: Facts On File.

[261] Gookin, D. (2008). *Troubleshooting your PC for dummies* (3rd ed.). Hoboken, N. J.: Wiley.

[262] Gardner, H. (2011). *Frames of mind: The theory of multiple intelligences*. New York: Basic Books.

Home | Mi Oasis (n.d.). *Mi Oasis*. Retrieved June 20, 2014, from MI Oasis website: http://multipleintelligencesoasis.org

[263] Adler, A. (1956). *The Individual Psychology of Alfred Adler: A systematic presentation in selections from his writings*. H. Ansbacher & R. Ansbacher (Eds.), New York: Basic Books.

Shulman, B. H. (1977a). Encouraging the pessimist: a confronting technique. *The Individual Psychologist, 14*(1), 7-9.

Shulman, B. H. & Dreikurs, S. G. (1978). The contributions of Rudolf Dreikurs to the theory and practice of Individual Psychology. *Journal of Individual Psychology, 34*(2), 153-169.

[264] Adler, A. (1958). *What life should mean to you*. A. Porter (Ed.). New York: Capricorn Books. (Original work published 1931)

265 Adler, A. (1926). *The neurotic constitution: Outlines of a comparative individualistic psychology and psychotherapy.* [Translated by Bernard Glueck and John E. Lind] New York: Dodd, Mead and Company.

Way, L. M. (1950). *Adler's place in psychology.* London: George Allen & Unwin LTD.

266 Lévy, P. (1997). *Collective intelligence: Mankind's emerging world in cyberspace.* New York: Plenum Trade.

Christakis, A. N., & Bausch, K. C. (2006). *How people harness their collective wisdom and power to construct the future in co-laboratories of democracy.* Greenwich, CT: Information Age Pub.

Yi, S. K., Steyvers, M., Lee, M. D., & Dry, M. J. (January 01, 2012). The wisdom of the crowd in combinatorial problems. *Cognitive Science, 36,* 3, 452-70.

267 Sartre, J.–P. (1989). *No exit and three other plays.* New York: Vintage International. (Original work published 1946), p. 45.

268 Eastburn, D. (2011). *What is hypnosis?: What every person should know about hypnosis.* Bloomington, IN: Trafford Pub.

Kroger, W. S. (1977). *Clinical and experimental hypnosis in medicine, dentistry, and psychology.* Philadelphia: Lippincott.

Coon, D., & Mitterer, J. O. (2008). *Psychology: Modules for active learning.* Belmont, CA: Wadsworth.

Blair, F. R. (2004). *Instant self-hypnosis: How to hypnotize yourself with your eyes open.* Naperville, Ill: Sourcebooks, Inc.

269 Krausz, E. O. (1973). Neurotic versus normal reaction categories. In H. H. Mosak (Ed.), *Alfred Adler: His influence on psychology today* (pp. 53-57). Park Ridge, N. J.: Noyes Press.

270 Mosak, H. H., & Maniacci, M. (1999). *A primer of Adlerian psychology: The analytic-behavioral-cognitive psychology of Alfred Adler.* Philadelphia, PA: Brunner/Mazel.

271 Kopp, R. R. (1986). Styles of striving for significance with and without social interest: An Adlerian typology. *Individual Psychology: Journal of Adlerian Theory, Research and Practice, 42,* 17-25.

272 Mosak, H. H., & Maniacci, M. (1999). *A primer of Adlerian psychology: The analytic-behavioral-cognitive psychology of Alfred Adler.* Philadelphia, PA: Brunner/Mazel.

273 Mosak, H. H. (1977). The controller: A social interpretation of the anal character. In H. H. Mosak (Ed.), *On purpose* (pp. 216-227). Chicago: Alfred Adler Institute. (Originally published in Alfred Adler: His influence on psychology today, 1973. Park Ridge, N. J.: Noyes Press.)

274 Mosak, H. H. (1977). The controller: A social interpretation of the anal character. In H. H. Mosak (Ed.), *On purpose* (pp. 216-227). Chicago: Alfred Adler Institute. (Originally published in Alfred Adler: His influence on psychology today, 1973. Park Ridge, N. J.: Noyes Press.)

275 Di Pietro, R. (2010). *The depression code: Deciphering the purposes of neurotic depression.* Raleigh, NC: Lulu.com.

276 Mosak, H. H. (1977). The controller: A social interpretation of the anal character. In H. H. Mosak (Ed.), *On purpose* (pp. 216-227). Chicago: Alfred Adler Institute. (Originally published in Alfred Adler: His influence on psychology today, 1973. Park Ridge, N. J.: Noyes Press.)

277 Mosak, H. H. (1977). The controller: A social interpretation of the anal character. In H. H. Mosak (Ed.), *On purpose* (pp. 216-227). Chicago: Alfred Adler Institute. (Originally published in Alfred Adler: His influence on psychology today, 1973. Park Ridge, N. J.: Noyes Press.)

278 Kaeppel, J. (2009). *Seasonal stock market trends: The definitive guide to calendar based*

stock market trading. Hoboken, NJ: Wiley.

[279] Mosak, H. H. & Maniacci, M. P. (2006). Of cookie jars and candy bars: Dysthymia in the light of Individual Psychology. *The Journal of Individual Psychology*, 62(4), 357-365.

[280] Mosak, H. H. & Maniacci, M. P. (2006). Of cookie jars and candy bars: Dysthymia in the light of Individual Psychology. *The Journal of Individual Psychology*, 62(4), 357-365.

[281] Metcalf, R. (2000). *The successful race car driver: A career development handbook.* Warrendale, Pa: Society of Automotive Engineers.

[282] Job, M. (1994). *Air disaster*. Weston Creek, ACT: Aerospace Publications.

[283] Dreikurs, R. (1953). *Fundamentals of Adlerian psychology.* Chicago: Alfred Adler Institute. (Original work published 1935)

[284] Dreikurs, R. (1953). *Fundamentals of Adlerian psychology.* Chicago: Alfred Adler Institute. (Original work published 1935)

[285] Dreikurs, R. (1953). *Fundamentals of Adlerian psychology.* Chicago: Alfred Adler Institute. (Original work published 1935)

Orgler, H. (1963). *Alfred Adler: The man and his work.* New York: Capricorn Books. (Original work published 1939)

Mosak, H. H. & Maniacci, M. P. (1999). *A primer of Adlerian psychology: The analytic-behavioral-cognitive psychology of Alfred Adler*. Philadelphia: Brunner/Mazel.

[286] Krauss, H. H. (1967). Anxiety: The dread of a future event. *Journal of Individual Psychology, 23*(1), 88-93.

[287] Adler, Alexandra. (1938). *Guiding human misfits: A practical application of Individual Psychology.* New York: Macmillan.

[288] Adler, A. (1958). *What life should mean to you.* A. Porter (Ed.). New York: Capricorn Books. (Original work published 1931)

[289] Adler, A. (1964b). *Social interest: A challenge to mankind.* New York: Capricorn Books.

[290] Mosak, H. H. & Maniacci, M. P. (1999). *A primer of Adlerian psychology: The analytic-behavioral-cognitive psychology of Alfred Adler.* Philadelphia: Brunner/Mazel.

[291] Adler, A. (1927). *Understanding human nature.* [Translated by Walter Béran Wolfe] Garden City, NY: Garden City Publishing Company, Inc.

[292] Darwin, C. (1859). *On the Origin of Species by Means of Natural Selection, or the Preservation of Favoured Races in the Struggle for Life* (1st ed.), London: John Murray, Retrieved February 14, 2009, from http://darwin-online.org.uk/content/frameset?itemID=F373&viewtype=text&pageseq=1

Dawkins, R. (1989). *The selfish gene.* New York: Oxford University Press.

[293] Mowrer, O. H. (1960). *Learning theory and the symbolic processes.* New York: Wiley.

Harley, T. A. (2014). *The psychology of language: From data to theory.* New York: Psychology Press.

[294] Adler, A. (1973). *Superiority and social interest.* (3rd. Rev. ed.). H. L. Ansbacher, & R. R. Ansbacher (Eds.). New York: Viking Press.

[295] Dreikurs, R. (1953). *Fundamentals of Adlerian psychology.* Chicago: Alfred Adler Institute. (Original work published 1935)

[296] Adler, Alexandra. (1938). *Guiding human misfits: A practical application of Individual Psychology.* New York: Macmillan.

[297] Dreikurs, R. (1953). *Fundamentals of Adlerian psychology.* Chicago: Alfred Adler Institute. (Original work published 1935)

[298] Dreikurs, R. (1953). *Fundamentals of Adlerian psychology.* Chicago: Alfred Adler Institute. (Original work published 1935)

[299] Adler, A. (1964). *Problems of neurosis.* P. Mairet (Ed.). New York: Harper & Row. (Original work published 1929)

Adler, Alexandra. (1938). *Guiding human misfits: A practical application of Individual*

Psychology. New York: Macmillan.

[300] Adler, A. (1996a). The structure of neurosis. *Individual Psychology, 52*(2), 351-362. (Original work published 1935)

[301] Dreikurs, R. & Stoltz, V. (1990). *Children: The challenge.* New York: Plume.

[302] Dreikurs, R. (1953). *Fundamentals of Adlerian psychology.* Chicago: Alfred Adler Institute. (Original work published 1935)

[303] Manaster, G. J. & Corsini, R. J. (1982). *Individual psychology: Theory and practice.* Itasca, IL: F. E. Peacock Publishers, Inc.

[304] Way, L. M. (1950). *Adler's place in psychology.* London: George Allen & Unwin LTD.

[305] Dreikurs, R. (1953). *Fundamentals of Adlerian psychology.* Chicago: Alfred Adler Institute. (Original work published 1935)

[306] Hyman, I. A. (1997). *The case against spanking: How to discipline your child without hitting.* San Francisco: Jossey-Bass.

Smith, B. L. (April, 2012) "The Case Against Spanking." *Monitor on Psychology, 43,* (4), p. 60. American Psychological Association. Retrieved November 1, 2013 from http://www.apa.org/monitor/2012/04/spanking.aspx

Cummings, M. S. (2001). *Beyond political correctness: Social transformation in the United States.* Colorado: Lynne Rienner Publishers.

[307] Adler, A. (1958). *What life should mean to you.* A. Porter (Ed.). New York: Capricorn Books. (Original work published 1931)

[308] Dreikurs, R. (1953). *Fundamentals of Adlerian psychology.* Chicago: Alfred Adler Institute. (Original work published 1935)

[309] Patterson, G. R. (1982). *Coercive family process.* Eugene, OR: Castalia.

[310] McGaugh, J. L. (2003). *Memory and emotion: The making of lasting memories.* New York: Columbia University Press.

Reisberg, D., & Hertel, P. (2004). *Memory and emotion.* Oxford: Oxford University Press.

[311] Gopnik, A. (2009). *The philosophical baby: What children's minds tell us about truth, love, and the meaning of life.* New York: Farrar, Straus and Giroux.

Meltzoff, A. N., & Moore, M. K. (June 01, 1983). Newborn Infants Imitate Adult Facial Gestures. *Child Development, 54,* 3, 702-9.

[312] Dreikurs, R. & Stoltz, V. (1990). *Children: The challenge.* New York: Plume.

[313] Dreikurs, R. (1953). *Fundamentals of Adlerian psychology.* Chicago: Alfred Adler Institute. (Original work published 1935)

[314] Orgler, H. (1963). *Alfred Adler: The man and his work.* New York: Capricorn Books. (Original work published 1939)

[315] Adler, A. (1973). *Superiority and social interest.* (3rd. Rev. ed.). H. L. Ansbacher, & R. R. Ansbacher, (Eds.), New York: Viking Press.

[316] Wexberg, E. (1929). *Individual psychology.* (Translated by W. Béran Wolfe). New York: Cosmopolitan Book

[317] Dreikurs, R. (1953). *Fundamentals of Adlerian psychology.* Chicago: Alfred Adler Institute. (Original work published 1935)

[318] Dreikurs, R. (1953). *Fundamentals of Adlerian psychology.* Chicago: Alfred Adler Institute. (Original work published 1935)

[319] Dreikurs, R. (1953). *Fundamentals of Adlerian psychology.* Chicago: Alfred Adler Institute. (Original work published 1935)

[320] Adler, A. (1958). *What life should mean to you.* A. Porter (Ed.). New York: Capricorn Books. (Original work published 1931)

[321] Gottman, J. (1994). *Why marriages succeed or fail.* New York: Fireside.

[322] Adler, A. (1927). *Understanding human nature.* (Walter Béran Wolfe, Trans.). Garden City, NY: Garden City Publishing Company, Inc.

[323] Mosak, H. H. & Todd, F. J. (1977). Selective perception in the interpretation of symbols. In H. H. Mosak (Ed.) *On purpose* (pp. 9-11). Chicago: Adler School of Professional Psychology.

[324] Adler, A. (1958). *What life should mean to you.* A. Porter (Ed.). New York: Capricorn Books. (Original work published 1931)

[325] Mosak, H. H. (1977). The psychological attitude in rehabilitation. American Archives Rehabilitation Therapy, 2, 9-10. In H. H. Mosak (Ed.), *On purpose* (pp. 52-54). Chicago: Adler School of Professional Psychology.

[326] Adler, A. (1956). *The Individual Psychology of Alfred Adler: A systematic presentation in selections from his writings.* H. Ansbacher & R. Ansbacher (Eds.), New York: Basic Books.

[327] Adler, A. (1929b). *The science of living.* New York: Greenberg, Publisher, Inc.

Adler, Alexandra. (1938). *Guiding human misfits: A practical application of Individual Psychology.* New York: Macmillan.

[328] Adler, A. (1930). *The neurotic constitution: Outlines of a comparative individualistic psychology and psychotherapy.* (B. Glueck & J. E. Lind, Trans.). New York: Dodd, Mead and Company.

[329] Adler, A. (1956). *The Individual Psychology of Alfred Adler: A systematic presentation in selections from his writings.* H. Ansbacher & R. Ansbacher (Eds.), New York: Basic Books.

[330] Adler, A. (1929a). *The practice and theory of Individual Psychology.* (P. Radin, Trans.). New York: Harcourt, Brace & Company, Inc.

[331] Adler, Alexandra. (1938). *Guiding human misfits: A practical application of Individual Psychology.* New York: Macmillan.

[332] Lundin, R. W. (1989). *Alfred Adler's basic concepts and implications.* Muncie, Indiana: Accelerated Development Inc.

[333] Adler, A. (1929b). *The science of living.* New York: Greenberg, Publisher, Inc.

[334] Adler, Alexandra. (1938). *Guiding human misfits: A practical application of Individual Psychology.* New York: Macmillan.

[335] Adler, A. (1929b). *The science of living.* New York: Greenberg, Publisher, Inc.

[336] Adler, A. (1964). *Problems of neurosis.* P. Mairet (Ed.). New York: Harper & Row. (Original work published 1929)

[337] Adler, A. (1964b). *Social interest: A challenge to mankind.* New York: Capricorn Books.

[338] Adler, A. (1964). *Problems of neurosis.* P. Mairet (Ed.). New York: Harper & Row. (Original work published 1929)

[339] Adler, A. (1927). *Understanding human nature.* (Walter Béran Wolfe, Trans.). Garden City, NY: Garden City Publishing Company, Inc.

[340] Adler, A. (1929b). *The science of living.* New York: Greenberg, Publisher, Inc. p. 218.

Lundin, R. W. (1989). *Alfred Adler's basic concepts and implications.* Muncie, Indiana: Accelerated Development Inc.

[341] Adler, A. (1929b). *The science of living.* New York: Greenberg, Publisher, Inc. p. 218.

[342] Adler, A. (1930). *The neurotic constitution: Outlines of a comparative individualistic psychology and psychotherapy.* (B. Glueck & J. E. Lind, Trans.). New York: Dodd, Mead and Company.

[343] Lundin, R. W. (1989). *Alfred Adler's basic concepts and implications.* Muncie, Indiana: Accelerated Development Inc.

[344] Adler, A. (1956). *The Individual Psychology of Alfred Adler: A systematic presentation in selections from his writings.* H. Ansbacher & R. Ansbacher (Eds.), New York: Basic Books.

Adler, A. (1964b). *Social interest: A challenge to mankind.* New York: Capricorn Books.

[345] Mosak, H. H. & LeFevre, C. (1976). The resolution of "intrapersonal" conflict. *Journal of Individual Psychology, 32*(1), 19-26.

[346] Cunningham, P. (1979, October 24), Words which should live in history. *Rockford Register Star*: Rockford, Illinois.

[347] Seligman, M. E. P. (1975). *Helplessness: On depression, development, and death.* San Francisco: W. H. Freeman.

Seligman, M. E. P., & Maier, S. F. (1967). *Failure to escape traumatic shock.* Washington: American Psychological Association.

[348] Krausz, E. O. (1973). Neurotic versus normal reaction categories. In H. H. Mosak (Ed.), *Alfred Adler: His influence on psychology today* (pp. 53-57). Park Ridge, NJ: Noyes Press.

Adler, A. (1973). *Superiority and social interest.* (3rd. Rev. ed.). H. L. Ansbacher, & R. R. Ansbacher, (Eds.), New York: Viking Press.

Adler, A. (1956). *The Individual Psychology of Alfred Adler: A systematic presentation in selections from his writings.* H. Ansbacher & R. Ansbacher (Eds.), New York: Basic Books.

[349] Krausz, E. O. (1973). Neurotic versus normal reaction categories. In H. H. Mosak (Ed.), *Alfred Adler: His influence on psychology today* (pp. 53-57). Park Ridge, NJ: Noyes Press.

Adler, A. (1973). *Superiority and social interest.* (3rd. Rev. ed.). H. L. Ansbacher, & R. R. Ansbacher, (Eds.), New York: Viking Press.

[350] Ashby, J. S. & Kottman, T. (1996). Inferiority as a distinction between normal and neurotic perfectionism. *Individual Psychology: Journal of Adlerian Theory, Research and Practice, 52*(3), 237-245.

[351] Krausz, E. O. (1973). Neurotic versus normal reaction categories. In H. H. Mosak (Ed.), *Alfred Adler: His influence on psychology today* (pp. 53-57). Park Ridge, NJ: Noyes Press.

[352] Krausz, E. O. (1973). Neurotic versus normal reaction categories. In H. H. Mosak (Ed.), *Alfred Adler: His influence on psychology today* (pp. 53-57). Park Ridge, NJ: Noyes Press.

Adler, A. (1956). *The Individual Psychology of Alfred Adler: A systematic presentation in selections from his writings.* H. Ansbacher & R. Ansbacher (Eds.), New York: Basic Books.

[353] Adler, A. (1929b). *The science of living.* New York: Greenberg, Publisher, Inc.

[354] Benson, H., Dusek, J. A., Sherwood, J. B., Lam, P., Bethea, C. F., et al. (January 01, 2006). Study of the Therapeutic Effects of Intercessory Prayer (STEP) in cardiac bypass patients: a multicenter randomized trial of uncertainty and certainty of receiving intercessory prayer. *American Heart Journal, 151,* 4, 934-42.

Masters, K. S., Spielmans, G. I., & Goodson, J. T. (January 01, 2006). Are there demonstrable effects of distant intercessory prayer? A meta-analytic review. *Annals of Behavioral Medicine : a Publication of the Society of Behavioral Medicine, 32,* 1, 21-6.

Hodge, D. (January 01, 2007). A Systematic Review of the Empirical Literature on Intercessory Prayer. *Research on Social Work Practice, 17,* 2, 174-187.

[355] Krausz, E. O. (1973). Neurotic versus normal reaction categories. In H. H. Mosak (Ed.), *Alfred Adler: His influence on psychology today* (pp. 53-57). Park Ridge, NJ: Noyes Press.

[356] Krausz, E. O. (1973). Neurotic versus normal reaction categories. In H. H. Mosak (Ed.), *Alfred Adler: His influence on psychology today* (pp. 53-57). Park Ridge, NJ: Noyes Press.

Orgler, H. (1963). *Alfred Adler: The man and his work.* New York: Capricorn Books. (Original work published 1939)

Adler, A. (1973). *Superiority and social interest.* (3rd. Rev. ed.). H. L. Ansbacher, & R. R. Ansbacher, (Eds.), New York: Viking Press.

[357] Krausz, E. O. (1973). Neurotic versus normal reaction categories. In H. H. Mosak (Ed.), *Alfred Adler: His influence on psychology today* (pp. 53-57). Park Ridge, NJ: Noyes Press.

[358] Krausz, E. O. (1973). Neurotic versus normal reaction categories. In H. H. Mosak (Ed.), *Alfred Adler: His influence on psychology today* (pp. 53-57). Park Ridge, NJ: Noyes Press. p. 55

[359] Adler, A. (1964b). *Social interest: A challenge to mankind.* New York: Capricorn Books.

[360] Krausz, E. O. (1973). Neurotic versus normal reaction categories. In H. H. Mosak (Ed.), *Alfred Adler: His influence on psychology today* (pp. 53-57). Park Ridge, NJ: Noyes Press.

[361] Adler, A. (1973). *Superiority and social interest.* (3rd. Rev. ed.). H. L. Ansbacher, & R. R. Ansbacher, (Eds.), New York: Viking Press.

[362] Krausz, E. O. (1973). Neurotic versus normal reaction categories. In H. H. Mosak (Ed.), *Alfred Adler: His influence on psychology today* (pp. 53-57). Park Ridge, NJ: Noyes Press.

[363] Krausz, E. O. (1973). Neurotic versus normal reaction categories. In H. H. Mosak (Ed.), *Alfred Adler: His influence on psychology today* (pp. 53-57). Park Ridge, NJ: Noyes Press.

[364] Krausz, E. O. (1973). Neurotic versus normal reaction categories. In H. H. Mosak (Ed.), *Alfred Adler: His influence on psychology today* (pp. 53-57). Park Ridge, NJ: Noyes Press.

[365] Adler, A. (1926). *The neurotic constitution: Outlines of a comparative individualistic psychology and psychotherapy.* [Translated by Bernard Glueck and John E. Lind] New York: Dodd, Mead and Company.

[366] Adler, A. (1958). *What life should mean to you.* A. Porter (Ed.). New York: Capricorn Books. (Original work published 1931)

[367] Way, L. M. (1950). *Adler's place in psychology.* London: George Allen & Unwin LTD.

[368] Plowman, S. A. & Smith, D. L. (2008). *Exercise physiology for health, fitness, and performance* (Reprinted 2nd ed.). Baltimore: Lippincott Williams & Wilkins.

West, B. J. & Griffin, L. A. (2004). *Biodynamics: Why the wirewalker doesn't fall.* Hoboken, N. J.: John Wiley & Sons.

[369] Porth, C. M. (2011). *Essentials of pathophysiology: Concepts of altered health states.* Philadelphia: Lippincott Williams & Wilkins.

Plaford, G. R. (2009). *Sleep and learning: The magic that makes us healthy and smart.* Lanham, Md: Rowman & Littlefield Education.

[370] Miller, A. D. (1993). Neuroanatomy and physiology. In M. H. Sleisenger (Ed.), *The Handbook of Nausea and Vomiting* (pp.1-10). New York: Parthenon Publishing.

Horn, C. C. (2008, March). Why is the neurobiology of nausea and vomiting so important? *Appetite, 50*(2-3), 430-434.

Davidson, G. P. (1991). Viral diarrhea. In M. Gracey (Ed.), *Diarrhea* (pp. 67-92). Boca Raton, Florida: Telford Press.

[371] Singer, A. J. & Clark, R. A. F. (2002). The biology of wound healing. In A. J. Singer, & J. E. Hollancher, (Eds.), *Lacerations and Acute Wounds: An Evidence-Based Guide* (pp. 1-8). Philadelphia: F. A. Davis Company.

Trott, A. (2005). *Wounds and lacerations: Emergency care and closure* (3rd ed.). Philadelphia: Mosby.

[372] Grierson, I. (2000). *The eye book: Eyes and eye problems explained.* Liverpool, UK:

Liverpool University Press.

Hofstetter, H. W., Griffin, J. R., Berman, M. S. & Everson, R. W. (2000). *Dictionary of visual science and related clinical terms* (5th ed.). Boston: Butterworth-Heinemann

373 Naslund, E., & Hellstrom, P. M. (2007, September). Appetite signaling: From gut peptides and enteric nerves to brain. *Physiology & Behavior, 92*(1-2), 256-262.

Gray, P. O. (2007). Chapter 6: Mechanisms of motivation and emotions. In *Psychology* (5th ed.) (pp. 179-224). New York: Worth Publishers.

Woods, S. C. & Stricker, E. M. (2008). Food intake and metabolism. In L. R. Squire, D. Berg, F. Bloom, S. du Lac, & A. Ghosh (Eds.), *Fundamental neuroscience* (3rd ed.) (pp. 873-888). Burlington, MA: Academic Press.

374 Rogers, D. F. (2004). Overview of airway mucus clearance. In B. K. Rubin, & C. P. van der Schans (Eds.), *Therapy for mucus-clearance disorders* (pp. 1-27). New York: Marcel Dekker, Inc.

Pus cell (2008, October 25). *Biology online.* Retrieved February 26, 2009 from http://www.biology-online.org/dictionary/Pus_cell

Sompayrac, L. M. (2008). *How the Immune System Works* (3rd ed.). Malden, M. A.: Blackwell publishing.

Griffin, J., Arif, S. & Mufti, A. (2003). *Crash course: Immunology and Haematology* (2nd ed.). St. Louis, MO: C. V. Mosby.

375 Lippincott Williams & Wilkins (2008). *Nursing: Interpreting signs & symptoms.* Ambler, PA: Lippincott Williams & Wilkins.

Watson Genna, C. & Sandora, L. (2013). Breastfeeding: Normal sucking and swallowing. In C. Watson Genna (Ed.). *Supporting sucking skills in breastfeeding infants* (pp. 1-42). Burlington, MA: Jones & Bartlett Learning.

376 Watson Genna, C. & Sandora, L. (2013). Breastfeeding: Normal sucking and swallowing. In C. Watson Genna (Ed.). *Supporting sucking skills in breastfeeding infants* (pp. 1-42). Burlington, MA: Jones & Bartlett Learning.

Grillner, S. (2008). Fundamentals of motor system. In L. R. Squire, D. Berg, F. Bloom, S. du Lac, & A. Ghosh (Eds.), *Fundamental neuroscience* (3rd ed.) (pp. 663-698). Burlington, MA: Academic Press.

377 Taylor, P. N., Wolinsky, I., & Klimis, D. J. (1999). Water in exercise and sport. In J. A. Driskell, I.. Wolinsky (Eds.), *Macroelements, water, and electrolytes in sports nutrition* (pp. 93-108). Boca Raton: CRC Press Inc.

Stricker, E. M. & Verbalis, J. G. (2008). Water intake and bodily fluids. In L. R. Squire, D. Berg, F. Bloom, S. du Lac, & A. Ghosh (Eds.), *Fundamental neuroscience* (3rd ed.) (pp. 889-930). Burlington, MA: Academic Press.

Rolls, B. J. (1993). Palatability and fluid intake. In B. M. Marriott (Ed.), *Fluid replacement and heat stress* (pp. 161-167). Washington, D. C.: Food and nutrition board, Institute of medicine, National Academy of Sciences.

Woods, S. C. & Stricker, E. M. (2008). Food intake and metabolism. In L. R. Squire, D. Berg, F. Bloom, S. du Lac, & A. Ghosh (Eds.), *Fundamental neuroscience* (3rd ed.) (pp. 873-888). Burlington, MA: Academic Press.

378 Krauss, H. H. (1967). Anxiety: The dread of a future event. *Journal of Individual Psychology, 23*(1), 88-93.

379 Krauss, H. H. (1967). Anxiety: The dread of a future event. *Journal of Individual Psychology, 23*(1), 88-93.

380 Yerkes R. M. & Dodson J. D. (1908). The relation of strength of stimulus to rapidity of habit-formation. *Journal of Comparative Neurology and Psychology 18*, 459–482.

381 Adler, A. (1929a). *The practice and theory of Individual Psychology.* (P. Radin, Trans.). New York: Harcourt, Brace & Company, Inc.

382 Mairet, P. (1928). *A B C of Adler's psychology.* London: Kegan Paul, Trench, Trubner & Co., LTD.

383 Adler, A. (1964). *Problems of neurosis.* P. Mairet (Ed.). New York: Harper & Row. (Original work published 1929)

384 Adler, A. (1996a). The structure of neurosis. *Individual Psychology, 52*(2), 351-362. (Original work published 1935).

385 Dreikurs, R. (1948). *The challenge of parenthood.* New York: Duell, Sloan & Pearce.

386 Dreikurs, R. & Grey, L. (1968). *Logical consequences: A new approach to discipline.* New York: Hawthorne Press.

387 Adler, A. (1927). *Understanding human nature.* (Walter Béran Wolfe, Trans.). Garden City, NY: Garden City Publishing Company, Inc.

388 Behan, B. In Behan, D. (1966). *My brother Brendan.* New York: Simon and Schuster. p. 158.
Wilde, O. (1908). *The picture of Dorian Gray.* Leipzig: B. Tauchnitz. p. 9.

389 Adler, A. (1958). *What life should mean to you.* A. Porter (Ed.). New York: Capricorn Books. (Original work published 1931)
Mosak, H. H. & Shulman, B. (1977). Various purposes of symptoms. In H. H. Mosak (Ed.), *On purpose* (pp. 118-132). Chicago: Adler School of Professional Psychology. (Originally published in Journal of Individual Psychology, 1967, 23, 79-87.)
Mosak, H. H., Brown, P. R. & Boldt, R. M. (1994). Various purposes of suffering. *Individual Psychology, 50*(2), 142-148.

390 Rasmussen, P. R. (2010). *The quest to feel good.* New York: Routledge.

391 Mosak, H. H. & Shulman, B. (1977). Various purposes of symptoms. In H. H. Mosak (Ed.), *On purpose* (pp. 118-132). Chicago: Adler School of Professional Psychology. (Originally published in Journal of Individual Psychology, 1967, 23, 79-87.)

392 Adler, A. (1964). *Problems of neurosis.* P. Mairet (Ed.). New York: Harper & Row. (Original work published 1929)
Adler, A. (1956). *The Individual Psychology of Alfred Adler: A systematic presentation in selections from his writings.* H. Ansbacher & R. Ansbacher (Eds.), New York: Basic Books.

393 Adler, A. (1964b). *Social interest: A challenge to mankind.* New York: Capricorn Books.

394 Adler, A. (1956). *The Individual Psychology of Alfred Adler: A systematic presentation in selections from his writings.* H. Ansbacher & R. Ansbacher (Eds.), New York: Basic Books.

395 Adler, A. (1964b). *Social interest: A challenge to mankind.* New York: Capricorn Books.

396 Oberst, U. O. & Stewart, A. E. (2003). *Adlerian psychotherapy: An advanced approach to Individual Psychology.* New York: Brunner-Routledge.

397 Adler, A. (1996b). What is neurosis? *Individual Psychology, 52*(4), 318-333. (Original work published 1935)

398 Bitter, J. R. (1996). On neurosis: An introduction to Adler's concepts and approach. *Individual Psychology: The Journal of Adlerian Theory, Research and Practice, 52*(4), 310-317.

399 Mairet, P. (1928). *A B C of Adler's psychology.* London: Kegan Paul, Trench, Trubner & Co., LTD.

400 Adler, A. (1973). *Superiority and social interest.* (3rd. Rev. ed.). H. L. Ansbacher, & R. R. Ansbacher, (Eds.), New York: Viking Press.

401 Adler, A. (1920). *The practice and theory of Individual Psychology.* Totowa, NJ: Littlefield, Adams, 1959.
Adler, A. (1973). *Superiority and social interest.* (3rd. Rev. ed.). H. L. Ansbacher, & R. R. Ansbacher, (Eds.), New York: Viking Press.

402 Adler, A. (1958). *What life should mean to you.* A. Porter (Ed.). New York: Capricorn Books.

(Original work published 1931)

Adler, A. (1930). *The neurotic constitution: Outlines of a comparative individualistic psychology and psychotherapy*. (B. Glueck & J. E. Lind, Trans.). New York: Dodd, Mead and Company.

[403] Adler, A. (1929b). *The science of living*. New York: Greenberg, Publisher, Inc.

[404] Adler, A. (1996a). The structure of neurosis. *Individual Psychology, 52*(2), 351-362. (Original work published 1935)

[405] Adler, A. (1996a). The structure of neurosis. *Individual Psychology, 52*(2), 351-362. (Original work published 1935)

[406] Adler, A. (1958). *What life should mean to you*. A. Porter (Ed.). New York: Capricorn Books. (Original work published 1931)

Adler, A. (1996a). The structure of neurosis. *Individual Psychology, 52*(2), 351-362. (Original work published 1935)

Adler, A. (1973). *Superiority and social interest*. (3rd. Rev. ed.). H. L. Ansbacher, & R. R. Ansbacher, (Eds.), New York: Viking Press.

[407] Adler, A. (1958). *What life should mean to you*. A. Porter (Ed.). New York: Capricorn Books. (Original work published 1931)

Adler, A. (1969). *The case of Mrs. A: The diagnosis of a life-style*. Chicago: Alfred Adler Institute. (Original work published 1931).

[408] Milliren, A., Clemmer, F., Wingett, W., & Testerment, T. (2005). The movement from "felt minus" to "perceived plus": Understanding Adler's concept of inferiority. In S. Slavik, & J. Carlson, (Eds.), *Readings in the theory of Individual Psychology* (pp. 351-363). New York: Routledge.

[409] Mosak, H. H. & Maniacci, M. P. (1999). *A primer of Adlerian psychology: The analytic-behavioral-cognitive psychology of Alfred Adler*. Philadelphia: Brunner/Mazel.

Milliren, A., Clemmer, F., Wingett, W., & Testerment, T. (2005). The movement from "felt minus" to "perceived plus": Understanding Adler's concept of inferiority. In S. Slavik, & J. Carlson, (Eds.), *Readings in the theory of Individual Psychology* (pp. 351-363). New York: Routledge.

Griffith, J., & Powers, B. (1984). *An Adlerian lexicon: Fifty-nine terms associated with the Individual Psychology of Alfred Adler*. Chicago: The Americas Institute of Adlerian Studies.

[410] Teichman, M. & Foa, U. G. (1972). Depreciation and accusation tendencies: Empirical support. *Journal of Individual Psychology, 28*(1), 45-50.

[411] Manaster, G. J. & Corsini, R. J. (1982). *Individual psychology: Theory and practice*. Itasca, IL: F. E. Peacock Publishers, Inc.

Crandall, J. E. (1981). *Theory and measurement of social interest: Empirical tests of Alfred Adler's concept*. New York: Columbia University Press.

[412] Adler, A. (1956). *The Individual Psychology of Alfred Adler: A systematic presentation in selections from his writings*. H. Ansbacher & R. Ansbacher (Eds.), New York: Basic Books.

[413] Adler, A. (1956). *The Individual Psychology of Alfred Adler: A systematic presentation in selections from his writings*. H. Ansbacher & R. Ansbacher (Eds.), New York: Basic Books.

[414] Adler, A. (1956). *The Individual Psychology of Alfred Adler: A systematic presentation in selections from his writings*. H. Ansbacher & R. Ansbacher (Eds.), New York: Basic Books.

[415] Adler, A. (1956). *The Individual Psychology of Alfred Adler: A systematic presentation in selections from his writings*. H. Ansbacher & R. Ansbacher (Eds.), New York: Basic

Books.

[416] Adler, A. (1956). *The Individual Psychology of Alfred Adler: A systematic presentation in selections from his writings.* H. Ansbacher & R. Ansbacher (Eds.), New York: Basic Books.

[417] Adler, A. (1956). *The Individual Psychology of Alfred Adler: A systematic presentation in selections from his writings.* H. Ansbacher & R. Ansbacher (Eds.), New York: Basic Books.

[418] Dreikurs, R. (1953). *Fundamentals of Adlerian psychology.* Chicago: Alfred Adler Institute. (Original work published 1935)

[419] Rasmussen, P. R. (2003). Emotional reorientation: A clinical strategy. *Journal of Individual Psychology, 59*(3), 345-359.

[420] Adler, A. (1964). *Problems of neurosis.* P. Mairet (Ed.). New York: Harper & Row. (Original work published 1929)

Dreikurs, R. (1953). *Fundamentals of Adlerian psychology.* Chicago: Alfred Adler Institute. (Original work published 1935)

[421] Adler, A. (1956). *The Individual Psychology of Alfred Adler: A systematic presentation in selections from his writings.* H. Ansbacher & R. Ansbacher (Eds.), New York: Basic Books.

[422] Starcevic, V. (2010). *Anxiety disorders in adults: A clinical guide.* New York: Oxford University Press.

[423] Dreikurs, R. & Soltz, V. (1990). *Children: The challenge.* New York: Plume.

[424] Adler, A. (1964). *Problems of neurosis.* P. Mairet (Ed.). New York: Harper & Row. (Original work published 1929)

[425] Way, L. M. (1950). *Adler's place in psychology.* London: George Allen & Unwin LTD.

[426] Adler, A. (1956). *The Individual Psychology of Alfred Adler: A systematic presentation in selections from his writings.* H. Ansbacher & R. Ansbacher (Eds.), New York: Basic Books.

[427] Adler, A. (1956). *The Individual Psychology of Alfred Adler: A systematic presentation in selections from his writings.* H. Ansbacher & R. Ansbacher (Eds.), New York: Basic Books.

[428] Adler, A. (1956). *The Individual Psychology of Alfred Adler: A systematic presentation in selections from his writings.* H. Ansbacher & R. Ansbacher (Eds.), New York: Basic Books.

[429] Adler, A. (1958). *What life should mean to you.* A. Porter (Ed.). New York: Capricorn Books. (Original work published 1931)

Dewey, E. A. (1984). The use and misuse of emotions. *Individual Psychology: Journal of Adlerian Theory, Research and Practice, 40*(2), 184-195.

[430] Manaster, G. J. & Corsini, R. J. (1982). *Individual psychology: Theory and practice.* Itasca, IL: F. E. Peacock Publishers, Inc.

[431] Adler, A. (1956). *The Individual Psychology of Alfred Adler: A systematic presentation in selections from his writings.* H. Ansbacher & R. Ansbacher (Eds.), New York: Basic Books.

[432] Adler, A. (1956). *The Individual Psychology of Alfred Adler: A systematic presentation in selections from his writings.* H. Ansbacher & R. Ansbacher (Eds.), New York: Basic Books.

Adler, A. (1964). *Problems of neurosis.* P. Mairet (Ed.). New York: Harper & Row. (Original work published 1929)

[433] Adler, A. (1956). *The Individual Psychology of Alfred Adler: A systematic presentation in selections from his writings.* H. Ansbacher & R. Ansbacher (Eds.), New York: Basic Books.

[434] Adler, A. (1964). *Problems of neurosis.* P. Mairet (Ed.). New York: Harper & Row. (Original work published 1929)

[435] Grayson, P. A. (1983). The self-criticism gambit: How to safeguard self-esteem through blaming the self. *Individual Psychology: Journal of Adlerian Theory, Research and Practice, 39*(1), 17-26.

Mosak, H. H. (1984). Adlerian psychotherapy. In R. J. Corsini (Ed.), *Current psychotherapies* (pp. 56-107). Itasca, IL: F. E. Peacock Press.

Mosak, H. H. (1987). Guilt, guilt feelings, regret and repentance. *Individual Psychology, 43*(3), 288-295.

[436] Mosak, H. H. (1987). Guilt, guilt feelings, regret and repentance. *Individual Psychology, 43*(3), 288-295.

[437] Adler, A., (1964). In Mairet, P. (Ed.), *Problems of neurosis: A book of case histories.* New York: Harper & Row. (Original work published 1929)

[438] Grayson, P. A. (1983). The self-criticism gambit: How to safeguard self-esteem through blaming the self. *Individual Psychology: Journal of Adlerian Theory, Research and Practice, 39*(1), 17-26.

[439] Adler, A. (1956). *The Individual Psychology of Alfred Adler: A systematic presentation in selections from his writings.* H. Ansbacher & R. Ansbacher (Eds.), New York: Basic Books.

[440] Shakespeare, W. (n.d.). *Hamlet.* Retrieved February 27, 2009 from http://shakespeare.mit.edu/hamlet/hamlet.3.1.html

[441] Adler, A. (1964b). *Social interest: A challenge to mankind.* New York: Capricorn Books.

Bitter, J. R. (1996). On neurosis: An introduction to Adler's concepts and approach. *Individual Psychology: The Journal of Adlerian Theory, Research and Practice, 52*(4), p. 310.

[442] Adler, A. (1964b). *Social interest: A challenge to mankind.* New York: Capricorn Books.

Adler, A. (1956). *The Individual Psychology of Alfred Adler: A systematic presentation in selections from his writings.* H. Ansbacher & R. Ansbacher (Eds.), New York: Basic Books.

[443] Adler, A. (1956). *The Individual Psychology of Alfred Adler: A systematic presentation in selections from his writings.* H. Ansbacher & R. Ansbacher (Eds.), New York: Basic Books.

[444] Nock, M., Borges, G., & Ono, Y. (2012). *Suicide: Global perspectives from the WHO World Mental Health Surveys.* Cambridge: Cambridge University Press.

Sareen J., Houlahan T., Cox B. J., Asmundson G. J. G. (2005). Anxiety disorders associated with suicidal ideation and suicide attempts in the National Comorbidity Survey. *Journal of Nervous and Mental Disease, 193*, 450-454.

Sareen J., Cox B. J., Afifi, T. O., de Graff, R., & Asmundson G. J. G. (2005). Anxiety Disorders and Risk for Suicidal Ideation and Suicide Attempts: A Population-Based Longitudinal Study of Adults. *Archives of General Psychiatry, 62*(11):1249-1257.

[445] Montgomery, S. A. (2011). *Handbook of generalised anxiety disorder.* London: Springer Healthcare Ltd.

Sareen J., Cox B. J., Afifi, T. O., de Graff, R., & Asmundson G. J. G. (2005). Anxiety Disorders and Risk for Suicidal Ideation and Suicide Attempts: A Population-Based Longitudinal Study of Adults. *Archives of General Psychiatry, 62*(11):1249-1257.

[446] Dreikurs, R. (1953). *Fundamentals of Adlerian psychology.* Chicago: Alfred Adler Institute. (Original work published 1935)

[447] Adler, A. (1956). *The Individual Psychology of Alfred Adler: A systematic presentation in selections from his writings.* H. Ansbacher & R. Ansbacher (Eds.), New York: Basic Books.

[448] Adler, A. (1958). *What life should mean to you.* A. Porter (Ed.). New York: Capricorn Books.

(Original work published 1931)

[449] Adler, A. (1956). *The Individual Psychology of Alfred Adler: A systematic presentation in selections from his writings.* H. Ansbacher & R. Ansbacher (Eds.), New York: Basic Books.

[450] Adler, A. (1956). *The Individual Psychology of Alfred Adler: A systematic presentation in selections from his writings.* H. Ansbacher & R. Ansbacher (Eds.), New York: Basic Books.

[451] Adler, A. (1956). *The Individual Psychology of Alfred Adler: A systematic presentation in selections from his writings.* H. Ansbacher & R. Ansbacher (Eds.), New York: Basic Books.

[452] Adler, Alexandra. (1938). *Guiding human misfits: A practical application of Individual Psychology.* New York: Macmillan.

[453] Adler, A. (1956). *The Individual Psychology of Alfred Adler: A systematic presentation in selections from his writings.* H. Ansbacher & R. Ansbacher (Eds.), New York: Basic Books.

Mosak, H. H. & Shulman, B. (1977). Various purposes of symptoms. In H. H. Mosak (Ed.), *On purpose* (pp. 118-132). Chicago: Adler School of Professional Psychology. (Originally published in Journal of Individual Psychology, 1967, 23, 79-87.)

[454] Adler, A. (1956). *The Individual Psychology of Alfred Adler: A systematic presentation in selections from his writings.* H. Ansbacher & R. Ansbacher (Eds.), New York: Basic Books.

[455] Adler, A. (1956). *The Individual Psychology of Alfred Adler: A systematic presentation in selections from his writings.* H. Ansbacher & R. Ansbacher (Eds.), New York: Basic Books.

Adler, A. (1958). *What life should mean to you.* A. Porter (Ed.). New York: Capricorn Books. (Original work published 1931)

Leifer, R. (1966). Avoidance and mastery: An interactional view of phobias. *Journal of Individual Psychology, 22*(1), 80-93.

[456] Adler, A. (1964). *Problems of neurosis.* P. Mairet (Ed.). New York: Harper & Row. (Original work published 1929)

[457] Adler, A. (1973). *Superiority and social interest.* (3rd. Rev. ed.). H. L. Ansbacher, & R. R. Ansbacher, (Eds.), New York: Viking Press.

[458] Adler, A. (1996a). The structure of neurosis. *Individual Psychology, 52*(2), 351-362. (Original work published 1935)

Adler, A. (1973). *Superiority and social interest.* (3rd. Rev. ed.). H. L. Ansbacher, & R. R. Ansbacher, (Eds.), New York: Viking Press.

Adler, A. (1926). *The neurotic constitution: Outlines of a comparative individualistic psychology and psychotherapy.* [Translated by Bernard Glueck and John E. Lind] New York: Dodd, Mead and Company.

[459] Adler, A. (1958). *What life should mean to you.* A. Porter (Ed.). New York: Capricorn Books. (Original work published 1931)

[460] Adler, A. (1973). *Superiority and social interest.* (3rd. Rev. ed.). H. L. Ansbacher, & R. R. Ansbacher, (Eds.), New York: Viking Press.

[461] Adler, A. (1929b). *The science of living.* New York: Greenberg, Publisher, Inc.

[462] Way, L. M. (1950). *Adler's place in psychology.* London: George Allen & Unwin LTD.

Dreikurs, R. (1953). *Fundamentals of Adlerian psychology.* Chicago: Alfred Adler Institute. (Original work published 1935)

[463] Adler, A. (1956). *The Individual Psychology of Alfred Adler: A systematic presentation in selections from his writings.* H. Ansbacher & R. Ansbacher (Eds.), New York: Basic Books.

[464] Way, L. M. (1950). *Adler's place in psychology.* London: George Allen & Unwin LTD.

[465] Mosak, H. H. (1977). The interrelatedness of the neuroses through central themes. In H. H. Mosak (Ed.), *On purpose* (pp. 138-143). Chicago: Adler School of Professional Psychology. (Originally published in the Journal of Individual Psychology, 1968, 24, 67-70.)

[466] Dreikurs, R. (1953). *Fundamentals of Adlerian psychology.* Chicago: Alfred Adler Institute. (Original work published 1935)

[467] Adler, A. (1973). *Superiority and social interest.* (3rd. Rev. ed.). H. L. Ansbacher, & R. R. Ansbacher, (Eds.), New York: Viking Press.

[468] Adler, A. (1958). *What life should mean to you.* A. Porter (Ed.). New York: Capricorn Books. (Original work published 1931)

[469] Adler, Alexandra. (1938). *Guiding human misfits: A practical application of Individual Psychology.* New York: Macmillan.

Adler, A. (1958). *What life should mean to you.* A. Porter (Ed.). New York: Capricorn Books. (Original work published 1931)

[470] Adler, A. (1964b). *Social interest: A challenge to mankind.* New York: Capricorn Books.

[471] Way, L. M. (1950). *Adler's place in psychology.* London: George Allen & Unwin LTD.

[472] Mosak, H. H. & Shulman, B. (1977). Various purposes of symptoms. In H. H. Mosak (Ed.), *On purpose* (pp. 118-132). Chicago: Adler School of Professional Psychology. (Originally published in Journal of Individual Psychology, 1967, 23, 79-87.)

[473] Grayson, P. A. (1983). The self-criticism gambit: How to safeguard self-esteem through blaming the self. *Individual Psychology: Journal of Adlerian Theory, Research and Practice, 39*(1), 17-26.

[474] Grayson, P. A. (1983). The self-criticism gambit: How to safeguard self-esteem through blaming the self. *Individual Psychology: Journal of Adlerian Theory, Research and Practice, 39*(1), 17-26.

[475] Adler, A. (1958). *What life should mean to you.* A. Porter (Ed.). New York: Capricorn Books. (Original work published 1931)

Adler, A. (1927). *Understanding human nature.* (Walter Béran Wolfe, Trans.). Garden City, NY: Garden City Publishing Company, Inc.

[476] Dreikurs, R. (1953). *Fundamentals of Adlerian psychology.* Chicago: Alfred Adler Institute. (Original work published 1935)

[477] Arkes, H. R. & Blumer, C. (2000). The psychology of sunk cost. In T. Connolly, H. R. Arkes, & K. R. Hammond (Eds.), *Judgment and decision making: An interdisciplinary reader* (2nd ed.) (pp. 97-113). New York: Cambridge University Press.

[478] Ghezzi, P. M. (2006). *Gambling: Behavior theory, research, and application.* Reno, NV: Context Press.

Morris, D. (2006). *Opportunity: Optimizing life's chances.* Amherst, NY: Prometheus Books.

[479] Martin, G., & Pear, J. (2015). *Behavior modification: What it is and how to do it.* Boston: Pearson Education.

[480] Glasser, W. (2003). *Warning: Psychiatry can be hazardous to your mental health.* New York: Harper Collins.

[481] Dewey, E. A. (1984). The use and misuse of emotions. *Individual Psychology: Journal of Adlerian Theory, Research and Practice, 40*(2), 184-195.

[482] Adler, A. (1958). *What life should mean to you.* A. Porter (Ed.). New York: Capricorn Books. (Original work published 1931)

Mosak, H. H. (1977). The controller: A social interpretation of the anal character. In H. H. Mosak (Ed.), *On purpose* (pp. 216-227). Chicago: Alfred Adler Institute. (Originally published in Alfred Adler: His influence on psychology today, 1973. Park Ridge, NJ: Noyes Press.)

[483] Hart, J. L. (1977). Perils of the pleaser. In J. P. Madden (Ed.), *Loneliness: Issues of living in an age of stress for clergy and religion* (pp. 41-55). Whitinsville, MA: Affirmation Books.

[484] Mosak, H. H. (1977). The controller: A social interpretation of the anal character. In H. H. Mosak (Ed.), *On purpose* (pp. 216-227). Chicago: Alfred Adler Institute. (Originally published in Alfred Adler: His influence on psychology today, 1973. Park Ridge, NJ: Noyes Press.)

[485] Adler, A. (1973). *Superiority and social interest.* (3rd. Rev. ed.). H. L. Ansbacher, & R. R. Ansbacher, (Eds.), New York: Viking Press.

[486] Mosak, H. H. & Shulman, B. (1977). Various purposes of symptoms. In H. H. Mosak (Ed.), *On purpose* (pp. 118-132). Chicago: Adler School of Professional Psychology. (Originally published in Journal of Individual Psychology, 1967, 23, 79-87.)

[487] Mosak, H. H. & Shulman, B. (1977). Various purposes of symptoms. In H. H. Mosak (Ed.), *On purpose* (pp. 118-132). Chicago: Adler School of Professional Psychology. (Originally published in Journal of Individual Psychology, 1967, 23, 79-87.)

[488] Nock, M., Borges, G., & Ono, Y. (2012). *Suicide: Global perspectives from the WHO World Mental Health Surveys.* Cambridge: Cambridge University Press.

Sareen J., Houlahan T., Cox B. J., Asmundson G. J. G. (2005). Anxiety disorders associated with suicidal ideation and suicide attempts in the National Comorbidity Survey. *Journal of Nervous and Mental Disease, 193*, 450-454.

Sareen J., Cox B. J., Afifi, T. O., de Graff, R., & Asmundson G. J. G. (2005). Anxiety Disorders and Risk for Suicidal Ideation and Suicide Attempts: A Population-Based Longitudinal Study of Adults. *Archives of General Psychiatry, 62*(11):1249-1257.

[489] Montgomery, S. A. (2011). *Handbook of generalised anxiety disorder.* London: Springer Healthcare Ltd.

Sareen J., Cox B. J., Afifi, T. O., de Graff, R., & Asmundson G. J. G. (2005). Anxiety Disorders and Risk for Suicidal Ideation and Suicide Attempts: A Population-Based Longitudinal Study of Adults. *Archives of General Psychiatry, 62*(11):1249-1257.

[490] Nikelly, A. G. (Ed.), (1971). *Techniques for behavior change.* Springfield, IL: Charles C. Thomas.

[491] Mosak, H. H. & Shulman, B. (1977). Various purposes of symptoms. In H. H. Mosak (Ed.), *On purpose* (pp. 118-132). Chicago: Adler School of Professional Psychology. (Originally published in Journal of Individual Psychology, 1967, 23, 79-87.)

[492] Partridge, E. & Beale, P. (1985). *A dictionary of catch phrases, American and British, from the sixteenth century to the present day.* New York: Stein and Day.

[493] Mosak, H. H., Brown, P. R. & Boldt, R. M. (1994). Various purposes of suffering. *Individual Psychology, 50*(2), 142-148.

[494] Mosak, H. H., Brown, P. R. & Boldt, R. M. (1994). Various purposes of suffering. *Individual Psychology, 50*(2), 142-148.

[495] Krausz, E. O. (1935). The pessimistic attitude. *International Journal of Individual Psychology, 1*(3), 86-99.

[496] Mosak, H. H., Brown, P. R. & Boldt, R. M. (1994). Various purposes of suffering. *Individual Psychology, 50*(2), 142-148.

[497] Mosak, H. H., Brown, P. R. & Boldt, R. M. (1994). Various purposes of suffering. *Individual Psychology, 50*(2), 142-148.

[498] Adler, A. (1973). *Superiority and social interest.* (3rd. Rev. ed.). H. L. Ansbacher, & R. R. Ansbacher, (Eds.), New York: Viking Press.

[499] Mosak, H. H., Brown, P. R. & Boldt, R. M. (1994). Various purposes of suffering. *Individual Psychology, 50*(2), 142-148.

[500] Mosak, H. H. (1971). Lifestyle. In H. H. Mosak (Ed.), *On purpose* (pp. 183-187). Chicago:

Alfred Adler Institute. p. 185. (Originally published in A. G. Nikelly (Ed.), *Techniques for behavior change*, 1971, 77-81. Springfield, IL: Charles C. Thomas.)

[501] Mosak, H. H. & Shulman, B. H. (1971). *The Life Style Inventory*. Chicago: Alfred Adler Institute.

Mosak, H. H., Brown, P. R. & Boldt, R. M. (1994). Various purposes of suffering. *Individual Psychology, 50*(2), 142-148.

[502] Adler, A. (1956). *The Individual Psychology of Alfred Adler: A systematic presentation in selections from his writings*. H. Ansbacher & R. Ansbacher (Eds.), New York: Basic Books.

[503] Mosak, H. H. (1977). The controller: A social interpretation of the anal character. In H. H. Mosak (Ed.), *On purpose* (pp. 216-227). Chicago: Alfred Adler Institute. (Originally published in Alfred Adler: His influence on psychology today, 1973. Park Ridge, NJ: Noyes Press.

Mosak, H. H. (1987). *Ha ha and aha: The role of humor in psychotherapy*. Muncie, IN: Accelerated Development.

[504] Adler, A. (1964). *Problems of neurosis*. P. Mairet (Ed.). New York: Harper & Row. (Original work published 1929)

[505] Adler, A. (1956). *The Individual Psychology of Alfred Adler: A systematic presentation in selections from his writings*. H. Ansbacher & R. Ansbacher (Eds.), New York: Basic Books.

[506] Adler, A. (1964). *Problems of neurosis*. P. Mairet (Ed.). New York: Harper & Row. (Original work published 1929)

[507] Adler, A. (1958). *What life should mean to you*. A. Porter (Ed.). New York: Capricorn Books. (Original work published 1931)

[508] Manaster, G. J. & Corsini, R. J. (1982). *Individual psychology: Theory and practice*. Itasca, IL: F. E. Peacock Publishers, Inc.

[509] Dreikurs, R. (1953). *Fundamentals of Adlerian psychology*. Chicago: Alfred Adler Institute. (Original work published 1935)

[510] Norcross, J. C., Mrykalo, M. S., & Blagys, M. D. (2002). Auld lang syne: Success predictors, change processes, and self-reported outcomes of New Year's resolvers and nonresolvers. *Journal of Clinical Psychology, 58*(4), 397-405.

Norcross, J. C., Ratzin, A. C., & Payne, D. (1989). Ringing in the new year: The change processes and reported outcomes of resolutions. *Addictive Behaviors*, 14(2), 205-212.

Norcross, J. C., Loberg, K., & Norcross, J. (2012). *Changeology: 5 steps to realizing your goals and resolutions*. New York: Simon & Schuster.

[511] Phillips, E. L. (1985). *Psychotherapy revised: New frontiers in research and practice*. Hillsdale, NJ: L. Erlbaum Associates.

Duncan, B. L., Miller, S. D., and Hubble, M. A. (1998). Uncommonly common therapy: Focusing on what works. In Matthews, W. and Edgette, J. (Eds.). *Current thinking and research in brief therapy: Solutions, strategies, narratives, volume 2* (pp. 203-227). New York: Brunner/Mazel.

Chaffee, R. B. (2007). Managed care and termination. In W. T. O'Donohue & M. Cucciare (Eds.), Terminating psychotherapy: A clinician's guide (pp 3 -14). New York Routledge.

[512] Cornelius, R. R. (2001) Crying and catharsis. In Vingerhoets, A. J. J. M., & Cornelius, R. R. (Eds.). *Adult crying: A biopsychosocial approach* (pp. 192-212). New York: Brunner-Routledge.

[513] Vingerhoets, A. J. J. M. (2013). *Why only humans weep: Unravelling the mysteries of tears*. Oxford: Oxford University Press.

[514] Cornelius, R. R. (2001) Crying and catharsis. In Vingerhoets, A. J. J. M., & Cornelius, R. R. (Eds.). *Adult crying: A biopsychosocial approach* (pp. 192-212). New York: Brunner-

Routledge.
[515] Adler, A. (1964). Two grade-school girls. In H. L. Ansbacher & R. R. Ansbacher (Eds.), *Superiority and social interest* (pp. 143-158). Evanston, IL: Northwestern University Press.
[516] Adler, A. (1958). *What life should mean to you*. A. Porter (Ed.). New York: Capricorn Books. (Original work published 1931)
Adler, A. (1964). Two grade-school girls. In H. L. Ansbacher & R. R. Ansbacher (Eds.), *Superiority and social interest* (pp. 143-158). Evanston, IL: Northwestern University Press.
[517] Mosak, H. H. & Shulman, B. (1977). Various purposes of symptoms. In H. H. Mosak (Ed.), *On purpose* (pp. 118-132). Chicago: Adler School of Professional Psychology. (Originally published in Journal of Individual Psychology, 1967, 23, 79-87.)
[518] Adler, A. (1956). *The Individual Psychology of Alfred Adler: A systematic presentation in selections from his writings*. H. Ansbacher & R. Ansbacher (Eds.), New York: Basic Books.
[519] Goldstein, A. N., Greer, S. M., Saletin, J. M., Harvey, A. G., Nitschke, J. B., & Walker. M. P. (2013). Tired and apprehensive: Anxiety amplifies the impact of sleep loss on aversive brain anticipation. *Journal of Neuroscience, 33* (26): pp.10607-10615.
[520] Way, L. M. (1950). *Adler's place in psychology*. London: George Allen & Unwin LTD.
[521] Dreikurs, R. (1953). *Fundamentals of Adlerian psychology*. Chicago: Alfred Adler Institute. (Original work published 1935)
[522] Adler, A. (1929b). *The science of living*. New York: Greenberg, Publisher, Inc.
Adler, Alexandra. (1938). *Guiding human misfits: A practical application of Individual Psychology*. New York: Macmillan.
[523] Corsini, R. J. (2002). *The dictionary of psychology*. New York, NY: Brunner/Routledge.
Adler, A., Stein, H., & Alfred Adler Institute of Northwestern Washington. (2006). *The general system of individual psychology: Overview and summary of classical Adlerian theory & current practice*. Bellingham, WA: Classical Adlerian Translation Project.
Mosak, H. H. (1977). The interrelatedness of the neuroses through central themes. In H. H. Mosak (Ed.), *On purpose* (pp. 138-143). Chicago: Adler School of Professional Psychology. (Originally published in the Journal of Individual Psychology, 1968, 24, 67-70.)
Glassman, W. E., & Hadad, M. (2006). *Approaches to psychology*. Maidenhead, Berkshire, England: Open University Press.
[524] Hitchcock, A. & Gottlieb, S. (2003). *Alfred Hitchcock: Interviews*. Jackson: Univ. Press of Mississippi.
Gottlieb, S., & Brookhouse, C. (2002). *Framing Hitchcock: Selected essays from the Hitchcock annual*. Contemporary film and television series. Detroit: Wayne State University Press.
[525] Mosak, H. H., Brown, P. R. & Boldt, R. M. (1994). Various purposes of suffering. *Individual Psychology, 50*(2), 142-148.
[526] Orgler, H. (1963). *Alfred Adler: The man and his work*. New York: Capricorn Books. (Original work published 1939)
[527] Mosak, H. H. & Shulman, B. (1977). Various purposes of symptoms. In H. H. Mosak (Ed.), *On purpose* (pp. 118-132). Chicago: Adler School of Professional Psychology. (Originally published in Journal of Individual Psychology, 1967, 23, 79-87.)
Mosak, H. H., Brown, P. R. & Boldt, R. M. (1994). Various purposes of suffering. *Individual Psychology, 50*(2), 142-148.
[528] Adler, A. (1964). *Problems of neurosis*. P. Mairet (Ed.). New York: Harper & Row. (Original work published 1929)
[529] Adler, A. (1964). *Problems of neurosis*. P. Mairet (Ed.). New York: Harper & Row. (Original

work published 1929)

[530] Kopp, R. R. (1986). Styles of striving for significance with and without social interest: An adlerian typology. *Individual Psychology, 42*(1), 17-25.

Leman, K. (1987). *The pleasers: Women who can't say no and the men who control them.* Old Tappan, NJ: F. H. Revell Co.

Mosak, H. H. (1971). Lifestyle. In A. G. Nikelly (Ed.), *Techniques for behavior change* (pp. 77-81). Springfield, IL: Charles C. Thomas Publisher.

[531] Mosak, H. H. & Maniacci, M. P. (1999). *A primer of Adlerian psychology: The analytic-behavioral-cognitive psychology of Alfred Adler.* Philadelphia: Brunner/Mazel.

[532] Nikelly, A. G. (Ed.). (1971). *Techniques for behavior change.* Springfield, IL: Charles C. Thomas.

[533] Hart, J. L. (1977). Perils of the pleaser. In J. P. Madden (Ed.), *Loneliness: Issues of living in an age of stress for clergy and religion* (pp. 41-55). Whitinsville, MA: Affirmation Books.

[534] Kopp, R. R. (1986). Styles of striving for significance with and without social interest: An adlerian typology. *Individual Psychology, 42*(1), 17-25.

[535] Kershaw-Bellemare, R. & Mosak, H. H. (1993). *Adult children of alcoholics: An Adlerian perspective. Journal of Alcohol and Drug Education, 38*(3), 105-119.

Mosak, H. H. & Maniacci, M. P. (1999). *A primer of Adlerian psychology: The analytic-behavioral-cognitive psychology of Alfred Adler.* Philadelphia: Brunner/Mazel.

[536] Nikelly, A. G. (Ed.), (1971). *Techniques for behavior change.* Springfield, IL: Charles C. Thomas.

[537] Mosak, H. H. & Maniacci, M. P. (1999). *A primer of Adlerian psychology: The analytic-behavioral-cognitive psychology of Alfred Adler.* Philadelphia: Brunner/Mazel.

[538] Hart, J. L. (1977). Perils of the pleaser. In J. P. Madden (Ed.), *Loneliness: Issues of living in an age of stress for clergy and religion* (pp. 41-55). Whitinsville, MA: Affirmation Books.

Mosak, H. H. & Maniacci, M. P. (1999). *A primer of Adlerian psychology: The analytic-behavioral-cognitive psychology of Alfred Adler.* Philadelphia: Brunner/Mazel.

[539] Hart, J. L. (1977). Perils of the pleaser. In J. P. Madden (Ed.), *Loneliness: Issues of living in an age of stress for clergy and religion* (pp. 41-55). Whitinsville, MA: Affirmation Books.

[540] Hart, J. L. (1977). Perils of the pleaser. In J. P. Madden (Ed.), *Loneliness: Issues of living in an age of stress for clergy and religion* (pp. 41-55). Whitinsville, MA: Affirmation Books.

[541] Nelms, H. (1969). *Magic and showmanship: A handbook for conjurers.* New York: Dover Publications.

Diagram Group. (2008). *Card & magic tricks.* New York: Sterling Publishing Co.

[542] Adler, A., Liebenau, G. L., Stein, H. T., & Alfred Adler Institute of Northwestern Washington. (2004). *Journal articles, 1821-1926: Talent & occupation, crime & revolution, philosophy of living.* Bellingham, WA: Classical Adlerian Translation Project.

Mosak, H. H. & Maniacci, M. P. (1999). *A primer of Adlerian psychology: The analytic-behavioral-cognitive psychology of Alfred Adler.* Philadelphia: Brunner/Mazel.

Adler, A. (1956). *The Individual Psychology of Alfred Adler: A systematic presentation in selections from his writings.* H. Ansbacher & R. Ansbacher (Eds.), New York: Basic Books.

[543] Mosak, H. H. & Maniacci, M. P. (1999). *A primer of Adlerian psychology: The analytic-behavioral-cognitive psychology of Alfred Adler.* Philadelphia: Brunner/Mazel.

[544] Mosak, H. H. (1977). The controller: A social interpretation of the anal character. In H. H. Mosak (Ed.), *On purpose* (pp. 216-227). Chicago: Alfred Adler Institute. (Originally

published in Alfred Adler: His influence on psychology today, 1973. Park Ridge, NJ: Noyes Press.)

[545] Dreikurs, R. (1953). *Fundamentals of Adlerian psychology.* Chicago: Alfred Adler Institute. (Original work published 1935)

[546] Manaster, G. J. & Corsini, R. J. (1982). *Individual psychology: Theory and practice.* Itasca, IL: F. E. Peacock Publishers, Inc.

[547] Mosak, H. H. (1987). *Ha ha and aha: The role of humor in psychotherapy.* Muncie, IN: Accelerated Development.

[548] Mosak, H. H. & Shulman, B. (1977). Various purposes of symptoms. In H. H. Mosak (Ed.), *On purpose* (pp. 118-132). Chicago: Adler School of Professional Psychology. (Originally published in Journal of Individual Psychology, 1967, 23, 79-87.)

[549] Stein, D. J. & Williams, D. (2010). Cultural and social aspects of anxiety disorders. In Stein, D. J., Hollander, E., & Rothbaum, B. O. *Textbook of anxiety disorders* (pp. 717-730). Washington, DC: American Psychiatric Pub.

Stein, D. J., Patel, V. & Heinze, G. (2010). Commentary on "Confirmatory factor analysis of common mental disorders across cultures" In Goldberg, D. P. *Diagnostic issues in depression and generalized anxiety disorder* (pp. 211-216). Arlington, VA: American Psychiatric Association.

[550] American Psychiatric Association. (2000). *Diagnostic and statistical manual of mental disorders: DSM-IV-TR.* Washington, DC: American Psychiatric Association.

World Health Organization. (1992). The ICD-10 classification of mental and behavioural disorders: Clinical descriptions and diagnostic guidelines. Geneva: World Health Organization.

Starcevic, V. (2005). Anxiety disorders in adults: A clinical guide. New York: Oxford University Press.

[551] Mosak, H. H. & Shulman, B. (1977). Various purposes of symptoms. In H. H. Mosak (Ed.), *On purpose* (pp. 118-132). Chicago: Adler School of Professional Psychology. (Originally published in Journal of Individual Psychology, 1967, 23, 79-87.)

[552] Adler, A. (1956). *The Individual Psychology of Alfred Adler: A systematic presentation in selections from his writings.* H. Ansbacher & R. Ansbacher (Eds.), New York: Basic Books.

Orgler, H. (1963). *Alfred Adler: The man and his work.* New York: Capricorn Books. (Original work published 1939)

[553] Adler, A. (1964). *Problems of neurosis.* P. Mairet (Ed.). New York: Harper & Row. (Original work published 1929)

[554] Adler, A. (1929a). *The practice and theory of Individual Psychology.* (P. Radin, Trans.). New York: Harcourt, Brace & Company, Inc.

Adler, A. (1956). *The Individual Psychology of Alfred Adler: A systematic presentation in selections from his writings.* H. Ansbacher & R. Ansbacher (Eds.), New York: Basic Books.

Mosak, H. H. & Maniacci, M. P. (1999). *A primer of Adlerian psychology: The analytic-behavioral-cognitive psychology of Alfred Adler.* Philadelphia: Brunner/Mazel.

[555] Adler, A. (1964). *Problems of neurosis.* P. Mairet (Ed.). New York: Harper & Row. (Original work published 1929)

Mosak, H. H. & Shulman, B. (1977). Various purposes of symptoms. In H. H. Mosak (Ed.), *On purpose* (pp. 118-132). Chicago: Adler School of Professional Psychology. (Originally published in Journal of Individual Psychology, 1967, 23, 79-87.)

[556] Adler, A. (1956). *The Individual Psychology of Alfred Adler: A systematic presentation in selections from his writings.* H. Ansbacher & R. Ansbacher (Eds.), New York: Basic Books.

Adler, A. (1964). *Problems of neurosis*. P. Mairet (Ed.). New York: Harper & Row. (Original work published 1929)

[557] Mosak, H. H. & Shulman, B. (1977). Various purposes of symptoms. In H. H. Mosak (Ed.), *On purpose* (pp. 118-132). Chicago: Adler School of Professional Psychology. (Originally published in Journal of Individual Psychology, 1967, 23, 79-87.)

[558] Mosak, H. H. (1977). The controller: A social interpretation of the anal character. In H. H. Mosak (Ed.), *On purpose* (pp. 216-227). Chicago: Alfred Adler Institute. (Originally published in Alfred Adler: His influence on psychology today, 1973. Park Ridge, NJ: Noyes Press.)

[559] Mosak, H. H. (1977). The controller: A social interpretation of the anal character. In H. H. Mosak (Ed.), *On purpose* (pp. 216-227). Chicago: Alfred Adler Institute. (Originally published in Alfred Adler: His influence on psychology today, 1973. Park Ridge, N. J.: Noyes Press.)

[560] Vingerhoets, A. J. J. M. (2013). *Why only humans weep: Unravelling the mysteries of tears.* Oxford: Oxford University Press.

[561] Mosak, H. H. (1977). The controller: A social interpretation of the anal character. In H. H. Mosak (Ed.), *On purpose* (pp. 216-227). Chicago: Alfred Adler Institute. (Originally published in Alfred Adler: His influence on psychology today, 1973. Park Ridge, NJ: Noyes Press.)

[562] Adler, A. (1964). *Problems of neurosis*. P. Mairet (Ed.). New York: Harper & Row. (Original work published 1929)

[563] Adler, A. (1927). *Understanding human nature*. (Walter Béran Wolfe, Trans.). Garden City, NY: Garden City Publishing Company, Inc.

[564] Hewstone, M., Rubin, M., & Willis, H. (January 01, 2002). Intergroup bias. *Annual Review of Psychology, 53,* 575-604.

[565] Adler, A. (1926). *The neurotic constitution: Outlines of a comparative individualistic psychology and psychotherapy.* [Translated by Bernard Glueck and John E. Lind] New York: Dodd, Mead and Company.

[566] Adler, A. (1927). *Understanding human nature*. (Walter Béran Wolfe, Trans.). Garden City, NY: Garden City Publishing Company, Inc.

[567] Adler, A. (1956). *The Individual Psychology of Alfred Adler: A systematic presentation in selections from his writings.* H. Ansbacher & R. Ansbacher (Eds.), New York: Basic Books.

[568] Adler, A. (1927). *Understanding human nature*. (Walter Béran Wolfe, Trans.). Garden City, NY: Garden City Publishing Company, Inc.

[569] Adler, A. (1930). *The neurotic constitution: Outlines of a comparative individualistic psychology and psychotherapy.* (B. Glueck & J. E. Lind, Trans.). New York: Dodd, Mead and Company.

[570] Adler, A. (1926). *The neurotic constitution: Outlines of a comparative individualistic psychology and psychotherapy.* [Translated by Bernard Glueck and John E. Lind] New York: Dodd, Mead and Company.

Adler, A. (1927). *Understanding human nature*. [Translated by Walter Béran Wolfe] Garden City, NY: Garden City Publishing Company, Inc.

Adler, A. (1996b). What is neurosis? *Individual Psychology, 52*(4), 318-333. (Original work published 1935)

Dreikurs, R. (1953). *Fundamentals of Adlerian Psychology.* Chicago: Alfred Adler Institute. (Original work published 1935)

[571] Dreikurs, R. (1953). *Fundamentals of Adlerian psychology.* Chicago: Alfred Adler Institute. (Original work published 1935)

[572] Mosak, H. H. (1977). The controller: A social interpretation of the anal character. In H. H.

Mosak (Ed.), *On purpose* (pp. 216-227). Chicago: Alfred Adler Institute. (Originally published in Alfred Adler: His influence on psychology today, 1973. Park Ridge, N. J.: Noyes Press.)

[573] Mosak, H. H. (1977). The controller: A social interpretation of the anal character. In H. H. Mosak (Ed.), *On purpose* (pp. 216-227). Chicago: Alfred Adler Institute. (Originally published in Alfred Adler: His influence on psychology today, 1973. Park Ridge, N. J.: Noyes Press.)

[574] Mosak, H. H. (1977). The controller: A social interpretation of the anal character. In H. H. Mosak (Ed.), *On purpose* (pp. 216-227). Chicago: Alfred Adler Institute. (Originally published in Alfred Adler: His influence on psychology today, 1973. Park Ridge, N. J.: Noyes Press.)

[575] Adler, A. (1964b). *Social interest: A challenge to mankind.* New York: Capricorn Books.

Adler, A. (1996b). What is neurosis? *Individual Psychology, 52*(4), 318-333. (Original work published 1935)

[576] Berne, E. (1964). *Games people play: The psychology of human relationships.* New York: Grove Press.

[577] Adler, K. A. (1961). Depression in the light of individual psychology. *Journal of Individual Psychology, 17*(1), 56-67.

[578] Adler, A. (1964b). *Social interest: A challenge to mankind.* New York: Capricorn Books.

[579] Adler, A. (1996b). What is neurosis? *Individual Psychology, 52*(4), 318-333. (Original work published 1935)

Orgler, H. (1963). *Alfred Adler: The man and his work.* New York: Capricorn Books. (Original work published 1939)

[580] Mosak, H. H. & Shulman, B. (1977). Various purposes of symptoms. In H. H. Mosak (Ed.), *On purpose* (pp. 118-132). Chicago: Adler School of Professional Psychology. (Originally published in Journal of Individual Psychology, 1967, 23, 79-87.)

Manaster, G. J. & Corsini, R. J. (1982). *Individual psychology: Theory and practice.* Itasca, IL: F. E. Peacock Publishers, Inc.

[581] Mosak, H. H., Brown, P. R. & Boldt, R. M. (1994). Various purposes of suffering. *Individual Psychology, 50*(2), 142-148.

[582] Mosak, H. H., Brown, P. R. & Boldt, R. M. (1994). Various purposes of suffering. *Individual Psychology, 50*(2), 142-148.

[583] Grayson, P. A. (1983). The self-criticism gambit: How to safeguard self-esteem through blaming the self. *Individual Psychology: Journal of Adlerian Theory, Research and Practice, 39*(1), 17-26.

[584] Beecher, W. (1959). Guilt feelings: Masters of our fate or our servants? In K. A. Adler & D. Deutsch (Eds.), *Essays in Individual Psychology: Contemporary application of Alfred Adler's theories.* New York: Grove Press, Inc.

Grayson, P. A. (1983). The self-criticism gambit: How to safeguard self-esteem through blaming the self. *Individual Psychology: Journal of Adlerian Theory, Research and Practice, 39*(1), 17-26.

[585] Grayson, P. A. (1983). The self-criticism gambit: How to safeguard self-esteem through blaming the self. *Individual Psychology: Journal of Adlerian Theory, Research and Practice, 39*(1), 17-26.

[586] Adler, A. (1929a). *The practice and theory of Individual Psychology.* (P. Radin, Trans.). New York: Harcourt, Brace & Company, Inc.

Adler, A. (1956). *The Individual Psychology of Alfred Adler: A systematic presentation in selections from his writings.* H. Ansbacher & R. Ansbacher (Eds.), New York: Basic Books.

[587] Grayson, P. A. (1983). The self-criticism gambit: How to safeguard self-esteem through

blaming the self. *Individual Psychology: Journal of Adlerian Theory, Research and Practice, 39*(1), 17-26.

[588] Grayson, P. A. (1983). The self-criticism gambit: How to safeguard self-esteem through blaming the self. *Individual Psychology: Journal of Adlerian Theory, Research and Practice, 39*(1), 17-26.

[589] Grayson, P. A. (1983). The self-criticism gambit: How to safeguard self-esteem through blaming the self. *Individual Psychology: Journal of Adlerian Theory, Research and Practice, 39*(1), 17-26.

[590] Adler, A. (1956). *The Individual Psychology of Alfred Adler: A systematic presentation in selections from his writings.* H. Ansbacher & R. Ansbacher (Eds.), New York: Basic Books.

[591] Grayson, P. A. (1983). The self-criticism gambit: How to safeguard self-esteem through blaming the self. *Individual Psychology: Journal of Adlerian Theory, Research and Practice, 39*(1), 17-26.

[592] Clance, P. R., & Imes, S. A. (1978). The Impostor Phenomenon in High Achieving Women: Dynamics and Therapeutic Interventions. *Psychotherapy: Theory Research and Practice, 15,* 241-247.

Clance, P. R. (1986). *The impostor phenomenon: When success make you feel like a fake.* Toronto: Bantam Books.

Matthews, G., & Clance, P. R. (1985). Treatment of the Impostor Phenomenon in Psychotherapy Clients. *Psychotherapy in Private Practice, 3*(1), 71-81.

Kamarzarrin, H., Khaledian, M., Shooshtari, M., Yousefi, E., & Ahrami, R. (2013). A study of the relationship between self-esteem and the imposter phenomenon in the physicians of Rasht city (Iran), *European Journal of Experimental Biology, 3*(2), 363-366.

[593] Sicher, L. (1950). Guilt and guilt feelings. *Individual Psychology Bulletin, 8,* 4-11.

[594] Beecher, W. (1959). Guilt feelings: Masters of our fate or our servants? In K. A. Adler & D. Deutsch (Eds.), *Essays in Individual Psychology: Contemporary application of Alfred Adler's theories.* New York: Grove Press, Inc. p. 65

[595] Feichtinger, F. (1950). The psychology of guilt feelings. *Individual Psychology Bulletin, 8,* 39-43.

[596] Mosak, H. H. (1977). The psychological attitude in rehabilitation. In H. H. Mosak (Ed.), *On purpose.* Chicago: Adler School of Professional Psychology. (Originally published in American Archives of Rehabilitation Therapy, 1954, 2(1), 9-10.)

[597] Beecher, W. (1959). Guilt feelings: Masters of our fate or our servants? In K. A. Adler & D. Deutsch (Eds.), *Essays in Individual Psychology: Contemporary application of Alfred Adler's theories.* New York: Grove Press, Inc.

Grayson, P. A. (1983). The self-criticism gambit: How to safeguard self-esteem through blaming the self. *Individual Psychology: Journal of Adlerian Theory, Research and Practice, 39*(1), 17-26.

Mosak, H. H. (1987). Guilt, guilt feelings, regret and repentance. *Individual Psychology, 43*(3), 288-295.

[598] Beecher, W. (1959). Guilt feelings: Masters of our fate or our servants? In K. A. Adler & D. Deutsch (Eds.), *Essays in Individual Psychology: Contemporary application of Alfred Adler's theories.* New York: Grove Press, Inc.

[599] Feichtinger, F. (1950). The psychology of guilt feelings. *Individual Psychology Bulletin, 8,* 39-43.

[600] Sicher, L. (1950). Guilt and guilt feelings. *Individual Psychology Bulletin, 8,* 4-11.

Mosak, H. H. (1987). Guilt, guilt feelings, regret and repentance. *Individual Psychology, 43*(3), 288-295.

[601] Sicher, L. (1950). Guilt and guilt feelings. *Individual Psychology Bulletin, 8,* 4-11.

[602] apology. (n.d.). *Oxford Dictionaries*. Retrieved May 10, 2013, from oxforddictionaries.com/us/ website: http://oxforddictionaries.com/us/definition/american_english/apology

[603] Sicher, L. (1950). Guilt and guilt feelings. *Individual Psychology Bulletin, 8*, 4-11.

[604] Mosak, H. H. (1987). Guilt, guilt feelings, regret and repentance. *Individual Psychology, 43*(3), 288-295.

[605] Feichtinger, F. (1950). The psychology of guilt feelings. *Individual Psychology Bulletin, 8*, 39-43.

[606] Mosak, H. H. (1987). Guilt, guilt feelings, regret and repentance. *Individual Psychology, 43*(3), 288-295.

[607] Beecher, W. (1959). Guilt feelings: Masters of our fate or our servants? In K. A. Adler & D. Deutsch (Eds.), *Essays in Individual Psychology: Contemporary application of Alfred Adler's theories*. New York: Grove Press, Inc.

Feichtinger, F. (1950). The psychology of guilt feelings. *Individual Psychology Bulletin, 8*, 39-43.

[608] Beecher, W. (1959). Guilt feelings: Masters of our fate or our servants? In K. A. Adler & D. Deutsch (Eds.), *Essays in Individual Psychology: Contemporary application of Alfred Adler's theories*. New York: Grove Press, Inc.

Mosak, H. H. (1987). Guilt, guilt feelings, regret and repentance. *Individual Psychology, 43*(3), 288-295.

[609] Beecher, W. (1959). Guilt feelings: Masters of our fate or our servants? In K. A. Adler & D. Deutsch (Eds.), *Essays in Individual Psychology: Contemporary application of Alfred Adler's theories*. New York: Grove Press, Inc.

[610] Dreikurs, R., & Mosak H. (1977). The tasks of life II: The fourth life task. In H. H. Mosak (Ed.), *On purpose*. Chicago: Adler School of Professional Psychology. (Originally published in Individual Psychologist, 1967, 4, 18-22.)

[611] Sicher, L. (1950). Guilt and guilt feelings. *Individual Psychology Bulletin, 8*, 4-11.

[612] Sicher, L. (1950). Guilt and guilt feelings. *Individual Psychology Bulletin, 8*, 4-11.

[613] Mosak, H. H. (1987). Guilt, guilt feelings, regret and repentance. *Individual Psychology, 43*(3), 288-295.

[614] Beecher, W. (1959). Guilt feelings: Masters of our fate or our servants? In K. A. Adler & D. Deutsch (Eds.), *Essays in Individual Psychology: Contemporary application of Alfred Adler's theories*. New York: Grove Press, Inc.

Feichtinger, F. (1950). The psychology of guilt feelings. *Individual Psychology Bulletin, 8*, 39-43.

[615] Di Pietro, R. (2010). *The depression code: Deciphering the purposes of neurotic depression*. Raleigh, NC: Lulu.com.

[616] Mosak, H. H. (1977). Lifestyle. In Harold H. Mosak (Ed.). *On purpose* (pp. 183-187). Chicago: Alfred Adler Institute. (Original work published 1971)

[617] Adler, A. (1958). *What life should mean to you*. A. Porter (Ed.). New York: Capricorn Books. (Original work published 1931)

[618] Dreikurs, R. (1953). *Fundamentals of Adlerian psychology*. Chicago: Alfred Adler Institute. (Original work published 1935)

[619] Adler, A. (1958). *What life should mean to you*. A. Porter (Ed.). New York: Capricorn Books. (Original work published 1931)

Dreikurs, R. (1953). *Fundamentals of Adlerian psychology*. Chicago: Alfred Adler Institute. (Original work published 1935)

[620] Dreikurs, R. (1953). *Fundamentals of Adlerian psychology*. Chicago: Alfred Adler Institute. (Original work published 1935)

[621] Orgler, H. (1963). *Alfred Adler: The man and his work*. New York: Capricorn Books.

(Original work published 1939)

[622] Krausz, E. O. (1935). The pessimistic attitude. *International Journal of Individual Psychology, 1*(3), 86-99.

[623] Adler, A. (1958). *What life should mean to you.* A. Porter (Ed.). New York: Capricorn Books. (Original work published 1931)

[624] Adler, A. (1964). *Problems of neurosis.* P. Mairet (Ed.). New York: Harper & Row. (Original work published 1929)

[625] Adler, A. (1964). *Problems of neurosis.* P. Mairet (Ed.). New York: Harper & Row. (Original work published 1929)

[626] Schwartz, B. (2004). *The paradox of choice: Why more is less.* New York: HarperCollins.

[627] Newberg, A & Waldman, M. R. (2007). *Born to believe: God, science, and the origin of ordinary and extraordinary beliefs.* New York: Free Press.

[628] Adler, A. (1930). *The neurotic constitution: Outlines of a comparative individualistic psychology and psychotherapy.* (B. Glueck & J. E. Lind, Trans.). New York: Dodd, Mead and Company.

[629] Kamler, H. (1994). *Identification and character: A book on psychological development.* Albany, NY: State University of New York Press.

Oldham, J. M., Skodol, A. E., Bender, D. S., & American Psychiatric Publishing. (2005). *The American Psychiatric Publishing textbook of personality disorders.* Washington, DC: American Psychiatric Pub.

Superson, A. M., & Cudd, A. E. (2002). *Theorizing backlash: Philosophical reflections on the resistance to feminism.* Lanham, Md: Rowman & Littlefield.

[630] Adler, A. (1958). *What life should mean to you.* A. Porter (Ed.). New York: Capricorn Books. (Original work published 1931)

[631] Adler, A. (1930). *The neurotic constitution: Outlines of a comparative individualistic psychology and psychotherapy.* (B. Glueck & J. E. Lind, Trans.). New York: Dodd, Mead and Company.

Adler, A. (1956). *The Individual Psychology of Alfred Adler: A systematic presentation in selections from his writings.* H. Ansbacher & R. Ansbacher (Eds.), New York: Basic Books.

[632] Adler, A. (1926). *The neurotic constitution: Outlines of a comparative individualistic psychology and psychotherapy.* [Translated by Bernard Glueck and John E. Lind] New York: Dodd, Mead and Company.

[633] Adler, A. (1973). *Superiority and social interest.* (3rd. Rev. ed.). H. L. Ansbacher, & R. R. Ansbacher, (Eds.), New York: Viking Press.

[634] Adler, A. (1996b). What is neurosis? *Individual Psychology, 52*(4), 318-333. (Original work published 1935)

Dreikurs, R. (1953). *Fundamentals of Adlerian Psychology.* Chicago: Alfred Adler Institute. (Original work published 1935)

[635] Mosak, H. H. & Di Pietro, R. (2005). *Early recollections: Interpretative method and application.* New York: Routledge.

[636] Adler, A. (1930). *The neurotic constitution: Outlines of a comparative individualistic psychology and psychotherapy.* (B. Glueck & J. E. Lind, Trans.). New York: Dodd, Mead and Company. p. 19.

[637] Reik, T. (1948). *Listening with the third ear.* New York: Farrar, Straus and Company.

[638] Adler, A. (1930). *The neurotic constitution: Outlines of a comparative individualistic psychology and psychotherapy.* (B. Glueck & J. E. Lind, Trans.). New York: Dodd, Mead and Company.

[639] Hanson, G. R., Fleckenstein, A. E., & Venturelli, P. J. (2011). *Drugs and Society.* Jones & Bartlett Learning, LLC.

Glassman, W. E., & Hadad, M. (2006). *Approaches to psychology.* Maidenhead, Berkshire, England: Open University Press.

Amen, D. G., & Routh, L. C. (2003). *Healing anxiety and depression.* New York: Putnam.

Buckworth, J., & Dishman, R. K. (2002). *Exercise psychology.* Champaign, IL: Human Kinetics.

Johnsgård, K. W. (2004). *Conquering depression and anxiety through exercise.* Amherst, NY: Prometheus Books.

Rippe, J. M. (2012). *Encyclopedia of lifestyle medicine & health.* Thousand Oaks, Calif: Sage Publications.

[640] Juliano, L. M. & Griffiths, R. R. (1997). Caffeine. In J. H. Lowinson (Ed.). *Substance abuse: A comprehensive textbook* (pp. 403-421). Baltimore: Williams & Wilkins.

Dopheide, J. A. (2010). Anxiety. In Tisdale, J. E., Miller, D. A., & American Society of Health-System Pharmacists. *Drug-induced diseases: Prevention, detection, and management* (2nd ed.) (pp. 333-343). Bethesda, Md: American Society of Health-System Pharmacists.

Noyes, R., & Hoehn-Saric, R. (1998). *The anxiety disorders.* Cambridge, UK: Cambridge University Press.

[641] Mosak, H. H. & Maniacci, M. P. (2010). Adlerian Psychotherapy. In Corsini, R. J., & Wedding, D. (Eds.). *Current psychotherapies* (9th ed.) (pp. 67-112). Belmont, CA: Brooks/Cole.

[642] Mosak, H. H. & Todd, F. J. (1977). Selective perception in the interpretation of symbols. In H. H. Mosak (Ed.) *On purpose* (pp. 9-11). Chicago: Adler School of Professional Psychology.

[643] Adler, A. (1973). *Superiority and social interest.* (3rd. Rev. ed.). H. L. Ansbacher, & R. R. Ansbacher, (Eds.), New York: Viking Press.

[644] Way, L. M. (1950). *Adler's place in psychology.* London: George Allen & Unwin LTD.

[645] Dreikurs, R. (1953). *Fundamentals of Adlerian psychology.* Chicago: Alfred Adler Institute. (Original work published 1935)

[646] Dreikurs, R. (1953). *Fundamentals of Adlerian psychology.* Chicago: Alfred Adler Institute. (Original work published 1935)

[647] Mosak, H. H. & Shulman, B. (1977). Various purposes of symptoms. In H. H. Mosak (Ed.), *On purpose* (pp. 118-132). Chicago: Adler School of Professional Psychology. (Originally published in Journal of Individual Psychology, 1967, 23, 79-87.)

Mosak, H. H. & Maniacci, M. P. (1999). *A primer of Adlerian psychology: The analytic-behavioral-cognitive psychology of Alfred Adler.* Philadelphia: Brunner/Mazel.

[648] Adler, A. (1929b). *The science of living.* New York: Greenberg, Publisher, Inc.

Adler, Alexandra. (1938). *Guiding human misfits: A practical application of Individual Psychology.* New York: Macmillan.

[649] Milgram, S. (1974). *Obedience to authority: An experimental view.* New York: Harper & Row.

[650] Zimbardo, P. G. (2007). *The Lucifer effect: Understanding how good people turn evil.* New York: Random House.

[651] Sherif, M., & University of Oklahoma. (1954). *Experimental study of positive and negative intergroup attitudes between experimentally produced groups: Robbers Cave Study.* Norman, Okla.

[652] Stone, J. R. (2006). *The Routledge book of world proverbs.* London: Routledge.

40167540R00250

Made in the USA
Lexington, KY
26 March 2015